MICRO
Economics
for
Life

Smart Choices for You

SECOND EDITION

Avi J. Cohen
York University
University of Toronto

Toronto

Vice-President, CMPS: Gary Bennett
Editorial Director: Claudine O'Donnell
Marketing Manager: Claire Varley
Program Manager: Joel Gladstone
Project Manager: Richard di Santo
Developmental Editor: Suzanne Simpson Millar
Developmental Team Lead: Suzanne Schaan
Media Editor: Victoria Naik
Production Services: Mohinder Singh, Aptara®, Inc.
Permissions Project Manager: Joanne Tang
Photo Permissions Research: Candice Velez, Q2A/Bill Smith
Text Permissions Research: Haydee Hidalgo, Electronic Publishing Services, Inc.
Cover Designer: Anthony Leung
Interior Designer: Anthony Leung, Pearson/Cenveo Publishing Services
Cover Image: Deryk Ouseley/derykouseley.com

Library and Archives Canada Cataloguing in Publication

Cohen, Avi J., author
    Microeconomics for life: smart choices for you / Avi J.
Cohen. — Second edition.

Includes index.
ISBN 978-0-13-313583-1 (pbk)

    1. Microeconomics—Textbooks.   I. Title.

HB172.C63 2014   338.5   C2014-905468-8

PEARSON

ISBN: 978-0-13-313583-1

To Susan — for encouraging me to find my voice.

A.J.C.

About the Author

Avi J. Cohen

Avi J. Cohen is Professor of Economics at York University and at the University of Toronto. He has a PhD from Stanford University; is a Life Fellow of Clare Hall, University of Cambridge; and is past Co-Chair of the Canadian Economics Association Education Committee.

Professor Cohen has been President of the History of Economics Society, a Senior Research Fellow at the Center for the History of Political Economy at Duke University, and has research interests in the history of economics, economic history, and economic education. He has published in *Journal of Economic Perspectives, Journal of Economic Education, History of Political Economy, Journal of the History of Economic Thought, Cambridge Journal of Economics, Journal of Economic History,* and *Explorations in Economic History,* among other journals and books.

Professor Cohen is co-author of the best-selling *Study Guide* that accompanied the first eight editions of Parkin/Bade's *Economics.* He is the winner of numerous teaching awards, including Canada's most prestigious national award for educational leadership, the 3M Teaching Fellowship.

Brief Contents

Table of Contents

Chapter 1

Chapter 2

Chapter 12

What Are You Worth?
Inputs, Incomes, and Inequality   310

Preface to Students

I wrote *Economics for Life* to show you how to use economic ideas to make smart choices in life. I focus on core concepts that you can use regularly, to make smart choices in your life as a consumer, as a businessperson, and as an informed citizen.

You, like most people, are probably not interested in economic concepts for their own sake. This book is not designed to train you as an economist. Instead, my goal is to present important ideas, concepts, and decision-making strategies — based on an economic way of thinking — that will help you be more successful throughout life. The stories in the book reflect real-life situations. You will, I hope, quickly see how you can make yourself better off by learning the economic lessons they contain.

The Three Keys shown are at the heart of making smart choices and are at the heart of this book. You can always spot them by the key icon in the margin.

You will first learn about the Three Keys to Smart Choices in Chapter 1, and they will reappear many times. The Three Keys are like a map, helping you choose a direction to take at decision points — forks in the road. When you face a decision, they focus your attention on the information that is most useful to making your smart choice.

If you learn to use the three keys well and start making smarter choices in life, then I will have done my job well and you will have gained strong tools in your quest for success. If you do not enjoy reading this book or do not learn to make smarter choices in life, then I will have failed.

The only way for me to know how close I've come to achieving the goal of helping you make smart choices is to hear from you. Let me know what works for you in this book — and, more importantly, what doesn't. You can write to me at **avicohen@yorku.ca.** In future editions I will acknowledge by name all students who help improve *Economics for Life.*

Now start learning how economics will help you make smarter choices in life!

Professor Avi J. Cohen
Economics
York University
University of Toronto

P.S. Your first smart choice will be to read the tour of the features in the book to find out how you can get the most out of your textbook.

Three Keys to Smart Choices

3 KEYS TO SMART CHOICES

1 CHOOSE ONLY WHEN ADDITIONAL BENEFITS ARE GREATER THAN ADDITIONAL OPPORTUNITY COSTS.

2 COUNT ONLY ADDITIONAL BENEFITS AND ADDITIONAL OPPORTUNITY COSTS.

3 BE SURE TO COUNT ALL ADDITIONAL BENEFITS AND COSTS, INCLUDING IMPLICIT COSTS AND EXTERNALITIES.

ADDITIONAL BENEFITS VS. OPPORTUNITY COSTS

Features of This Book

Welcome to *Microeconomics for Life: Smart Choices for You*. This tour of your textbook is designed to help you use this book effectively and complete your course successfully.

Chapter Opener

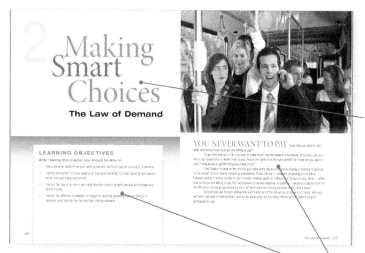

Every chapter begins with a two-page spread. These two pages set the theme for the chapter. Like a trailer for a movie, this opening spread gives you a preview of what is coming and prepares you for the "feature presentation."

Every chapter has a title and a subtitle. The main title summarizes the content of the chapter in plain language. The subtitle for the chapter is in the language economists use when referring to the concepts.

Every chapter is divided into main sections, and each of these sections is accompanied by a learning objective. The learning objective describes what you will have learned after reading each section. Once you have read the chapter, you can review these learning objectives to test your understanding of the chapter material.

Every chapter begins with an overview that introduces you to the main ideas and themes in the chapter. This introduction connects the economic principles discussed in the chapter to the choices and decisions you make in your everyday life.

Learning Objectives

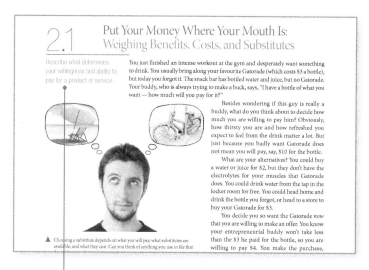

Learning objectives are repeated at the beginning of each main section of every chapter and provide an important reminder of what you will learn in each section.

Special Features

badly you want it plays a role. But just as important is what your alternative choices are. There are substitutes for everything — water for Gatorade, a yoga class for a gym workout, long underwear or a move to Florida for winter coats. Substitutes need not be exactly the same product or service. Substitutes just have to basically satisfy the same want. For any choice, what you are willing and able to pay, or to give up, depends on what substitutes are available, and what they cost.

The final factor determining how much you are willing and able to give up is how much you can afford. Are you able to pay the price of the product or service you want? Can you afford to take the time to relax all evening when you have a test tomorrow?

The list of things we want is endless. But the choices we actually make reflect our willingness — and ability — to give up something in exchange. Economists use the term **demand** to describe consumers' willingness and ability to pay for a particular product or service. Demand is *not* just what consumers want. You must put your money (or time) where your mouth is in order to demand a product or service. And those demands, or choices, are smart choices only when expected benefits are greater than opportunity costs.

demand consumers' willingness and ability to pay for a particular product or service

Refresh 2.1

1. What is the difference between wants and demands?
2. What is the key factor that would make you choose to download a song for free rather than pay for it on iTunes? Explain your choice.
3. You have just started at a school that is a 30-minute drive from home or a 90-minute transit ride. Which is your smart choice, taking the transit or buying a car? Justify your choice.

MyEconLab
For answers to these Refresh Questions, visit MyEconLab.

Refresh

The Refresh feature provides three questions that require you to review and apply the concepts in the preceding section. These questions give you the opportunity to assess your understanding of the principles developed in the section. Answers to these questions are located on MyEconLab (www.myeconlab.com) that accompanies this book.

---

headphones (listening pleasure and blocking out the world) is greater than the additional cost (the $200 price tag). You are willing and able to pay $200. Sold! An economist would say that, at the price of $200, your *quantity demanded* of Beats Solo headphones is one.

Quantity demanded, as we will see, is not the same as *demand*. **Quantity demanded** is the amount you actually plan to buy at a given price, taking into account everything that affects your willingness and ability to pay.

We saw in the previous section that if circumstances change the additional benefit, your choice may change. The second bottle of Gatorade wasn't worth as much as the first, and the value of the headphones would change if you were driving to school in a car with a good sound system instead of riding the bus. But our focus here is not on benefits. Our focus is on *what happens to your buying decision when the price — the additional cost you pay — changes*. In order to focus on the relationship between price and quantity demanded, we will keep all other influences on demand the same.

quantity demanded amount you actually plan to buy at a given price

Key Terms

Key terms are bolded in the text where they first appear, and definitions for key terms are in the margin. A complete list of all key terms and definitions are in the glossary at the end of the book.

Your willingness to pay, determined at the margin by changing circumstances including quantity, is important in determining prices, ranging from low prices for water to high prices for diamonds.

Economics *Out There*

Coke's Automatic Price Gouging

In the late 1990s, Coca-Cola Co. worked on technology to automatically raise prices in soft-drink vending machines on hot days. Critics — calling the plan "shameful" and a "cynical ploy" to exploit consumers "when they are most susceptible to price gouging" — suggested Coca-Cola should abandon the plan. The company claimed it was fair that the price should rise with demand, and that the machines simply automate that process. Unconvinced, critics warned that the plan would alienate customers, with the reminder that "archrival Pepsi is out there, and you can hardly tell the difference."

- The public reaction to these variable-price vending machines was so negative that Coca-Cola never introduced them.

- However, the strategy is based on the correct observation that willingness to pay changes with circumstances — the principle of marginal benefit.
- The strategy failed not because the economics were wrong, but because the idea of paying different prices for the same product seemed so unfair — "price gouging." (However, in Chapter 9 we will look at examples where consumers accept businesses charging different consumers different prices for the same product — cellphone minutes cost providers the same, whether daytime, evening, or weekend. Why are prices different? [*Hint:* Consumer willingness to pay.])
- Notice the line about Pepsi — substitutes are always available, which limits willingness to pay for any product, regardless of the marginal benefit.

Source: "Coke's Automatic Price Gouging," *San Francisco Chronicle*, October 29, 1999, p. A22.

Economics Out There

These feature boxes provide real-world examples of the economic principle being discussed. The stories told in Economics Out There help you make connections between the concepts in the chapter and everyday life.

Notes

In the margin, you will see notes that provide a quick explanation of the idea, concept, or principle being discussed in the narrative.

Three Keys Icon

In keeping with the theme of making smart choices, you will also find an icon in the margin beside text that discusses the Three Keys to Smart Choices. The key (or keys) being discussed is indicated by the number on the key icon.

NOTE
Rising prices create two incentives for increased quantity supplied — higher profits and covering higher marginal opportunity costs of production.

quantity supplied the quantity you actually plan to supply at a given price

As your eye goes down the columns in Figure 3.1, note that as the price rises, the quantity supplied increases. (What happens to quantity demanded as price rises?) In general, when prices rise, individuals and businesses devote more of their time or resources to producing or supplying — more money stimulates more quantity supplied. The two reasons for this are the desire for profits (higher prices usually mean higher profits) and the need for a higher price to cover higher marginal opportunity costs — your weekend time is worth more to you than your *World of Warcraft* time.

Quantity supplied, as we will see, is not the same as supply. **Quantity supplied** is a more limited concept — the quantity you actually plan to supply at a given price, taking into account everything that affects your willingness to supply work hours.

Let's take the economist's idea of supply and apply it to Paola's willingness to supply a particular quantity of piercings at a particular price.

Body Piercings or Nail Sets?

Businesses, like consumers, make smart choices based on Key 1 — Choose only when additional benefits are greater than additional *opportunity costs*.

Paola's first choice is *what to produce* with her resources — the labour and equipment she has in her shop. She can do body piercing, and she can also paint fingernails. Let's limit her choices to full body piercings and full sets of fingernails to allow the simple, made-up numbers below.

Paola's Parlour has special tools for piercing and for nail painting. There are four people working (including Paola). All four are equally skilled at piercing (the business started with just piercing), but their fingernail skills differ from expert (Paola) to beginner (Parminder). The table in Figure 3.2 shows the different combinations of fingernail sets and piercings that Paola's Parlour can produce in a day.

Study Guide

Study Guide

CHAPTER 2 SUMMARY

2.1 Put Your Money Where Your Mouth Is:
Weighing Benefits, Costs, and Substitutes

Your willingness to buy a product or service depends on your ability to pay, comparative benefits and costs, and the availability of substitutes.

- **Preferences** — your wants and their intensities.
- **Demand** — consumers' willingness and ability to pay for a particular product or service.
- For any choice, what you are willing to pay or give up depends on the cost and availability of substitutes.

2.2 Living on the Edge:
Smart Choices Are Marginal Choices

Key 2 states, "Count only *additional* benefits and *additional* costs." Additional benefits mean marginal benefits — not total benefits — and marginal benefits change with circumstances.

- **Marginal benefit** — the additional benefit from a choice, changing with circumstances.
- Marginal benefit explains the diamond/water paradox. Why do diamonds cost more than water, when water is more valuable for survival? Willingness to pay depends on marginal benefit, not total benefit. Because water is abundant, marginal benefit is low. Because diamonds are scarce, marginal benefit is high.

2.3 Move On When the Price Isn't Right:
The Law of Demand

The demand curve combines two forces — switch to substitutes; willingness and ability to pay — determining quantity demanded, and can be read as a demand curve and as a marginal benefit curve.

- **Quantity demanded** — the amount you actually plan to buy at a given price.
- **Market demand** — the sum of demands of all individuals willing and able to buy a particular product or service.

- **Law of demand** — if the price of a product or service rises, quantity demanded decreases, other things remaining the same.
- **Demand curve** — shows the relationship between price and quantity demanded, other things remaining the same.

2.4 Moving the Margins:
What Can Change Demand?

Quantity demanded changes only with a change in price. All other influences on consumer choice change demand.

- Demand is a catch-all term summarizing all possible influences on consumers' willingness and ability to pay for a particular product or service.
  - **Increase in demand** — increase in consumers' willingness and ability to pay. Rightward shift of demand curve.
  - **Decrease in demand** — decrease in consumers' willingness and ability to pay. Leftward shift of demand curve.
- Demand changes with changes in preferences, prices of related goods, income, expected future price, and number of consumers. For example, demand increases with:
  - increase in preferences.
  - rise in price of a **substitute** — products or services used in place of each other to satisfy the same want.
  - fall in price of a **complement** — products or services used together to satisfy the same want.
  - increase in income for **normal goods** — products or services you buy more of when your income increases.
  - decrease in income for **inferior goods** — products or services you buy less of when your income increases.
  - rise in expected future prices.
  - increase in number of consumers.

Study Guide

At the end of each chapter you will find a study guide designed to assist you in reviewing and testing your understanding of the material in the chapter. The study guide for each chapter includes:

- Chapter Summary
- 15 True/False Questions
- 15 Multiple Choice Questions

Chapter Summary

Organized by section, the summary recaps the main ideas in each chapter. The first item (in red) under each section head is the most important point in that section. All key terms are in bold.

TRUE/FALSE

Circle the correct answer. Solutions to these questions are available at the end of the book and on MyEconLab. You can also visit the MyEconLab Study Plan to access additional questions that will help you master the concepts covered in this chapter.

2.1 Weighing Benefits, Costs, and Substitutes

1. Demand is the same as wants.   T   F

2. Your willingness to pay for a product depends on what substitutes are available, and what they cost.   T   F

3. What you can afford is just about money.   T   F

2.2 Smart Choices Are Marginal Choices

4. Marginal cost is the same as additional cost.   T   F

5. The flat fee charged at an all-you-can-eat restaurant should not influence how much food you eat once you are seated.   T   F

6. Marginal benefit always equals average benefit.   T   F

7. Willingness to pay depends on marginal benefit, not total benefit.   T   F

2.3 The Law of Demand

8. Quantity demanded is the same as demand.   T   F

9. If the price of a product or service changes, quantity demanded changes.   T   F

10. Market demand is the sum of the demands of all individuals.   T   F

11. Demand curves may be straight lines or curves, but always slope downward to the left.   T   F

2.4 What Can Change Demand?

12. If your willingness to pay decreases, demand decreases.   T   F

13. If your ability to pay decreases, demand increases.   T   F

14. Throughout the month of December, the quantity of video game consoles purchased increases even as the price rises. This violates the law of demand.   T   F

15. A decrease in income always shifts the demand curve leftward.   T   F

True/False Questions

There are 15 true/false questions, organized by learning objective. The heading next to each learning objective number gives you the topic of the questions that follow. Each question is answered at the end of the book, with a brief explanation.

MULTIPLE CHOICE

Circle the best answer. Solutions to these questions are available at the end of the book and on MyEconLab. You can also visit the MyEconLab Study Plan to access similar questions that will help you master the concepts covered in this chapter.

2.1 Weighing Benefits, Costs, and Substitutes

1. Economists describe the list of your wants and their intensities as
   a) demand.
   b) supply.
   c) benefit.
   d) preferences.

2. Costs are
   a) worth money.
   b) whatever we are willing to give up.
   c) the answer to the question "What do we want?"
   d) whatever we are willing to get.

3. Your preferences measure
   a) the availability of substitutes.
   b) how limited your time is.
   c) the price of a product.
   d) how badly you want something.

2.2 Smart Choices Are Marginal Choices

4. All-you-can-eat buffet restaurants charge a fixed fee for eating. With each plate that Anna eats, she experiences
   a) decreasing marginal costs.
   b) increasing marginal costs.
   c) decreasing marginal benefits.
   d) increasing marginal benefits.

5. Thinking like economists, a dating couple should break up when the
   a) total benefits of dating are greater than the total costs of dating.
   b) total costs of dating are greater than the total benefits of dating.
   c) additional benefits of dating are greater than the additional costs of dating.
   d) additional costs of dating are greater than the additional benefits of dating.

48   CHAPTER 2   MAKING SMART CHOICES

Multiple Choice Questions

There are 15 multiple choice questions organized by learning objective. The heading next to each learning objective number gives you the topic of the questions that follow. Each question is answered at the end of the book, with a brief explanation.

Using Your Textbook to Achieve Success in Your Course

This textbook is set up for your success. Each element is designed to help you organize, understand, and learn the material efficiently and easily. Here is a four-step guide to being successful in this course.

1: Fully understand the learning objectives

The learning objectives in each chapter are presented in the chapter opener and repeated in the margin at the beginning of each section of the chapter. If you can do what each learning objective asks, you will understand what is most important in each section. These learning objectives are the core of the course. Master these and you have mastered the course. The most important point in each section — a one- to two-sentence summary of what each learning objective asks — appears in red after each section head in the Study Guide's Chapter Summary.

2: Check your understanding of the learning objectives

At the end of each complete section, there are three questions titled Refresh. When you complete a section, take the 5 to 10 minutes required to answer the Refresh questions. These questions are designed for you to assess how well you have mastered the learning objective. They will help you make sure you understand what is important.

Research shows that small quizzes help students get higher grades and retain more of what they learn than spending the same amount of time highlighting and rereading material.

3: Complete the Study Guide material

After finishing the chapter, complete the Study Guide pages — it will save you study time and reinforce what you have mastered. The Study Guide is divided into two main sections, a chapter summary and a set of exam-like questions.

Chapter Summary The Chapter Summary contains the key points you need to know. It is organized using the same major sections as the chapter. The first item in red under each section head is the most important point in that section. The Chapter Summary is an excellent study aid for the night before a test. It's a final check of the ideas — the learning objectives — you have studied.

Exam-Like Questions Do the true/false and multiple-choice questions *without looking at the answers*. This is the single most important tip for profitably using the Study Guide. Struggling for the answers to questions you find challenging is one of the most effective ways to learn. The athletic saying of "No pain, no gain" applies equally to studying. You will learn the most from right answers you have had to struggle for and from your wrong answers and mistakes. Look at the answers only *after* you have attempted all the questions. When you finally do check the answers, be sure to understand where you went wrong and why your right answers are right.

4: Know it before you go on

Master each chapter by taking the above actions *before* moving on. Feel confident that you understand the chapter's objectives. By following this simple four-point plan you will be making a smart choice for learning, and you will do well in the course.

Preface
to
Instructors

When people ask me what I do, I say, "I teach Economics." While I am a full professor at two universities, a productive academic with an active research program (past president of the History of Economics Society) and honourable service commitments to my schools, my professional identity is largely tied to my teaching.

As a young assistant professor, the immortality of publishing articles in journals that would forever be in libraries was an important goal. But over time, I came to realize how few people would read those articles, let alone be affected by them. Most of my, and I suspect your, "academic footprint" on this earth will be through our students. Over a career, we teach tens of thousands students.

As economists and teachers, what do we want our lasting "economic footprint" to be? There is a wonderful old *Saturday Night Live* skit by Father Guido Sarducci called "The Five Minute University" (**http://www.youtube.com/watch?v=kO8x8eoU3L4**). Watch it. His premise is to teach in five minutes what an average college or university graduate remembers five years after graduating. For economics, he states it's the two words "supply and demand." That's it.

The serious question behind the skit, the one that motivates this book, is "What do we really want our students to remember of what we teach them in an introductory economics class?"

The vast, vast majority of students in introductory economics never take another economics course. *Economics for Life* is designed to help those students learn what they need to know to be economically literate citizens. If we can teach students the fundamentals of thinking like an economist, they will be equipped to make smarter choices in their lives as consumers, as businesspeople, and as citizens evaluating policies proposed by politicians.

For microeconomics, the essentials are grounded in the Three Keys to Smart Choices, which form the core of *Microeconomics for Life: Smart Choices for You*.

Key 1: Choose only when additional benefits are greater than additional *opportunity costs*.

Key 2: Count only *additional* benefits and *additional* opportunity costs.

Key 3: Be sure to count *all* additional benefits and costs, including *implicit costs* and *externalities*.

We can teach all topics in micro with those three keys.

Because economists disagree far more about macroeconomics than microeconomics, I incorporated that disagreement into the core of the macro textbook as **"the fundamental macroeconomic question."**

If left alone by government, do the price mechanisms of market economies adjust quickly to maintain steady growth in living standards, full employment, and stable prices?

Not only do economists disagree over the answer to this question, so do the politicians our students will be voting for, for the rest of their lives. I believe the essential macroeconomic concepts students must know in order to answer that question for themselves — the macroeconomics they need to know *as citizens* — are included in *Macroeconomics for Life: Smart Choices for All?*

Focusing on essential concepts means letting go of many of the more technical concepts and tools that most introductory courses include to prepare students to become economics majors. I consider these exclusions to be a major strength of the textbooks. The excluded concepts detract from the student's accepting the value of the basic economic analysis that will enhance her decision-making throughout her life. As one strays beyond the core concepts and stories set out in *Economics for Life*, diminishing returns set in rapidly.

It is far more valuable, I believe, for students to understand and apply the core economic concepts well than to be exposed to a wide range of concepts they will not master and therefore will likely soon forget.

Economics for Life is also designed to get students **interested** in economics as a way of thinking that will help them make smarter choices in their lives. Concepts are not presented as theoretical ideas that must be learned in isolation, or as formulas for a set of problems. Instead, each chapter begins with a scenario, and the concepts emerge logically as the narrative unfolds.

Vision (and Graphs) for the Second Edition

The first edition had narratives based on tables of numbers — implicit graphs — but very few graphs. The second edition makes these implicit graphs explicit. The addition of simple demand and supply graphs and production possibilities frontiers fits smoothly into the existing flow of the book's narrative, providing the students an additional powerful tool for their understanding of the material. Graphs now appear in chapters on demand and supply, rent controls and minimum wages, explanation of choosing output where marginal revenue equals marginal cost, externalities, labour-hiring decisions, and in the macro text, in chapters on aggregate demand and aggregate supply (complete with output gaps and shocks), and the money, loanable funds and foreign exchange markets.

The vision of focusing on the core economic concepts remains the foundation of the second edition. There are still no indifference curves or detailed models of market structure in micro. Although I believe that the many detailed firm cost curves are not core concepts (once students master marginal cost and marginal revenue), for those who want to teach the complete model of perfect competition, there is a concise treatment in the new Appendix to Chapter 9. (Contact me if you would like to discuss my reasons for excising cost curves beyond marginal cost.) In macro there are no derivations of aggregate demand from the aggregate expenditure model, detailed multiplier formulas (whether spending, tax, transfer, or money) or aggregate production functions.

Micro still focuses on the Three Keys for Smart Choices, and the macro narrative focuses on using the expanded circular flow diagram and simple aggregate demand and aggregate supply graphs to explore the question: "How well do markets adjust to provide steady growth in living standards, full employment, and stable prices?" Students are asked throughout the macro text, "Should the government keep it's hands off of the economy, or does it need to be hands on?" I try to present sympathetically the strongest case for both the hands-off and hands-on positions.

ADDITIONAL BENEFITS VS. OPPORTUNITY COSTS

Join Me!

The second edition of *Economics for Life* retains the focus on the question "What do we really want our students to remember of what we teach them in an introductory economics class?" The focus is on essential economic concepts students need to know to become economically literate citizens, delivered in an engaging, narrative style. **Those concepts are now illustrated with the core graphs that are at the heart of thinking like an economist.** Because fewer topics are covered in more depth, this literacy-targeted approach allows instructors to spend more time in the classroom helping students master the core concepts, supported by active learning exercises, group work, economic experiments, and other forms of engagement that are integrated into both the student exercises and the Instructor's Manual. Have a look for more details.

What I find exciting about these books is the possibility of helping far more students "get" the benefit of thinking like an economist. If these books succeed in doing what they set out to do — and you and your students will be the judges of that — then your students will be more actively engaged with the material. Students will learn economics in a way that will stay with them — even five years after leaving your classroom.

This brings us back to the question of your "economic footprint." You will cover fewer topics using *Economics for Life* (the 12 micro or 9 macro chapters can be covered in a semester, with room for discussion), but your students will retain more. If we do our jobs well, after five years, your students will actually be *ahead* of students who were exposed to the full range of topics. Your economic footprint will be larger. You will have produced more students who have better learned the fundamentals of thinking like an economist, and who are making smarter choices in their lives as consumers, as businesspeople, and as citizens evaluating policies proposed by politicians.

You will have succeeded in helping your students learn how to use economics in life.

Avi Cohen
Toronto

Supplements

This textbook is supported by many supplemental materials designed to help instructors quickly customize their courses and enhance student learning.

All of the supplements have been developed and edited by Professor Avi Cohen, the author of the text. Professor Cohen has over 30 years of experience teaching introductory economics, is an award-winning teacher, and is a 3M National Teaching Fellow. He is the author of the *Study Guide* accompanying the first eight editions of Michael Parkin's and Robin Bade's *Economics: Canada in the Global Environment*. He served for many years at York University as Dean's Advisor on Technology Enhanced Learning (TEL), where he developed and ran *do TEL*, a faculty development program for instructors interested in transforming their face-to face courses to blended or fully online formats.

The following support materials developed by Professor Cohen are available for instructors.

Instructor's Manual

The Instructor's Manual (IM) will assist you in preparing for and teaching this course, whether you are a neophyte teaching the course for the first time, or an experienced instructor looking for ways to enliven your classroom or to adapt to the growing world of fully or partially online courses. The IM is organized by chapter, paralleling the textbook organization.

To make it easy and efficient for you to customize your lectures, each chapter includes an overview and concise summary of the main ideas, concepts and key graphs. You will find class discussion questions and answers to the student Refresh questions for each chapter.

Whether you are teaching 30 students or 500, we provide proven strategies for enhancing the interactivity of your classroom or online environment. Strategies, current discussion topics, economic data, and media stories will be updated regularly on Professor Cohen's teaching blog. See the Instructor's Manual for details.

PowerPoint Presentations

The PowerPoint® slides are a set of lectures based on the textbook content, paralleling the Chapter Summary found in the end-of-chapter Study Guide material. Professor Cohen selected, developed, and edited all of the content in the slides to allow you to be able to prepare and present a focused and manageable lecture without having to wade through an excessive number of slides. You can, of course, still elaborate on each slide's material. The parallels between the slides and the Study Guide's Chapter Summary make it easier for students to connect the textbook material, your classroom presentation, and the Study Guide exercises.

The design of the slides matches the textbook design so students connect more easily the material they have read and the content of your classroom presentation. The font sizes of the slides have been tested for readability from the back of a 500-seat lecture hall as well as on mobile devices. The graphs' slides are dynamic — as you click through them, curves shift and new equilibrium points appear.

Narrated Dynamic Graphs

The PowerPoint graphs, built from the textbook graphic files, are the basis of the Narrated Dynamic Graphs. For each analytical graph in the textbook, there is a short MP4 video. In a voice-over, Professor Cohen talks the student through the meaning of the graph, and traces shifts of curves and changes in outcomes. There is a moving cursor directing students' attention to the portion of the graph being discussed in the narration. These MP4 files, which tell the story of each graph, can be viewed online or downloaded to a student's computer or mobile device.

Pearson TestGen

Professor Cohen created or edited all multiple choice and true/false questions in the testbank. Multiple choice questions have five good choices. "None of the above" and "All of the above" are actually used as correct answers, and sometimes the fifth choice is humorous. Questions are classified by level of difficulty (1 – 3) and as recall or analytical.

This computerized test item file enables instructors to view and edit existing test questions, add questions, generate tests, and print tests in a variety of formats. Powerful search and sort functions make it easy to locate questions and arrange them in any order desired. TestGen also enables instructors to administer tests on a local area network, have the tests graded electronically, and have the results prepared in electronic or printed reports. These questions are also available in MyTest, which is available through MyEconLab at www.myeconlab.com.

MyEconLab

Pearson Canada's online resource, MyEconLab, offers instructors and students all of their resources in one place, written and designed to accompany this text. MyEconLab creates a perfect pedagogical loop that provides not only text-specific assessment and practice problems, but also tutorial support to make sure students learn from their mistakes.

At the core of MyEconLab are the following features:

NEW Dynamic Study Modules: Canadian study modules allow students to work through groups of question and check their understanding of foundational Economics topics. As students work through questions, the Dynamic Study Modules assess their knowledge and only show questions that still require practice. Dynamic Study Modules can be completed online using your computer, tablet, or mobile device.

NEW Learning Catalytics: Learning Catalytics is a "bring your own device" student engagement, assessment, and classroom intelligence system. It allows instructors to engage students in class with a variety of questions types designed to gauge student understanding.

Study Plan: As students work through the Study Plan, they can clearly see which topics they have mastered — and, more importantly, which they need to work on. Each question has been carefully written to match the concepts, language, and focus of the text, so students can get an accurate sense of how well they've understood the chapter content.

Adaptive Assessment: Integrated directly into the MyEconLab Study Plan, Pearson's adaptive assessment is the latest technology for individualized learning and mastery. As students work through each question, they are provided with a custom learning path tailored specifically to the concepts they need to practise and master.

Unlimited Practice: Most Study Plan exercises contain algorithmically generated values to ensure that students get as much practice as they need. Every problem links students to learning resources that further reinforce the concepts they need to master.

Auto-Graded Tests and Assignments: MyEconLab comes with two preloaded Sample Tests for each chapter. Students can use these tests for self-assessment and obtain immediate feedback. Instructors can assign the Sample Tests or use them along with Test Bank questions or their own exercises to create tests or quizzes.

Economics Video Questions: Instructors also have access to a series of video questions that tie current events to key concepts from the text.

Learning Resources: Each assessment contains a link to the eText page that discusses the concept being applied. Students also have access to guided solutions, dynamic narrated graphs, news feeds, and glossary flash cards.

Experiments in MyEconLab: Experiments are a fun and engaging way to promote active learning and mastery of important economic concepts. Pearson's Experiments program is flexible and easy for instructors and students to use. They include single-player experiments that allow students to play against virtual players from anywhere at any time and multiplayer experiments allow you to assign and manage a real-time experiment with your class.

Acknowledgments

Joseph Gladstone, Project Developer, had the original vision for this book. While we have developed that vision collaboratively, Joseph has been the guiding force and, in all but title, a co-author. Without his counsel, wisdom, and vast experience in teaching and publishing, this book would not have come to life.

Ian Howe wrote the Study Guide for the first edition and helped polish all of the original textbook chapters. His humour and vast knowledge of StatsCan data and policy issues continue to enliven many questions at the end of each chapter and in the Instructor's Manual. Andrew Dickens searched out and compiled most data for tables and charts. Deryk Ouseley drew the marvelous illustrations on the covers and others inside that capture the spirit of the *Economics for Life* books.

Much of what is good (I think; you judge) in this book comes from my long association with Robin Bade and Michael Parkin. During more than 20 years as an author to the Study Guide accompanying their *Economics: Canada in the Global Environment*, I have learned so much from their skills as teachers, writers, and economists. Their commitment to clarity, conciseness, and helping students learn has made them both an inspiration and role models. Although this textbook is intended for a slightly different audience, I hope that it will be judged to be in their league.

Many students in both my York and University of Toronto classes caught typos, ambiguities, and offered suggestions for improving the text, including Zaid Faiz, Harpal Hothi, Catherine Huntley, Vadim Slukovich, and Mia Viswanathan. Lior Krimus and Mahsa Nasseri plastered a first edition textbook with dozens of sticky notes containing detailed suggestions for better explaining concepts in ways students would "get it." The time-machine analogy for explaining marginal revenue and pricing decisions with the one-price rule in Chapter 9 is their idea.

Thanks to Dwayne Benjamin, who invited me to teach the ECO105Y course at the St. George campus, and has steadfastly supported giving the many science, public policy, and international relations students at the University of Toronto a different way to learn introductory economics, while retaining the option to become Economics majors and minors.

The team Pearson assembled — Susan Bindernagel, Richard di Santo, Joel Gladstone, Leigh-Ann Graham, Jurek Konieczny, Suzanne Simpson Millar, Victoria Naik, Mohinder Singh, Karen Townsend, Nurlan Turdaliev, and Claire Varley — have shown me how much hard work and skill go into transforming a manuscript into a product for the now-digital marketplace. I have learned that I am not simply an author, but a "digital content creator!" Thank you all.

Claudine O'Donnell deserves pride-of-place thanks for this second edition, as did Gary Bennett and Allan Reynolds for the first. It is because of their abiding faith and support that the *Economics for Life* books are before you.

Avi J. Cohen
Toronto
September 2014

The author and the publisher thank the reviewers and consultants for their time, ideas, and suggestions that have helped make this textbook better. Their input has been extremely positive and their expertise invaluable in making this new economics book more accessible and useful to both professors and students.

Aurelia Best, Centennial College
Darren Chapman, Fanshawe College
Carol Derksen, Red River College
Paritosh Ghosh, Red Deer College
Jamal Hejazi, University of Ottawa
Randy Hull, Fanshawe College
Sacha Des Rosiers, Dawson College
Gail English, New Brunswick Community College
Agostino Menna, Niagara College of Applied Arts & Technology
John O'Laney, New Brunswick Community College
Stephanie Powers, Red Deer College
Geoffrey Prince, Centennial College
Charles Ramsay, Dawson College
Sheila Ross, Southern Alberta Institute of Technology
John Saba, Champlain Regional College
Patrick Sherlock, Nova Scotia Community College
Sarah Stevens, Georgian College
Nurlan Turdaliev, University of Windsor
Franc A. Weissenhorn, Nova Scotia Community College
Carl Weston, Mohawk College

MICRO

Economics *for* Life

Smart Choices for You

1 What's in Economics for You?

Scarcity, Opportunity Cost, Trade, and Models

LEARNING OBJECTIVES

After reading this chapter, you should be able to:

1.1 Explain scarcity and describe why you must make smart choices among your wants.

1.2 Define and describe opportunity cost.

1.3 Describe how comparative advantage, specialization, and trade make us all better off.

1.4 Explain how models like the circular flow of economic life make smart choices easier.

1.5 Differentiate microeconomic and macroeconomic choices, and explain the Three Keys model for smart choices.

sellingpix/Shutterstock

EBFoto/Shutterstock

makeitdouble/Shutterstock

WHAT DO YOU WANT OUT OF LIFE?

Riches? Fame? Love? Adventure? A successful career? To make the world a better place? To live a life that respects the environment? To express your creativity? Happiness? Children? A long and healthy life? All of the above?

Many people believe economics is just about money and business, but economics can help you get what you want out of life.

The title of this book comes from a quote by Nobel Prize–winning author George Bernard Shaw: "Economy is the art of making the most of life." Economics is partly about getting the most for your money, but it is also about making smart choices generally. I wrote this book because I believe that if you learn a little economics, it will help you make the most of your life, whatever you are after. That same knowledge will also help you better understand the world around you and the choices you face as a citizen.

You don't need to be trained as an economist to lead a productive and satisfying life. But if you can learn *to think like an economist,* you can get more out of whatever life you choose to lead, and the world will be better for it.

1.1 Are You Getting Enough?
Scarcity and Choice

Explain scarcity and describe why you must make smart choices among your wants.

Can you afford to buy everything you want? If not, every dollar you spend involves a choice. If you buy the Xbox One, you might not be able to afford your English textbook. If you treat your friends to a movie, you might have to work an extra shift at your job or give up your weekend camping trip.

It would be great to have enough money to buy everything you want, but it would not eliminate the need to make smart choices. Imagine winning the biggest lottery in the world. You can buy whatever you want for yourself, your family, and your friends. But you still have only 80-some years on this planet (if you are lucky and healthy), only 24 hours in a day, and a limited amount of energy. Do you want to spend the week boarding in Whistler or surfing in Australia? Do you want to spend time raising your kids or exploring the world? Will you go to that third party on New Year's Eve or give in to sleep? Do you want to spend money on yourself, or set up a charitable foundation to help others? Bill Gates, one of the richest people on Earth, has chosen to set up the Bill and Melinda Gates Foundation. With billions of dollars in assets, the Foundation still receives more requests for worthy causes than it has dollars. How does it choose which requests to fund?

scarcity the problem that arises from our limited money, time, and energy

Economists call this inability to satisfy all of our wants the problem of **scarcity**. Scarcity arises from our limited money, time, and energy. All mortals, even billionaires, face the problem of scarcity. We all have to make choices about what we will get and what we will give up. Businesses with limited capital must choose between spending more on research or on marketing. Governments must make similar choices in facing the problem of scarcity. Spending more on colleges and universities leaves less to spend on health care. Or if governments try to spend more on all social programs, the higher taxes to pay for them mean less take-home pay for all of us.

Because none of us — individuals, businesses, governments — can ever satisfy all of our wants, smart choices are essential to making the most of our lives.

economics how individuals, businesses, and governments make the best possible choices to get what they want, and how those choices interact in markets

Economics is about how individuals, businesses, and governments make the best possible choices to get what they want, and how those choices interact in markets.

Refresh 1.1

MyEconLab

For answers to these Refresh Questions, visit MyEconLab.

1. Define scarcity and give one example from your own experience.

2. Write a definition of economics in your own words that includes the word *scarcity*.

3. Social activists argue that materialism is one of the biggest problems with society: If we all wanted less, instead of always wanting more, there would be plenty to go around for everyone. Do you agree with this statement? Why or why not?

Give It Up for Opportunity Cost!
Opportunity Cost

Scarcity means you must choose, and if you want the most out of what limited money and time you have, you need to make smart choices. A choice is like a fork in the road. You have to compare the alternatives — where does each path take you — and then pick one. You make a smart choice by weighing benefits and costs.

Choose to Snooze?

What are you going to do with the next hour? Since you are reading this, you must be considering studying as one choice. If you were out far too late last night, or up taking care of a crying baby, sleep might be your alternative choice. If those are your top choices, let's compare benefits of the two paths from this fork. For studying, the benefits are higher marks on your next test, learning something, and (if I have done my job well) perhaps enjoying reading this chapter. For sleep, the benefits are being more alert, more productive, less grumpy, and (if I have done my job poorly) avoiding the pain of reading this chapter.

If you choose the studying path, what is *the cost of your decision*? It is the hour of sleep you give up (with the benefits of rest). And if you choose sleep, the cost is the studying you give up (leading to lower marks).

In weighing the benefits and costs of any decision, we compare what we get from each path with what we give up from the other. For any choice (what we get), its true cost is what we have to give up to get it. The true cost of any choice is what economists call **opportunity cost**: the cost of the best alternative given up.

▲ The true cost of any choice you make is what you must give up to get it.

Opportunity Cost Beats Money Cost

For smart decisions, it turns out that opportunity cost is more important than money cost. Suppose you win a free trip for one to Bermuda that has to be taken the first week in December. What is the money cost of the trip? (This is not a trick question.) Zero — it's free.

But imagine you have a business client in Saskatoon who can meet to sign a million-dollar contract *only* during the first week in December. What is the opportunity cost of your "free" trip to Bermuda? $1 million. A smart decision to take or not take the trip depends on opportunity cost, not money cost.

Or what if your current significant other lives out of town, and the only time you can get together is during the first week in December? What is the opportunity cost of taking your "free" trip for one? Besides losing out on the benefits of time together, you may be kissing that relationship goodbye.

All choices are forks in the road, and the cost of any path taken is the value of the path you must give up. Because of scarcity, every choice involves a trade-off — to get something, you must give up something else. *To make a smart choice, the value of what you get must be greater than the value of what you give up*. The benefits of a smart choice must outweigh the opportunity costs.

opportunity cost the cost of the best alternative given up

what you have to give up to get the best option/opportunity

scarcity = every choice has costs + benefits

NOTE
Scarcity means every choice involves a trade-off.

Economics *Out There*

Where Have All the Men Gone?

Women make up 60 percent of undergraduate college and university students. Why do women so outnumber men? There are many explanations, from women's liberation to schools rewarding girls' more obedient behaviour and punishing boys' ADD (attention deficit disorder). There is also a simple economic explanation based on opportunity cost.

- Think of going or not going to college or university as a fork in the road.

- Weigh the costs and benefits of each choice. Everyone pays the same tuition and fees, but the benefits given up with each choice are different for women and men.

- More women than men go to college and university because the cost of *not* going is higher for women — men's alternative is higher-paying blue-collar jobs. Women's alternative tends to be lower-paying clerical or retail jobs.

Women with post-secondary education earn 50 to 80 percent more a year than women with only a high-school diploma. Men with the same post-secondary education earn only 25 to 30 percent more a year than men with only a high-school diploma. *The gap in pay* between high-school and post-secondary women is larger than the same gap for men.

Because of the differences in opportunity cost — women who don't go to college or university *give up* a bigger income gain than men do — the rate of return for a college diploma or university degree is 9 percent for women, and only around 6 percent for men. Incentives matter, and people respond to the incentives. For women, it pays more to get a post-secondary education.

---

incentives rewards and penalties for choices

Incentives Work   Since smart choices compare costs and benefits, your decisions will change with changes in costs or benefits. We all respond to **incentives** — rewards and penalties for choices. You are more likely to choose a path that leads to a reward, and avoid one with a penalty. A change in incentives causes a change in choices. If your Saskatoon business deal is worth only $100 instead of $1 000 000, you might take the trip to Bermuda. If you were up most of last night, you are more likely to sleep than to study. If you have a test tomorrow instead of next week, you are more likely to study than to sleep.

To make the most out of life and make smart decisions, you must always ask the questions, "What is the opportunity cost of my choice?" and "Do the benefits outweigh the opportunity costs?"

Refresh 1.2

MyEconLab

For answers to these Refresh Questions, visit MyEconLab.

1. What is the opportunity cost of any choice?

2. This weekend, your top choices are going camping with your friends or working extra hours at your part-time job. List three facts (think rewards and penalties) that, if they changed, would influence your decision.

3. Your sister is trying to decide whether to go to college or get a job after high school. What would you advise her to do based only on the money cost of attending college? Based on the opportunity cost of her attending college?

Why Don't You Cook Breakfast?
Gains from Trade

What did you have for breakfast today? Did you have cereal and orange juice at home, or did you buy coffee and a bagel at Tim Hortons on the way to school? Either way, you made a choice — to make breakfast for yourself, or to buy it from a business. This is the most basic choice you and everyone else makes in trying to do the best you can: Do you yourself produce the products and services you want, or do you earn money at a job and then buy (or trade money for) products and services made by others?

These days, that basic choice sounds crazy. We all work (or hope to) at jobs, earning money by specializing in a particular occupation. We use that money to buy what we want. Even a "homemade" breakfast uses cereal and juice bought at a grocery store. But if you go back only a few hundred years in Canadian history, most Aboriginal peoples and pioneers were largely self-sufficient, making for themselves most of what they needed — hunting and growing their own food, making clothes from animal hides, and building shelters from available resources.

Voluntary Trade

What happened to lead us all away from self-sufficiency toward specializing and trading? The historical answer to that question is complex, but the simple economic answer is that specializing and trading make us better off, so of course people made that basic choice. It's simple self-interest at work.

Our standard of living, in terms of material products and services, is much higher than it was hundreds of years ago in Canada. (What we have done to the environment, which in the past was better than in the present, is another story that I will also explain in terms of self-interest in Chapter 11.) The irony is that *as individuals,* we are hopeless at supporting ourselves compared to our ancestors. Yet *collectively,* our standard of living is much better.

Trade is the key to our prosperity. Trade makes all of us better off. Why? Trade is voluntary. Any time two people make a voluntary trade, each person feels that what they get is of greater value than what they give up. If there weren't mutual benefits, the trade wouldn't happen. But how does trade make us better off?

Bake or Chop? Again, opportunity cost is the key to the mutual benefits from trade. To illustrate, let's take a simple imaginary example of two early Canadians who are each self-sufficient in producing food and shelter.

Jill grows her own wheat to make bread, and chops her own wood for fire and shelter. If she spends an entire month producing only bread, she can make 50 loaves. Alternatively, if she spends all her time chopping wood, she can cut 100 logs. Her monthly choice of how to spend her time looks like the picture in the margin.

Since Jill is self-sufficient, that means she can consume only what she produces herself, so she must divide her time and produce some bread and some wood. The table in Figure 1.1 shows different possible combinations (*A – F*) of bread and wood she can produce, depending on how she divides up her time during the month. From these production possibilities, Jill chooses to produce possibility *D,* 20 loaves of bread and 60 logs of wood. We will get to the graph in a moment.

voluntary - a trade you make because you think it is worth it

NOTE
When you "trade" money for coffee at Tim Hortons, that is a voluntary exchange. If you thought you would be better off keeping the money instead of the coffee, you wouldn't pay. If Tims weren't better off with your money instead of the coffee, it wouldn't sell.

▲ Since she's self-sufficient, Jill must choose how much bread to bake and wood to chop in order to survive.

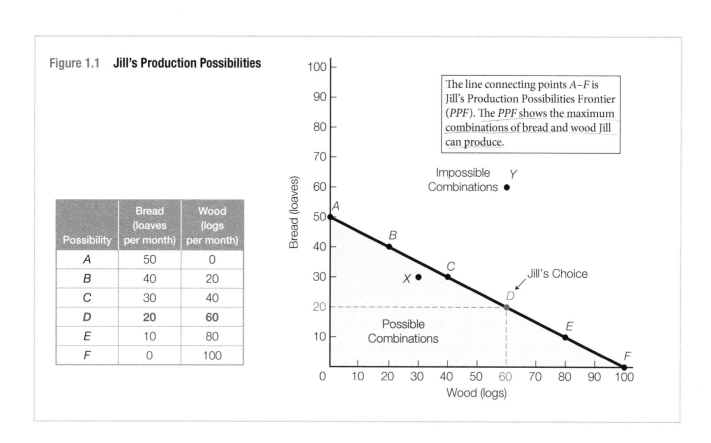

Figure 1.1 Jill's Production Possibilities

Possibility	Bread (loaves per month)	Wood (logs per month)
A	50	0
B	40	20
C	30	40
D	20	60
E	10	80
F	0	100

The line connecting points *A–F* is Jill's Production Possibilities Frontier (*PPF*). The *PPF* shows the maximum combinations of bread and wood Jill can produce.

Marie, Jill's nearest neighbour, also grows her own wheat to make bread, and chops her own wood for fire and shelter. The table in Figure 1.2 shows the possible monthly combinations of bread and wood she can produce, depending on how she divides up her time.

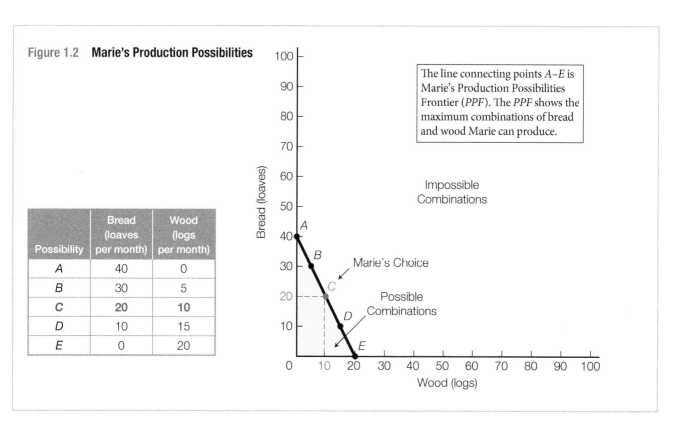

Figure 1.2 Marie's Production Possibilities

Possibility	Bread (loaves per month)	Wood (logs per month)
A	40	0
B	30	5
C	20	10
D	10	15
E	0	20

The line connecting points *A–E* is Marie's Production Possibilities Frontier (*PPF*). The *PPF* shows the maximum combinations of bread and wood Marie can produce.

Marie is weaker than Jill, so if Marie spends an entire month producing only bread, she can make 40 loaves (possibility *A* in Figure 1.2). Alternatively, if she spends all her time chopping wood, she can cut only 20 logs (possibility *E*). Since Marie is also self-sufficient, and can consume only what she produces herself, she divides her time and produces some bread and some wood. From these production possibilities, Marie chooses to produce possibility *C*, 20 loaves of bread and 10 logs of wood.

Production Possibilities Frontier   A **production possibilities frontier —** *PPF* for short — shows the maximum combinations of products or services that can be produced with existing inputs. The graphs in Figures 1.1 and 1.2 show the production possibilities of our two pioneers.

Look first at Jill's *PPF* in the Figure 1.1 graph. The monthly quantity of wood she can produce is measured on the horizontal axis. The monthly quantity of bread is measured on the vertical axis. When you connect the points representing her possible combinations of wood and bread (*A – F* from the Figure 1.1 table), you get the straight black line that is Jill's production possibilities frontier. The points on Jill's *PPF* show the *maximum* combinations of bread and wood she can produce if she uses all of her time, tools, and other inputs. Jill chose combination *D, 20 loaves and 60 logs*.

Jill could also choose not to work so hard and produce less. She could choose to produce any combination of bread and wood *inside* her production possibilities frontier. For example, she could decide to produce the combination of 30 loaves and 30 logs (possibility *X*). The shaded area inside her *PPF* represents all of her "possible combinations." These combinations are possible, but are not maximum.

Combinations of bread and wood *outside* of Jill's *PPF* are impossible for her to produce. Jill, like all of us, faces the problem of scarcity. She has limited time and energy, and can't produce everything she might want. A combination of 60 loaves of bread and 60 logs of wood (possibility *Y*) might make Jill happier and more comfortable, but that combination is impossible for her to produce.

Similarly, Marie's *PPF* in the Figure 1.2 graph shows the maximum possible combinations of bread and wood she can produce. Marie chose combination *C*. Her other possible production combinations are inside her *PPF*. Impossible combinations are outside her *PPF*. Marie has fewer possible combinations of bread and wood production than Jill.

Deal or No Deal? Do the Numbers

Can trade make both Jill and Marie better off? It doesn't look promising, especially for Jill. She is a better bread maker than Marie (50 loaves versus 40 loaves) *and* a better wood chopper (100 logs versus 20 logs). An economist would describe Jill as having an **absolute advantage** — the ability to produce a product or service at a *lower absolute cost* than another producer — over Marie in both bread production and wood production. That is, Jill is more productive as a bread maker and as a wood chopper. If we were to measure dollar costs (which I have left out to keep the example as simple as possible), absolute advantage would mean Jill could produce both bread and wood at lower absolute dollar costs than Marie could.

If you are not keen on history, then in place of Jill and Marie, think China and Canada. If China can produce everything at lower cost than Canada, can there be mutually beneficial gains from trade for both countries? What's the benefit for China? Won't all Canadians end up unemployed?

production possibilities frontier   maximum combinations of products or services that can be produced with existing inputs

absolute advantage   the ability to produce a product or service at a lower absolute cost than another producer

*cost of
a choice*

Comparative Advantage But mutually beneficial gains from trade do not depend on absolute advantage. They depend on what economists call **comparative advantage** — the ability to produce a product or service at a *lower opportunity cost* than another producer. To figure out comparative advantage, we need to calculate *opportunity costs* for Jill and Marie.

Opportunity costs are always calculated by comparing two alternative possibilities — two choices. Comparing possibilities A and F in the Figure 1.1 table or graph, Jill can produce 50 loaves of bread and zero wood or 100 logs of wood and zero bread. If she chooses to bake 50 loaves of bread, the opportunity cost is 100 logs of wood. If she instead chooses to chop 100 logs of wood, the opportunity cost is 50 loaves of bread. Opportunity cost is the value of the path — the choice — *not taken*.

To compare opportunity costs, it is easier if we measure them per unit of the product chosen. Here is a simple, useful formula for finding opportunity cost:

$$\text{Opportunity cost} = \frac{\text{Give Up}}{\text{Get}}$$

So Jill's opportunity cost of producing more bread is

$$\text{Opportunity cost of additional bread} = \frac{100 \text{ logs of wood}}{50 \text{ loaves of bread}} = \frac{2 \text{ logs of wood}}{1 \text{ loaf of bread}}$$

Jill must give up 2 logs of wood to get each additional loaf of bread.

What is Jill's opportunity cost of producing more wood?

$$\text{Opportunity cost of additional wood} = \frac{50 \text{ loaves of bread}}{100 \text{ logs of wood}} = \frac{\frac{1}{2} \text{ loaf of bread}}{1 \text{ log of wood}}$$

Jill must give up ½ loaf of bread to get each additional log of wood.

If you calculate opportunity costs for Marie (compare possibilities A and E in Figure 1.2), her opportunity cost of getting an additional loaf of bread is giving up ½ log of wood, and her opportunity cost of getting an additional log of wood is giving up 2 loaves of bread. These opportunity cost calculations are summarized in Figure 1.3. Since comparative advantage is defined as lowest opportunity cost (not lowest absolute cost), you can see that Marie has a comparative advantage in bread-making (give up ½ log of wood versus Jill's 2 logs of wood), while Jill has a comparative advantage in wood-chopping (give up ½ loaf of bread versus Marie's 2 loaves of bread).

Figure 1.3 Opportunity Costs for Jill and Marie

	Opportunity Cost of 1 Additional	
	Loaf of Bread	Log of Wood
Jill	Gives up 2 logs of wood	Gives up ½ loaf of bread
Marie	Gives up ½ log of wood	Gives up 2 loaves of bread
Comparative Advantage	Marie has comparative advantage (lower opportunity cost) in bread-making	Jill has comparative advantage (lower opportunity cost) in wood-chopping

Smart Deals

Here's the payoff to these calculations. Instead of each pioneer being self-sufficient, and producing everything she needs herself, look what happens if our pioneers specialize in producing what each is best at, and then trading.

According to comparative advantage, Jill should specialize in only chopping wood, and Marie should specialize in only making bread. In this way, Jill will produce 100 logs of wood and no bread, and Marie will produce 40 loaves of bread and no wood. If they then trade 20 logs of wood for 20 loaves of bread:

- Jill ends up with 20 loaves of bread (0 produced plus 20 traded for) and 80 logs of wood (100 produced minus 20 traded away);
- Marie ends up with 20 loaves of bread (40 produced minus 20 traded away) and 20 logs of wood (0 produced plus 20 traded for).

Figure 1.4 tells the story of Jill and Marie's specialization and trade.

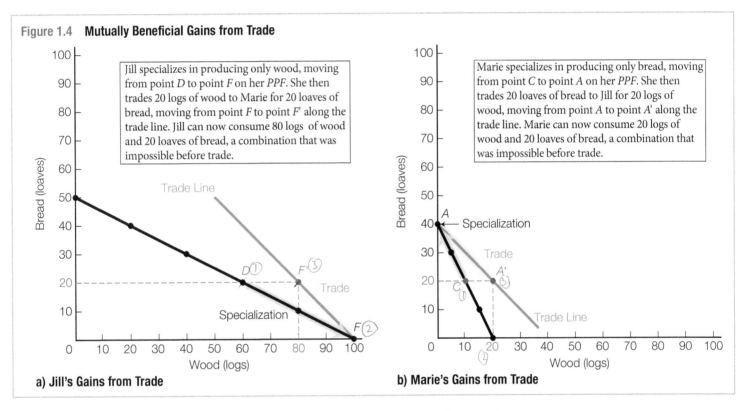

Figure 1.4 **Mutually Beneficial Gains from Trade**

Jill specializes in producing only wood, moving from point D to point F on her PPF. She then trades 20 logs of wood to Marie for 20 loaves of bread, moving from point F to point F' along the trade line. Jill can now consume 80 logs of wood and 20 loaves of bread, a combination that was impossible before trade.

Marie specializes in producing only bread, moving from point C to point A on her PPF. She then trades 20 loaves of bread to Jill for 20 logs of wood, moving from point A to point A' along the trade line. Marie can now consume 20 logs of wood and 20 loaves of bread, a combination that was impossible before trade.

a) **Jill's Gains from Trade**

b) **Marie's Gains from Trade**

Jill (Figure 1.4a) starts out at point D on her PPF (20 loaves and 60 logs). Choosing to specialize in only chopping wood, she moves down along her production possibilities frontier to point F, producing 100 logs of wood and no bread.

Marie (Figure 1.4b) starts out at point C on her PPF (20 loaves and 10 logs). Choosing to specialize in only baking bread, she moves up along her production possibilities frontier to point A, producing 40 loaves of bread and no wood.

Trade occurs along the blue trade lines. As either Jill or Marie moves along the trade lines to exchange wood for bread, 1 log of wood trades for 1 loaf of bread.

Jill moves from her point F (100 logs, 0 loaves) to the new point F' along the trade line, trading 20 logs of wood for 20 loaves of bread. She ends up with 80 logs of wood and 20 loaves of bread.

Marie moves from her point A (40 loaves, 0 logs) along the trade line to the new point A', trading 20 loaves of bread for 20 logs of wood. She ends up with 20 loaves and 20 logs.

Achieving the Impossible Check it out. *After trading, Jill and Marie are both better off than when they were each self-sufficient.* Before trade, the best Jill could produce with 20 loaves of bread was 60 logs of wood (point *D*). After trade, Jill has the same amount of bread and more wood. Before trade, the best Marie could produce with 20 loaves of bread was just 10 logs of wood (point *C*). After trade, Marie has the same amount of bread and more wood.

Jill and Marie each reach a combination of wood and bread that was impossible before trade. After specialization and trade, each can now consume a combination of wood and bread that is outside of her production possibilities frontier. Voluntary trade is not a zero-sum game, where one person's gain is the other's loss. Both traders gain.

What is remarkable is that these *gains from trade,* which improve both Jill's and Marie's standards of living (with more wood they can stay warmer or build better houses), *happen without anyone working harder, or without any improvement in technology or new inputs.* Both are better off because they have made smart decisions to specialize and trade, rather than each trying to produce only what each will consume. Both can have toast for breakfast (bread roasted over a fire), even though each produced only part of what was necessary to make the breakfast.

Notice also that there are gains for both Jill and Marie, even though Jill can produce more bread and wood than Marie can. Despite Jill's absolute advantage in producing everything at lower cost, there are still differences in opportunity costs, or comparative advantage. *Comparative advantage is the key to mutually beneficial gains from trade.* The trade can be between individuals, or between countries. That is why China trades with Canada, even though China can produce most things more cheaply than Canada can. There are still differences in comparative advantage based on opportunity costs. Trade allows us all to work smarter and live better.

So the next time you buy breakfast, don't feel guilty about spending the money when you could have cooked it yourself — feel smart about specializing and trading — a smart choice that makes you better off!

NOTE
Specialization according to comparative advantage is the key to mutually beneficial gains from trade. All arguments you will ever hear for freer trade are based on comparative advantage.

Refresh 1.3

MyEconLab

For answers to these Refresh Questions, visit MyEconLab.

1. Explain the difference between absolute advantage and comparative advantage.

2. If you spend the next hour working at Canadian Tire, you will earn $10. If instead you spend the next hour studying economics, your next test score will improve by five marks. Calculate the opportunity cost of studying in terms of dollars given up per mark. Calculate the opportunity cost of working in terms of marks given up per dollar.

3. The best auto mechanic in town (who charges $120/hour) is also a better typist than her office manager (who earns $20/hour). The mechanic decides to do her own typing. Is this a smart choice for her to make? Explain your answer.
[*Hint:* The best alternative employment for the office manager is another office job that also pays $20/hour.]

Economists as Mapmakers and Scientists: Thinking Like an Economist

Explain how models like the circular flow of economic life make smart choices easier.

Canada is a very large country, the second largest in the world in terms of geographical area. Have you ever had the urge to follow in the footsteps of our ancestors and explore the land — perhaps a trip to the northernmost tip of the Northwest Territories, or a cross-country trip from Newfoundland to British Columbia?

Economics is the study of mankind in the ordinary business of life.

— Alfred Marshall (1890)

Why Maps (and Economists) Are Useful

How do you start planning your trip? The satellite photo of Canada below, while amazing to look at, is not very useful. It contains too much information and too little information. How can that be? The photo captures every aspect of Canada that can be seen from space — lakes, rivers, mountains, and forests. But the photo doesn't reveal smaller details that are important for your trip — most importantly, roads, railways, or ferry services.

A map of the same area shows you the auto route along the Trans-Canada Highway (you've decided it's too cold to go up north). Why is the map so much more useful than the satellite photo? Because it focuses your attention on the information that is most relevant for your task, and leaves all other information in the background.

Learning to think like an economist allows the key "roads" to making smart choices stand out — like looking at life on the map. This kind of thinking makes difficult decisions and understanding the complex world around you easier.

There are an almost infinite number of choices we could look at, so to keep things manageable, let's limit ourselves to the opening definition of economics: *Economics is about how individuals, businesses, and governments make the best possible choices to get what they want, and about how those choices interact in markets.* (We will look at markets more closely in Chapter 4, but for the moment, think of a market as the interaction of buyers and sellers.)

Another good definition of economics was presented in 1890 by Alfred Marshall, a legendary professor who first created economics as a separate subject at the University of Cambridge. Marshall said: "Economics is the study of mankind in the ordinary business of life."

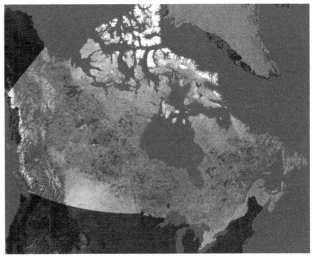

▲ Satellite photo of Canada — not useful for trip planning.

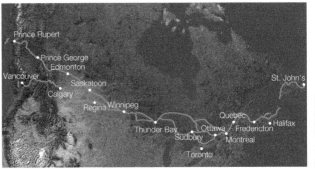

▲ Map of Canada with the Trans-Canada Highway — useful for trip planning.

The Circular Flow of Economic Life

Even limiting ourselves to these definitions of economics, the choices are still overwhelming. Imagine 35 million people spread out over 10 million square kilometres, engaged in the "ordinary business of life," earning a living, specializing in producing products and services, selling, and buying. Instead of trying to capture every detail of every action and choice (like the satellite photo), Figure 1.5 shows a map version of the same economic activity.

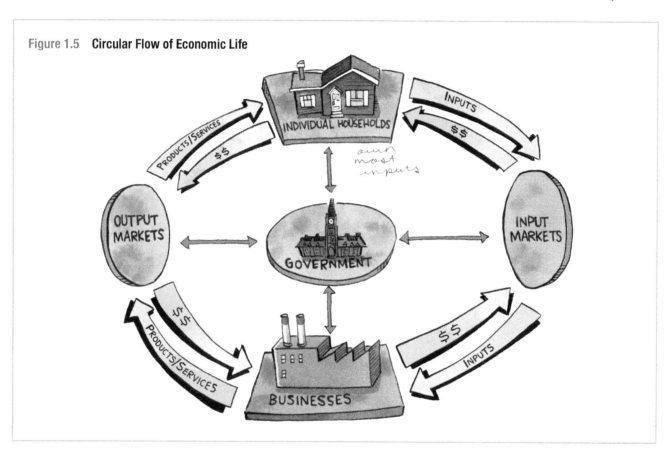

Figure 1.5   **Circular Flow of Economic Life**

model   a simplified representation of the real world, focusing attention on what's important for understanding

inputs   the productive resources — labour, natural resources, capital equipment, and entrepreneurial ability — used to produce products and services

long lasting goods used to produce other commodities ex trucks

Economic Models   The maps that economists use are called economic models. A **model** is a simplified representation of the real world, focusing attention on what's important for understanding a specific idea or concept.

Figure 1.5 is an economic model called the "circular flow of economic life." It shows you the simplest big picture of how an economist thinks about economic choices. All the complexity of the Canadian economy is reduced to three sets of players: households, businesses, and governments. Individuals in households ultimately own all of the **inputs** of an economy — the productive resources used to produce products and services. The four types of inputs are labour (the ability to work), natural resources, capital equipment, and entrepreneurial ability. Even the assets of the largest corporations, such as Imperial Oil, Ford, or BlackBerry, are ultimately owned by individual shareholders.

Households and businesses interact in two sets of markets — input markets (where businesses buy the inputs they need to produce products and services), and output markets (where businesses sell their products and services). Governments (in the middle) set the rules of the game and can choose to interact, or not, in almost any aspect of the economy.

Follow the Flow Clockwise   Follow the circle, starting at the top. Individuals in households sell or rent to businesses the labour, resources, capital, and entrepreneurial abilities they own. This is the outer blue flow on the right-hand side of the circle, from top to bottom. In exchange, businesses pay wages and other money rewards to households. This is the inner green flow on the right-hand side of the circle, from bottom to top. These exchanges, or trades, happen in input markets, where households are the sellers and businesses are the buyers. When Mr. Sub hires you to work in its stores, that interaction happens in an input market — the labour market.

Businesses then use those inputs to produce products and services, which they sell to households. This is the outer blue flow on the left-hand side of the circle, from bottom to top. In exchange, households use the money they have earned in input markets to pay businesses for these purchases. This is the inner green flow on the left-hand side of the circle, from top to bottom. These exchanges, or trades, happen in output markets, where households are the buyers and businesses are the sellers. These are markets where you buy your breakfast from a store or supermarket, your cars from Ford or Toyota, your piercings from a neighbourhood piercing parlour, and so on.

At the end of the trip around the circle, households have the products and services they need to live, and businesses end up with the money. That sets the stage for the next trip around the circle, where businesses again buy inputs from individuals in households, and the flow goes on.

So there you have it — an economic model, a sort of map, to guide you on your economics road trip toward understanding and making smart choices.

Models as the Economist's Laboratory

An economic model, like a map, is useful because it is focused and leaves out unnecessary information. But how do you know if the information your model leaves out is important, preventing you from making a smart choice? The test of a good map is if it gets you quickly and safely to where you want to go, without your getting lost. What is the test of a good economic model?

A good economic model helps you make smart choices, or helps you better understand the observed facts of the economic world around you. The test is in comparing the simplified picture of the model with the facts. If the model helps you understand or predict the facts, it's a good model.

But testing an economic model is difficult because the facts we observe are affected by many factors, including factors the model leaves out. For example, the circular flow model in Figure 1.5 leaves out economic factors like international trade between Canada and other countries, the value of the Canadian dollar, and competition between specific banks like RBC or TD Bank. The model also leaves out non-economic factors like the weather, global warming, and military conflicts. Yet all of those factors affect the Canadian economy. Is the simple model still useful even though it ignores those complicating factors?

input market: households = sellers businesses = buyers

output market: households = buyers businesses = sellers

All Other Things Unchanged To test models against the facts, economists do what natural scientists do. We assume that "other things are unchanged," to remove the influence of the factors left out of the simplified model. Here is a natural science example.

The law of gravity predicts that, all other factors unchanged, objects fall at the same rate regardless of their mass. So if we drop a bowling ball and a feather from a tall building, and find the bowling ball hits the ground first, does that disprove the law of gravity? No, because we are not controlling for air resistance, which changes the path of the feather more than the bowling ball. To accurately test the law of gravity, we must perform the same experiment in a laboratory vacuum, so that we eliminate, or control for, the influence of air resistance as an "other factor." We need to keep all other factors unchanged.

A good economic example is the model of demand and supply. In Chapter 2 you will learn about the "law of demand," which predicts that, all other factors unchanged, as the price of a product rises, the quantity demanded by consumers decreases. If the price of wine rises, and consumers buy more wine, does that disprove the law of demand? Not necessarily, because we are not controlling for changes in other factors, like increasing income, which could lead consumers to buy more wine even as the price rises. To accurately test the "law of demand," we need to keep all other factors, like income, unchanged.

Economists, and citizens like you, have it much tougher than scientists. We can't pause everything in the world while focusing only on the factors we are interested in. Instead, we have to use economic models to isolate the factors we think are important. The economic models you will learn here focus attention on what is important by assuming that all other things not in the model are unchanged. Thinking like an economist and using economic models is the mental equivalent of the controlled experiments of the laboratory!

NOTE
Economic models, which assume all other things not in the model are unchanged, are the mental equivalent of controlled experiments in a laboratory.

Economics *Out There*

Do You Want to Be an Online Gamer Economist?

More and more online gaming businesses are hiring economists. As an academic economist, Yanis Varoufakis was well aware of economists'

> "inability to run experiments on a macroeconomy such as rewinding time to, say, 1932, in order to see whether the US would have rebounded [from the Great Depression] without the New Deal [a policy of massive government spending] . . . . Even at the level of the microeconomy, keeping faith with the *ceteris paribus* assumption (. . . keeping all other things equal [unchanged] in order to measure, e.g., the relationship between the price of and the demand for milk) is impossible."

Varfoufakis signed on to work with Valve, a major video game company behind hits like *Half-Life*, *Portal*, *Team Fortress*, and *Dota*. The attraction was

"In sharp contrast to our incapacity to perform truly scientific tests in 'normal' economic settings, Valve's digital economies are a marvelous test-bed for meaningful experimentation. . . . we can change the economy's underlying values, rules and settings, and then sit back to observe how the community responds, how relative prices change, the new behavioural patterns that evolve. An economist's paradise indeed . . ."

Online gaming businesses aren't limited to creating models of the economy. They have complete digital gaming economies and can literally change one factor at a time and digitally capture all of the resulting changes.

If you like gaming, perhaps economics is for you — or better still, if you love economics, maybe online gaming is for you!

Source: Yanis Varoufakis, "It All Began with a Strange Email," *Valve Economics,* June 14, 2012, http://blogs.valvesoftware.com/economics/it-all-began-with-a-strange-email/.

Positive and Normative Statements   In trying to explain the facts of the world, economists, like other scientists, distinguish facts from opinions.

Positive statements are about what is; about things that can be checked. "Toronto is closer to Vancouver than to St. John's, Newfoundland" is a positive statement. It can be evaluated as true or false by checking the facts. (False. Vancouver is 3354 kilometres away from Toronto; St. John's is 2112 kilometres away.)

Normative statements involve value judgments or opinions; things that cannot be factually checked. "You should go to Vancouver for your holiday instead of St. John's" is a normative statement. A normative statement is based on personal values, which differ among individuals. Normative statements cannot be tested or shown to be true or false.

The distinction between positive statements and normative statements will also help you make smart choices. To make smart choices in life, you first have to decide on your goals — What do you value? Should you spend your life getting rich or helping others? Those are normative questions. Once you choose your goals, thinking like an economist and using economic models and positive statements will help you effectively achieve them, and get you to where you want to go.

positive statements   about what is; can be evaluated as true or false by checking the facts

normative statements   about what you believe should be; involve value judgments

positive = fact
normative = opinion

Refresh 1.4

1. Who are the three sets of players in the circular flow model of economic life?

2. Write a positive statement linking increasing government taxes on tobacco and smoking habits. Now rewrite it as a normative statement.

3. If you are trying to decide whether to buy a car, what are the most important factors to focus on when making your decision? What are some of the factors that you ignore, or leave out of your decision? Explain how your thinking resembles an economic model.

MyEconLab

For answers to these Refresh Questions, visit MyEconLab.

Where and How to Look: Models for Microeconomics and Macroeconomics

1.5

Differentiate microeconomic and macroeconomic choices, and explain the Three Keys model for smart choices.

"One size fits all" does not apply to maps or to models. The map of Canada with the highlighted Trans-Canada Highway may be fine for planning the big picture of your trip, but when you are trying to get to a hostel in downtown Fredricton, New Brunswick, from the Trans-Canada, a detailed city map is far more useful. Different needs require different kinds of maps. Depending on the task, economists also use different kinds of models.

The economic way of thinking, while always concerned with smart choices and their interactions in markets, can be applied on different scales to understand microeconomics and macroeconomics.

It's All Greek to Me: Microeconomics or Macroeconomics?

Microeconomics   "Micro" comes from the Greek word *mikros*, meaning "little" or "small." A microscope lets us see little details of an object. A micromanager supervises every tiny detail of an employee's work (ever had a boss like that?). A detailed city map has a micro scale. **Microeconomics** analyzes the choices made by individuals in households, individual businesses, and governments, and how those choices interact in markets.

Microeconomic choices for individuals include whether to go to college or to get a job, whether to be self-sufficient or to specialize and trade, whether to take out a bank loan or to run up a credit card balance, and whether to get married or to stay single. (Yes, there is even a microeconomic analysis comparing the benefits and costs of marriage!)

Microeconomic choices for businesses include what product or service to produce, how much to spend on research and development of new products, which technology to use, which marketing strategy to use, and whether to outsource manufacturing to China or produce in Canada.

Microeconomic choices for governments focus on individual industries. For example, should the government step in and regulate the wireless phone industry (including Bell, Telus, Rogers, and smaller providers), or let competition determine the winners and losers? How would a carbon tax affect car sales?

Macroeconomics   When we step back from individual details and look at the big picture, we are taking a "macro" view. Macro comes from the Greek word *makros*, meaning "large." The macrocosm is the cosmos, or the whole of a complex structure. A macrobiotic diet consists of whole, pure foods based on Taoist principles of the overall balance of yin and yang. **Macroeconomics** analyzes the performance of the whole Canadian economy and the global economy, the combined outcomes of all individual microeconomic choices. For the circular flow model in Figure 1.5, instead of focusing on the individual exchanges in markets, macroeconomics focuses on the whole circle, the combined outcomes of all of the individual interactions in markets.

Macroeconomics focuses on overall outcomes of market interactions, including Canadian unemployment, inflation rates, government deficits and surpluses, interest rates set by the Bank of Canada, the value of the Canadian dollar, and international trade. Macroeconomics also examines the policy choices governments make that affect the whole economy — for example, whether to play an active economic role by spending and taxing (more likely for New Democrats or Liberals) or to leave the economy alone (more likely for Conservatives), whether to raise or lower taxes, whether to raise or lower interest rates, and whether to defend the value of the Canadian dollar or let it be determined by economic forces. Since government macroeconomic policy choices will affect your personal economic fortunes, as a citizen you have a personal incentive to learn some macroeconomics so you can make more informed choices when voting for politicians.

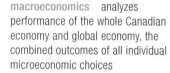

microeconomics analyzes choices that individuals in households, individual businesses, and governments make, and how those choices interact in markets

macroeconomics analyzes performance of the whole Canadian economy and global economy, the combined outcomes of all individual microeconomic choices

Looking at the Trees or the Forest? The difference between micro and macro views is reflected in the subtitle of these books — *Microeconomics for Life: Smart Choices for You* and *Macroeconomics for Life: Smart Choices for All?* The microeconomics book, with the subtitle *Smart Choices for You*, is about individual choices. The macroeconomic book, with the subtitle *Smart Choices for All?*, is about the combined market outcomes of all choices. Micro looks at the individual trees, while macro looks at the forest.

Three Keys to Smart Choices: Weigh Marginal Benefits and Marginal Costs

Whether you are taking a course in microeconomics, macroeconomics, or both, all roads to smart choices begin with microeconomic choices.

Good road maps make travel easier, and economic models make smart choices easier. Figure 1.6 shows a second economic model to help guide all of your microeconomic choices toward being smart choices. This model consists of three keys to consider when standing at any fork in the road, when making any choice. While this model doesn't look like a traditional map (no cities, roads, or lines), it serves the same function as all maps and models do — focusing your attention on the information that is most useful for making a smart choice, and leaving all other information in the background.

For each key, pay special attention to the words in **BOLDED CAPS** in the explanations.

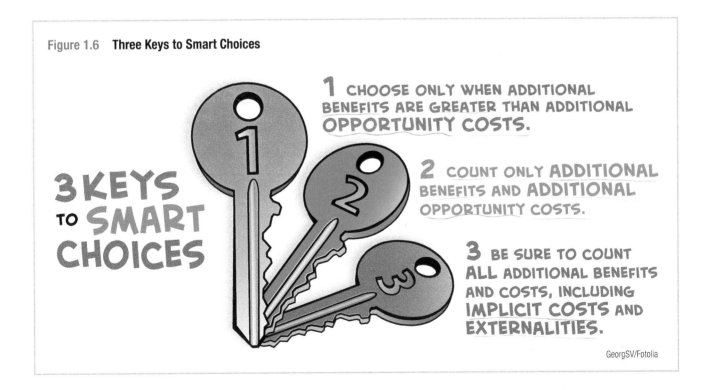

Figure 1.6 **Three Keys to Smart Choices**

1 CHOOSE ONLY WHEN ADDITIONAL BENEFITS ARE GREATER THAN ADDITIONAL OPPORTUNITY COSTS.

2 COUNT ONLY **ADDITIONAL** BENEFITS AND **ADDITIONAL** OPPORTUNITY COSTS.

3 BE SURE TO COUNT **ALL** ADDITIONAL BENEFITS AND COSTS, INCLUDING **IMPLICIT COSTS** AND **EXTERNALITIES.**

GeorgSV/Fotolia

Key 1: Opportunity Costs Rule To make a smart choice, when you weigh benefits against costs, additional benefits must be greater than additional *opportunity costs*. When counting costs, people who make dumb decisions usually count only money costs, rather than including opportunity costs as well. Remember the "free" trip to Bermuda? The money cost was zero, but the opportunity cost was the $1-million deal you would have given up. Or think about your decision to go to college. For that fork in the road, the additional benefits include the higher lifetime income you will earn from your education. The additional costs are the money you spend on tuition and books (these money costs are also opportunity costs, as you could have spent the same money to buy other things), as well as the income you give up by not working full time. The additional benefits must be greater than all additional opportunity costs (and the data show that they are — so congratulations on making a smart choice!).

Key 2: Look Forward Only to Additional Benefits and Opportunity Costs If you are deciding whether or not to study for the next hour, the tuition you paid for this course is irrelevant. You can't get it back whether you choose to study or not. When standing at a fork in the road, don't look back, only look forward. Your previous decisions or the money you already spent are history and can't be undone. The past is the same no matter which fork you choose now, so it shouldn't influence your choice.

Your choices should weigh the *additional* benefit from the next hour of studying against the *additional* cost (giving up sleep, or perhaps working an extra hour at your part-time job). It's not the total benefit of all hours spent studying or the average benefit of an hour of studying that matters, only the additional benefit. Economists use the word "marginal" instead of "additional," so you can also read Key 2 as "Count only **marginal benefits** — additional benefits from your next choice — and **marginal opportunity costs** — additional opportunity costs from your next choice." Chapter 2 will explain marginal benefits, and Chapter 3 will explain marginal costs. Thinking like an economist means thinking at the margin.

marginal benefits additional benefits from the next choice

marginal opportunity costs additional opportunity costs from the next choice

Key 3: Implicit Costs and Externalities Count, Too If you invest $1000 in your own business, and expect to get $1100 back in a year, is that a smart choice? You can't know until you compare the best alternative use of your money. If the best your bank pays is $1050 in a year, invest in your business. But if the bank is paying 20 percent interest, paying $1200 in a year, your business investment is not a smart choice. Economists use the term **implicit costs** to describe the opportunity costs of investing your own money or time. These *implicit costs* will not show up on the books your accountant would prepare, as we will see in Chapter 7. But smart choices must incorporate implicit costs.

implicit costs opportunity costs of investing your own money or time

Negative Externalities   Driving a car is expensive. Think of the gas bill alone for driving clear across Canada! But your costs also include car payments, insurance, repairs, licence fees, tolls, and parking. What's more, as expensive as those costs are, they don't cover the total cost of driving a car. Your car also emits pollution, but you don't pay for the costs of damage to the environment from acid rain, or for the increased medical costs to treat patients suffering from asthma and other pollution-related illnesses. Economists call these costs that you create, but don't pay for directly, **negative externalities**. They are costs that affect others who are external to a choice or trade. But from an environmentalist's or economist's point of view, *external costs* should be included in making smart decisions.

costs you create but don't pay for directly

negative (or positive) externalities   costs (or benefits) that affect others external to a choice or a trade

Positive Externalities   There are also **positive externalities**, benefits that affect others who are external to a choice or trade. If you plant a beautiful garden in your front lawn, you certainly benefit, but so do all of your neighbours who take in the colours and smells. Again, from an economist's point of view, *positive externalities* should be included in making smart decisions, but they are not.

As we will see in Microeconomics Chapter 11, market economies like ours in Canada tend to produce too many products and services that have negative externalities, and too few products and services that have positive externalities. Government policy can play an important role in adjusting for external costs and benefits to result in smart decisions for society.

Moving On

The Three Keys will guide all of your microeconomic choices. If you go on to study macroeconomics, they and the circular flow model of economic life will continue to guide you.

Now that you have been introduced to the economic models, let's get on with the journey. You will use the Three Keys model to make smart decisions many times over the coming chapters. Don't worry if they seem a bit sketchy for now. Each time we use them, we will fill in some of the details that might seem to be missing.

The models in Figures 1.5 and 1.6 will help you learn to think like an economist, which will help you get more out of whatever life you choose to lead, as well as help you make better decisions as a citizen.

Refresh 1.5

1. List the three keys to smart choices, and highlight the most important words in each key.

2. Find one story in today's news that you think is about microeconomics, and one that is about macroeconomics. How did you decide whether the story was about micro or macro economics?

3. Highway 407 ETR in Toronto is a toll road that uses transponders to keep track of how many kilometres you drive on it, and then sends you a monthly bill. Highway 401 runs parallel to Highway 407 and is free. Why do drivers voluntarily pay the tolls? (Use opportunity cost in your answer.) Suppose the government could calculate the cost per kilometre of the pollution damage from your driving, and send you a similar monthly bill. How might that additional cost affect your decision to drive?

MyEconLab

For answers to these Refresh Questions, visit MyEconLab.

Study Guide

1.1 Are You Getting Enough? Scarcity and Choice

Because you can never satisfy all of your wants, making the most out of your life requires smart choices about what to go after, and what to give up.

- The problem of **scarcity** arises because of limited money, time, and energy.
- **Economics** is how individuals, businesses, and governments make the best possible choices to get what they want, and how those choices interact in markets.

1.2 Give It Up for Opportunity Cost! Opportunity Cost

Opportunity cost is the single most important concept both in economics and for making smart choices in life.

- Because of scarcity, every choice involves a trade-off — you have to give up something to get something else.
- The true cost of any choice is the **opportunity cost** — the cost of the best alternative given up.
- For a smart choice, the value of what you get must be greater than value of what you give up.
- **Incentives** — rewards and penalties for choices.
- You are more likely to choose actions with rewards (positive incentives), and avoid actions with penalties (negative incentives).

1.3 Why Don't You Cook Breakfast? Gains from Trade

Opportunity cost and comparative advantage are key to understanding why specializing and trading make us all better off.

- With voluntary trade, each person feels that what they get is of greater value than what they give up.
- **Production possibilities frontier** (*PPF*) — graph showing the maximum combinations of products or services that can be produced with existing inputs.
- **Absolute advantage** — the ability to produce a product or service at a lower absolute cost than another producer.

- **Comparative advantage** — the ability to produce a product or service at a lower opportunity cost than another producer.
- Trade makes individuals better off when each specializes in the product or service where they have a comparative advantage (lower opportunity cost) and then trades for the other product or service.
- Specialization according to comparative advantage and trade allows each trader to consume outside her *PPF*, a combination that was impossible without trade. All arguments you will ever hear for freer trade are based on comparative advantage.
- Even if one individual has an absolute advantage in producing everything at lower cost, as long as there are differences in comparative advantage, there are mutually beneficial gains from specializing and trading.

1.4 Economists as Mapmakers and Scientists: Thinking Like an Economist

The circular-flow model, like all economic models, focuses attention on what's important for understanding and shows how smart choices by households, businesses, and governments interact in markets.

- An economic **model** is a simplified representation of the real world, focusing attention on what's important for understanding.
- The circular flow model of economic life reduces the complexity of the Canadian economy to three sets of players who interact in markets — households, businesses, and governments.
  - In input markets, households are sellers and businesses are buyers.
  - In output markets, households are buyers and businesses are sellers.
  - Governments set rules of the game and can choose to interact in any aspect of the economy.
  - **Inputs** are the productive resources — labour, natural resources, capital equipment, and entrepreneurial ability — used to produce products and services.
- Economic models, which assume all other things not in the model are unchanged, are the mental equivalent of controlled experiments in a laboratory.

- **Positive statements** — about what is; can be evaluated as true or false by checking the facts.
- **Normative statements** — about what you believe *should* be; involve value judgments.
  - Cannot be factually checked.

1.5 Where and How to Look: Models for Microeconomics and Macroeconomics

The Three Keys model summarizes the core of microeconomics, providing the basis for smart choices in all areas of your life.

- **Microeconomics** analyzes choices that individuals in households, individual businesses, and governments make, and how those choices interact in markets.
- **Macroeconomics** analyzes performance of the whole Canadian economy and global economy, the combined outcomes of all individual microeconomic choices.

- The Three Keys Model to Smart Choices:
  1. Choose only when additional benefits are greater than additional *opportunity costs.*
  2. Count only *additional* benefits and *additional* opportunity costs.
  3. Be sure to count *all* additional benefits and costs, including *implicit costs* and *externalities.*
- Important concepts in the Three Keys model:
  - Marginal = "additional"
  - **Marginal benefits** — additional benefits from the next choice.
  - **Marginal opportunity costs** — additional opportunity costs from the next choice.
  - **Implicit costs** — opportunity costs of investing your own money or time.
  - **Negative** (or **positive**) **externalities** — costs (or benefits) that affect others external to a choice or a trade.

TRUE/FALSE

Circle the correct answer. Solutions to these questions are available at the end of the book and on MyEconLab. You can also visit the MyEconLab Study Plan to access additional questions that will help you master the concepts covered in this chapter.

1.1 Scarcity and Choice

1. Economics is about how individuals, businesses, and governments make the best possible choices to get what they want, and how those choices interact in markets. **T** F

2. People who win the lottery don't have to make smart choices. T **F**

1.2 Opportunity Cost

3. Opportunity cost equals money cost. T **F**

4. The Government of Canada announced a $1000 Apprenticeship Incentive Grant to pay for tuition, travel, and tools for apprentices in the sealing trades. This will eliminate the opportunity cost of being an apprentice. **T** F

5. According to Economics Out There on p. 6, men have a larger incentive to get a post-secondary education because *not* getting a post-secondary education results in a relatively worse outcome compared to women. T **F**

1.3 Gains from Trade

6. Traditionally, women specialized in unpaid work at home and men specialized in paid work outside the house. One possible explanation is that men have a comparative advantage in performing housework (for example, cooking, cleaning, and child care). T **F**

7. Combinations of products inside a production possibilities frontier are impossible to produce. T **F**

8. Comparative advantage is the ability to produce at a lower absolute cost, compared to another producer. **T** F

9. Voluntary trade is a zero-sum game, where one person's gain is the other's loss. T **F**

1.4 Thinking Like an Economist

10. In input markets, households are sellers and businesses are buyers; in output markets, households are buyers and businesses are sellers. **T** F

11. Economists can perform controlled experiments just like natural scientists. T F

12. The statement "Tuition fees should be reduced" is a normative statement. T F

1.5 Models for Microeconomics and Macroeconomics

13. Decisions to go to college or take out a loan are macroeconomic choices. T **F**

14. Microeconomics analyzes choices that individuals in households, individual businesses, and governments make, and how those choices interact in markets. **T** F

15. Negative externalities are benefits that affect others external to a choice or a trade. T **F**

MULTIPLE CHOICE

Circle the best answer. Solutions to these questions are available at the end of the book and on MyEconLab. You can also visit the MyEconLab Study Plan to access similar questions that will help you master the concepts covered in this chapter.

1.1 Scarcity and Choice

1. You can't get everything you want because you are limited by
   a) time.
   b) money.
   c) energy.
   d) all of the above.

2. Scarcity is
   a) not a challenge for governments.
   b) not a challenge for celebrities.
   c) not a challenge for people who win the lottery.
   d) a challenge for everyone.

3. Economics does *not* focus on
   a) individuals.
   b) animals.
   c) businesses.
   d) government.

1.2 Opportunity Cost

4. Opportunity cost includes
   a) time you give up.
   b) energy you spend.
   c) money you spend.
   d) all of the above.

5. In deciding whether to study or sleep for the next hour, you should consider all of the following *except*
   a) how much tuition you paid.
   b) how tired you are.
   c) how productive you will be in that hour.
   d) how much value you place on sleeping in that hour.

6. Recently, the proportion of 25- to 29-year-old women with university degrees rose from 21 percent to 34 percent, while the proportion of 25- to 29-year-old men with degrees rose from 16 percent to 21 percent. There is a similar trend for college diplomas. More woman than men are getting post-secondary education because
   a) the gap in pay between post-secondary and high-school graduates is higher for women.
   b) the cost of not going to post-secondary education is higher for women.
   c) the opportunity cost of going to post-secondary education is lower for women.
   d) all of the above.

7. If the resource-rich sector of Alberta's economy slows down,
   a) opportunity costs of upgrading to a college diploma increase.
   b) opportunity costs of upgrading to a college diploma decrease.
   c) incentives to drop out of college increase.
   d) all of the above.

1.3 Gains from Trade

8. Mutually beneficial gains from trade come from
   a) absolute advantage.
   b) comparative advantage.
   c) self-sufficiency.
   d) China.

9. The easiest way to calculate opportunity cost is
   a) $\dfrac{\text{give up}}{\text{get}}$
   b) $\dfrac{\text{get}}{\text{give up}}$
   c) give up – get
   d) get – give up

10. In one hour, Chloe can bake 24 cookies or 12 muffins. Zabeen can bake 6 cookies or 2 muffins. For mutually beneficial trade, Chloe should
    a) bake cookies because she has a comparative advantage.
    b) bake cookies because she has an absolute advantage.
    c) bake muffins because she has a comparative advantage.
    d) bake muffins because she has an absolute advantage.

1.4 Thinking Like an Economist

11. Which of the following statements is normative?
    a) Economists should not make normative statements.
    b) Warts are caused by handling toads.
    c) As smartphone prices fall, people will buy more of them.
    d) As test dates get closer, students study more hours.

12. In the circular-flow model,
    a) households ultimately own all inputs of an economy.
    b) governments set the rules of the game.
    c) businesses are sellers and households are buyers in output markets.
    d) all of the above.

13. Which of the following is *not* a microeconomic choice for businesses?
    a) what interest rate to set
    b) what products to supply
    c) what quantity of output to produce
    d) how many workers to hire

14. Which of the following is *not* a microeconomic choice for governments?
    a) increasing tuition rates
    b) taxing automobile emissions
    c) increasing the exchange rate of the Canadian dollar
    d) increasing the number of taxi licences

15. All of the following should be considered when making smart choices, *except*
    a) external costs and benefits.
    b) past costs and benefits.
    c) implicit costs.
    d) additional costs and additional benefits.

2 Making Smart Choices

The Law of Demand

LEARNING OBJECTIVES

After reading this chapter, you should be able to:

2.1 Describe what determines your willingness and ability to pay for a product or service.

2.2 Identify why smart choices depend on marginal benefits, not total benefits, and explain what changes marginal benefits.

2.3 Explain the law of demand, and describe the roles of substitutes and willingness and ability to pay.

2.4 Explain the difference between a change in quantity demanded and a change in demand, and identify five factors that change demand.

YOU NEVER WANT TO PAY more than you have to. But

what determines how much you are willing to pay?

To get the most out of life, you need to make smart choices between alternatives. Should you use your time to go to school or to work? How do you choose the right job or the right partner? And how can you spend your money wisely to get the things you value most?

This chapter focuses on the choices you make every day as a consumer, buying products and services in the market. Choice means comparing alternatives. Those choices — between competing phone plans, between getting to school by bike or car or transit, between water or coffee or pop to quench your thirst — affect how much you are willing to pay. Your willingness to pay also depends on quantity — would you pay as much for the fifth slice of pizza as you would for the first? And how much money you have is definitely a factor.

Economists use the term *demand* to summarize all of the influences on consumer choice. Here you will learn the keys to making smart choices by separating out the many influences that determine your willingness to pay.

2.1

Put Your Money Where Your Mouth Is: Weighing Benefits, Costs, and Substitutes

Describe what determines your willingness and ability to pay for a product or service.

You just finished an intense workout at the gym and desperately want something to drink. You usually bring along your favourite Gatorade (which costs $3 a bottle), but today you forgot it. The snack bar has bottled water and juice, but no Gatorade. Your buddy, who is always trying to make a buck, says, "I have a bottle of what you want — how much will you pay for it?"

sellingpix/Shutterstock

EBFoto/Shutterstock

makeitdouble/Shutterstock

▲ Choosing a substitute depends on what you will pay, what substitutes are available, and what they cost. Can you think of anything you use in life that doesn't have a substitute?

Besides wondering if this guy is really a buddy, what do you think about to decide how much you are willing to pay him? Obviously, how thirsty you are and how refreshed you expect to feel from the drink matter a lot. But just because you badly want Gatorade does not mean you will pay, say, $10 for the bottle.

What are your alternatives? You could buy a water or juice for $2, but they don't have the electrolytes for your muscles that Gatorade does. You could drink water from the tap in the locker room for free. You could head home and drink the bottle you forgot, or head to a store to buy your Gatorade for $3.

You decide you so want the Gatorade *now* that you are willing to make an offer. You know your entrepreneurial buddy won't take less than the $3 he paid for the bottle, so you are willing to pay $4. You make the purchase, quench your thirst — and then ditch the buddy.

ADDITIONAL
BENEFITS
VS.
OPPORTUNITY
COSTS

We all make hundreds of choices a day that are similar — what to eat; what to wear; what to buy; whether to spend time studying, working, working out, or relaxing; whom to vote for. . . . All these choices are based (consciously or unconsciously) on a comparison of expected benefits and costs. This is Key 1 of the Three Keys to Smart Choices from Chapter 1: Choose only when additional benefits are greater than additional *opportunity costs*.

How Badly Do You Want It?

The first part of the comparison requires you to have a sense of the expected benefits from your choice. The expected benefit question is, "How badly do you want it?" What satisfaction do you expect to get from this choice? The want and the satisfaction might be quite logical — I want a warm coat so I won't freeze during the winter in Regina. I want water because I am thirsty. I want to spend the evening studying because I have a test tomorrow. Or your desire for the latest, biggest-screen phone may be based on more emotional reasons — wanting to look cool, or to impress others, or just because, well, you want it. Businesses spend money on advertising, in part, to convince you to want their product. Economists describe all of your wants — and how intense each want is — as your **preferences**.

preferences your wants and their intensities

What Will You Give Up?

For the second part of the comparison, the cost question is, "How much are you willing and able to give up for it?" I purposely chose the words *give up* when you might have expected me to say, "How much are you willing and able to *pay* for it?" There's a reason for this choice, just as there are reasons for all of your choices. Many things we want — Gatorade or phones — we have to pay for with money. But for many other things we want, what we have to give up is our time or our effort. Spending the evening studying means not seeing your friends, playing with your kids, or working at your part-time job. Cost always means *opportunity cost* — what you are willing to give up.

What determines *how much* you are willing to give up? Certainly, how badly you want it plays a role. But just as important is what your alternative choices are. There are substitutes for everything — water for Gatorade, a yoga class for a gym workout, long underwear or a move to Florida for winter coats. Substitutes need not be exactly the same product or service. Substitutes just have to basically satisfy the same want. For any choice, what you are willing and able to pay, or to give up, depends on what substitutes are available, and what they cost.

The final factor determining how much you are willing and able to give up is how much you can afford. Are you able to pay the price of the product or service you want? Can you afford to take the time to relax all evening when you have a test tomorrow?

The list of things we want is endless. But the choices we actually make reflect our willingness — and ability — to give up something in exchange. Economists use the term **demand** to describe consumers' willingness and ability to pay for a particular product or service. Demand is *not* just what consumers want. You must put your money (or time) where your mouth is in order to demand a product or service. And those demands, or choices, are smart choices only when expected benefits are greater than opportunity costs.

demand consumers' willingness and ability to pay for a particular product or service

Refresh 2.1

1. What is the difference between wants and demands?

2. What is the key factor that would make you choose to download a song for free rather than pay for it on iTunes? Explain your choice.

3. You have just started at a school that is a 30-minute drive from home or a 90-minute transit ride. Which is your smart choice, taking the transit or buying a car? Justify your choice.

MyEconLab

For answers to these Refresh Questions, visit MyEconLab.

Living on the Edge:
Smart Choices Are Marginal Choices

Identify why smart choices depend on marginal benefits, not total benefits, and explain what changes marginal benefits.

You make a smart choice only when expected benefits are greater than opportunity costs. But the benefits or satisfaction you expect to get depend on the circumstances.

Marginal Benefits Change with Circumstances

To see how benefits change with circumstances, let's return to the Gatorade example. Suppose you remembered to bring a bottle to the gym, and gulped it all after your workout. If your greedy buddy then asked you how much you were willing to pay for another bottle, chances are it would be much less than the $4 you were willing to pay when you had few convenient Gatorade alternatives. The *additional* benefit you will get from his second bottle is less than the benefit you got from your thirst-quenching first bottle. So your willingness to pay is less for the second bottle.

What if you have a test tomorrow, and you have to choose between spending the evening studying or going out with a friend? If you have been studying like mad for days already, the *additional* benefit of a few more hours might not help much, so you choose to visit. But if you have been busy working at your job all week and haven't cracked a book, the *additional* benefit of studying will be large, and you give up the friend time.

In both cases, the *additional* benefit you expect, and your willingness to pay (either in money or giving up friend time you value), depends on the circumstances. The economist's term for *additional* benefit is **marginal benefit**. Marginal means "on or at the edge," just like the margins of these textbook pages are at the edges of the pages.

marginal benefit the additional benefit from a choice, changing with circumstances

Key 2 of the Three Keys to Smart Choices says that when you compare expected benefits and costs, count only *additional* benefits and *additional* costs, or marginal benefits and marginal costs. Here we are explaining marginal benefits; in Chapter 3 we will explain marginal costs.

A smart decision to study (or not) does not depend on the total value of all hours spent studying, or the average value of an hour spent studying, but only on the *marginal* value of the additional time spent studying (compared with the additional cost of giving up those hours).

What if you choose to spend the evening studying, and your friend gets angry and shouts, "Is your stupid economics course more important than I am?" At the margin, the answer is yes. Your choice to study tonight doesn't necessarily mean that, overall, you value the course more than the friend (well, depending on the friend, you might). What your choice means is that tonight, at the margin, you value the next few hours spent studying more than you value spending the next few hours with your friend.

▲ The difference between total growth and marginal growth is the difference between "How tall are you?" and "How much have you grown?" The *difference* between the second-highest mark and the highest represents your *marginal*, or *additional*, growth during the past year.

But margins, and circumstances, change. Your choice would be different if you had another week before the test, or if you hadn't seen your friend for months. The value you place on an activity or thing depends on the margin, and *that* additional value is marginal benefit.

Your friend's angry accusation comes from the common mistake (not smart) of looking at choices as all or nothing — friend versus economics. That's not the (smart) choice you made at the margin — the marginal benefit of the time spent studying tonight was greater than the value, or marginal benefit, of the same time spent with your friend.

[handwritten: changes margin depending on the circumstances]

Marginal Benefits Decrease with Quantity

The Gatorade and studying examples share a common circumstance that regularly changes marginal benefit — quantity. The first Gatorade after a workout is very satisfying — it has a high marginal benefit. The second Gatorade is less satisfying, and a third or fourth might make you sick. Your first hour studying might raise your test mark by 40 marks. But as you spend more hours studying, each additional hour provides fewer additional marks. Additional quantities consumed give you decreasing marginal benefit.

Since marginal benefit is the key to how much you are willing to pay, decreasing marginal benefit means decreasing willingness to pay for additional quantities of the same product or service.

Your willingness to pay, determined at the margin by changing circumstances including quantity, is important in determining prices, ranging from low prices for water to high prices for diamonds.

[handwritten: the first marginal benefit is worth most]

Economics *Out There*

Coke's Automatic Price Gouging

In the late 1990s, Coca-Cola Co. worked on technology to automatically raise prices in soft-drink vending machines on hot days. Critics — calling the plan "shameful" and a "cynical ploy" to exploit consumers "when they are most susceptible to price gouging" — suggested Coca-Cola should abandon the plan. The company claimed it was fair that the price should rise with demand, and that the machines simply automate that process. Unconvinced, critics warned that the plan would alienate customers, with the reminder that "archrival Pepsi is out there, and you can hardly tell the difference."

- The public reaction to these variable-price vending machines was so negative that Coca-Cola never introduced them.

- However, the strategy is based on the correct observation that willingness to pay changes with circumstances — the principle of marginal benefit.
- The strategy failed not because the economics were wrong, but because the idea of paying different prices for the same product seemed so unfair — "price gouging." (However, in Chapter 9 we will look at examples where consumers accept businesses charging different consumers different prices for the same product — cellphone minutes cost providers the same, whether daytime, evening, or weekend. Why are prices different? [*Hint:* Consumer willingness to pay.])
- Notice the line about Pepsi — substitutes are always available, which limits willingness to pay for any product, regardless of the marginal benefit.

Source: "Coke's Automatic Price Gouging," *San Francisco Chronicle*, October 29, 1999, p. A22.

The Diamond/Water Paradox

NOTE

Willingness to pay, a key part of demand, depends on marginal benefits, not total benefits. If you think about total benefits you will get confused in section 2.3. Think marginal!

The distinction between looking at choices at the margin (smart) instead of as "all or nothing" or total-value choices helps make sense of the diamond/water paradox you may have heard about. What's more valuable in providing benefit or satisfaction — diamonds or water? One answer is water. Water is essential for survival, while diamonds are an unnecessary frill. But then why do diamonds cost far more than water?

You can solve the paradox by distinguishing marginal benefit from total benefit. You would die without any water, so you would be willing to pay everything you can for the first drink. But when water is abundant and cheap, and you are not dying of thirst, what would you be willing to pay, at the margin, for your next drink today? Not much. Marginal benefit is low, even though the total benefit of all water consumed (including the first, life-saving drink) is high.

Diamonds won't keep you alive, but they are relatively scarce, and desirable for that very reason. What would you pay for what is likely your first diamond? A lot. *Marginal benefit* is high. Because diamonds are scarce, there aren't many out there (compared to drinks of water), so *total benefit* is low. But willingness to pay depends on marginal benefit, not total benefit, so people are generally willing to pay more for a diamond (high marginal benefit) than for a glass of water (low marginal benefit).

Marginal benefit, as we will see in Chapter 4, is important not only for making smart choices, but also for explaining how prices are determined in the real world.

Refresh 2.2

MyEconLab

For answers to these Refresh Questions, visit MyEconLab.

1. In your own words, define *marginal benefit*.

2. Explain why we are willing to pay more for a diamond than a glass of water even though water is essential for survival and diamonds are an unnecessary luxury.

3. You and your entrepreneurial buddy have a concession stand on the beach. It is a hot, sunny, crowded day, and you are selling a few $5 collapsible umbrellas as sun shades. The skies suddenly darken, rain begins to pour, and your buddy quickly switches the umbrella price sign to $10. Will you sell more or fewer umbrellas? Explain your thinking, including your analysis of the customer's decision.

Move On When the Price Isn't Right: The Law of Demand

After weeks of boring bus rides to school and overhearing too many other riders' personal phone conversations, you finally decide to buy a good pair of headphones. You research the alternatives and decide to buy the Beats Solo model in green. You would have loved the Beats Pro model, or Bose Quiet Comfort headphones, but decided you couldn't afford those.

Explain the law of demand, and describe the roles of substitutes and willingness and ability to pay.

Quantity Demanded

Let's presume you made a smart choice, so the additional benefit of these headphones (listening pleasure and blocking out the world) is greater than the additional cost (the $200 price tag). You are willing and able to pay $200. Sold! An economist would say that, at the price of $200, your *quantity demanded* of Beats Solo headphones is one.

Quantity demanded, as we will see, is not the same as *demand.* **Quantity demanded** is the amount you actually plan to buy at a given price, taking into account everything that affects your willingness and ability to pay.

We saw in the previous section that if circumstances change the additional benefit, your choice may change. The second bottle of Gatorade wasn't worth as much as the first, and the value of the headphones would change if you were driving to school in a car with a good sound system instead of riding the bus. But our focus here is not on benefits. Our focus is on *what happens to your buying decision when the price — the additional cost you pay — changes.* In order to focus on the relationship between price and quantity demanded, we will keep all other influences on demand the same.

quantity demanded amount you actually plan to buy at a given price

Changing Prices Change Quantity Demanded   What if this Beats model were priced at $225 instead of $200? How might that change your decision to buy? You might want these headphones so badly that you would be willing to pay $225, judging that the additional benefit is still greater than the $200 cost. (That means that at $200, you felt you were getting a bargain!) But since you are a smart shopper and have limited income, you would still be thinking carefully about alternatives. There are substitutes for everything. For listening to music and sound-blocking there are cheaper headphones, and the not-so-great earbuds that came with your phone. The extra $25 cost might be enough to change your choice from the Beats Solo headphones to one of these substitutes. And if the price were $250, you, along with many more consumers out there, would definitely change your smart choice away from these specific headphones to a substitute. At a price of $250, your quantity demanded is zero.

What if Apple puts these headphones on sale for $150 instead of $200? Given your willingness and ability to pay, this is such a bargain that you decide to buy two — one for you, and one as a gift for your boyfriend or girlfriend. At a price of $150, your quantity demanded is two.

If we put your combinations of prices (willing and able to pay) and quantities demanded into a table, it looks like Figure 2.1.

NOTE
When the price of a product rises, consumers switch to cheaper substitutes. The quantity demanded of the original product, at the now higher price, decreases.

Figure 2.1 Your Demand for Beats Headphones

Price (willing and able to pay)	Quantity Demanded
$150	2
$200	1
$250	0

As your eye goes down the two columns, notice that as the price rises, the quantity demanded decreases. In general, when prices rise, consumers look for substitutes. When something becomes more expensive, people economize on its use.

A change to a new behaviour is often encouraged by an increase in the cost of an old behaviour. What might make this man change from using a hose and water to using a broom to clean his walk?

Water or Brooms? Households in the City of Toronto used to pay a fixed monthly price for water that didn't change with the quantity of water used. So the *additional* cost of using more water was zero. With "free" marginal water, many residents would "sweep" their sidewalks and driveways with a hose. But when water became metered, so that users paid for each additional cubic metre (m^3), many gave up this practice and started sweeping with a broom. (Only economics teaches you that water and brooms are substitutes!) Other reactions to higher water prices included placing flow regulators on showers, taking showers instead of baths, installing water-saving dual flush toilets, and planting ground cover that consumes less water than grass. With a higher price for water, the quantity demanded decreased.

The Law of Demand

The market for any product or service consists of millions of potential customers, each trying to make a smart choice about what to buy. **Market demand** is the sum of the demands of all individuals willing and able to buy a particular product or service.

Whether it is the market for headphones, water, or anything else, substitutes exist, so that consumers buy a smaller quantity at higher prices, and a larger quantity at lower prices. This inverse relationship (when one goes up, the other goes down) between price and quantity demanded is so universal that economists call it (somewhat grandiosely) the **law of demand**: If the price of a product or service rises, the quantity demanded of the product or service decreases. If the price falls, the quantity demanded increases. The law of demand works as long as other influences on demand besides price do not change. The next section will explore what happens when other influences do change. Will the law of demand then fail? Stay tuned.

market demand sum of demands of all individuals willing and able to buy a particular product or service

law of demand if the price of a product or service rises, quantity demanded decreases, other things remaining the same

Philip Harvey/CORBIS

Market Demand Curve for Water   The table of numbers in Figure 2.2 illustrates the inverse relationship between price and quantity demanded for the market demand for water. If you graph the combinations of prices and quantity demanded, you get the *market demand curve* in Figure 2.2.

Figure 2.2   Market Demand for Water

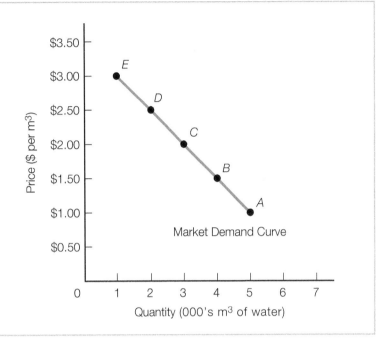

Row	Price ($ per m³)	Quantity Demanded (000's of m³ per month)
A	$1.00	5
B	$1.50	4
C	$2.00	3
D	$2.50	2
E	$3.00	1

A **demand curve** shows the relationship between price and quantity demanded, when all other influences on demand besides price do not change.

For example, the table in Figure 2.2 shows that when the price of a cubic metre (m^3) of water is $1, the quantity demanded is 5000 m^3 per month (row *A*). When the price is $3, the quantity demanded is 1000 m^3 (row *E*). The other rows in the table show the quantities demanded for prices in between $1 and $3.

We can draw the market demand curve for water by plotting these combinations on a graph that has *quantity* on the horizontal axis and *price* on the vertical axis. The points on the demand curve labelled *A* to *E* correspond to the rows of the table.

demand curve shows the relationship between price and quantity demanded, other things remaining the same

Economizing Decisions   The law of demand, represented by a demand curve, is yet another way of saying that when something becomes more expensive, people economize on its use. This law helps explain many decisions beyond shopping decisions or how to sweep a sidewalk.

Mother Teresa's charity wanted to open a shelter for the homeless in New York City. When city bureaucrats insisted on expensive but unnecessary renovations to the building, the charity abandoned the project. Mother Teresa didn't abandon her commitment to the poor. When the cost of helping the poor in New York went up, she decided that, at the margin, her efforts would do more good elsewhere. For her charity, a shelter elsewhere was a substitute for a New York shelter.

Because there are substitutes for everything, higher prices create incentives for smart consumers to reduce their purchases of more expensive products or services and look for alternatives.

NOTE
Demand curves can be straight lines (like this simple one) or curves, but they all slope downward to the right — as the price falls, quantity demanded increases.

Two Ways to Read a Demand Curve

The demand curve shows graphically the relationship between price and quantity demanded, when all other influences on demand do not change. The demand curve is a simple yet powerful tool summarizing the two forces that determine quantity demanded — the switch to substitutes and willingness and ability to pay.

Because there are two forces determining quantity demanded, there are two ways to "read" a demand curve — as a demand curve and as a marginal benefit curve. Both readings are correct, but each highlights a different force. You can see the two readings in Figure 2.3.

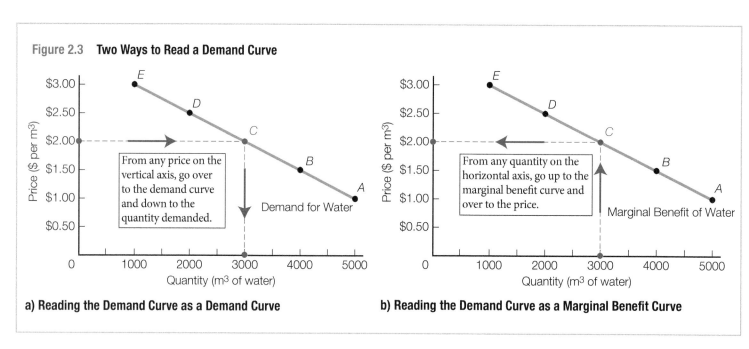

Figure 2.3   Two Ways to Read a Demand Curve

a) Reading the Demand Curve as a Demand Curve

b) Reading the Demand Curve as a Marginal Benefit Curve

Demand Curve   To read Figure 2.3a as a demand curve, start with price. For any given price, the demand curve tells you the quantity demanded. For example, start with the price of $2 on the vertical axis (Price). To find quantity demanded at $2, you trace a line from the $2 price over to the demand curve and then down to the horizontal axis (Quantity) to read the quantity demanded, which is 3000 m³ of water per month. You can do the same for any price — from any chosen price, go over to the demand curve and then down to read the corresponding quantity demanded.

To see how a price rise from $2 to $3 causes a switch to substitutes, and a decrease in quantity demanded, for each price go over to the demand curve and then down to the quantity demanded. The rise in price of $1 causes a decrease in quantity demanded of 2000 m³ of water per month (3000 – 1000).

Marginal Benefit Curve To read Figure 2.3b as a marginal benefit curve, start with quantity. For a given quantity, the marginal benefit curve tells you the maximum price people are willing and able to pay for the last unit available. Start with the quantity 3000 m^3 of water on the horizontal axis (Quantity). To find the maximum price people are willing and able to pay for the 3000th cubic metre of water, you trace a line up to the marginal benefit curve and over to the vertical (Price) axis to read the price, which is $2. You can do the same for any quantity — from any chosen quantity, go up to the marginal benefit curve and then over to read the corresponding price, which is the maximum price people are willing and able to pay for that last available unit of water.

To see how an increase in quantity from 3000 to 4000 m^3 causes a decreased marginal benefit and decreases willingness and ability to pay, for each quantity go up to the marginal benefit curve and then over to the price. $2 is the most someone is willing and able to pay for the 3000th cubic metre of water, and $1.50 is the most someone is willing and able to pay for the 4000th cubic metre of water. The 4000th m^3 of water, compared to the 3000th m^3 of water, provides a decreased marginal benefit. The increase in quantity of 1000 m^3 causes a decrease in marginal benefit of $0.50 ($2.00 – $1.50).

The Demand Curve Is Also a Marginal Benefit Curve You read a demand curve over and down. You read a marginal benefit curve up and over. While the demand curve has a double identity both as a demand curve and as a marginal benefit curve, we generally refer to it as a demand curve. Sometimes, though, the marginal benefit reading will make it easier to understand smart choices.

Both readings are movements along an unchanged demand curve. But what about the other influences on demand that we have been keeping constant? What happens if they change? The two ways to read a demand curve will help you answer that question.

NOTE
You read a demand curve over and down. You read a marginal benefit curve up and over.

Refresh 2.3

1. In just a couple of sentences, explain the law of demand to a friend who is not taking this economics course.

2. You own a car and work at a job that you cannot get to by public transit. If the price of gasoline goes up dramatically, does the law of demand apply to you? Explain the choices you might make in responding to this price rise.

3. You have tickets for a concert tonight that you have been looking forward to. Your mother, who is helping you pay your tuition, phones and says that it's very important to her that you come to Grandma's birthday party tonight. Using the law of demand, explain your decision — the concert or Grandma's party? [*Hint:* Think about opportunity cost.]

MyEconLab

For answers to these Refresh Questions, visit MyEconLab.

Moving the Margins: What Can Change Demand?

The price of gasoline in Halifax rose from $0.99 per litre to $1.39 per litre between 2010 and 2012. But the quantity of gasoline motorists bought actually *increased*. Does that disprove the "law of demand"?

If nothing else changed except the price of gasoline, the answer would be yes — and I'd have to quit this job as an economist and do something more socially useful, like being a trash collector.

But I, and other economists, have enough confidence in the law of demand that if we observe a rise in price leading to an *increase* in purchases, we take it as a signal that something else must have changed at the same time.

Economists use the concept of *demand* to summarize all the influences on consumer choice. Your demand for any product or service reflects your willingness and ability to pay. In the examples of Gatorade, headphones, and water, we have seen that your willingness to pay depends on things like your preferences, what substitutes are available, and marginal benefit. Your ability to pay depends on your income.

As long as all these factors (and a few more) do not change, the law of demand holds true: If the price of a product or service rises, the quantity demanded decreases.

But when change happens, economists distinguish between two kinds of change:

- If the price of a product or service changes, that affects *quantity demanded*. This is represented graphically by a movement along an unchanged demand curve.

- If anything else changes, that affects *demand*. This is represented graphically by a shift of the entire demand curve.

Quantity demanded is a much more limited term than *demand*. Only a change in price changes quantity demanded. A change in any other influence on consumer choice changes demand. This may sound like semantic hair-splitting — quantity demanded versus demand — but it is important for avoiding not-smart thinking.

Why Bother Distinguishing between Quantity Demanded and Demand?

Suppose you observe a witch placing a curse on some poor young man, who dies a month later. The apparent conclusion is that the curse was fatal. But if the witch had been secretly poisoning his food with arsenic all along, what was the real cause of death? Something else changed that was really behind the observed result.

What if a gasoline supplier decides to raise his prices to increase his sales, based on the observed result that when gasoline prices rose between 2010 and 2012, motorists bought more gasoline. What do you think would happen? Would this be a smart choice?

We live in a complicated world, where everything depends on everything else. There are obvious connections between events like a lottery win increasing your spending, or high ticket prices increasing movie downloads. But non-economic events like the weather can affect coffee prices, and a whiff of a terrorist threat can sink airline stock prices. So when you observe a change in the economy like increased gasoline purchases, how do you decide what caused it when so many interdependent things can change at the same time? (Was the young man's death caused by curse, arsenic, or natural causes?)

Controlled Experiments   Scientists deal with this interdependence problem by performing controlled experiments in a laboratory. The law of gravity claims that, all other factors unchanged, objects fall at the same rate regardless of their mass. So if we drop a bowling ball and a feather from a tall building, and find the bowling ball hits the ground first, does that disprove the law of gravity? No, because we are not controlling for air resistance, which changes the path of the feather more than the bowling ball. To accurately test the law of gravity, we must perform the same experiment in a laboratory vacuum, so that we eliminate, or control for, the influence of air resistance as an "other factor." We need to keep all other factors unchanged.

Economists, and citizens like you, have it much tougher than scientists. We can't pause everything in the world while changing only the factors we are interested in. Instead, we have to use economic thinking to make sense of the changes. The distinction between a change in quantity demanded and a change in demand is the economist's way of trying to mentally imitate a controlled experiment.

The law of demand is the simplest of all the interdependent relationships. *If nothing else changes,* a rise in the price of gasoline will cause a decrease in the quantity demanded of gasoline.

Let's look at the more complicated parts (like air resistance for the law of gravity) — all the important "other things" that can cause a change in demand.

NOTE
It is difficult to distinguish an event's actual causes from apparent causes. Scientists use controlled laboratory experiments to isolate one cause while keeping all other factors unchanged. Economists use distinctions like change in quantity demanded versus change in demand to mentally imitate controlled experiments.

Five Ways to Change Demand and Shift the Demand Curve

Only a change in the price of a product or service itself changes *quantity demanded* of that product or service. But there are five important other factors that can change market demand — the willingness and ability to pay for a product or service. They are:

- Preferences
- Prices of related products
- Income
- Expected future prices
- Number of consumers

A change in any of these five factors shifts the demand curve.

Preferences   There are many reasons why businesses advertise, but ultimately they are trying to get you to want their product, to persuade you that you need what they sell. Remember that economists use the term "preferences" to describe your wants and their intensities — so, for an economist, advertising is about increasing your preferences for a product or service.

Most car commercials are not about information but about showing you a fabulous, fun driving experience that the manufacturer wants you to believe will be yours only if you buy its car.

All businesses want to increase your preferences, because if they succeed in increasing the intensity of your want or desire for their product you will be willing to pay more for it. If Apple runs a successful ad campaign that makes you and many other consumers feel you can't live (and be cool) without Beats headphones, what would happen to your willingness and ability to pay, according to our earlier example? Look at Figure 2.4 on the next page.

Figure 2.4 An Increase in Demand for Beats Headphones

Price	Quantity Demanded (originally)	Quantity Demanded (after advertising)
$150	2	3
$200	1	2
$250	0	1
$300	0	0

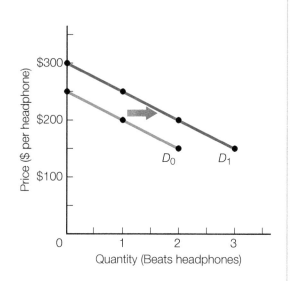

Look first at demand curve D_0, which shows your original plans, before advertising, to buy no headphones if the price is $250, one if the price is $200, and two headphones if the price is $150. Reading the demand curve as a marginal benefit curve — up and over — makes most sense here. For the first set of headphones, go up to demand curve D_0 and over to the price axis. You were willing and able to pay $200. For the second set, go up to demand curve D_0 and over to the price axis. You were willing and able to pay $150. Connecting those points yields the demand curve D_0.

After the successful ad campaign, your willingness and ability to pay has increased, represented by demand curve D_1. For each set of headphones, your willingness and ability to pay is now described by the points on demand curve D_1. Going up to D_1 and over, for the first set, you are now willing and able to pay $250 instead of $200. For the second set, you are now willing and able to pay $200 instead of $150. Before advertising, you were not willing to pay anything for a third set of headphones. Now you are willing and able to pay $150.

Your ability to pay has not changed, it's just that you are willing to give up more of your unchanged income because the intensity of your wants increased. Advertising succeeded in moving the margin, increasing both the marginal benefit you expect to get from the Beats headphones and your willingness to pay. Economists call any increase in consumers' willingness and ability to pay an **increase in demand**. Consumers are now willing to pay a higher price for the same quantity of a product.

Changes in preferences can also cause a decrease in demand. What if a Health Canada study shows conclusively that regular listening with Beats headphones causes serious hearing loss and mushrooms to grow out of your ears? If you and other consumers believe the study, consumers' willingness and ability to pay decreases, resulting in a **decrease in demand** for headphones. Consumers are now willing to pay only a lower price for the same quantity of a product.

increase in demand increase in consumers' willingness and ability to pay

decrease in demand decrease in consumers' willingness and ability to pay

NOTE
An increase in preferences causes
an increase in demand, not a
change in quantity demanded.

In January 2014, the National Hockey League held its once-a-year outdoor hockey game in Ann Arbor, Michigan, at the University of Michigan football stadium. Ann Arbor has a population of 115 000, and the Michigan stadium, the largest in North America, holds 110 000 people. What happened to the demand for hotel rooms in Ann Arbor? The large number of fans attending the game increased the willingness to pay and *increased the demand* for hotel rooms. On the other hand, think of the demand by tourists for hotel rooms in Toronto before and after a 2012 outbreak of bedbugs. The fear of bug bites decreased tourists' preferences for Toronto hotel bookings. With decreased willingness to pay, there was a decrease in demand for Toronto hotel rooms.

Any change in preferences causes a change in demand. An increase in preferences causes an increase in demand. A decrease in preferences causes a decrease in demand.

Prices of Related Products   Many products or services you choose to buy are related. Changes in price of a different, related product or service will affect your demand for the original product or service. There are two main types of related products: substitutes and complements.

Substitutes are products or services that can be used in place of each other to satisfy the same want. Examples of substitutes are headphones and earbuds for listening to music, or water and Gatorade for quenching thirst.

What happens to your demand for Beats headphones when the price of other headphones falls drastically? You are not willing to pay as much for the Beats, as your smart choice now involves much cheaper alternatives. A fall in the price of a substitute decreases the demand for the related product.

If the price of water skyrockets because of a drought, your willingness to pay for Gatorade increases. A rise in the price of a substitute increases demand for the related product.

substitutes   products or services used in place of each other to satisfy the same want

Economics *Out There*

Diamond Engagement Rings Were Not Forever

More than 80 percent of North American brides receive a diamond engagement ring, at an average cost of over $3000.

It wasn't always that way. The tradition of diamond engagement rings only began in the late 1800s when the discovery of diamond mines in South Africa drove down the price of diamonds. Then, in 1919, diamond sales plunged and didn't recover for over 20 years! But diamond prices and demand changed forever when the De Beers diamond company hired the firm N. W. Ayers to create a national advertising campaign, which included paying Hollywood actresses to wear diamond rings in public.

Sales rose over 50 percent in three years. In 1947, a female copywriter at Ayers created the tag line "A diamond is forever." De Beers used that line with a steady stream of photos showing happy newlyweds with the brides all wearing diamond engagement rings. Sales rose all through the 1950s, and by 1965, 80 percent of brides had diamond engagement rings. The advertising campaign also introduced the guideline for how much grooms should spend on a diamond ring — it started at one month's salary, quickly doubled to two months' salary, and most recently stood at three months' salary.

This was perhaps one of the most successful ad campaigns ever for increasing preferences, willingness to pay, and demand.

Source: Meghan O'Rourke, "Diamonds Are a Girl's Worst Friend," *Slate*, June 11, 2007, http://www.slate.com/articles/news_and_politics/weddings/2007/06/diamonds_are_a_girls_worst_friend.html.

Complements are products or services that are used together to satisfy the same want. Music players and headphones are complementary products, as are hot dogs and hot dog buns, or cars and gasoline.

If music player prices fall, that makes owning headphones more attractive, and will increase your willingness to pay for Beats headphones. A fall in the price of a complement increases demand for the related product because the cost of using both products together decreases.

When gasoline prices rose significantly in 2012, gas-guzzling eight-cylinder SUVs became much more expensive to operate. The rise in gas prices decreased the demand for eight-cylinder SUVs. A rise in the price of a complement decreases demand for the related product because the cost of using both products together increases.

Income Winning a million dollars in a lottery would have a large effect on your demand for products and services. Demand reflects your willingness and ability to pay. With more money, or more income, you are more able (and still willing) to pay for things and not worry about it. But not always.

Take your demand for Beats headphones from Figure 2.4, before any advertising (demand curve D_0). If your income increases, the effect on your willingness and ability to pay is similar to the effect of an increase in preferences (demand curve D_1). At each quantity you are still willing and now *able to pay more,* so the increase in income increases demand. The intensity of your wants doesn't change with a change in income, but what you have to *give up in other products or services* decreases. With more income, you can spend more on headphones and still have lots of extra cash to buy other things. Higher income lowers your real opportunity cost of spending. There is more "get" and less "give up."

If unfortunately your income falls, so does your ability to pay, and your demand for headphones decreases.

Economists call products like headphones **normal goods** — products and services that you buy more of when your income increases. For a normal good, an increase in income increases demand, and a decrease in income decreases demand.

But not all products are normal goods. Can you think of products or services you buy as a poor student that you will buy *less of* when your income goes up? If you have been living on Kraft Dinner, you may never want to eat it again once you can afford real food. And what about those endless bus rides? If you could afford a car, what would happen to your demand for public transit?

Economists call these products and services, for which an increase in income *decreases* demand, **inferior goods** — products and services that you buy less of when your income increases. Similarly, a decrease in income increases demand for inferior goods.

Businesses care about the distinction between normal and inferior goods. If incomes are rising and your business sells a normal good, the increase in demand increases sales. But if you sell an inferior good, prepare for a possible drop in sales and reduce inventory so you don't get stuck with unsold goods. The demand for inferior goods is more likely to increase during a downturn in the economy, where unemployed people economize on their food budget and buy more Kraft Dinner and Hamburger Helper.

Expected Future Prices   Smart choices depend not only on prices and incomes today, but also on our expectation of future prices. Consumers choose between substitutes, and one of many possible substitutions is a purchase tomorrow for a purchase today. We do this all the time with gasoline. If it's the weekend and you decide to wait until mid-week to buy gas because you expect the price to fall, that decreases your demand for gasoline today. Likewise, if you are expecting prices to rise, you fill up now, increasing your demand for gasoline today. Notice that your decision is not determined by the current price (that would be a quantity demanded decision), but by whether you expect the current price (whatever it may be) to fall or rise in the future.

An expected future price fall decreases demand today. An expected future price rise increases demand today.

NOTE
A rise in expected future price causes an increase in demand today.

hurricanes in
ny + gas

Number of Consumers   So far, the explanation for all the factors that change demand are the same for an individual as for all consumers whose combined willingness and ability to pay make up market demand. Looking at willingness and ability to pay, it makes more sense to look at the demand curve as a marginal benefit curve. For any quantity, we examine how a change in each factor affects the price the consumer is willing and able to pay. Each such change in demand changes marginal benefit and moves the margin. As marginal benefits increase or decrease, demand increases or decreases.

For the last factor, the number of consumers, the explanation makes more sense if we read the demand curve as a demand curve. Start with any price, and examine how a change in consumer numbers affects quantity demanded. For each price, if the number of consumers increases, we need to add together all the quantities demanded by all consumers at that price.

Let's take our earlier table of the market demand for water, and add a third column showing the quantity demanded after many new households move into the city and start using water. Look at Figure 2.5 on the next page.

Figure 2.5 More Consumers Increase the Market Demand for Water

Price ($ per m³)	Quantity Demanded (000's of m³ per month)	Quantity Demanded with More Households (000's of m³ per month)
$1.00	5	10
$1.50	4	9
$2.00	3	8
$2.50	2	7
$3.00	1	6

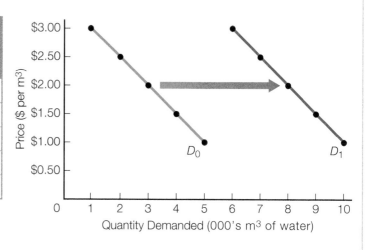

NOTE
An increased number of consumers increases demand.

At any price (first column), it is no surprise that with additional households (last column), quantity demanded is greater than it was originally (middle column). The increased number of consumers increases demand, just as an increase in preferences or an increase in income (for normal goods) increases demand. A decrease in the number of consumers decreases demand, just as a decrease in the price of a substitute product or service or a decrease in expected future prices decreases demand.

Moving Along or Shifting the Demand Curve
Any increase (or decrease) in demand caused by the five factors can be described in alternative ways. For the first four factors, the description for an increase in demand is:

- At any given quantity, consumers are willing and able to pay a higher price. This is the marginal benefit reading of the demand curve.

For the fifth factor, number of consumers, the description for an increase in demand is:

- At any given price, consumers plan to buy a larger quantity. This is the demand curve reading of the demand curve.

While the marginal benefit reading of the demand curve provides the best intuition behind changes in demand, the demand curve reading will be most useful for understanding the economic world around you, and is used most often.

NOTE
An increase in demand is a rightward shift of the demand curve. A decrease in demand is a leftward shift of the demand curve.

In the demand curve reading, an increase in demand is also called a rightward shift of the demand curve. A decrease in demand is a leftward shift of the demand curve. We will always call an increase in demand a rightward shift, and a decrease in demand a leftward shift of the demand curve.

When none of the five factors change, we can focus on the relationship between price and quantity demanded. That is represented in Figure 2.6a as a movement along the demand curve D_0. If the price rises, and all other things do not change, that is a movement up along the demand curve to a smaller quantity demanded. If the price falls, all other things unchanged, that is a movement down along the demand curve to a larger quantity demanded.

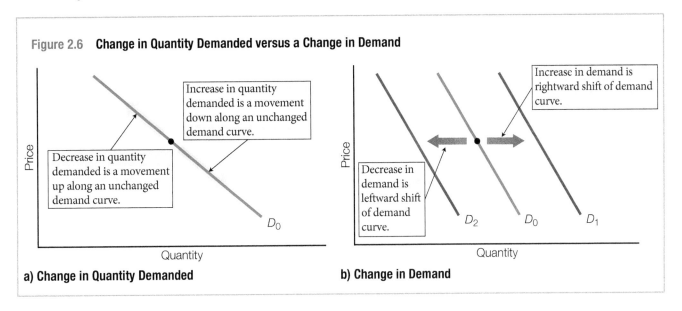

Figure 2.6   Change in Quantity Demanded versus a Change in Demand

Increase in quantity demanded is a movement down along an unchanged demand curve.

Decrease in quantity demanded is a movement up along an unchanged demand curve.

D_0

Increase in demand is rightward shift of demand curve.

Decrease in demand is leftward shift of demand curve.

D_2 D_0 D_1

a) Change in Quantity Demanded

b) Change in Demand

Figure 2.6b shows an increase in demand as the rightward shift from D_0 to D_1. The leftward shift from D_0 to D_2 is a decrease in demand. These shifts in demand are caused by changes in any of the five factors — preferences, prices of related products, income, expected future prices, and number of consumers.

Saving the Law of Demand

You have learned to distinguish between a change in quantity demanded (caused by a change in the price of the product) and a change in demand (caused by changes in preferences, prices of related products, income, expected future prices, and number of consumers). Can we now explain why, when gasoline prices increased from $0.99 per litre to $1.39 per litre between 2010 and 2012, the quantity of gasoline motorists bought actually increased? Can we save the law of demand?

According to the law of demand, if the price of a product rises, the quantity demanded of the product decreases (as long as other factors besides price do not change). The rise in gas prices alone would have decreased the quantity demanded, *but other things also changed.*

While a complete explanation is more complex (involving supply factors from Chapter 3 as well as demand), a major change was the increased number of drivers and cars on the road. This increase in the number of consumers increased demand for gasoline. The effect of the increase in demand outweighed the price effect of the decrease in quantity demanded.

To conclusively explain whether the witch's curse or the arsenic killed the poor young man, you need a controlled experiment. And without the economist's equivalent of a controlled experiment — the mental distinction between quantity demanded and demand — you never would have been able to explain what happened in the gasoline market.

Figure 2.7 is a good study device for reviewing the difference between the law of demand (focusing on quantity demanded and movements along the demand curve) and the factors that change demand (and shift the demand curve).

Figure 2.7   Law of Demand and Changes in Demand

The Law of Demand *The quantity demanded of a product or service*	
Decreases if:	*Increases if:*
• price of the product or service rises	• price of the product or service falls

Changes in Demand *The demand for a product or service*	
Decreases if:	*Increases if:*
• preferences decrease	• preferences increase
• price of a substitute falls	• price of a substitute rises
• price of a complement rises	• price of a complement falls
• income decreases (normal good)	• income increases (normal good)
• income increases (inferior good)	• income decreases (inferior good)
• expected future price falls	• expected future price rises
• number of consumers decreases	• number of consumers increases

Refresh 2.4

MyEconLab

For answers to these Refresh Questions, visit MyEconLab.

1. Explain the difference between a change in quantity demanded and a change in demand. Identify the five factors that can change demand.

2. Roses sell for about $40 a bouquet most of the year, and at that price, worldwide sales are 6 million bouquets per month. Every February, the price of roses doubles to $80 a bouquet, but the quantity of roses demanded and sold also increases, to 24 million bouquets per month. The cost of producing roses doesn't change throughout the year. Explain what else is going on that saves the law of demand.

3. There are some "status goods," like Rolex watches, that people want to own *because* they are expensive. In contradiction to the law of demand, if Rolex watches were less expensive, fewer "status-seeking" consumers would demand them. Reconcile status products or services with the law of demand. How does the existence of cheap "knock-off" imitations of Rolex watches fit with the law of demand?

Study Guide

2.1 Put Your Money Where Your Mouth Is: Weighing Benefits, Costs, and Substitutes

Your willingness to buy a product or service depends on your ability to pay, comparative benefits and costs, and the availability of substitutes.

- **Preferences** — your wants and their intensities.

- **Demand** — consumers' willingness and ability to pay for a particular product or service.

- For any choice, what you are willing to pay or give up depends on the cost and availability of substitutes.

2.2 Living on the Edge: Smart Choices Are Marginal Choices

Key 2 states, "Count only *additional* benefits and *additional* costs." Additional benefits mean marginal benefits — not total benefits — and marginal benefits change with circumstances.

- **Marginal benefit** — the additional benefit from a choice, changing with circumstances.

- Marginal benefit explains the diamond/water paradox. Why do diamonds cost more than water, when water is more valuable for survival? Willingness to pay depends on marginal benefit, not total benefit. Because water is abundant, marginal benefit is low. Because diamonds are scarce, marginal benefit is high.

2.3 Move On When the Price Isn't Right: The Law of Demand

The demand curve combines two forces — switch to substitutes; willingness and ability to pay — determining quantity demanded, and can be read as a demand curve and as a marginal benefit curve.

- **Quantity demanded** — the amount you actually plan to buy at a given price.

- **Market demand** — the sum of demands of all individuals willing and able to buy a particular product or service.

- **Law of demand** — if the price of a product or service rises, quantity demanded decreases, other things remaining the same.

- **Demand curve** — shows the relationship between price and quantity demanded, other things remaining the same.

2.4 Moving the Margins: What Can Change Demand?

Quantity demanded changes only with a change in price. All other influences on consumer choice change demand.

- Demand is a catch-all term summarizing all possible influences on consumers' willingness and ability to pay for a particular product or service.

  - **Increase in demand** — increase in consumers' willingness and ability to pay. Rightward shift of demand curve.

  - **Decrease in demand** — decrease in consumers' willingness and ability to pay. Leftward shift of demand curve.

- Demand changes with changes in preferences, prices of related goods, income, expected future price, and number of consumers. For example, demand increases with:

  - increase in preferences.

  - rise in price of a **substitute** — products or services used in place of each other to satisfy the same want.

  - fall in price of a **complement** — products or services used together to satisfy the same want.

  - increase in income for **normal goods** — products or services you buy more of when your income increases.

  - decrease in income for **inferior goods** — products or services you buy less of when your income increases.

  - rise in expected future prices.

  - increase in number of consumers.

TRUE/FALSE

Circle the correct answer. Solutions to these questions are available at the end of the book and on MyEconLab. You can also visit the MyEconLab Study Plan to access additional questions that will help you master the concepts covered in this chapter.

2.1 Weighing Benefits, Costs, and Substitutes

1. Demand is the same as wants. T **F**

2. Your willingness to pay for a product depends on what substitutes are available, and what they cost. **T** F

3. What you can afford is just about money. T **F**

2.2 Smart Choices Are Marginal Choices

4. Marginal cost is the same as additional cost. T **F**

5. The flat fee charged at an all-you-can-eat restaurant should not influence how much food you eat once you are seated. **T** F

6. Marginal benefit always equals average benefit. T **F**

7. Willingness to pay depends on marginal benefit, not total benefit. **T** F

2.3 The Law of Demand

8. Quantity demanded is the same as demand. T **F**

9. If the price of a product or service changes, quantity demanded changes. **T** F

10. Market demand is the sum of the demands of all individuals. **T** F

11. Demand curves may be straight lines or curves, but always slope downward to the left. T **F**

2.4 What Can Change Demand?

12. If your willingness to pay decreases, demand decreases. **T** F

13. If your ability to pay decreases, demand increases. T **F**

14. Throughout the month of December, the quantity of video game consoles purchased increases even as the price rises. This violates the law of demand. T **F**

15. A decrease in income always shifts the demand curve leftward. **T** F

MULTIPLE CHOICE

Circle the best answer. Solutions to these questions are available at the end of the book and on MyEconLab. You can also visit the MyEconLab Study Plan to access similar questions that will help you master the concepts covered in this chapter.

2.1 Weighing Benefits, Costs, and Substitutes

1. Economists describe the list of your wants and their intensities as
   a) demand.
   b) supply.
   c) benefit.
   d) preferences.

2. Costs are
   a) worth money.
   b) whatever we are willing to give up.
   c) the answer to the question "What do we want?"
   d) whatever we are willing to get.

3. Your preferences measure
   a) the availability of substitutes.
   b) how limited your time is.
   c) the price of a product.
   d) how badly you want something.

2.2 Smart Choices Are Marginal Choices

4. All-you-can-eat buffet restaurants charge a fixed fee for eating. With each plate that Anna eats, she experiences
   a) decreasing marginal costs.
   b) increasing marginal costs.
   c) decreasing marginal benefits.
   d) increasing marginal benefits.

5. Thinking like economists, a dating couple should break up when the
   a) total benefits of dating are greater than the total costs of dating.
   b) total costs of dating are greater than the total benefits of dating.
   c) additional benefits of dating are greater than the additional costs of dating.
   d) additional costs of dating are greater than the additional benefits of dating.

6. Peter wants two cars, one for everyday and the other for special occasions. He has only $15 000, so he buys only one car. His quantity demanded of cars is
   a) 1.
   b) 2.
   c) 15 000.
   d) 30 000.

7. The price of diamonds is higher than the price of water because
   a) total benefits from water are relatively low.
   b) total benefits from diamonds are relatively high.
   c) marginal benefits from water are relatively high.
   d) marginal benefits from diamonds are relatively high.

2.3 The Law of Demand

8. When the price of a product rises,
   a) consumers look for more expensive substitutes.
   b) quantity demanded increases.
   c) consumers look for cheaper substitutes.
   d) consumers use more of the product.

9. If homeowners were charged for garbage collection by the number of garbage bags used, there would be a(n)
   a) increase in demand for garbage collection.
   b) decrease in demand for garbage collection.
   c) increase in quantity demanded of garbage collection.
   d) decrease in quantity demanded of garbage collection.

10. A sociology class is a substitute for an economics class if
    a) attending the two classes has the same opportunity cost.
    b) the two classes satisfy the same want.
    c) both classes are at the same time.
    d) both classes are taught by the same instructor.

2.4 What Can Change Demand?

11. What is most likely to be an inferior good?
    a) fast food
    b) antique furniture
    c) school bags
    d) textbooks

12. Demand
    a) increases with a rise in price.
    b) is the same as quantity demanded.
    c) changes with income.
    d) decreases with a rise in price.

13. If the price of cars rises, the demand for tires
    a) increases.
    b) decreases.
    c) stay the same.
    d) depend on the price of tires.

14. Which of the following could cause a leftward shift of the demand curve for a product?
    a) increase in income
    b) decrease in income
    c) increase in the price of a substitute
    d) all of the above

15. If Kraft Dinner is an inferior good, a rise in the price of Kraft Dinner
    a) decreases demand for Kraft Dinner.
    b) increases demand for Kraft Dinner.
    c) increases the quantity demanded of Kraft Dinner.
    d) decreases the quantity demanded of Kraft Dinner.

3

Show Me the Money

The Law of Supply

LEARNING OBJECTIVES

After reading this chapter, you should be able to:

3.1 Explain why marginal costs are ultimately opportunity costs.

3.2 Define sunk costs and explain why they do not influence smart, forward-looking decisions.

3.3 Explain the law of supply and describe the roles of higher profits and higher marginal opportunity costs of production.

3.4 Explain the difference between a change in quantity supplied and a change in supply, and list six factors that change supply.

MONEY IS THE MARKET'S REWARD

to individuals or businesses who give up something of value. Your boss rewards you with an hourly wage for supplying labour services. A business producing a top-selling product is rewarded with profits (as long as revenues are greater than costs).

What goes into decisions to sell or supply services or products to the market? What price do you need to get to be willing to work? How much money does it take before a business is willing to supply?

This chapter focuses on choices businesses make every day in producing and selling. Economists use the term *supply* to summarize all of the influences on business decisions. You will learn about influences that change business supply, which include new technologies like noodle-slicing robots!

Business decisions seem more "objective" than consumer decisions that seem to be based on "subjective" desires and preferences. After all, there is a bottom line in business with prices, costs, and profits. But business supply decisions are not as straightforward or objective as you might think.

3.1 What Does It Really Cost?
Costs Are Opportunity Costs

ADDITIONAL
BENEFITS
VS.
OPPORTUNITY
COSTS

Supply, like demand, starts with decision makers choosing among alternative opportunities by comparing expected benefits and costs at the margin.

How Much to Work?

It's Sunday night and your boss calls in a panic, begging you to work as many hours as possible next week. You normally work 10 hours a week, but the extra money would come in handy. The timing, however, couldn't be worse. You have two midterms the following week, and your out-of-town best friend is coming in next weekend for the only visit you will have in six months. How many hours then are you willing to work?

Of course you will make a smart choice, weighing the additional benefits and costs of working extra hours. The additional, or marginal, benefits are the $15 per hour you earn. The additional costs are opportunity costs — the alternative uses of the time you have to give up.

You want to attend all your classes, keep time for studying for midterms, and definitely keep the weekend free. You are willing to give up the 10 hours a week you spend playing *World of Warcraft*. When your boss hears you are willing to work only a total of 20 hours, while she is hoping for 60 hours, she instantly replies, "What if I pay you double time for all your hours next week?"

Well, that changes things. At $30 per hour, you will willingly give up your game time, skip a few classes where you are not having a test, but still keep the weekend free. You are up to 35 hours of work, but your boss is totally desperate and asks again, "What if I pay you triple time?"

At that price, you will also cut back on your sleep, reduce your study time, and try to reschedule your weekend visit. (Is the visit worth giving up $700 for a weekend's work?) Your boss relaxes a bit when you promise 55 hours.

Notice that the quantity of work or time that you are willing to supply to your boss increases as the price she is willing to pay you rises. In order to get you to switch more of your time from alternative uses, she has to offer you more money (which increases her costs).

For your supply decision, there are always alternative uses of your time, and each use has a different cost to you. Your game time is worth the least to you, the weekend time the most. Your willingness to work changes with circumstances, depending on the price offered and the opportunity cost — the value you place on alternative uses of your time.

Marginal Cost   The economist's term for the additional opportunity cost of alternative uses of your time is **marginal cost** — the additional opportunity cost of increasing the quantity of whatever is being supplied. For you, the opportunity cost, or marginal cost, of an hour of game time is less than the opportunity cost, or marginal cost, of an hour of weekend time. As you shift your time away from alternative uses to work, *the marginal cost of your time increases*. You give up the least valuable time first, and continue giving up increasingly valuable time as the price you are offered rises.

How Demand and Supply Choices Are Similar   There are similarities between the demand choices from Chapter 2 and your supply choices.

As a demander, think about products or services you might buy. There are always substitutes available, which is why consumers buy less of a product or service as the price rises — we all switch to cheaper alternatives. Willingness to pay depends on available substitutes and changes with circumstances — the marginal benefit of the first bottle of Gatorade is greater than the marginal benefit of the second bottle.

As a supplier, think about the number of hours you might work. There are always alternative uses of your time, with different values to you. Willingness to supply hours depends on those alternatives and changes with circumstances — the opportunity cost of giving up your gaming hours is less than the opportunity cost of giving up your weekend hours with your best friend. That is one reason why suppliers supply more as the price rises — higher prices are necessary to compensate for the higher opportunity costs as you give up additional time (or other resources).

How Demand and Supply Choices Are Different   There are also important differences between smart demand and smart supply choices.

As a demander buying products and services, marginal benefit — the maximum you are willing to pay — decreases as you buy more. As a supplier of labour hours or other resources, marginal cost — the minimum you need to be paid — increases as you supply more.

For demand and supply, the comparison of benefits and costs is also reversed. As a demander of products and services, marginal benefit is your subjective satisfaction, and marginal cost is measured in dollars — the price you must pay. As a supplier of labour, marginal benefit is measured in dollars — the hourly wage rate you earn — and marginal cost is an opportunity cost, the value of alternative uses of the time that you must give up.

What Do Inputs *Really* Cost?

Any business supply decision involves the same smart choice between marginal benefit and marginal cost as your work decision. The marginal benefit or reward from selling is measured in the dollar price you receive, and all marginal costs are ultimately opportunity costs.

Let's look at a business: Paola's Parlour for Piercing and Nails. To supply her services to the market, Paola, like any businessperson, has to buy inputs (studs, tools, polish), pay rent to her landlord, and pay wages to her employees. What do those hard dollar actual costs have to do with opportunity costs? Which costs are *real* costs?

Take the nickel studs Paola buys for $1 each from a stud supplier. If the world price of nickel rises because of increasing demand from China for the metal, Paola has to pay more for her studs. The stud supplier will sell to Paola only as long as she pays as much as the best price he can get from another customer, whether in China or Canada. Paola's stud cost has to cover the opportunity cost of the stud supplier.

The same goes for Paola's rent or the wages she pays to her employees. If Paola's landlord finds another tenant willing to pay more for the shop space, then once Paola's lease is up, she has to pay that higher amount or the landlord will rent to the other tenant. If Paola's employees, like you, have alternative uses of their time that they value more than what she pays, or if they can get job offers elsewhere at higher wages, Paola has to match the offers or start advertising for help wanted.

Zach Weiner

▲ There are always alternative uses of your time. You must decide how much your game time is worth to you.

▲ Paola's inputs include studs, polish and labour, Like all businesspeople, Paola must pay an input owners at least the best alternative price the input owner can get.

NOTE

The marginal cost a business pays for an input is ultimately an opportunity cost, the value of the best alternative use of that input.

Marginal Costs Are Ultimately Opportunity Costs   To hire or buy inputs, a business must pay a price matching the best opportunity cost of the input owner. The real cost of any input is determined by the best alternative use of that input. All marginal costs are ultimately opportunity costs. Marginal costs can be measured in dollars, but they are an opportunity cost — the value of the best alternative use of that input.

As we will see in the next section, Paola's smart business supply decisions depend on whether the price (the marginal benefit) she receives for a piercing is greater than her marginal opportunity costs.

Refresh 3.1

MyEconLab

For answers to these Refresh Questions, visit MyEconLab.

1. Explain why marginal costs are ultimately opportunity costs.

2. In 2013, Microsoft released a limited supply of Xbox Ones with a list price of $500. The units immediately started selling on eBay and other online auction websites for far more than $500. What factors determined that increase in price of an Xbox One?

3. During a recession, it is much harder for workers to find better-paying jobs. Explain how a recession might affect Paola's labour costs.

3.2 Forget It, It's History: Sunk Costs Don't Matter for Future Choices

Define sunk costs and explain why they do not influence smart, forward-looking decisions.

NOTE

Past expenses are not marginal opportunity costs and have no influence on smart choices.

sunk costs   past expenses that cannot be recovered

Paola bases her business supply decisions on her costs, which are ultimately opportunity costs. But some expenses are not opportunity costs. This is another part of supply decisions that is not as straightforward as you might think.

Past expenses that cannot be reversed or recovered are *not* opportunity costs. If Paola has signed a year's lease for her rent that she cannot get out of, then her rent becomes irrelevant for her future decisions. How can that be?

Paola's or your decisions are always forward looking. A smart decision about which fork in the road to take compares the expected future benefits and the expected future costs of each path. When Paola has to decide whether to supply more piercings or fingernail sets, or to choose between buying new tools or hiring more employees, the rent expense is the same, so its influence cancels out. The past expense of rent paid (or legally contracted for) is the same for either fork Paola chooses, so it shouldn't influence her decision.

These irreversible costs are called **sunk costs** — past, already-paid expenses that cannot be recovered. In other words, they are history — they can't be changed. Decisions that have already been made and can't be changed don't matter for forward-looking economic decisions.

Suppose you paid your tuition for this semester, and the refund date has passed. Your boss's request for extra hours comes at a time when you are finding it hard to balance work and school, and you are considering dropping out.

Your decision to drop out and work full-time (making your boss very happy), versus staying in school, depends on how you evaluate the expected benefits and costs of each fork in your career road. Dropping out and working more means more income right away, while staying in school means less income now but probably more in the future. (We will look at data connecting education and income in Chapter 12.) The tuition you paid is history. You can't get it back no matter which fork you choose — staying in school or dropping out — so it is not part of the opportunity costs of either choice.

ADDITIONAL
BENEFITS
& COSTS

Refresh 3.2

1. Why aren't sunk costs part of the opportunity costs of forward-looking decisions?

2. If you bought a $100 textbook for a course, and then dropped out after the tuition refund date, is that $100 a sunk cost? Explain your answer.

3. Suppose you have just paid your bus fare. A friend in a car pulls up and offers you a ride. Explain how you would decide between staying on the bus or taking the ride, and the influence of the paid fare on your choice.

MyEconLab

For answers to these Refresh Questions, visit MyEconLab.

More for More Money:
The Law of Supply

3.3

Demand is not just what you want. It is your willingness and ability to pay for a product or service — putting your money where your mouth is. Similarly, the economist's idea of supply is not just offering things for sale. **Supply** is the overall willingness of businesses (or individuals) to sell a particular product or service because the price covers all opportunity costs of production.

Explain the law of supply, and describe the roles of higher profits and higher marginal opportunity costs of production.

Quantity Supplied

Let's look at how an economist would describe your supply decision about how many hours to work at your part-time job. Figure 3.1 combines price information — the lowest wage you are willing to accept — and the quantity of work you will supply at each wage.

supply   businesses' willingness to produce a particular product or service because price covers all opportunity costs

Figure 3.1   Your Supply of Hours Worked

Price (minimum willing to accept per hour)	Quantity Supplied (hours of work at that price)
$15	10 – 20
$30	35
$45	55

At a price of $15 per hour, your quantity supplied of work could be anywhere between 10 and 20 hours. At $30 per hour, your quantity supplied of work is 35 hours, and at $45 per hour, your quantity supplied is 55 hours.

quantity supplied   the quantity you actually plan to supply at a given price

As your eye goes down the columns in Figure 3.1, note that as the price rises, the quantity supplied increases. (What happens to quantity demanded as price rises?) In general, when prices rise, individuals and businesses devote more of their time or resources to producing or supplying — more money stimulates more quantity supplied. The two reasons for this are the desire for profits (higher prices usually mean higher profits) and the need for a higher price to cover higher marginal opportunity costs — your weekend time is worth more to you than your *World of Warcraft* time.

Quantity supplied, as we will see, is not the same as supply. **Quantity supplied** is a more limited concept — the quantity you actually plan to supply at a given price, taking into account everything that affects your willingness to supply work hours.

Let's take the economist's idea of supply and apply it to Paola's willingness to supply a particular quantity of piercings at a particular price.

Body Piercings or Nail Sets?

Businesses, like consumers, make smart choices based on Key 1 — Choose only when additional benefits are greater than additional *opportunity costs*.

Paola's first choice is *what to produce* with her resources — the labour and equipment she has in her shop. She can do body piercing, and she can also paint fingernails. Let's limit her choices to full body piercings and full sets of fingernails to allow the simple, made-up numbers below.

Paola's Parlour has special tools for piercing and for nail painting. There are four people working (including Paola). All four are equally skilled at piercing (the business started with just piercing), but their fingernail skills differ from expert (Paola) to beginner (Parminder). The table in Figure 3.2 shows the different combinations of fingernail sets and piercings that Paola's Parlour can produce in a day.

Figure 3.2   Paola's Parlour Production Possibilities Frontier

Combination	Fingernails (full sets)	Piercings (full body)
A	15	0
B	14	1
C	12	2
D	9	3
E	5	4
F	0	5

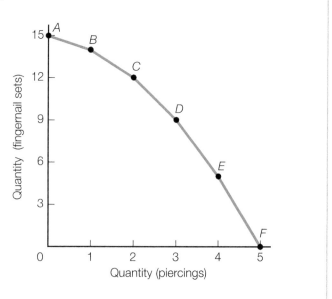

At one extreme (combination *A*) all four workers do fingernails only, so they produce 15 fingernail sets and no piercings. If Paola starts shifting some staff from fingernails to piercings, she moves to combination *B* (14 fingernail sets and 1 full body piercing). Shifting more staff and equipment out of fingernails and into piercing gives combination *C* (12 fingernail sets and 2 piercings), and then combinations *D* (9 fingernail sets and 3 piercings) and *E* (5 fingernail sets and 4 piercings). Combination *F* is the other extreme, where the Paola's Parlour produces only piercings — 5 piercings and 0 fingernail sets. As you will see, the pattern of numbers in the table in Figure 3.2 has a lot to do with differences in fingernail painting skills.

Paola's Parlour's Production Possibilities Frontier We can graph the table of numbers in Figure 3.2 as Paola's production possibilities frontier (*PPF*). The graph in Figure 3.2 shows Paola's Parlour's *PPF*, with daily output of piercings measured on the horizontal axis, and daily output of fingernail sets measured on the vertical axis. Each point (*A – F*) on the frontier corresponds to a combination in the table.

Increasing Marginal Opportunity Costs

The numbers and graph in Figure 3.2 don't make much business sense — they are just maximum possible combinations of piercings and nail sets that Paola's Parlour can produce. To use the numbers for Paola's business supply decisions, we must translate them into marginal costs. (And eventually into profits in Chapter 8.)

Remember that costs are ultimately opportunity costs. The cost of acquiring or producing products or services is the value of the best alternative opportunity we must give up to get them. To get more piercings, Paola gives up doing nail sets. Opportunity cost is what we give up divided by what we get:

$$\text{Opportunity Cost} = \frac{\text{Give Up}}{\text{Get}}$$

Figure 3.3 (on the next page) shows, in the last column, the marginal opportunity costs to Paola of producing more piercings.

Figure 3.3 Paola's Parlour's Marginal Opportunity Costs

Combination	Fingernails (full sets)	Piercings (full body)	Marginal Opportunity Cost of Producing More Piercings (fingernail sets given up)
A	15	0	
			$\dfrac{(15 - 14)}{1} = 1$
B	14	1	
			$\dfrac{(14 - 12)}{1} = 2$
C	12	2	
			$\dfrac{(12 - 9)}{1} = 3$
D	9	3	
			$\dfrac{(9 - 5)}{1} = 4$
E	5	4	
			$\dfrac{(5 - 0)}{1} = 5$
F	0	5	

What is the marginal opportunity cost of producing the first piercing? To move from 0 to 1 piercing (from combination *A* to *B*), Paola gives up 1 fingernail set, because fingernail production drops from 15 to 14 sets as some staff time switches from fingernails to piercing. In exchange, she gets 1 piercing. So substituting into the formula, the marginal opportunity cost of the first piercing is

$$\frac{1 \text{ fingernail set}}{1 \text{ piercing}} = 1 \text{ fingernail set per piercing}$$

To produce a second piercing (moving from combination *B* to *C*), Paola gives up 2 fingernail sets (14 – 12 sets). The marginal opportunity cost of the second additional piercing is 2 fingernail sets given up per piercing. The third piercing (moving from combination *C* to *D*) has a marginal opportunity cost of 3 fingernail sets given up (12 – 9 sets) per piercing. In moving the last of her staff to piercing, for the fifth piercing she gives up 5 fingernail sets (5 – 0 sets). The marginal opportunity cost of the last additional piercing — the fifth — is 5 fingernail sets given up per piercing.

Opportunity Costs Are Marginal Costs If you are wondering what the difference is between opportunity cost, marginal cost, and marginal opportunity cost — since they seem like the same thing — good for you! You are not confused, you're right. *All opportunity costs are marginal costs, and all marginal costs are opportunity costs.*

Opportunity cost and marginal cost are two sides of the same coin. Opportunity cost focuses on the value of the opportunity *given up* when you make a decision. On the flip side, marginal cost focuses on the *additional cost* of that decision. Paola must give up 5 fingernail sets in deciding to produce the fifth piercing. So the marginal opportunity cost of the fifth piercing is 5 fingernail sets. **Marginal opportunity cost** is the complete term for any cost relevant to a smart decision. We will usually use the shorter name — *marginal cost* — when describing supply decisions.

Figure 3.4a begins to illustrate the economic sense of these numbers. The numbers in the table for marginal opportunity costs and quantity of piercings come from Figure 3.3 (columns 4 and 3). Each point on the graph in Figure 3.4a shows the marginal opportunity cost measured in fingernail sets given up per piercing (along the vertical axis) for each quantity of piercings supplied (along the horizontal axis).

marginal opportunity cost
complete term for any cost relevant to a smart decision
marginal cost
shortened name

Figure 3.4   Increasing Marginal Opportunity Cost

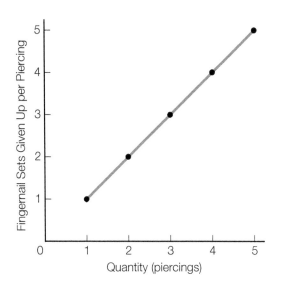

Marginal Opportunity Cost of Additional Piercings (fingernail sets given up)	Quantity Supplied (piercings)
1	1
2	2
3	3
4	4
5	5

a) Marginal Opportunity Cost of Additional Piercings Measured in Fingernail Sets

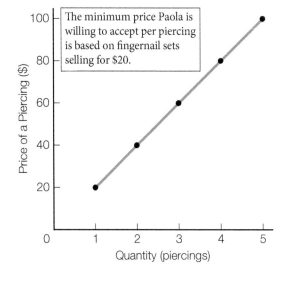

The minimum price Paola is willing to accept per piercing is based on fingernail sets selling for $20.

Price (marginal opportunity cost or minimum willing to accept per piercing)	Quantity Supplied (piercings)
$ 20	1
$ 40	2
$ 60	3
$ 80	4
$100	5

must be at least what she would have made w fingernail sets

b) Marginal Opportunity Cost of Additional Piercings Measured in $

Note in Figure 3.4a that as Paola increases her quantity supplied of piercings, her marginal opportunity costs increase, from 1 fingernail set given up for the first piercing to 5 fingernail sets given up for the fifth piercing. This is the same pattern in the decision to shift your time away from alternative uses to work more hours — the marginal cost of additional time given up increases as you give up increasingly more valuable uses of your time.

Paying for Opportunity Costs   So far, the numbers in Paola's example are measured in piercings or fingernail sets. But Paola, as a profit-seeking entrepreneur, wants to make a smart supply decision based on dollar prices. Luckily, it is easy to convert body decorations to dollars. Suppose that fingernail full sets sell for $20. Then the marginal opportunity costs for supplying additional piercings appear in the table in Figure 3.4b on the previous page.

The marginal opportunity cost of producing and supplying the first piercing is $20 (the cost of 1 nail set given up); of the second piercing, $40 (2 nail sets given up); all the way up to $100 for the fifth piercing. So for Paola to be willing to supply 1 piercing, she needs to receive a price of at least $20 to cover the costs of the alternative use of her inputs. To continue to supply more piercings, she needs to receive higher prices to cover her higher marginal opportunity costs. Paola won't supply the fifth piercing unless she receives at least $100 for it, because that is what she would be giving up from the best alternative use of her inputs (5 fingernail sets at $20 each).

The graph in Figure 3.4b shows, for each quantity of piercings supplied (along the horizontal axis), the minimum price Paola will accept to cover her increasing marginal opportunity costs (along the vertical axis). Because of increasing marginal opportunity costs, the minimum price rises as Paola's quantity supplied increases.

Why Marginal Opportunity Costs Increase   Are the reasons for Paola's increasing marginal opportunity costs the same as for your work decision? And is there a connection between the increasing marginal opportunity costs of Paola's curved-shaped *PPF*, compared to the straight-line *PPF*s in Chapter 1 for Jill and Marie making bread and wood?

The answers to these important questions come from differences among inputs to production. Paola's increasing marginal opportunity costs arise because her staff and equipment are not equally good at piercing and painting. Paola is better (more productive) at doing fingernails than is Parminder, and the tools can't be easily switched between tasks — nail-polish brushes and emery boards aren't much help in piercing.

These differences in productivity cause increasing marginal opportunity costs. Think about Paola as she decides to reduce fingernail output and produce the first piercing. Remember that all staff are equally skilled at piercing. Who will she switch first to piercing? As an economizer, she will switch the person who is least productive for fingernails — Parminder. So her given up, or forgone, fingernail production is small (1 set). To increase piercing output more, she has to then switch staff who are slightly better at doing fingernails, so the opportunity cost is higher (2 fingernail sets). And who is the last person she switches when moving entirely to piercing? Of course, it is Paola herself — the best nail painter — so the opportunity cost of that fifth piercing is the highest, at 5 fingernail sets given up.

Increasing marginal opportunity costs arise because inputs are not equally productive in all activities. There are always opportunity costs in switching between activities because time spent on piercing can no longer be spent on fingernails. But *increasing* opportunity costs arise because of the differing skill levels of the staff being switched.

The reasons for Paola's increasing marginal opportunity costs are not quite the same as the reasons for your decision to supply more work hours as the price rises, but there is much in common. For your work decision, increasing marginal opportunity costs arise from differences in the value of alternative uses of your time (from gaming to weekend fun). For Paola's decision to supply additional piercings, increasing marginal opportunity costs arise from differences in employee skill levels and equipment in producing alternative services. The common reason is alternative uses (of time or inputs) with increasing opportunity costs.

When Marginal Opportunity Costs Are Constant

If all of Paola's staff and equipment were equally good at piercing and fingernail painting, the opportunity costs would always be the same, no matter what combinations of piercings and fingernails she produced.

NOTE
Marginal opportunity costs are constant when inputs are equally productive in all activities.

The *PPF* examples of Jill and Marie in Chapter 1 have such constant marginal opportunity costs. Jill's straight line *PPF* means that as she switches between combinations of bread and wood, her marginal opportunity costs do not change. Jill's skills don't change as she switches between making bread and chopping wood. All that changes is the amount of time she spends on each task. The same is true for Marie. While Marie's skills and abilities differ from Jill's, Marie's skills don't change as she switches her time between tasks. For each person, marginal opportunity costs are constant as she switches between combinations of bread and wood.

In the real world, marginal opportunity costs may be increasing or constant. We will examine both cases in Chapter 9. Most businesses have inputs that are *not* equally productive in all activities, and so have increasing marginal opportunity costs. That is the case we will focus on here.

The Law of Supply

Just as you are willing to supply more hours of work only if the price you are paid rises, Paola's business must receive a higher price to be willing to supply a greater quantity to the market. She needs the higher price to cover her increasing marginal opportunity costs as she increases production.

Market supply is the sum of the supplies of all businesses willing to produce a particular product or service. Suppose there are 100 piercing businesses just like Paola's. The market supply of piercings is the sum of the supplies of all piercing businesses, and looks like the table in Figure 3.5.

market supply   sum of supplies of all businesses willing to produce a particular product or service

Figure 3.5   Market Supply of Piercings

Row	Price (marginal opportunity cost or minimum willing to accept per piercings)	Quantity Supplied (piercings)
A	$ 20	100
B	$ 40	200
C	$ 60	300
D	$ 80	400
E	$100	500

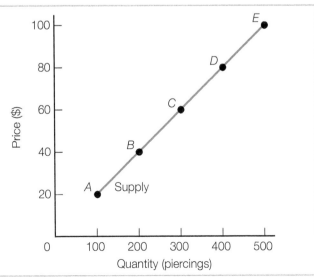

The positive relationship between price and quantity supplied (both go up together) is so universal that economists call it the **law of supply**: If the price of a product or service rises, the quantity supplied increases. Higher prices create incentives for increased production through higher profits and by covering higher marginal opportunity costs of production.

The law of supply works as long as other factors besides price do not change. Section 3.4 explores what happens when other factors do change.

Supply Curve of Piercings In Figure 3.5 on the previous page, if you take the combinations of prices and quantity supplied from the table and graph them, you get the upward-sloping supply curve.

For example, when the price of a piercing is $20, the quantity supplied by all businesses is 100 piercings (point *A*). When the price is $100, the quantity supplied is 500 (point *E*). Other points on the supply curve show the quantities supplied for prices between $20 and $100.

We draw the market supply curve for piercings by plotting these combinations on a graph that has *quantity* on the horizontal axis and *price* on the vertical axis. The points labelled *A* to *E* correspond to the rows of the table.

A **supply curve** shows the relationship between price and quantity supplied, when all other influences on supply besides price do not change.

Two Ways to Read a Supply Curve

The supply curve shows graphically the relationship between price and quantity supplied, when all other influences on supply do not change. The supply curve is a simple yet powerful tool summarizing the two forces determining quantity supplied — the desire for higher profits and the need to cover increasing marginal opportunity costs of production.

Because there are two forces determining quantity supplied, there are two ways to "read" a supply curve — as a supply curve and as a marginal cost curve. Both readings are correct, but each highlights a different force. You can see the two readings in Figures 3.6a and 3.6b.

Figure 3.6 Two Ways to Read a Supply Curve

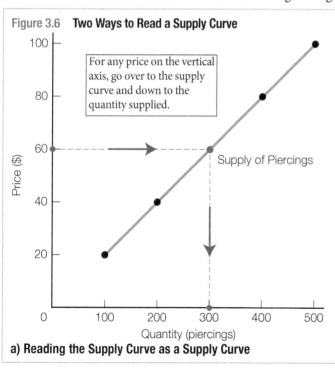

For any price on the vertical axis, go over to the supply curve and down to the quantity supplied.

Supply of Piercings

a) Reading the Supply Curve as a Supply Curve

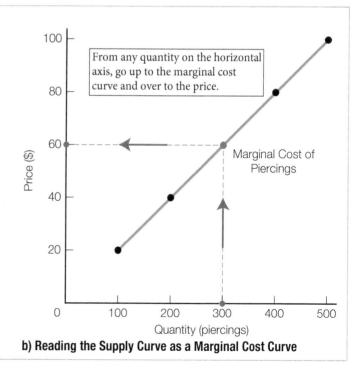

From any quantity on the horizontal axis, go up to the marginal cost curve and over to the price.

Marginal Cost of Piercings

b) Reading the Supply Curve as a Marginal Cost Curve

Supply Curve   To read Figure 3.6a as a supply curve, start with price. For any price, the supply curve tells you the quantity businesses are willing to supply. For example, start with the price of $60 on the vertical axis (Price). To find quantity supplied at $60, trace a line from the $60 price over to the supply curve and then down to the horizontal axis (Quantity) to read the quantity supplied, which is 300 piercings per day. You can do the same for any price — from any price, go over to the supply curve and then down to read the corresponding quantity supplied.

To think about how a price rise from $60 to $80 increases the quantity businesses are willing to supply, for each price, go over to the supply curve and then down to the quantity supplied. The rise in price of $20 increases quantity supplied by 100 piercings per day (400 – 300).

start w the opposite axis of the name

Marginal Cost Curve   To read Figure 3.6b as a marginal cost curve, start with quantity. For any quantity, the marginal cost curve tells you the minimum price businesses will accept that covers all marginal opportunity costs of production. Start with the quantity 300 piercings on the horizontal axis (Quantity). To find the minimum price businesses will accept to produce the 300th piercing, trace a line up to the marginal cost curve and over to the vertical (Price) axis to read the price, which is $60. You can do the same for any quantity — from any quantity, go up to the marginal cost curve and then over to read the corresponding price, which is the minimum price businesses will accept for that last piercing.

To think about how an increase in quantity supplied from 300 to 400 piercings increases marginal opportunity cost and the minimum price businesses will accept, for each quantity, go up to the marginal cost curve and then over to the price. Sixty dollars is the lowest price a business will accept for the 300th piercing, and $80 is the lowest price someone will accept for the 400th piercing. The increase in quantity of 100 units causes an increase in marginal opportunity cost of $20 per unit ($80 – $60).

The Supply Curve Is Also a Marginal Cost Curve   You read a supply curve over and down. You read a marginal cost curve up and over. While the supply curve has a double identity both as a supply curve and as a marginal cost curve, we generally refer to it as a supply curve. Sometimes, though, the marginal cost reading makes it easier to understand smart choices.

Both readings are movements along an unchanged supply curve. But what about the other influences on supply that we have been keeping constant? What happens if they change? The two ways to read a supply curve will help you answer that question.

Refresh 3.3

1. Explain why Paola needs a higher price to be willing to supply more piercings.

2. If you could spend the next hour studying economics or working at your part-time job, which pays $11 an hour, what is your personal opportunity cost, in dollars, of studying?

3. Suppose Paola's Parlour was producing only piercings and no fingernail sets. If Paola wanted to start producing some fingernail sets, which staff person should she switch to fingernails first? Who should she switch last? Explain your answers.

MyEconLab

For answers to these Refresh Questions, visit MyEconLab.

Changing the Bottom Line: What Can Change Supply?

Explain the difference between a change in quantity supplied and a change in supply, and list five factors that change supply.

The average price of an ultrabook computer in Canada fell from around $2000 in 2010 to under $800 in 2013. But the quantity of ultrabook computers businesses sold *increased*.

Does that contradict the "law of supply"?

If nothing else changed except the price of ultrabooks, the answer would be yes. Why would ultrabook producers be willing to supply more ultrabooks at lower prices? Something is not right. But like evidence that appears to disprove the law of demand, a fall in price that increases quantity supplied is a signal that something else must have changed at the same time.

Economists use the term *supply* to summarize all of the influences on business decisions. In the examples of your work decision or Paola's piercings, that willingness to supply depends on the value of alternative uses of time or inputs and on marginal opportunity costs.

As long as these factors (and some others that we are about to look at) do not change, the law of supply holds true: If the price of a product or service rises, quantity supplied increases.

But change happens, and economists distinguish two kinds of change:

- If the price of a product or service changes, that affects *quantity supplied*. This is represented graphically by moving along an unchanged supply curve.

- If anything else changes, that affects *supply*. This is represented graphically by a shift of the entire supply curve.

This distinction is the same as the distinction in Chapter 2 between quantity demanded and demand.

Economics *Out There*

Uncorking the Okanagan

In the Okanagan region of British Columbia. — an area known for its fruit production — large excavation machines are ripping out apple trees to make way for a new crop: grapes. Local landowners hope the switch will allow them to make more profits from their property by jumping into the province's booming wine industry. Landowner Bryan Hardman says that in the past he has been a price taker, but is setting up his own winery because he "wants to be a price maker, and believes the wine business is the place to do it."

- This story beautifully illustrates the law of supply. Higher prices and profits are creating incentives to increase quantity supplied of grapes and wine.

- It also illustrates how all inputs must be paid their opportunity costs. Even though the Okanagan Valley is a world-class area for apple-growing, landowners can make more money switching to grapes — more than covering their opportunity costs — so they do.

- If land is not equally productive for grape-growing, which apple orchards would you expect to be dug up and replanted with grapes first? Which would be replanted last?

- Consider Mr. Hardman's comment about wanting to be a price maker instead of a price taker. We will use those exact terms in Chapter 8 when we discuss competition among businesses in an industry.

Source: Wendy Stueck, "Uncorking the Okanagan," *The Globe and Mail*, October 7, 2006, p. B4.

Six Ways to Change Supply and Shift the Supply Curve

Only a change in the price of a product or service itself changes *quantity supplied* of that product or service. There are six other important factors that change market supply — the willingness to produce a product or service. They are:

- Technology
- Environment
- Prices of inputs
- Prices of related products or services produced
- Expected future prices
- Number of businesses

A change in any of these six factors shifts the supply curve.

Technology   Paola is overjoyed because she just bought a new piercing gun that allows her employees to do more piercings in a day. This increase in productivity from the new technology reduces her costs. Word spreads quickly, and all of the other piercing parlour owners realize that to stay competitive, they also must adopt the new technology. The result is an increase in market supply, which is shown in Figure 3.7 and can be described either by reading the supply curve as a supply curve or as a marginal cost curve.

Figure 3.7   Increase in Market Supply of Piercings

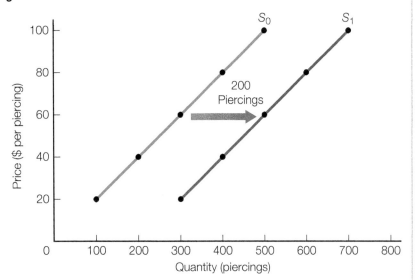

Price (marginal opportunity cost or minimum willing to accept per piercing)	Quantity Supplied (before technology improvement)	Quantity Supplied (after technology improvement)
$ 20	100	300
$ 40	200	400
$ 60	300	500
$ 80	400	600
$100	500	700

Let's start with the supply curve reading, which begins with price and goes over and down to the quantity supplied. At a price of $20 (the first row in the table), before the new technology, businesses were willing to supply 100 piercings (column 2). On the graph, from the price of $20 on the vertical axis, go over to supply curve S_0 and down to the quantity of 100 piercings.

Still in the first row of the table, at the unchanged price of $20, with the new technology, businesses will now supply 300 piercings (column 3). On the graph, from the price of $20, go over to the new supply curve S_1 and down to the quantity of 300 piercings. That is an increase in supply of 200 piercings (300 − 100).

As you look down the rest of the rows of the table, at every price businesses will supply 200 more piercings with the new technology. Economists call this an **increase in supply** — an increase in business's willingness to supply at any price. This increase in supply is represented on the graph by a rightward shift of the supply curve, from S_0 to S_1. The horizontal distance between S_0 and S_1 is 200 piercings.

The increase in supply can also be described by reading the supply curve as a marginal cost curve — up and over from quantity supplied to price. Before the new technology, to supply 300 piercings, businesses needed a minimum price of $60 per piercing to cover marginal opportunity costs. On the graph, from the quantity 300 on the horizontal axis, go up to supply curve S_0 and over to the price of $60. After the new technology, to supply 300 piercings businesses now need a price of only $20 per piercing — from the quantity 300, go up to supply curve S_1 and over to the price of $20.

The new technology lowers Paola's and other piercers' marginal opportunity costs, so they can accept a lower price while still covering all costs. For any quantity supplied, after the new technology, the minimum price businesses are willing to accept falls because marginal costs are lower.

Either way, whether you read the supply curve as a supply curve or a marginal cost curve, the result is an increase in supply — a rightward shift of supply curve.

increase in supply increase in businesses' willingness to supply; rightward shift of supply curve

NOTE
An improvement in technology increases supply, and does not change quantity supplied.

Economics *Out There*

Army of Noodle-Shaving Robots Invades Restaurants

Chinese restaurant owner and entrepreneur Cui Runguan developed a robot (see photo on page 51) that hand-slices noodles into a pot of boiling water.

The robots "can slice noodles better than human chefs, they never get tired or bored, and it is much cheaper than a real human chef" says Liu Maohu, a noodle shop owner. Each robot costs under $2000, but replaces a chef costing $4700 per year.

- This technological change decreases costs and increases supply.
- If I am a restaurant owner, noodle robots "show me more money," so I increase supply.

Source: Paula Forbes, "China Is Building an Army of Noodle-Making Robots," *Eater*, August 17, 2012, http://eater.com/archives/2012/08/17/china-is-building-an-army-of-noodle-making-robots.php; Raymond Wong, "Army of Noodle-Shaving Robots Invade Restaurants in China," *Dvice*, August 20, 2013, http://www.dvice.com/archives/2012/08/noodle_shaving.php.

Environment   Extreme weather — droughts, storms, tornadoes, earthquakes — can have a powerful effect on supply. Extreme environmental events can reduce or destroy wheat crops, decreasing market supply, and shifting the supply curve for wheat leftward. The reverse is also true. Good weather conditions produce bumper crops, increasing wheat supply and shifting the market supply curve for wheat rightward.

Water temperature can affect fish stocks. A change in the temperature of water may lower reproduction rates, fewer fish are born, market supply decreases, and the supply curve for fish shifts leftward. If the change in water temperature encourages reproduction, fish supply increases, and the supply curve for fish shifts rightward.

NOTE
A positive environmental change increases supply.

Price of Inputs   Paola and other businesses must pay a price for inputs matching the best opportunity cost of the input owner. If those opportunity costs and input prices fall, Paola's costs decrease. At any price for piercings, lower costs for studs or electricity mean Paola earns higher profits, so she will want to supply more. The effect of lower input prices on market supply is the same as a technology improvement. Lower input prices increase market supply and shift the supply curve rightward.

The reverse is also true: Higher input prices mean higher costs for Paola and, at any price, lower profits. Therefore, market supply decreases. The supply curve shifts leftward.

NOTE
A fall in input prices increases supply.

Prices of Related Products and Services   Paola's Parlour produces both piercings and fingernail sets. What happens to Paola's supply of piercings when the price of fingernail sets falls from $20 to $10 per set? Since Paola wants to earn maximum profits, which service will she supply more of, and which less, when the price of fingernail sets falls? Take a minute to see if you can answer that question before reading on.

When the price of fingernail sets falls, Paola will supply more piercings and fewer fingernail sets. You probably reasoned that when the price of fingernail sets falls, they are less profitable to produce, so Paola will shift more of her resources to producing piercings. You are correct. A fall in the price of fingernail sets increases the supply of piercings. The supply curve of piercings shifts rightward.

NOTE
Lower prices for a related product or service a business produces increase supply of alternative products or services.

You can also reason out the answer to the question of what happens to Paola's supply of piercings when the price of fingernail sets falls by thinking of the supply curve as a marginal cost curve. The lower price of fingernail sets lowers Paola's marginal opportunity cost of producing piercings. The real opportunity cost of producing more piercings is the fingernail sets Paola must give up. When those fingernail sets fall in price, Paola's marginal opportunity cost for producing piercings decreases. So the minimum price Paola will accept to supply any quantity of piercings falls. The supply curve of piercings shifts rightward.

In reverse, a rise in the price of fingernail sets decreases the supply of piercings. The supply curve of piercings shifts leftward. This is a **decrease in supply** — a decrease in business's willingness to produce.

A change in the price of related products or services supplied leads a business to reconsider its most profitable choices. A business will supply more of one product or service when alternative products or services it produces fall in price, and supply less when alternative products or services it produces rise in price.

Expected Future Prices

What happens to the supply of a product or service when the expected future price of the product or service changes? In Chapter 2, you learned that consumer demand changes if consumers expect lower or higher prices in the future. The same is true for businesses. If Paola expects falling piercing prices in the future, she will try to supply more now, while the price is relatively high. When future prices are expected to fall, supply increases in the present. The supply curve shifts rightward.

If Paola expects future prices to rise, she may reduce her current supply and increase her supply when prices and profits are higher. When future prices are expected to rise, supply decreases in the present. The supply curve shifts leftward.

Number of Businesses

An increase in the number of businesses increases market supply and shifts the supply curve rightward. It is no surprise that at any price, more businesses will supply a greater quantity. The increased number of businesses increases supply, just as an improvement in technology or a fall in input prices increases supply. A decrease in the number of businesses decreases supply, just as a rise in the price of a related product or service or an increase in expected future prices decreases supply.

Why would businesses enter (increase supply) or exit (decrease supply) a market? Usually, when profits are high, new competitors enter a market, increasing market supply. If profits are lower than elsewhere in the economy, competitors exit from the market, decreasing market supply. Those exiting businesses search for more profitable uses of their resources. You will learn more about these entry and exit stories in Chapter 7.

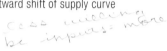

Moving Along or Shifting the Supply Curve   Any increase (or decrease) in supply caused by changes in any of the six factors discussed can be described in alternative ways. You can read the supply curve either as a supply curve or as a marginal cost curve.

- At any price, businesses will supply a larger quantity. This is the supply curve reading of an increase in supply.

- At any quantity supplied, businesses will accept a lower price because their marginal opportunity costs of production are lower. This is the marginal cost reading of an increase in supply.

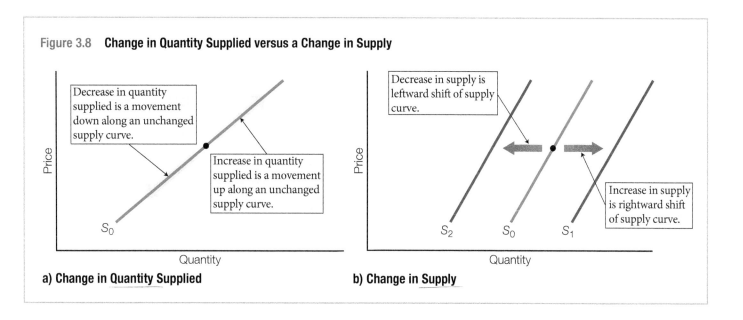

Figure 3.8   **Change in Quantity Supplied versus a Change in Supply**

Decrease in quantity supplied is a movement down along an unchanged supply curve.

Increase in quantity supplied is a movement up along an unchanged supply curve.

S_0

Quantity

a) Change in Quantity Supplied

Decrease in supply is leftward shift of supply curve.

Increase in supply is rightward shift of supply curve.

S_2 S_0 S_1

Quantity

b) Change in Supply

In both readings, an increase in supply is also called a rightward shift of the supply curve. A decrease in supply is called a leftward shift of the supply curve.

When none of the six factors change to shift the supply curve, we can focus on the relationship between price and quantity supplied. That is represented in Figure 3.8a as moving along the supply curve S_0. If the price rises, and all other things do not change, that is a movement up along the supply curve to a larger quantity supplied. If the price falls, all other things unchanged, that is a movement down along the supply curve to a smaller quantity supplied.

Figure 3.8b shows an increase in supply, as the rightward shift from S_0 to S_1. The leftward shift from S_0 to S_2 is a decrease in supply. These shifts in supply are caused by changes in any of the six factors — technology, environment, prices of inputs, prices of related products or services produced, expected future prices, or number of businesses.

NOTE

An increase in supply is a rightward shift of the supply curve. A decrease in supply is a leftward shift of the supply curve.

Saving the Law of Supply

A change in quantity supplied (caused by a change in the price of the product or service itself) differs from a change in supply (caused by changes in technology, environment, prices of inputs, prices of related products or services produced, expected future prices, or the number of businesses). Can you now see why, when ultrabook computer prices fell from $2000 to under $800, the quantity of ultrabooks sold actually *increased*? Is the "law of supply" really a law?

If the price of a product or service falls, the quantity supplied decreases, *as long as other factors do not change*. The fall in ultrabook prices alone would *decrease* quantity supplied, not increase it. But other things changed. While a complete explanation involves demand factors as well as supply, major changes included technological improvements in computer chips and falling input prices. These *increased the supply* of ultrabook computers. Using the marginal cost reading of an increase in supply, at any quantity supplied, businesses were willing to accept a lower price because marginal opportunity costs of production were lower. The effect of the increase in supply outweighed the lower prices decreasing quantity supplied.

Figure 3.9 is a good study device for reviewing the difference between the law of supply and the factors that change supply.

Figure 3.9   Law of Supply and Changes in Supply

The Law of Supply *The quantity supplied of a product or service*	
Decreases if:	*Increases if:*
• price of the product or service falls	• price of the product or service rises

Changes in Supply *The supply for a product or service*	
Decreases if:	*Increases if:*
• _____	• technology improves
• environmental change harms production	• environment change helps production
• price of an input rises	• price of an input falls
• price of a related product or service rises	• price of a related product or service falls
• expected future price rises	• expected future price falls
• number of businesses decreases	• number of businesses increases

---

Refresh 3.4

1. Explain the difference between a change in quantity supplied and a change in supply. In your answer, distinguish the six factors that can change supply.

2. Suppose you have two part-time jobs, babysitting and pizza delivery. After younger babysitters start working for less, babysitting clients pay only $8 instead of $10 per hour. What happens to your supply of hours for delivering pizzas? Explain.

3. When the price of nail sets falls, Paola's hard dollar costs do not change. Will the quantity of piercings Paola supplies increase or decrease? Explain.

Study Guide

3.1 What Does It Really Cost? Costs Are Opportunity Costs

Businesses must pay higher prices to obtain more of an input because opportunity costs change with circumstances. The marginal costs of additional inputs (like labour) are ultimately opportunity costs — the best alternative use of the input.

- **Marginal cost** — additional opportunity cost of increasing quantity supplied, changing with circumstances.
  - For the working example, you are supplying time, and the marginal cost of your time increases as you increase the quantity of hours supplied.

- Differences between smart supply choices and smart demand choices:
  - For supply, marginal cost increases as you supply more.
  - For demand, marginal benefit decreases as you buy more.
  - For supply, marginal benefit is measured in $ (wages you earn); marginal cost is the opportunity cost of time.
  - For demand, marginal benefit is the satisfaction you get; marginal cost is measured in $ (the price you pay).

3.2 Forget It, It's History: Sunk Costs Don't Matter for Future Choices

Sunk costs that cannot be reversed are not part of opportunity costs. Sunk costs do not influence smart, forward-looking decisions.

- **Sunk costs** — past expenses that cannot be recovered.

- Sunk costs are the same no matter which fork in the road you take, so they have no influence on smart choices.

3.3 More for More Money: The Law of Supply

If the price of a product or service rises, quantity supplied increases. Businesses increase production when higher prices either create higher profits or cover higher marginal opportunity costs of production.

- **Supply** — businesses' willingness to produce a particular product or service because price covers all opportunity costs.

- **Quantity supplied** — quantity you actually plan to supply at a given price.

- **Marginal opportunity cost** — complete term for any cost relevant to a smart decision.
  - All opportunity costs are marginal costs; all marginal costs are opportunity costs.

- Increasing marginal opportunity costs arise because inputs are not equally productive in all activities.
  - Where inputs are equally productive in all activities, marginal opportunity costs are constant.

- **Market supply** — sum of supplies of all businesses willing to produce a particular product or service.

- **Law of supply** — if the price of a product or service rises, quantity supplied increases.

- **Supply curve** — shows the relationship between price and quantity supplied, other things remaining the same.
  - There are two ways to read a supply curve.
  - As a supply curve, read over and down from price to quantity supplied.
  - As a marginal cost curve, read up and over from quantity supplied to price. A marginal cost curve shows the minimum price businesses will accept that covers all marginal opportunity costs of production.

3.4 Changing the Bottom Line: What Can Change Supply?

Quantity supplied is changed only by a change in price. Supply is changed by all other influences on business decisions.

- Supply is a catch-all term summarizing all possible influences on businesses' willingness to produce a particular product or service.

- Supply changes with changes in technology, environment, prices of inputs, prices of related products or services produced, expected future prices, and number of businesses. For example, supply increases with:
  - improvement in technology
  - environmental change helping production
  - fall in price of an input
  - fall in price of a related product or service
  - fall in expected future price
  - increase in number of businesses

- **Increase in supply** — increase in businesses' willingness to supply. Can be described in two ways:
  - At any unchanged price, businesses are now willing to supply a greater quantity.
  - For producing any unchanged quantity, businesses are now willing to accept a lower price.

- **Decrease in supply** — decrease in business's willingness to supply.

TRUE / FALSE

Circle the correct answer. Solutions to these questions are available at the end of the book and on MyEconLab. You can also visit the MyEconLab Study Plan to access additional questions that will help you master the concepts covered in this chapter.

3.1 Costs Are Opportunity Costs

1. When higher-paying jobs are harder to find for workers, a business will pay more to hire labour. — T (F)

2. Any smart business supply decision involves a choice between a business's marginal benefit (or reward) from supplying (or selling) its product and the business's marginal opportunity cost of producing the product. — T F

3. Any smart worker supply decision involves a choice between a worker's marginal benefit (or reward) from supplying (or selling) her work and the worker's marginal opportunity cost of working. — T F

4. Gordie's marginal opportunity cost of spending an extra hour on Facebook increases if he suddenly has the opportunity to go on a date with his high school crush. — T F

3.2 Sunk Costs Don't Matter for Future Choices

5. Businesses should consider the monthly rent when deciding whether to produce more of a product or service. — T F

6. Sunk costs are part of opportunity costs. — T F

3.3 The Law of Supply

7. Businesses must receive higher prices as output increases to compensate for increasing marginal opportunity costs. — T F

8. Opportunity cost equals what you get divided by what you give up. — T F

9. As you shift time *away* from watching TV to working more hours, the marginal opportunity cost of working decreases. — T (F)

10. All opportunity costs are marginal costs, and all marginal costs are opportunity costs. — T F

11. To read a supply curve as a marginal cost curve, you start with price and go over and down to quantity supplied. — T F

3.4 What Can Change Supply?

12. A rise in the price of inputs used by businesses decreases market supply. — T F

13. A rise in the price of a related product a business produces increases market supply of the other product. — T F

14. A rise in expected future prices shifts today's supply curve leftward. — T F

15. Moving up along a supply curve is an increase in supply. — T F

MULTIPLE CHOICE

Circle the best answer. Solutions to these questions are available at the end of the book and on MyEconLab. You can also visit the MyEconLab Study Plan to access similar questions that will help you master the concepts covered in this chapter.

3.1 Costs Are Opportunity Costs

1. Your opportunity cost of watching *The Big Bang Theory* increases if
   a) it is your favourite TV show.
   b) you have an expensive television.
   c) you have an exam the next day.
   d) all of the above.

2. The opportunity cost of going to school is highest for someone who
   a) has to give up a job paying $10 an hour.
   b) has to give up a job paying $15 an hour.
   c) loves school.
   d) has to give up a volunteer opportunity.

3. Which statement is *false*?
   a) Marginal costs are opportunity costs.
   b) Opportunity costs are marginal costs.
   c) Sunk costs are marginal costs.
   d) Marginal opportunity costs increase as quantity supplied increases.

3.2 Sunk Costs Don't Matter for Future Choices

4. Gamblers on slot machines often believe that the more they lose, the greater are their chances of winning on the next turn. However, the chances of winning on any turn are actually random — they do not depend on past turns. Therefore, the money lost on the previous turn is a(n)
   a) total cost.
   b) sunk cost.
   c) smart cost.
   d) opportunity cost.

5. Your friend Larry is deciding whether to break up with his current girlfriend, Lucy. He tells you that his number-one reason for staying with her is his tattoo, which says "I love Lucy." Based on economic thinking, you advise him to ignore his tattoo because it is a(n)
   a) opportunity cost.
   b) marginal cost.
   c) sunk cost.
   d) total cost.

3.3 The Law of Supply

6. If all workers and equipment are equally productive in all activities, the opportunity cost of increasing output is always
   a) increasing.
   b) decreasing.
   c) the same.
   d) low.

7. The law of supply applies to an individual's decision to work because
   a) as the wage rises, the quantity of hours a worker is willing to supply increases.
   b) as the price workers receive rises, the quantity of hours a worker is willing to supply increases.
   c) workers need to be compensated with higher wages to work more hours to cover increasing marginal opportunity costs.
   d) all of the above.

8. When a fall in price causes businesses to decrease the quantity supplied of a product, this illustrates
   a) the law of supply.
   b) the law of demand.
   c) a decrease in supply.
   d) an increase in supply.

9. Suppose that all inputs in a business are equally productive at all activities. As the business increases its output, marginal opportunity cost
   a) increases.
   b) decreases.
   c) is constant.
   d) is zero.

3.4 What Can Change Supply?

10. Which factor below does *not* change supply?
    a) prices of inputs
    b) expected future prices
    c) price of the supplied product or service
    d) number of businesses

11. The supply of a product or service increases with a(n)
    a) improvement in technology producing it.
    b) rise in the price a related product or service produced.
    c) rise in the price of an input.
    d) rise in the future price of the product or service.

12. The market supply of tires decreases if
    a) the price of oil — a major input used to produce tires — rises.
    b) tire-making technology improves.
    c) the expected future price of tires falls.
    d) new tire businesses enter the market.

13. The furniture industry shifts to using particleboard (glued wood chips), rather than real wood, which reduces costs. This
    a) increases supply.
    b) decreases supply.
    c) leaves furniture supply unchanged.
    d) effect on supply depends on demand.

14. Which factor below can change supply?
    a) income
    b) environmental change
    c) number of consumers
    d) price of a complement

15. Popeye's Parlour supplies both piercing and tattoo services. Higher prices for piercings will cause Popeye's
    a) quantity supplied of tattoos to increase.
    b) quantity supplied of tattoos to decrease.
    c) supply of tattoos to increase.
    d) supply of tattoos to decrease.

4

Coordinating Smart Choices

Demand and Supply

HAVE YOU EVER organized a milestone birthday party (20th, 50th, 80th?)

and felt like it was a miracle everything worked out? There are so many details to coordinate — who's helping with the food, who's decorating the cake, who's tending bar, and what about toilet paper? Now imagine organizing one day in the life of a small town — or, if your imagination is up to it, in Toronto. Think about the millions of consumers who each make hundreds of decisions about what to eat or which headphones to buy. Now think about the thousands of businesses that decide what to produce, where to find inputs, who to hire. Somehow, businesses produce just about everything consumers want to buy — for a price. With no one in charge, it seems miraculous. How are all those billions of decisions coordinated so that you (and everyone else) can find the food you want for breakfast and the headphones you want at the electronics store, let alone places to live, water, jobs, and gas?

If all that doesn't seem enough of a miracle, consider that the coordination problem is a fast-moving target. Japanese food becomes fashionable, condos replace houses, new immigrants arrive with different tastes — and yet businesses adjust, and we all continue to find the changing items we are looking for.

Markets and prices are the keys to these apparent miracles. As consumers, we each make smart choices in our own interests. Businesses make smart choices in pursuit of profits. Markets, when they work well, create incentives that coordinate the right products and services being produced in the right quantities and at the right locations to satisfy our wants. This chapter explains how markets form prices, which provide signals and incentives that coordinate the smart choices of consumers and businesses.

4.1 What's a Market?

market the interactions between buyers and sellers

Rolling Stone magazine named Jimi Hendrix the number-one rock guitarist of all time. Suppose you really want a vinyl copy of his first album, *Are You Experienced*? You can check out the local used record stores, you can prowl garage sales for 60-something-year-olds cleaning out their basement album collections, or you can go online to eBay. These are all markets. A **market** is not a place (physical or virtual) or a thing: It's a process — the interactions between buyers and sellers. Markets exist wherever there is a process of competing bids (from buyers or demanders) and offers (from sellers or suppliers). What is common to all markets is a negotiation between a buyer and a seller that results in an exchange.

Markets Mix Competition and Cooperation

Markets are an unlikely mix of competition and cooperation. There is competition between buyers trying to get the same product. This is most obvious in auction markets like eBay, where you bid against other buyers and the highest bid wins. But even in a store with fixed prices or at a garage sale, you are competing with other potential buyers on a first-come, first-gets basis.

Sellers also compete with each other for customers. Whether offering an album or artichokes, sellers try to get customers to buy from them by offering a lower price, better service, or higher quality than their competitors.

It is harder to see the cooperation in markets between buyers and sellers. Because any purchase or sale is voluntary, an exchange between a buyer and seller happens only when both sides end up better off. If you paid $100 for that rare Jimi Hendrix album, you must have felt that the benefit or satisfaction you would get is worth at least $100 (or you wouldn't have bought it). If the seller accepted $100, she felt that was at least the minimum she wanted to receive to give up the album (or she wouldn't have sold it).

ADDITIONAL BENEFITS VS. OPPORTUNITY COSTS

Using the economist's terms for smart choices from Chapters 2 and 3, for you, the buyer, the marginal benefit of the album is at least as great as its price (your marginal opportunity cost). For the seller, the price is at least as great as her estimate of marginal opportunity cost (the next best offer for the album). As long as the album — or any other product — sells voluntarily in a market, both sides are better off. Both buyer and seller have made smart choices.

Sure, you would have loved to pay less than $100, and the seller would have preferred to get $200. "Better off" doesn't require the buyer to get the lowest possible price or the seller to get the highest possible price. Both participants in the exchange are better off just as long each one has made a smart choice.

Voluntary exchange is essentially cooperative, and both sides win. Businesses want satisfied customers who will return, and businesses make money when they supply products or services that consumers want to buy. Consumers are better off when businesses supply products or services that provide satisfaction that is worth (or of greater value than) the price.

The Rules of the Game

For markets to work and voluntary exchanges to happen, some basic rules of the game are necessary. Through laws, government must define and protect property rights and enforce contracts between buyers and sellers. **Property rights** are rules that ensure that when you own something, no one can take it away from you by force. Property can be physical property (land, buildings, cars), financial property (stocks, bonds, savings), and intellectual property (music, books, or software resulting from creative effort, and protected by copyright and patents).

Without property rights, there would be no incentive to produce anything for exchange. Imagine that you operate a car-detailing business and have just finished a beautiful and time-consuming job on a 2015 Honda Acura. The owner of the car comes along, says thanks, and drives away without paying. If no laws protected you against theft, what incentive would you have to continue your business? While this example may sound outrageous, it's not much different from the case of a band that produces an album for sale, only to have it downloaded for free without the band or the record company being paid. Without property rights, most of our time and energy would have to go into protecting our property, rather than producing products or services.

While property rights are a prerequisite for anything to be produced, governments must also enforce agreements between buyers and sellers. For a successful exchange, both buyer and seller must deliver what they agreed to, and there must be some legal "referee" to settle disagreements.

Can I Trust You ?   Consider the enormous amount of trust involved when you make an online purchase on eBay. The seller trusts you will pay. You trust the product will be delivered. This trust does not happen accidentally.

Part of the reason eBay has been successful is that it has implemented rules that promote the necessary trust. The PayPal system guarantees that payments made by the buyer are received by the seller. And the ability of buyers to give anonymous and public feedback about their experiences with a seller creates enormous incentives for sellers to "produce" happy customers. If these informal rules don't work, the legal system is still the ultimate referee. This enormous trust between complete strangers is the foundation for the billions of voluntary exchanges that happen every day in all markets. Even passionate supporters of "free markets" acknowledge that there is an important role for government in defining and enforcing property rights so that free and voluntary exchanges can happen in markets.

property rights legally enforceable guarantees of ownership of physical, financial, and intellectual property

Refresh 4.1

1. In your own words, define what a market is.

2. You are negotiating over the price of a new car with a car dealer. Explain how this process contains both cooperation and competition.

3. The Recording Industry Association of America's (RIAA) mission is "to foster a business and legal climate that supports and promotes our members' . . . intellectual property rights worldwide." Have you ever downloaded music? Write a short argument (three or four sentences) defending people's right to download music for free. Now, write a short argument against that position, including the concept of property rights. Which do you agree with? Explain why.

MyEconLab

For answers to these Refresh Questions, visit MyEconLab.

Where Do Prices Come From?
Price Signals from Combining Demand and Supply

Explain how shortages and surpluses affect prices.

Why do most stores sell Gatorade for $3 a bottle, and doughnuts for 99 cents? Think back to the smart choices that consumers (Chapter 2) and businesses (Chapter 3) make: Prices play a central role. Consumers compare prices and marginal benefits *(buy if the marginal benefit is greater than the price)*, while businesses compare prices and marginal opportunity costs *(sell if the price is greater than the marginal opportunity costs)*. Where do these prices come from?

Prices are the outcome of a market process of competing bids and offers. These negotiations between buyers and sellers may be obvious on eBay or at garage sales, but when you buy Gatorade at the corner store or a coffee and bagel at Tim Hortons, the store has set the price and there is no negotiation. The only "process" seems to be the cashier tapping your debit card or making change. For most purchases we make as consumers, the answer to the question "Where do prices come from?" seems to be "Businesses set prices." What gives?

It's true that in a market economy, businesses are free to set any price they choose. But no one can force consumers to buy at any price, and competing businesses may set lower or higher prices. So why do prices settle at particular numbers?

The economist's short answer to these questions about where prices come from is . . . (drum roll) . . . the interaction of demand and supply in markets with appropriate property rights! But that answer, while true, is pretty useless. We can point to anything that happens in an economy and say, in our best educated voice, "It is all determined by the laws of demand and supply." The longer and more useful answer exposes the hidden interactions between buyers and sellers, and also explains the miracles of markets in providing the products and services we want.

Jonathan Larsen/Diadem Images / Alamy

▲ This Canadian women's soccer team plays by the same rules as other soccer teams. Consistent rules make the game safe, fair, predictable, and understandable — features also needed for a well-functioning market.

Economics *Out There*

Rules of the Game Are Necessary for All Games, Not Just Markets

The game of football can be considered a model for how markets have developed. The earliest version, folk football, was played in medieval England — there were few rules, and the ones that were in place came about spontaneously and based on custom. There was "little skill . . . just muscle." The sport continued this way for centuries, until folk football morphed into soccer and rugby, and official rules were adopted. Skill started to matter, and the new forms of football were embraced the world over.

Typical markets grow in the way folk football did — evolving spontaneously, driven by participants, unstructured to the point when rules begin to develop. Only when the rules become formal does a market reach its full potential. "An absolutely free market is like folk football, a free-for-all brawl. A real market is like American football, an ordered brawl."

Like other markets, eBay is not a free-for-all brawl because of the rules and procedures that have evolved to ensure trust and enforce contracts. Instead of competition between two football teams, there is competition between thousands of buyers, and between thousands of sellers. But the rules allow cooperative deals to be struck.

Source: John McMillan, *Reinventing the Bazaar*, Norton, 2002, pp. 12–13.

Prices in Action

Paradoxically, the best way to understand why prices settle at particular numbers is to look at what happens in markets when prices have not settled. Let's begin the story of "Where do prices come from?" by looking at what happens when markets are *not* working to coordinate smart choices, leaving frustrated consumers and producers.

Since the story has to explain particular numbers, it will be helpful to have . . . particular numbers! Let's use a simple set of made-up numbers for the market for piercings (recall our example of Paola's Parlour for Piercing and Nails introduced in Chapter 3).

NOTE

Prices come from the interaction of demand and supply, in markets with appropriate property rights.

Figure 4.1 Market Demand and Supply for Piercings

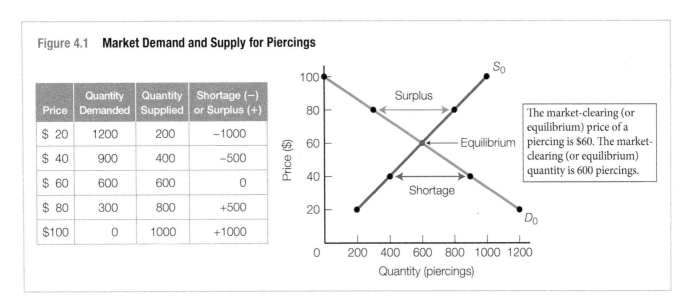

Price	Quantity Demanded	Quantity Supplied	Shortage (−) or Surplus (+)
$ 20	1200	200	−1000
$ 40	900	400	−500
$ 60	600	600	0
$ 80	300	800	+500
$100	0	1000	+1000

The market-clearing (or equilibrium) price of a piercing is $60. The market-clearing (or equilibrium) quantity is 600 piercings.

Demand Meets Supply   Figure 4.1 combines the market demand and market supply for piercings. The graph of the demand and supply curves is based on the numbers in the table. Let's look at the table first.

The three columns in the table in Figure 4.1 show alternative market prices for piercings (column 1), and, for each price, the quantity of piercings demanded (column 2) and supplied (column 3). If you look down columns 1 and 2 together, you see that as the price rises, the quantity demanded decreases. This is the law of demand. As a product becomes more expensive, consumers economize on its use and search for cheaper substitutes. If you look down columns 1 and 3 together, you see that as the price rises, the quantity supplied increases. This is the law of supply. Higher prices increase business's willingness to supply, because higher prices mean higher profits and the ability to profitably cover higher marginal opportunity costs. Higher prices generally lead to decreased quantity demanded and to increased quantity supplied in almost all markets.

Plotting those combinations of price and quantity demanded, and then price and quantity supplied, gives us the downward-sloping demand curve (D_0) and the upward-sloping supply curve (S_0) in the graph. (We will get to the surplus and shortage arrows soon.) In answering the question "Where do prices come from?" we will read the curves as demand and supply curves. For example, for a price of $20, we go over to the demand curve, and down to the quantity demanded of 1200 piercings. For that same $20 price, we go over to the supply curve and down to the quantity supplied of 200 piercings. For both the table of numbers and the graph, we read from price to quantity.

We know from the law of demand that consumers prefer lower prices, and we know from the law of supply that businesses prefer higher prices. How do prices get set in a way that reconciles these opposing goals?

Frustrated Buyers   What if the market price of piercings were $40 in parlours all around town? You might think that this relatively low price would make for happy consumers, but the numbers in Figure 4.1 tell another story. Look at row 2 of the table, where the price of a piercing is $40. Consumers want to buy 900 piercings, but Paola and her competitors are willing to supply only 400 piercings. While the 400 people who are able to buy a piercing for $40 will be happy, there are 500 frustrated buyers (900 − 400 = 500) who are willing and able to pay $40 but who can't get a parlour to do the piercing. This is a **shortage**, where quantity demanded exceeds quantity supplied. In markets with shortages, or **excess demand**, consumers experience long lineups and out-of-stock items at stores. Businesses experience products flying off the shelves and any inventories quickly dropping to zero.

On the graph, the horizontal distance between the supply and demand curves at the price of $40 represents that shortage of 500 piercings. This is the red arrow labelled *shortage*.

Shortages encourage competition among buyers. The consumers who most want the piercing will be willing to pay a bit more than $40, rather than being left with nothing. Buyers may bid for the scarce piercings (just like on eBay), driving up the price. Even if buyers don't actively bid up prices (when was the last time you offered to pay extra at Tim Hortons in hopes that they would find one more glazed doughnut for you?), sellers find that they can raise prices and still sell everything they have produced. Either way, shortages create pressure for prices to rise.

Rising prices provide signals and incentives, which are the key to how markets meet our wants. For businesses, higher prices are a signal, like a hand waving persistently in a classroom, saying, "Higher profits over here!" Higher prices and higher profits create an incentive for businesses to produce more and increase their quantity supplied. For consumers, higher prices mean we must revisit our smart choices. As prices go up, some consumers will give up on buying piercings and switch their planned purchases to some cheaper form of body decoration, like henna tattoos or costume jewellery. Quantity demanded decreases with higher prices.

Both adjustments — the increase in quantity supplied, and the decrease in quantity demanded — work to eliminate the shortage.

shortage or excess demand   quantity demanded exceeds quantity supplied

NOTE
Shortages create pressure for prices to rise.
Rising prices provide signals and incentives for businesses to increase quantity supplied and for consumers to decrease quantity demanded, eliminating the shortage.

Frustrated Sellers   Instead of $40, what if the market price of piercings were $80? Look at row 4 of the table in Figure 4.1. At the relatively high price of $80, consumers want to buy only 300 piercings, but piercing parlours are eagerly willing to supply 800 piercings. So, all over town, parlours are expecting customers who don't show up, and idle piercers are sitting and checking Facebook. Parlours happily sell 300 piercings at $80, but are frustrated to the tune of 500 unsold piercings (800 − 300 = 500) they were willing to supply at that price. This is a **surplus**, where quantity supplied exceeds quantity demanded. In markets with surpluses, or **excess supply**, businesses experience underemployed resources, unsold products sitting on shelves, or rising inventories in warehouses. Those consumers willing and able to buy at the high price experience their choice of where to buy and sellers who are eager to please.

surplus or excess supply   quantity supplied exceeds quantity demanded

On the graph, the horizontal distance between the demand and supply curves at the price of $80 represents that surplus of 500 piercings. This is the blue arrow labelled *surplus*.

Surpluses encourage competition among sellers. The businesses that are most efficient or desperate for sales will cut their prices rather than be faced with empty piercing beds or unsold products. Some businesses will hold sales, or offer extras in trying to woo customers (free nail set with any piercing!). As discounts appear, consumers will be less willing to pay the $80 price. Surpluses create pressure for prices to fall.

NOTE
Surpluses create pressure for prices to fall.
Falling prices provide signals and incentives for businesses to decrease quantity supplied and for consumers to increase quantity demanded, eliminating the surplus.

Falling prices also provide signals and incentives, but in the opposite direction to rising prices. For consumers, falling prices are an incentive to buy more of now less expensive products or services, switching from substitutes whose prices have not changed. And as prices fall, more people can afford to buy. More smart decisions result in buying products or services with lower prices. Quantity demanded increases.

For businesses, falling prices are bad news — a warning signal of "lower profits ahead." They will decrease the quantities they are willing to supply, and switch inputs to more profitable opportunities. Paola will move some of her staff from piercings to fingernails. Quantity supplied decreases.

Both adjustments — increased quantity demanded, and decreased quantity supplied — work to eliminate the surplus.

Adjusting Prices and Quantities   When there are shortages and surpluses, price adjustments play the key role. You may be thinking that the prices you observe in most markets don't adjust continuously and, in fact, settle for long times at particular values. Even the question I posed — "Why do prices settle at particular numbers?" — seems inconsistent with the stories about prices rising or falling in reaction to shortages and surpluses — but there is a reconciliation.

Most businesses have some *market power* (a concept coming in Chapter 8), which means they have some control over setting prices. Businesses pick a price point that they expect will make the most profits, taking into account all cooperative and competitive forces. For a mutually beneficial exchange with a cooperating customer, price must be less than the customer's marginal benefit but also must profitably cover the business's marginal opportunity costs. The price point also must be competitive with what other similar businesses charge. Once a business picks a price point, it may turn out to be too low (shortages develop and products sell out quickly) or too high (resulting in surpluses, underemployed resources, and rising inventories). But over time, especially in the face of competition, businesses react to market conditions of shortages or surpluses and adjust price points.

ADDITIONAL
BENEFITS
VS.
OPPORTUNITY
COSTS

Quantity adjustments also play an important role in the stories of how markets react to shortages or surpluses. When your local electronics store is always selling out of Beats headphones and frustrated customers come to the desk looking for them, the store orders more. Shortages lead to step-by-step increases in quantity supplied. If your local corner store regularly orders one case of Gatorade a week, but finds not all of the bottles are selling, it cuts back to ordering one case every other week. Surpluses lead to step-by-step decreases in quantity supplied. In response to excess demand or excess supply, businesses adjust quantities continuously, and can do so in small steps to match changing market conditions. When your boss asks you to work an extra shift next week, or your neighbourhood Tim Hortons bakes 10 dozen chocolate doughnuts a day instead of 13 dozen, those are quantity adjustments.

Self-Interest at Work   What is remarkable about all of these price adjustments (not so frequent) and quantity adjustments (frequent) is that no consumer or business needs to know anything about anyone's personal wants or production capabilities. Prices (and quantities) serve as signals to consumers and businesses, and all anyone has to do is consider his or her own self-interest. As long as there is an imbalance between quantity demanded and quantity supplied, prices will eventually adjust and send signals for consumers and businesses to change their smart decisions.

Consumers and businesses take all of these signals, and each makes self-interested smart decisions based on the price. As a byproduct of all these individual decisions made by complete strangers, markets provide the products and services we want.

It is not from the benevolence of the butcher, the brewer, or the baker that we expect our dinner, but from their regard to their own interest.
—*Adam Smith,*
The Wealth of Nations, *1776*

Refresh 4.2

MyEconLab

For answers to these Refresh Questions, visit MyEconLab.

1. In your own words, define what a shortage is. Explain who competes and what happens to prices when there is a shortage.

2. Old Navy decides to price a new line of jeans at $95, which covers all marginal opportunity costs as well as a healthy profit margin. If Old Navy has priced the jeans too high, what signals will the company receive? Based on those signals, what actions might Old Navy take next?

3. Most provincial parks charge a fixed price for a camping permit, and allow you to reserve specific campsites in advance. By the time the summer holiday weekends arrive, all the permits are usually taken. There is excess demand but no price adjustment. Suggest a pricing system for provincial parks that allows them to take advantage of the higher demand for campsites on holiday weekends. Your system should explain who is competing and who is cooperating.

When Prices Sit Still:
Market-Clearing or Equilibrium Prices

So, after reading stories of rising prices (from shortages) and falling prices (from surpluses), you may be wondering, "When do prices finally sit still, and settle at particular values?" Look at row 3 of Figure 4.1 on page 81, where the price of a piercing is $60. At $60, consumers want to buy 600 piercings, and all of the piercing parlours combined want to supply 600 piercings. At last, quantity demanded equals quantity supplied. On the graph in Figure 4.1, this is point where the demand curve and the supply curve intersect. With no shortages or surpluses, there are no competitive forces pushing prices up or down. Consumers are happy because every person who is willing and able to pay $60 gets a piercing. Businesses are happy because the $60 price profitably covers their marginal opportunity costs for the 600 piercings they supply.

There are consumers out there who would demand a piercing at $20, but think $60 is outrageous. They don't get pierced. But they made a smart decision: For them, a piercing isn't worth $60, or $60 is more than they can reasonably afford. They make a smart choice to spend their money elsewhere, and thus are not putting pressure on piercing prices. Likewise, there are parlours out there that would supply more piercings if the price were $80, but $60 doesn't cover their marginal opportunity costs so they use their resources to produce something else (nail sets? pedicures?) that they can sell at a price that profitably covers marginal opportunity costs.

The price that coordinates quantity demanded and quantity supplied is so important that economists have two names for it. (Don't you have a few names — nicknames — for people who are important to you?)

Market-Clearing Price

Market-clearing price is one name for the price equalizes quantity demanded and quantity supplied. At the market-clearing price, there are no longer frustrated buyers or sellers. There is a match for every buyer and seller, and all go home happy. Everyone who volunteers to exchange $60 for a piercing (both consumers buying and parlours selling) is better off, or they wouldn't have bought and sold.

market-clearing price the price that equalizes quantity demanded and quantity supplied

Equilibrium Price

The second name for the price that equalizes quantity demanded and quantity supplied is **equilibrium price**. *Equilibrium* is a term from physics that means a balance of forces resulting in an unchanging outcome. The equilibrium price exactly balances forces of competition and cooperation to coordinate the smart choices of consumers and businesses. At the equilibrium price, there is no tendency for change (until some new event occurs to disturb the balance, as we will see) and no incentives for anyone — consumers or businesses — to change their own, self-interested, smart decisions. No one is kicking himself for making a mistaken purchase or missing a better opportunity. Everyone has done the best they can in their exchanges, given the wants and resources they started with.

equilibrium price the price that equalizes quantity demanded and quantity supplied, balancing the forces of competition and cooperation, so that there is no tendency for change

Why is this particular "price that sits still" so important that it gets two names? It is the culmination of the forces of cooperation and competition that explains the miracle of markets. Ironically, when markets are functioning well and clearing, we don't pay much attention to this miracle. We find what we want for breakfast at Tim Hortons, the headphones we like are on the shelf at the electronics store, and we find jobs, gas for our cars, and all the other products and services that satisfy our wants. And businesses find customers for all the products and services they want to profitably supply. Often, it's only when something goes wrong — perhaps a labour dispute or a natural disaster that disrupts supplies — that we realize how conveniently we usually find what we want to buy.

The fact that consumers find that businesses have produced just about everything they want to buy, and with no one in charge, and that billions of decisions get coordinated is due to . . . (drum roll reprise) . . . the interaction of demand and supply, in markets with appropriate property rights! The law of demand is shorthand for the smart choices of consumers. The law of supply is shorthand for the smart choices of businesses. Market-clearing prices (and quantities) result when smart choices are coordinated. The forces of competition (between consumers, and between businesses) are balanced with the forces of cooperation (voluntary, mutually beneficial exchanges between consumers and businesses). The key to this outcome is that price signals in markets create incentives so that while each person acts only in her own self-interest, the unintended consequence is the coordinated production of all the products and services we want.

The Invisible Hand   Perhaps the most famous phrase in economics that describes this outcome is Adam Smith's "invisible hand" in his 1776 book, *The Wealth of Nations*:

> When an individual makes choices, "he intends only his own gain, and he is in this . . . led by an invisible hand to promote an end which was no part of his intention. . . . By pursuing his own interest he frequently promotes that of the society more effectually than when he really intends to promote it."

The miracle is that markets channel self-interest, as though "by an invisible hand," so that society produces the products and services we want, without the government doing anything beyond setting the rules of the game.

Refresh 4.3

1. List and define the two other names for "prices that sit still."

2. In an attempt to promote the social good of energy conservation, Toronto Hydro introduced the Peaksaver Program. Participating households received a $25 reward for allowing a "peaksaver" switch to be installed on their central air conditioners, which briefly turns off the air conditioner during peak demand times on hot summer days. Do you think the program would work without the $25 reward? Why or why not?

3. Explain the idea of Adam Smith's "invisible hand." Your explanation should illustrate the balance between the forces of competition and cooperation at "prices that sit still." (I can't give away the answer to question 1, can I?)

Moving Targets: What Happens When Demand and Supply Change?

We live in a fast-paced society where change happens regularly. Food and clothing go in and out of style, technology is constantly changing, and businesses may boom in Alberta and bust in New Brunswick. Even if markets succeed in temporarily coordinating the plans of consumers and businesses and settle at equilibrium prices, what happens when something changes? Will markets still be efficient — coordinating the right products and services being produced in the right quantities at the right locations to satisfy our wants when the "right" target keeps moving?

Believe it or not, all stories about shortages, surpluses, mutually beneficial trades, and adjusting prices and quantities we've looked at so far actually had very limited change. Yes, prices and quantities changed, and smart decisions changed — but in the background, I was holding almost everything else constant.

All the stories began with the numbers in Figure 4.1 on page 81, which illustrate the law of demand (when price rises, quantity demanded decreases) and the law of supply (when price rises, quantity supplied increases). We could focus carefully on those price-quantity relationships because *we were holding all other influences on consumers' choices and on businesses' choices constant.*

Recall the Chapter 2 distinction between a change in quantity demanded and a change in demand. Five factors can cause a change in demand. Name at least three and win a prize! Answer: changes in preferences, prices of related products, income, expected future prices, and number of consumers. All of those are unchanged in the numbers in Figure 4.1. And remember that Chapter 3 distinction between a change in quantity supplied and a change in supply? The six factors that can cause a change in supply (changes in technology, environment, prices of inputs, prices of related products produced, expected future prices, number of businesses) also are all unchanged in Figure 4.1.

Don't give up on this chapter because you fear I plan to slog through changes in all 11 factors. I won't. I have combined the explanations into groups: what happens to equilibrium prices and quantities when there are increases or decreases in demand, increases or decreases in supply, and combinations where demand and supply both change. As a bonus, I will let you in on the secret to thinking like an economist and making smart choices in this ever-changing world.

Changes in Demand

NOTE
For an increase in demand, the equilibrium price rises, and quantity supplied increases.

Increase in Demand When the Japanese food craze hit years ago, there was an increase in demand for sushi, triggered by this change in preferences. The demand curve for sushi shifted rightward. Increased demand drives up the market price, and restaurants responded to that signal of higher profits by increasing the quantity supplied of sushi. Any factor that increases demand causes a rise in the equilibrium price and an increase in the quantity supplied.

Figure 4.2 shows a similar *increase in demand* for the piercing market. The demand curve shifts rightward from D_0 to D_1. The equilibrium price rises from P_0 to P_1 and the equilibrium quantity increases from Q_0 to Q_1.

Figure 4.2   Increase in Demand

Price	Quantity Demanded		Quantity Supplied
	Original (D_0)	New (D_1)	(S_0)
$40	900 →	1150	400
$50	750 →	900	500
$60	600 →	850	600
$70	450 →	700	700
$80	300 →	550	800

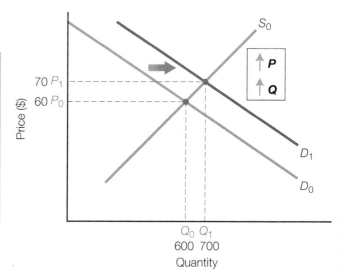

In the table in Figure 4.2, start with the original equilibrium in the piercing market, where the price (P_0) is $60. At that price, quantity demanded (D_0) equals quantity supplied (S_0), which is 600 piercings.

When demand increases (from D_0 to D_1), at every price, the new quantity demanded is now 250 piercings more than the original quantity demanded. At the price of $60, the original quantity demanded was 600. Then the new quantity demanded increases by 250 to 850 piercings. There is no change in supply — the supply curve and the numbers for quantity supplied (S_0) remain the same.

After the increase in demand, the new equilibrium price (P_1) is $70. At that price, the new quantity demanded (Q_1) equals quantity supplied (Q_1), which is 700 piercings.

The increase in demand raises the equilibrium price (↑ P) and increases the equilibrium quantity (↑ Q).

Decrease in Demand   When business boomed in Alberta from oil revenues, many people moved out west from New Brunswick. What did this decrease in population do to the real estate market in New Brunswick? There was a decrease in demand. The demand curve for housing shifts leftward, driving down the market price, and decreasing the quantity supplied of houses for sale. Any factor that decreases demand causes a fall in the equilibrium price and a decrease in the quantity supplied.

NOTE
For a decrease in demand, the equilibrium price falls, and quantity supplied decreases.

Figure 4.3 shows a similar *decrease in demand* for the piercing market. The demand curve shifts leftward from D_0 to D_1. The equilibrium price falls from P_0 to P_1 and the equilibrium quantity decreases from Q_0 to Q_1.

Figure 4.3   Decrease in Demand

| Price | Quantity Demanded | | Quantity Supplied |
	Original (D_0)	New (D_1)	(S_0)
$40	900 $\rightarrow$	650	400
$50	750 $\rightarrow$	500	500
$60	600 $\rightarrow$	350	600
$70	450 $\rightarrow$	200	700
$80	300 $\rightarrow$	50	800

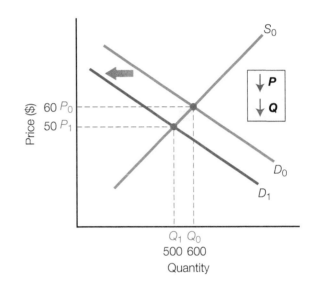

In the table in Figure 4.3, start with the original equilibrium in the piercing market, where the price (P_0) is $60. At that price, quantity demanded (D_0) equals quantity supplied (S_0), which is 600 piercings.

When demand decreases (from D_0 to D_1), at every price, the new quantity demanded is now 250 piercings less than the original quantity demanded. At the price of $60, the original quantity demanded was 600. Then the new quantity demanded decreases by 250 to 350 piercings. There is no change in supply — the supply curve and the numbers for quantity supplied (S_0) remain the same.

After the decrease in demand, the new equilibrium price (P_1) is $50. At that price, the new quantity demanded (Q_1) equals quantity supplied (Q_1), which is 500 piercings.

The decrease in demand lowers the equilibrium price (↓ P) and decreases the equilibrium quantity (↓ Q).

Changes in Supply

NOTE
For an increase in supply, the equilibrium price falls, and quantity demanded increases.

Increase in Supply The continuous improvement in semiconductor technology makes it cheaper to produce tablets and increases their supply. The supply curve for tablets shifts rightward. Market price falls as Amazon, Samsung, and Apple compete for customers by lowering prices to reflect their lower costs of production. Consumers respond to lower prices by increasing their quantity demanded of tablets. Any factor that increases supply causes a fall in the equilibrium price and an increase in the quantity demanded.

Figure 4.4 shows a similar *increase in supply* for the piercing market. The supply curve shifts rightward from S_0 to S_1. The equilibrium price falls from P_0 to P_1 and the equilibrium quantity increases from Q_0 to Q_1.

Figure 4.4 **Increase in Supply**

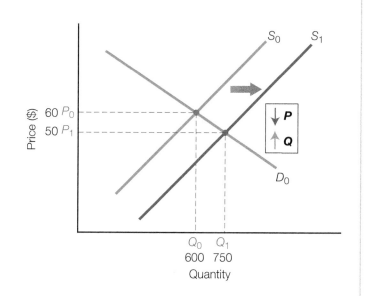

Price	Quantity Demanded (D_0)	Quantity Supplied	
		Original (S_0)	New (S_1)
$40	900	400 → 650	
$50	750	500 → 750	
$60	600	600 → 850	
$70	450	700 → 950	
$80	300	800 →1050	

In the table in Figure 4.4, start with the original equilibrium in the piercing market, where the price (P_0) is $60. At that price, quantity demanded (D_0) equals quantity supplied (S_0) which is 600 piercings.

When supply increases (from S_0 to S_1), at every price, the new quantity supplied is now 250 piercings more than the original quantity supplied. For example, at the price of $60, the original quantity supplied was 600. Then the new quantity supplied increases by 250 to 850 piercings. There is no change in demand — the demand curve and the numbers for quantity demanded (D_0) remain the same.

After the increase in supply, the new equilibrium price (P_1) is $50. At that price, the new quantity demanded (Q_1) equals quantity supplied (Q_1), which is 750 piercings.

The increase in supply lowers the equilibrium price (↓ P) and increases the equilibrium quantity (↑ Q).

NOTE
For a decrease in supply, the equilibrium price rises, and quantity demanded decreases.

Decrease in Supply The business boom in Alberta drove up wages, as businesses competed for scarce workers. The average hourly wage, even at fast-food restaurants, rose from $10 to $15. This rise in inputs costs decreases supply. The supply curve of fast food shifts leftward from S_0 to S_1. Restaurants are only willing to supply meals at higher prices, and the market price of meals rises. Rising prices cause customers to rethink their smart food choices, and quantity demanded of restaurant meals decreases. Any factor that decreases supply causes a rise in the equilibrium price and a decrease in the quantity demanded.

Figure 4.5 shows a similar *decrease in supply* for the piercing market. The supply curve shifts leftward from S_0 to S_1. The equilibrium price rises from P_0 to P_1 and the equilibrium quantity decreases from Q_0 to Q_1.

Figure 4.5 **Decrease in Supply**

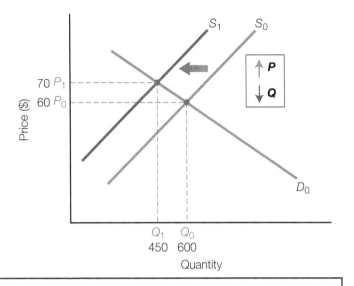

Price	Quantity Demanded (D_0)	Quantity Supplied		
		Original (S_0)		New (S_1)
$40	900	400	$\rightarrow$	150
$50	750	500	$\rightarrow$	250
$60	600	600	$\rightarrow$	350
$70	450	700	$\rightarrow$	450
$80	300	800	$\rightarrow$	550

In the table in Figure 4.5, start with the original equilibrium in the piercing market, where the price (P_0) is $60. At that price, quantity demanded (D_0) equals quantity supplied (S_0), which is 600 piercings.

When supply decreases (from S_0 to S_1), at every price, the new quantity supplied is now 250 piercings less than the original quantity supplied. For example, at the price of $60, the original quantity supplied was 600. Now the new quantity supplied has decreased by 250 to 350 piercings. There is no change in demand — the demand curve and the numbers for quantity demanded (D_0) remain the same.

After the decrease in supply, the new equilibrium price (P_1) is $70. At that price, the new quantity demanded (Q_1) equals quantity supplied (Q_1), which is 450 piercings.

The decrease in supply raises the equilibrium price ($\uparrow$ P) and decreases the equilibrium quantity ($\downarrow$ Q).

Economics *Out There*

Lobsters Galore!

Unusually warm ocean temperatures near the Atlantic coast in the spring of 2013 dramatically increased the supply of lobsters. A Nova Scotia lobster broker predicted that "If the price [of lobster] doesn't drop, I'll eat my shirt."

He was spared from having his shirt for lunch because, sure enough, lobster prices dropped from $10 a pound in the winter to $5 a pound in May. As catches continued to increase during the spring, the price dropped to a low of $3 a pound.

- This is a classic case of an environmental change increasing supply. With no change in demand, the price falls and lobster lovers get to eat more. The fall in price increases quantity demanded to bring supply and demand back into equilibrium.

Source: Chris Lambie, "Lobster prices set to drop as volume increases," *The Chronicle Herald*, May 3, 2013, http://thechronicleherald.ca/business/1127543-lobster-prices-set-to-drop-as-volume-increases

Roy LANGSTAFF / Alamy

Combining Changes in Demand and Supply

Once you allow both demand and supply to change at the same time, the effects on the equilibrium price and quantity are a bit more complicated. If demand and supply change together, for any of the reasons above, the effects are illustrated in Figure 4.6. P_0 and Q_0 are the original equilibrium price and quantity before the change. P_1 and Q_1 are the new equilibrium price and quantity after the changes in both demand and supply.

Increase in Both Demand and Supply   An increase in demand alone (D_0 to D_1) raises the equilibrium price and increases the equilibrium quantity. An increase in supply alone (S_0 to S_1) lowers the equilibrium price and increases the equilibrium quantity. Figure 4.6a combines these effects. Because both the increase in demand and the increase in supply increase the quantity, we know for sure that the equilibrium quantity increases (Q_0 to Q_1).

But the effect on the price is not so clear because price is being pushed in opposite directions. The increase in demand puts pressure on the price to rise, while the increase in supply puts pressure on the price to fall. I have drawn the shifts of the demand and supply curves so that these pressures cancel out, and the equilibrium price does not change — it remains at P_0. But a slightly larger or smaller shift in either the demand curve or the supply curve could cause the price to rise (if the rightward shift in demand is larger than the rightward shift in supply) or to fall (if the rightward shift in demand is smaller than the rightward shift in supply). Without more precise information, we cannot predict what will happen to the equilibrium price.

Decrease in Both Demand and Supply   A decrease in demand alone (D_0 to D_1) lowers the equilibrium price and decreases the equilibrium quantity. A decrease in supply alone (S_0 to S_1) raises the equilibrium price and decreases the equilibrium quantity. Figure 4.6b combines these effects. Because both the decrease in demand and the decrease in supply decrease the quantity, we know for sure that the equilibrium quantity decreases (Q_0 to Q_1).

Again, the effect on the price is not clear because price is being pushed in opposite directions. Without more precise information about how large or small are the (leftward) shifts of demand and supply, we cannot predict what will happen to the equilibrium price.

Increase in Demand and Decrease in Supply   An increase in demand alone (D_0 to D_1) raises the equilibrium price and increases the equilibrium quantity. A decrease in supply alone (S_0 to S_1) raises the equilibrium price and decreases the equilibrium quantity. Figure 4.6c combines these effects. Because both the increase in demand and the decrease in supply increase the price, we know for sure that the equilibrium price rises (P_0 to P_1).

But in this case the effect on the quantity is not so clear because quantity is being pushed in opposite directions. The increase in demand puts pressure on the quantity to increase, while the decrease in supply puts pressure on the quantity to decrease. Without more precise information about how large or small are the shifts of demand (rightward) and supply (leftward), we cannot accurately predict what will happen to the equilibrium quantity.

Decrease in Demand and Increase in Supply   A decrease in demand alone
(D_0 to D_1) lowers the equilibrium price and decreases the equilibrium quantity.
An increase in supply alone (S_0 to S_1) lowers the equilibrium price and increases
the equilibrium quantity. Figure 4.6d combines these effects. Because both the
decrease in demand and the increase in supply decrease the price, we know for
sure that the equilibrium price falls.

Again, the effect on the quantity is not clear because quantity is being pushed
in opposite directions. Without more precise information about how large or
small are the shifts of demand (leftward) and supply (rightward), we cannot
predict what will happen to the equilibrium quantity.

Figure 4.6   The Effects of Combined Changes in Demand and Supply

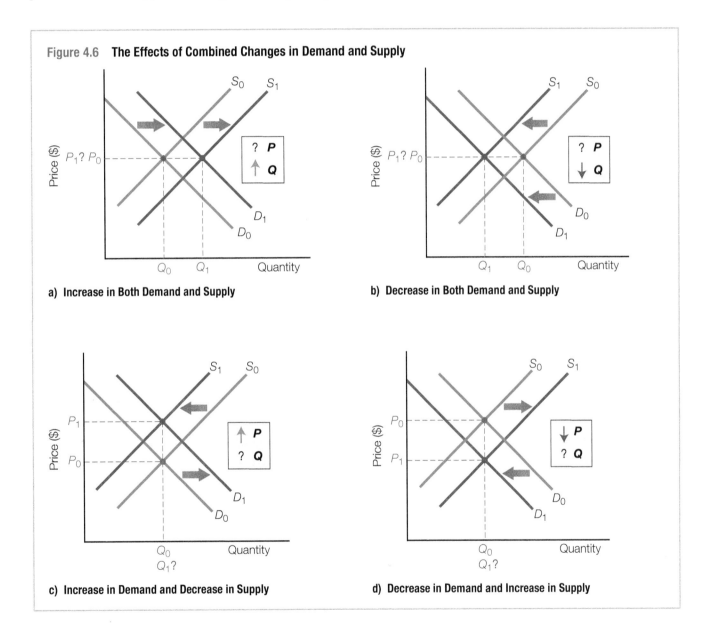

a) **Increase in Both Demand and Supply**

b) **Decrease in Both Demand and Supply**

c) **Increase in Demand and Decrease in Supply**

d) **Decrease in Demand and Increase in Supply**

Putting It All Together

Figure 4.7 is a good study device for reviewing all of the effects on price and quantity of any changes in demand and supply.

Figure 4.7 Effects of Changes in Demand or Supply

Change	Shifts of Curves	Effect on Equilibrium Price	Effect on Equilibrium Quantity
Increase in Demand	Demand shifts rightward	↑	↑
Decrease in Demand	Demand shifts leftward	↓	↓
Increase in Supply	Supply shifts rightward	↓	↑
Decrease in Supply	Supply shifts leftward	↑	↓
Increase in Demand and Increase in Supply	Demand shifts rightward; Supply shifts rightward	Need exact numbers to predict outcome	↑
Decrease in Demand and Decrease in Supply	Demand shifts leftward; Supply shifts leftward	Need exact numbers to predict outcome	↓
Increase in Demand and Decrease in Supply	Demand shifts rightward; Supply shifts leftward	↑	Need exact numbers to predict outcome
Decrease in Demand and Increase in Supply	Demand shifts leftward; Supply shifts rightward	↓	Need exact numbers to predict outcome

Economists Do It with Models

Think of all the simple demand and supply graphs in this chapter as models. They focus our attention on the reasons why mutually beneficial trades happen in a market, and select just enough information to predict where market-clearing prices and quantities will end up. As well, the models tell us when we do not have enough information to make those predictions.

In the real world, all 11 factors that influence consumers' and businesses' choices are changing constantly. Demand and supply graphs are like controlled laboratory experiments. They hold all influences constant except one (or two), so we can see the effect of that one influence alone. Let me explain.

Start in Equilibrium   When I draw a demand curve and a supply curve that intersect at price P_0 and quantity Q_0, I am holding constant all 11 factors that can shift the demand or supply curves and influence consumers' and businesses' choices. Once prices sit still at the market-clearing price there is no tendency for change. This is our starting point — the original equilibrium outcome.

One Change at a Time   In each "thought experiment" in Figures 4.2 through 4.5, I change one factor that affects demand or supply, while continuing to hold all other influences constant. That change is modelled as the shift of the demand or supply curve.

The results of these controlled thought experiments are the new market-clearing prices of P_1 and Q_1. When prices sit still at the new market-clearing price P_1 and quantity Q_1, once is again no further tendency for change. This is the new equilibrium outcome.

Even in Figure 4.6, when two factors change, we are still comparing an original equilibrium outcome (P_0 and Q_0) with a second equilibrium outcome (P_1 and Q_1), while continuing to hold all other influences constant.

This simplified way of using a model to isolate the impact of one (or two) factors in the economy is called **comparative statics** — the comparison of two equilibrium outcomes. Static means unchanging. Each equilibrium is static — there is no tendency for change. We start with one equilibrium outcome, change a single factor that affects demand or supply, and then compare it to the new equilibrium outcome. We compare two static, equilibrium outcomes. That simplified comparison allows us to predict changes in price and quantity, despite all of the complexities in the real world.

My favourite saying for this way of thinking is "Economists do it with models."

comparative statics   comparing two equilibrium outcomes to isolate the effect of changing one factor at a time

NOTE
"Economists do it with models" describes the economic way of thinking

Refresh 4.4

1. What happens to the market-clearing price and quantity of a product or service when demand increases? When demand decreases? When supply increases? When supply decreases?

2. Predicting changes in market-clearing prices and quantities is harder when *both* demand *and* supply change at the same time. You run a halal butcher shop in Ottawa. There is expected to be an increase in the number of practising Muslims in Ottawa who prefer halal meat. Rents for retail space are also falling all over town. Predict what will happen to the market-clearing price for halal meat. Predict what will happen to the market-clearing quantity. Explain your predictions.

3. In response to the business boom in Alberta, the city of Edmonton offered $200-per-month rent subsidies to low-income families so they could afford to live and work in the city. If you were asked to advise the city on this policy, what would you tell them about the impact it will have on rents? Will the rents go up or down? Explain your reasoning to the city officials.

MyEconLab

For answers to these Refresh Questions, visit MyEconLab.

Getting More Than You Bargained For: Consumer Surplus, Producer Surplus, and Efficiency

Explain the efficiency of markets using the concepts of consumer surplus and producer surplus.

When markets clear at equilibrium prices, lots of good things happen. There are no frustrated buyers or sellers. There is a balance between the forces of competition and cooperation, and quantity demanded equals quantity supplied. Mutually beneficial trades result in the miracle of markets — the right products and services being produced in the right quantities and at the right locations to satisfy our wants.

But wait, the results are even better than that! With an efficient market outcome, consumers get more benefits than they pay for, and businesses receive more money than they need to cover their opportunity costs. To see how this happens, we need to read demand and supply curves as marginal benefit and marginal cost curves.

Consumer Surplus

The market demand curve in Figure 4.1 on page 81 is also a marginal benefit curve. Figure 4.8 reproduces that demand curve and labels it also as a marginal benefit (*MB*) curve. A *market* demand curve combines the willingness and ability to pay of *all* consumers in this market. Some consumers, with a high willingness and ability to pay, are located up at the top left of the demand curve. Others, with less willingness and ability to pay, are located further down along the demand curve. Let me explain.

To read this demand curve as a marginal benefit curve, start with a quantity and go up and over to see the maximum price someone is willing and able to pay for that unit. For the 150th piercing, going up to the marginal benefit curve and over to the vertical axis tells us that someone is willing and able to pay $90 for that 150th piercing.

When the market-clearing price settles at $60, every consumer pays the same price — $60 per piercing. So the consumer who

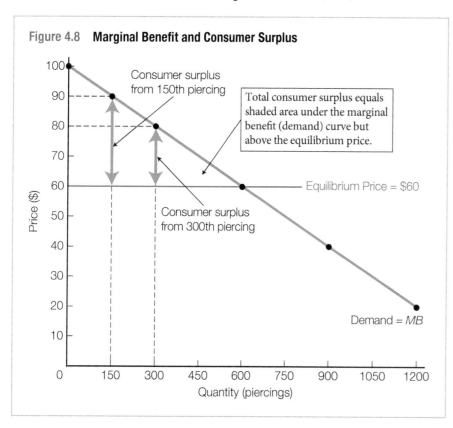

Figure 4.8 Marginal Benefit and Consumer Surplus

Consumer surplus from 150th piercing

Total consumer surplus equals shaded area under the marginal benefit (demand) curve but above the equilibrium price.

Equilibrium Price = $60

Consumer surplus from 300th piercing

Demand = *MB*

Price ($)

Quantity (piercings)

buys the 150th piercing gets an extra $30 worth of benefit ($90 − $60 = $30) — money that she was willing to pay but doesn't have to. On the graph in Figure 4.8, that extra benefit is the vertical distance between the marginal benefit curve and the market price.

Economists call this extra benefit **consumer surplus** — the difference between the amount a consumer is willing and able to pay, and the price actually paid. If we combine the consumer surplus for every piercing sold, from 1 to 600 piercings, the consumer surplus equals the green shaded area under the marginal benefit (demand) curve, but above the market price.

Did you ever go to a store where the receipt shows the total amount that you saved — the difference between the regular price and the sale price, added up for all of your purchases? Consumer surplus is like that total "saving." The green area under the marginal benefit curve but above the equilibrium price is total consumer surplus — the extra money all consumers were willing and able to pay for piercings but didn't have to. A bargain!

Producer Surplus

The market supply curve in Figure 4.1 on page 81 is also a marginal cost curve. Figure 4.9 reproduces the market supply curve in Figure 4.1 and labels it as a marginal cost (*MC*) curve. A *market* supply curve combines the supply decisions of *all* businesses in a market — the minimum prices businesses are willing to accept, covering all marginal opportunity costs of production, in order to supply piercings in this market. Businesses, with low marginal opportunity costs of production, are located down at the bottom of the supply curve. Others, with higher marginal opportunity costs of production, are located further up the supply curve.

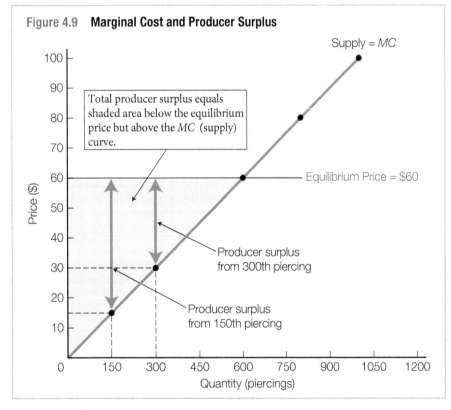

Figure 4.9 **Marginal Cost and Producer Surplus**

To read the supply curve in Figure 4.9 as a marginal cost curve, start with a quantity and go up and over to see the minimum price a business is willing to accept for producing that unit. For the 300th piercing, going up to the marginal cost curve and over to the vertical axis tells us that some business is willing to accept $30 for supplying that 300th piercing.

But when the market-clearing price settles at $60, every business receives $60 per piercing. So the business that was willing to sell the 300th piercing at $20 is getting an extra $40 worth of revenue ($60 − $20 = $40) over its marginal costs. On the graph, that extra revenue above marginal cost is the vertical distance between the marginal cost curve and the market price.

Economists call this extra revenue **producer surplus** — the difference between the amount a producer is willing to accept, and the price actually received. If we combine the producer surplus for every piercing sold, from 1 to 600 piercings, the producer surplus equals the shaded blue area below the market price but above the marginal cost (supply) curve.

Producer surplus represents the revenues that are greater than marginal opportunity costs of production when selling at the equilibrium price.

Economic Efficiency

When markets work well, producing the right products and services that consumers want, at competitive prices that are profitable for businesses, everyone is happy. This outcome is the miracle of markets.

But happiness is relative. How do we know there isn't a better outcome out there? *Consumer surplus* and *producer surplus* are useful measures for comparing outcomes.

Figure 4.10 combines the demand (marginal benefit) and the supply (marginal cost) curves from Figures 4.8 and 4.9.

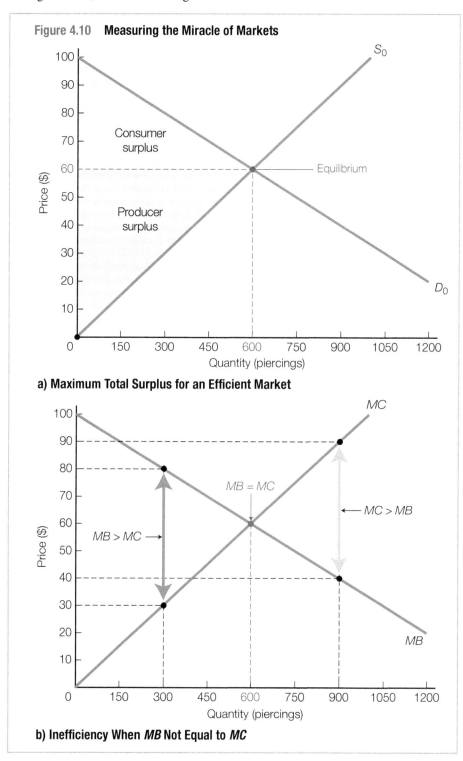

Figure 4.10 Measuring the Miracle of Markets

a) Maximum Total Surplus for an Efficient Market

b) Inefficiency When *MB* Not Equal to *MC*

Combining the green area of consumer surplus and the blue area of producer surplus — the total shaded area in Figure 4.10a — gives us the **total surplus**. The quantity of piercings that results in the "best" outcome is the quantity with the largest total surplus.

total surplus   consumer surplus plus producer surplus

The invisible hand leads smart consumers and businesses to the outcome with the largest total surplus. This comes from following Key 1: Choose only when additional benefits are greater than additional *opportunity costs*. Figure 4.10b is key for understanding why.

Marginal Benefit Greater Than Marginal Cost   In Figure 4.10b, look at the quantity of 300 piercings and compare marginal benefits and marginal costs. Go up to the marginal benefit curve and over to price. Some consumer is willing and able to pay $80 for that 300th piercing. Now go up to the marginal cost curve and over to price. A business is willing to produce that 300th piercing for a price of $30. Marginal benefit ($80) is greater than marginal cost ($30) for the 300th piercing.

Will this 300th piercing be produced and sold? Yes, because there is a mutually beneficial trade. With a consumer willing and able to pay $80, and a business willing to accept $30, an exchange takes place. The consumer and the business are both better off. For every quantity between 1 and 600 piercings, marginal benefit is greater than marginal cost, and it is smart for both consumers and businesses to trade dollars for piercings. The self-interest of consumers and producers increases output and sales until the quantity reaches 600 piercings and the price settles at $60 per piercing.

Marginal Cost Greater Than Marginal Benefit   The story is reversed for any quantities greater than 600 piercings. Again, look at Figure 4.10b. Start at the quantity of 900 piercings, go up to the marginal benefit curve and over to price. Some consumer is willing and able to pay $40 for that 900th piercing. Now go up to the marginal cost curve and over to price. A business will only produce that 900th piercing for a price of $90. Marginal cost ($90) is greater than marginal benefit ($40) for the 900th piercing.

Will this 900th piercing be produced and sold? Not if consumers and businesses are making smart choices. A consumer is willing and able to pay only $40 for that piercing, but a business needs at least $90 for it. No mutually beneficial trade is possible. There will *not* be an exchange.

For every quantity greater than 600 piercings, marginal cost is greater than marginal benefit. There are no mutually beneficial trades. If output was more than 600 piercings, people would *not* be making smart choices. Self-interest reduces output and sales until the quantity decreases to 600 piercings, and the price settles at $60 per piercing.

Comparing Total Surplus Figure 4.11 shows the total surplus for these examples of outputs of 300 piercings (Figure 4.11a) and 900 piercings (Figure 4.11b).

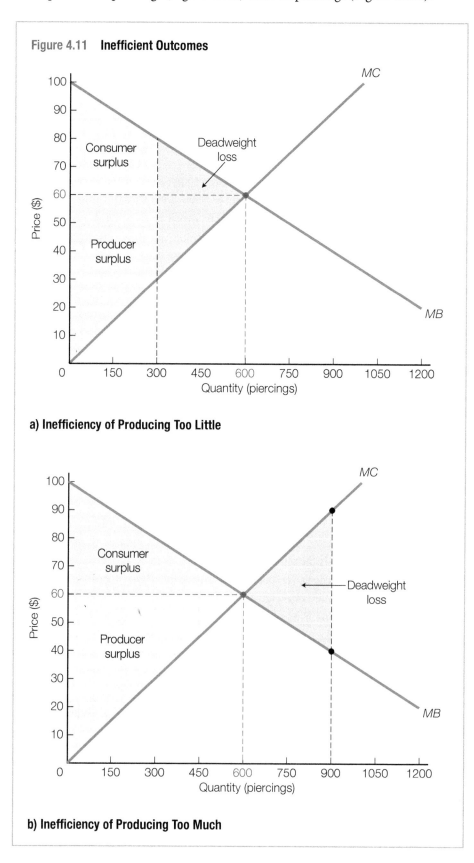

Figure 4.11   **Inefficient Outcomes**

a) **Inefficiency of Producing Too Little**

b) **Inefficiency of Producing Too Much**

The total surplus for 300 piercings (Figure 4.11a) is the areas of consumer surplus (green) plus producer surplus (blue). That total area is less than total surplus for 600 piercings in Figure 4.10a. The difference between the two areas of total surplus is the grey triangle in Figure 4.11a labelled **deadweight loss**. The output of 300 piercings is *inefficient* because there are mutually beneficial trades that are *not* happening. Producing and selling all piercings between 300 and 600 would make both consumers and producers better off because marginal benefits are greater than marginal costs. A society that stopped producing at 300 piercings would not be making the best use of its scarce resources. This inefficiency is *deadweight loss* — the decrease in total surplus compared to an efficient market outcome.

deadweight loss the decrease in total surplus compared to an economically efficient outcome

The output of 900 piercings (Figure 4.11b) also results in a deadweight loss, but from producing too *many* piercings relative to the economically efficient outcome. The grey deadweight loss triangle represents the not-smart use of resources, which cost more than the benefits they provide. This deadweight loss must be subtracted from the green consumer and blue producer surplus areas. Again, the total surplus is less than the total surplus for 600 piercings.

Efficient Market Outcome   An **efficient market outcome** does more than just coordinate smart choices of businesses and consumers to produce the miracle of markets. Consumers buy only products and services where marginal benefit is greater than price. These products and services are produced at the lowest cost, and their price just covers all opportunity costs of production. This is the outcome where the demand (marginal benefit) curve and supply (marginal cost) curve intersect.

efficient market outcome consumers buy only products and services where marginal benefit is greater than marginal cost; products and services produced at lowest cost, with price just covering all opportunity costs of production

Marginal benefit equals marginal cost at the quantity of an efficient market outcome. The benefit that consumers get from the last unit bought just equals the marginal cost of producing that unit. For all units up to the last unit, there is consumer surplus because marginal benefit is greater than marginal cost. For all units up to the last unit, there is producer surplus because price is greater than marginal cost. Total surplus = consumer surplus plus producer surplus — at the equilibrium quantity is greater than for any other outcome.

NOTE
At the quantity of an efficient market outcome, marginal benefit equals marginal cost.

Too Good to Be True?   If the efficient market outcome seems too good to always be true, you are right. Sometimes markets fail to produce such desirable, efficient outcomes. Some inefficiencies result from unintended consequences of government policies like rent controls (see Chapter 6). Other inefficiencies result from monopoly power (see Chapters 9 and 10) or externalities (see Chapter 11). We will use the concepts of consumer surplus and producer surplus in those chapters to measure inefficiencies from market failures.

Refresh 4.5

1. "At the quantity of an efficient market outcome, marginal benefit equals marginal cost." Explain this statement in your own words.

2. In the market for e-readers, at the prices of $40, $60, $80, $100, and $120, the following quantities are demanded: 2000, 1600, 1200, 800, and 600 units. The quantities supplied at those prices are 400, 800, 1200, 1600, and 2000 units. Draw a graph of this market. For the 800th unit, what is the consumer surplus? What is the producer surplus ?

3. For the e-reader market above, explain the reduction in total surplus that happens if the quantity of output increases beyond the efficient market outcome.

MyEconLab

For answers to these Refresh Questions, visit MyEconLab.

Study Guide

CHAPTER 4 SUMMARY

4.1 What's a Market?

Markets connect competition between buyers, competition between sellers, and cooperation between buyers and sellers. Government guarantees of property rights allow markets to function.

- **Market** — the interactions between buyers and sellers.

- Because any purchase or sale is voluntary, an exchange between a buyer and seller happens only when both sides end up better off.
  - Buyers are better off when businesses supply products or services that provide satisfaction (marginal benefit) that is at least as great as the price paid.
  - Sellers are better off when the price received is at least as great as marginal opportunity costs.

- **Property rights** — legally enforceable guarantees of ownership of physical, financial, and intellectual property.

4.2 Where Do Prices Come From?
Price Signals from Combining Demand and Supply

When there are shortages, competition between buyers drives prices up. When there are surpluses, competition between sellers drives prices down.

- Prices are the outcome of a market process of competing bids (from buyers) and offers (from sellers).

- When the market price turns out to be too low:
  - **shortage, or excess demand** — quantity demanded exceeds quantity supplied.
  - shortages create pressure for prices to rise.
  - rising prices provide signals and incentives for businesses to increase quantity supplied and for consumers to decrease quantity demanded, eliminating the shortage.

- When the market price turns out to be too high:
  - **surplus, or excess supply** — quantity supplied exceeds quantity demanded.
  - surpluses create pressure for prices to fall.
  - falling prices provide signals and incentives for businesses to decrease quantity supplied and for consumers to increase quantity demanded, eliminating the surplus.

- Even when prices don't change, shortages and surpluses also create incentives for frequent *quantity adjustments* to better coordinate smart choices of businesses and consumers.

4.3 When Prices Sit Still:
Market-Clearing or Equilibrium Prices

Market-clearing or equilibrium prices balance quantity demanded and quantity supplied, coordinating the smart choices of consumers and businesses.

- The price that coordinates the smart choices of consumers and businesses has two names:
  - **market-clearing price** — the price that equalizes quantity demanded and quantity supplied.
  - **equilibrium price** — the price that balances forces of competition and cooperation, so that there is no tendency for change.

- Price signals in markets create incentives, so that while each person acts only in her own self-interest, the result (coordinated through Adam Smith's invisible hand of competition) is the miracle of continuous, ever-changing production of the products and services we want.

4.4 Moving Targets: What Happens When Demand and Supply Change?

When demand or supply change, equilibrium prices and quantities change. The price changes cause businesses and consumers to adjust their smart choices. Well-functioning markets supply the changed products and services demanded.

- For a change in demand (changes in preferences, prices of related products, income, expected future prices, number of consumers)
  - an increase in demand (rightward shift of demand curve) causes a rise in the equilibrium price, and an increase in quantity supplied.
  - a decrease in demand (leftward shift of demand curve) causes a fall in the equilibrium price, and a decrease in quantity supplied.

- For a change in supply (changes in technology, environment, prices of inputs, prices of related products produced, expected future prices, number of businesses)
  - an increase in supply (rightward shift of supply curve) causes a fall in the equilibrium price and an increase in quantity demanded.
  - a decrease in supply (leftward shift of supply curve) causes a rise in the equilibrium price and a decrease in quantity demanded.

- When both demand and supply change at the same time, we can predict the change in either the equilibrium price or in the equilibrium quantity. But without information about the relative size of the shifts of the demand and supply curves, we cannot predict what will happen to the other equilibrium outcome.
  - when both demand and supply increase, the equilibrium price may rise/fall/remain constant, and the equilibrium quantity increases.
  - when both demand and supply decrease, the equilibrium price may rise/fall/remain constant, and the equilibrium quantity decreases.
  - when demand increases and supply decreases, the equilibrium price rises and the equilibrium quantity may rise/fall/remain constant.
  - when demand decreases and supply increases, the equilibrium price falls, and the equilibrium quantity may rise/fall/remain constant.
- **Comparative statics** — comparing two equilibrium outcomes to isolate the effect of changing one factor at a time.

4.5 Getting More Than You Bargained For: Consumer Surplus, Producer Surplus, and Efficiency

An efficient market outcome has the largest total surplus, prices just cover all opportunity costs of production and consumers' marginal benefit equals businesses' marginal cost.

- Reading demand and supply curves as marginal benefit and marginal cost curves reveals the concepts of:
  - **consumer surplus** — the difference between the amount a consumer is willing and able to pay, and the price actually paid. The area under the marginal benefit curve but above the market price.
  - **producer surplus** — the difference between the amount a producer is willing to accept, and the price actually received. The area below the market price but above the marginal cost curve.
  - **total surplus** — consumer surplus plus producer surplus.
  - **deadweight loss** — decrease in total surplus compared to an economically efficient outcome.
- **Efficient market outcome** — coordinates smart choices of businesses and consumers so
  - consumers buy only products and services where marginal benefit is greater than price.
  - product and services are produced at lowest cost, with prices just covering all opportunity costs of production.
  - at the quantity of an efficient market outcome, marginal benefit equals marginal cost ($MB = MC$).

TRUE/FALSE

Circle the correct answer. Solutions to these questions are available at the end of the book and on MyEconLab. You can also visit the MyEconLab Study Plan to access additional questions that will help you master the concepts covered in this chapter.

Apu Nahasapeemapetilon opens an outdoor iced cappuccino stand on his street in order to sell coffee to neighbours during peak hours of the day. Apu's product is unique enough that it allows him some choice in what price to charge. Use this scenario to answer questions 1 to 6.

4.1 What's a Market?

1. If customers are allowed to steal the iced cappuccinos without paying, this would still be a market. **T F**

2. The price should cover what it costs to make the iced cappuccinos, but not the cost of Apu's time. **T F**

4.2 Price Signals from Combining Demand and Supply

3. In order for price and quantity adjustments to occur in this market, Apu needs to be aware of the personal wants of his neighbours. **T F**

4. If Apu prices above the maximum price that consumers are willing to pay, he will end up with excess supply. **T F**

5. If Apu prices below the maximum price that consumers are willing to pay, he will lose out on potential profits. **T F**

4.3 Market-Clearing or Equilibrium Prices

6. If Apu sets a price that leaves him with no excess demand and no excess supply, he has found the equilibrium price. **T F**

7. When a market is in equilibrium, consumers who are not willing to pay the market-clearing price have made a smart choice. **T F**

8. When a market is in equilibrium, the market-clearing quantity equals the quantity demanded at the equilibrium price. **T F**

4.4 What Happens When Demand and Supply Change?

9. If new businesses enter the steel market, the equilibrium price of steel falls and the equilibrium quantity decreases. **T F**

10. Suppose the demand for earbuds increases while the cost of producing them decreases. The market-clearing quantity of earbuds increases and the price always falls. **T F**

11. Durham University researchers report Scottish grey seals are having more sex thanks to global warming. This is because, as drinking water becomes scarce, the females must travel farther distances and other males are able to seduce them. The market price for seal coat fur will likely increase. **T F**

12. Ontario recently had a ratio of 27 students for each full-time professor, while other provinces had a ratio of 18-to-one. It is estimated that Ontario needs 11 000 more professors by the end of the decade. If universities reduced qualification requirements to allow students with college degrees to teach introductory university courses, this would help reduce the shortage. **T F**

4.5 Consumer Surplus, Producer Surplus, and Efficiency

13. Producer surplus is the marginal cost of producing a product minus the price of the product. **T F**

14. Deadweight loss is the difference between consumer surplus and producer surplus at the economically efficient outcome. **T F**

15. The economically efficient outcome has the smallest deadweight loss. **T F**

MULTIPLE CHOICE

Circle the best answer. Solutions to these questions are available at the end of the book and on MyEconLab. You can also visit the MyEconLab Study Plan to access similar questions that will help you master the concepts covered in this chapter.

4.1 What's a Market?

1. The place where buyers and sellers meet is called a(n)
   a) store.
   b) economy.
   c) party.
   d) market.

2. Voluntary exchange happens in a market as long as the
   a) price is less than the marginal opportunity cost of the seller.
   b) marginal benefit for the buyer is less than the price.
   c) price equals or exceeds the marginal opportunity cost of the buyer.
   d) marginal benefit for the buyer exceeds the price.

3. For markets to work,
   a) governments must establish fair market prices.
   b) governments must establish an online trading system.
   c) governments must define and protect property rights.
   d) all of the above are true.

4.2 Price Signals from Combining Demand and Supply

4. If a market is not at the market-clearing price,
   a) prices adjust.
   b) prices send signals for consumers and businesses to change their smart decisions.
   c) quantities adjust.
   d) all of the above.

5. Which of the following is *not* a quantity adjustment?
   a) Tim Hortons asking its workers to work overtime
   b) bookstores ordering extra copies of *The Hunger Games*
   c) Leon's Furniture eliminating sales tax on all patio furniture
   d) a fish processing plant laying off 10 percent of its workers

6. When the price is too low we see
   a) unsold products.
   b) excess supply.
   c) shortages.
   d) frustrated sellers.

4.3 Market-Clearing or Equilibrium Prices

7. A price at which there are no shortages and no surpluses is a
   a) maximum price.
   b) minimum price.
   c) affordable price.
   d) market-clearing price.

8. In equilibrium,
   a) the price consumers are willing to pay equals the prices suppliers are willing to accept.
   b) consumers would like to buy more at the current price.
   c) producers would like to sell more at the current price.
   d) all of the above.

4.4 What Happens When Demand and Supply Change?

9. If demand increases and supply decreases, this leads to
   a) higher prices.
   b) lower prices.
   c) chaos.
   d) a shortage in the market.

10. Which will cause prices to fall?
    a) demand increases and supply decreases
    b) demand increases and supply increases
    c) demand decreases and supply decreases
    d) demand decreases and supply increases

11. A surplus can be eliminated by
    a) increasing supply.
    b) decreasing the quantity demanded.
    c) allowing the price to fall.
    d) allowing the market-clearing quantity to fall.

12. The Children's Fitness Tax Credit was introduced by the Government of Canada to provide parents with a tax credit (benefit) of up to $500 to register a child under the age of 16 in a program of physical activity. Therefore,
    a) demand for *The Hunger Games* novels may increase.
    b) demand for *The Hunger Games* novels may decrease.
    c) supply of *The Hunger Games* novels may increase.
    d) supply of *The Hunger Games* novels may decrease.

4.5 Consumer Surplus, Producer Surplus, and Efficiency

13. Consumer surplus is the
    a) difference between the amount a consumer is willing to accept and the price actually received.
    b) difference between the amount a consumer is willing and able to pay and the price actually paid.
    c) difference between the amount a consumer is willing and able to pay and the amount a producer is willing to accept.
    d) area under the marginal benefit curve.

14. For any quantity produced, total surplus is the
    a) deadweight loss.
    b) area under the marginal benefit curve but above the marginal cost curve.
    c) area above the marginal cost curve but below the market price.
    d) area under the marginal benefit curve but above the market price.

15. If the quantity produced is more than the efficient market outcome,
    a) deadweight loss is eliminated.
    b) total surplus is greater than total surplus for the efficient market outcome.
    c) marginal cost is greater than marginal benefit.
    d) marginal benefit is greater than marginal cost.

5 Just How Badly Do You Want It?

Elasticity

LEARNING OBJECTIVES

After reading this chapter, you should be able to:

5.1 Define and calculate elasticity of demand, and explain three factors that determine it.

5.2 Explain how the relationship between elasticity of demand and total revenue determines business pricing strategies.

5.3 Explain elasticity of supply and how it helps businesses avoid disappointed customers.

5.4 Define cross elasticity and income elasticity of demand, and explain how they measure substitutes and normal goods.

5.5 Use elasticity to explain who pays sales taxes and government tax choices.

DON'T YOU LOVE A GOOD SALE — 40 percent

off, 70 percent off? Most consumers do. No matter how much you are willing and able to pay, it's always a treat to pay less, which leaves you with cash to buy more of anything you want.

But do *businesses* love a good sale? Profit-seeking businesses would rather charge higher prices for what they sell. But to get consumers to buy, businesses must pick price points that match the market's — all consumers' — willingness and ability to pay. Higher prices might not always be best for business. Why do businesses have 70-percent-off sales, voluntarily lowering prices and bringing in less per unit?

I'm sure you have heard the answer to this question: "They'll make it up on volume!" Lower prices mean lower profit margins per unit, but a greater quantity sold. How do businesses decide whether it's a smart choice to set a higher price or a lower price?

In this chapter you will learn about *elasticity*, which is the most important tool used by anyone working in marketing or sales. Elasticity also helps explain supply shortages, why movie theatres won't let you bring in your own snacks, why governments tax alcohol and cigarettes, and who pays the HST. You may think you know who pays the tax, but I bet you'll be surprised by the answer.

Next to opportunity cost, elasticity is probably the most helpful concept for making smart choices by businesses and governments.

Measuring Your Responsiveness: Price Elasticity of Demand

Define and calculate elasticity of demand, and explain three factors that determine it.

We know from the law of demand that (all other things unchanged) a rise in price decreases quantity demanded, and a fall in price (sale's on!) increases quantity demanded (more volume). A smart business pricing decision depends on *by how much* quantity demanded changes when price changes. This responsiveness of quantity demanded to a change in price is related to just how badly consumers want the product or service — how much more or less people will buy of a good or service as its price falls or rises.

The tool that businesses use to measure consumer responsiveness and make pricing decisions is what economists call the **price elasticity of demand** (try saying *that* three times fast). This section will help you make sense of that tool, which businesses thankfully abbreviate to elasticity. **Elasticity** measures by how much quantity demanded responds to a change in price.

elasticity (or price elasticity of demand) measures by how much quantity demanded responds to a change in price

Measuring Your Responsiveness

Elasticity is all about responsiveness. When you pull on an elastic, by how much does it stretch or respond? When the price of a product changes, price elasticity of demand measures by how much quantity demanded responds.

NOTE
Whenever you see the word "elasticity," think "responsiveness."

Inelastic Demand A diabetic has a high willingness to pay for insulin. What happens to the quantity of insulin demanded when the price rises? Not much decrease. If the price rises enough, quantity demanded may decrease slightly as the poorest diabetics perhaps try to get by with a little less per dose. But in the market for insulin, there is very little response of quantity demanded to a rise in price. The demand for insulin is **inelastic**.

inelastic demand small response in quantity demanded when price rises

Look at the steeply sloped market demand curve for insulin in Figure 5.1a. Even a large rise in price, from P_0 to P_1, causes only a small decrease in the quantity demanded for insulin, from Q_0 to Q_1. The demand for a product or service is inelastic if there is a small response in quantity demanded when its price rises.

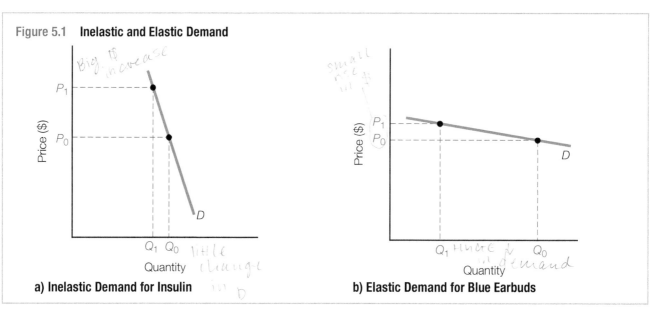

Figure 5.1 **Inelastic and Elastic Demand**

a) Inelastic Demand for Insulin

b) Elastic Demand for Blue Earbuds

Elastic Demand What about the market demand for blue earbuds? If the price of blue earbuds rises, what happens? A huge decrease in quantity demanded. Most consumers consider black or white earbuds to be identical substitutes, and aren't willing to pay extra for blue. Consumers switch to non-blue earbuds, so the quantity demanded of blue earbuds decreases drastically. There is a large response of quantity demanded to a rise in price. The demand for blue earbuds is called **elastic**. The market demand curve for blue earbuds in Figure 5.1b is very flat. Just a small rise in price, from P_0 to P_1, causes a large decrease in quantity demanded, from Q_0 to Q_1.

elastic demand   large response in quantity demanded when price rises

Calculating Elasticity of Demand

Businesses use this simple formula to calculate elasticity.

$$\text{Price elasticity of demand} = \frac{\text{Percentage change in quantity demanded}}{\text{Percentage change in price}}$$

The formula assumes that all of the other five factors that can affect demand are unchanged, so this is like a controlled experiment measuring just the relationship (in the law of demand) between quantity demanded and price.

Let's substitute some numbers from our examples into the formula.

For insulin, if a 10-percent rise in price causes a 2-percent decrease in quantity demanded, the calculation is

$$\text{Price elasticity of demand for insulin} = \frac{2 \text{ percent}}{10 \text{ percent}} = 0.2$$

The answer, 0.2, is less than 1. Any elasticity value less than 1 is considered to be inelastic. (If you are thinking that my math isn't quite right, good for you! Technically, the correct answer is –0.2. However, economists ignore the negative sign in calculating price elasticity of demand. You will be pleased to know that economists don't like negative numbers any more than you do.)

For blue earbuds, if a 10-percent rise in price causes a 50-percent decrease in quantity demanded, the calculation is

$$\text{Price elasticity of demand for blue earbuds} = \frac{50 \text{ percent}}{10 \text{ percent}} = 5$$

NOTE
When demand is inelastic the number from the calculation is less then 1.

Any elasticity value greater than 1 is considered to be elastic.

Are you wondering what demand is called when elasticity is exactly equal to 1? No, I didn't think so. But for the sake of completeness, here's the answer: When elasticity equals 1, economists say that demand is "unit elastic." The percentage change in quantity equals the percentage change in price. The key thing to remember about elasticity of demand is if it is less than 1 it is inelastic, and greater than 1 it is elastic.

NOTE
When demand is inelastic the number from the calculation is greater then 1.

Perfect Elasticities

perfectly inelastic demand price elasticity of demand equals zero; quantity demanded does not respond to a change in price

perfectly elastic demand price elasticity of demand equals infinity; quantity demanded has an infinite response to any change in price

Perfect Elasticities There are two extreme cases that are never observed in the real world, but that may help you understand elasticity better.

The most extreme inelastic demand is elasticity equal to zero. The vertical demand curve in Figure 5.2a has zero elasticity. There is no change in quantity demanded no matter what the change in price. This is called **perfectly inelastic demand**. The most extreme elastic demand is elasticity equal to infinity. The horizontal demand curve in Figure 5.2b has infinite elasticity. There is near infinite response in the quantity demanded to the slightest change in price. This is called **perfectly elastic demand**.

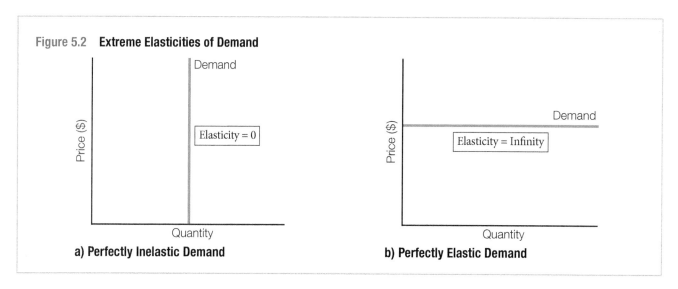

Figure 5.2 **Extreme Elasticities of Demand**

a) **Perfectly Inelastic Demand**

b) **Perfectly Elastic Demand**

Elasticity is about responsiveness. Perfectly inelastic demand has zero responsiveness. In the real world, insulin and addictive drugs probably come closest to perfectly inelastic demand. When there are no substitutes for a product or service, the elasticity of demand approaches zero.

For perfectly elastic demand, even the smallest change in price produces a huge — almost infinite — response in quantity demanded. The example of blue earbuds would come close to having infinite elasticity. A tiny increase in the price of blue earbuds would cause the quantity demanded to collapse toward zero. As the substitutes available for a product or service get better, the elasticity of demand gets larger. The elasticity of demand for perfect substitutes approaches infinity.

Shopping Elsewhere Another way to think about the different values for elasticity is your willingness to shop elsewhere if you don't get a low enough price.

If the price rises for products or services with:

- *inelastic demands,* consumers have a low willingness to shop elsewhere. The extreme case is elasticity equal to zero — perfectly inelastic demand. No matter how high the price goes, consumers continue to buy the same quantity and do not shop for substitutes.

- *elastic demands,* consumers have a high willingness to shop elsewhere. The extreme case is elasticity equal to infinity — perfectly elastic demand. If the price rises by even a penny, quantity demanded drops to zero. Everyone shops elsewhere for substitutes.

The Midpoint Formula for Measuring Elasticity of Demand   The simple formula allows you to calculate the elasticity of a demand curve between any two points like (Q_0, P_0) and (Q_1, P_1) on any demand curve, whether for insulin or earbuds. It is all you need to use for analyzing most business pricing decisions.

$$\text{Price elasticity of demand} = \frac{\text{Percentage change in quantity demanded}}{\text{Percentage change in price}}$$

But the simplification hides a problem. Suppose the price of a pair of earbuds in Figure 5.1b rises from $10 to $11 — a 10% change ($1 divided by $10 equals 10%). But if we reverse the story and have the price fall from $11 to $10, then the change is only 9.1% ($1 divided by $11 equals 9.1%). Since we are calculating elasticity between two points on the demand curve, it makes no sense to have a different number just because we describe the change as a rise rather than a fall in price.

To accurately measure the elasticity between two points on a demand curve and overcome the price-change problem, economists use the *average* of the two prices and the *average* of the two quantities demanded. The more accurate formula — called the midpoint formula — for price elasticity of demand is

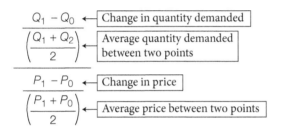

The midpoint formula is not as scary as it looks. Starting at the top, $(Q_1 - Q_0)$ is the change in quantity demanded. And $(Q_1 + Q_0) \div 2$ is the average quantity demanded between the two points on the demand curve. The change in quantity demanded divided by the average change in quantity demanded gives us the percentage change in quantity demanded. *This is the same as in the numerator of the simple formula.*

Continuing down to the bottom half of the midpoint formula, $(P_1 - P_0)$ is the change in price. And $(P_1 + P_0) \div 2$ is the average price between the two points on the demand curve. The change in price divided by the average change in price gives us the percentage change in price. *This is the same as in the denominator of the simple formula.*

By using *average* quantity demanded and *average* price, the midpoint formula gives the same answer whether you calculate for a price rise (where P_1 is greater than P_0) or a price fall (where P_1 is less than P_0).

Because economists don't use negative numbers for elasticity of demand, you can ignore any minus signs in the final answer, which is a bonus!

I will show you a worked-out example using the midpoint formula in section 5.2. But don't sweat the math. It's much more important that you understand the basic idea behind the simple formula and the factors that determine whether demand is elastic or inelastic.

Why Are You (Un)Responsive?
Factors Determining Elasticity

Three main factors influence price elasticity of demand, or "willingness to shop elsewhere to get a low enough price": available substitutes, time to adjust, and proportion of income spent on a product or service. Let's look at each.

Available Substitutes   The law of demand says that when something becomes more expensive, people economize on its use and look for substitutes. The more substitutes there are, the easier it is to switch away from a product or service whose price rises, and the more elastic is demand. Insulin has almost no substitutes, so the demand for insulin is inelastic. Blue earbuds have excellent substitutes, so the demand for earbuds is elastic.

There is a connection between whether substitutes are available and whether a product or service is a *necessity* or a *luxury*. Necessities like insulin for diabetics, or heat in the winter, usually have few substitutes and are necessary for your well-being. As price rises for a necessity, consumers still buy it. Most necessities have inelastic demand. Luxuries, like good restaurants, or Caribbean vacations, on the other hand, are not essential for your well-being and usually have many substitutes. Because you don't need a luxury product or service, when its price rises you may not buy at all or switch to one of the many available substitutes. Luxuries have more elastic demand.

Time to Adjust   When prices rise, it often takes time to adjust and to find substitutes. If gasoline prices rise and you have to drive to work, you can't do much initially to decrease your quantity of gasoline demanded — you can cut back on pleasure driving and errands. With more time though, you could arrange a car pool, and with much more time, you might buy a more fuel-efficient car or move closer to work. Time allows consumers to find substitutes. The longer the time to adjust to a price rise, the more elastic demand becomes.

Proportion of Income Spent   Suppose the price of salt increases by 100%, from $1 per kilo to $2 per kilo. By how much will you reduce your quantity demanded of salt? Not much. What if the price of a car increases by 100%, from $20 000 to $40 000? The quantity demanded of cars will collapse. A key difference between the examples is in the proportion of income spent on the product. We spend a tiny fraction of our income on salt, so a big percentage price rise doesn't increase our total spending much. But buying a car is one the largest purchases you will make: A big percentage price rise makes it unaffordable. The greater the proportion of income spent on a product, the greater the elasticity of demand.

No matter what elasticity of demand is, its importance for smart business decisions is all about total revenue, and that's our next topic.

NOTE
The more, and better, substitutes available, the greater elasticity of demand.

NOTE
The longer time to adjust to a price rise, the more elastic demand becomes.

NOTE
The greater the proportion of income spent on a product, the greater elasticity of demand.

Refresh 5.1

MyEconLab

For answers to these Refresh Questions, visit MyEconLab.

1. Explain the relationship between price and quantity demanded for inelastic demand and for elastic demand.

2. A jewellery store cuts its prices on specialty watches by 20 percent and finds that its quantity sold increases by 40 percent. Calculate the price elasticity of demand for its specialty watches. Is it elastic or inelastic?

3. In the women's clothing market, which is likely to be more inelastic, demand for the latest fashions or demand for clothing in general? If you were the marketing manager of a women's clothing chain, use your answer to explain to store managers why they should or should not exclude the latest arrivals in their upcoming sale.

Will You Make It Up in Volume?
Elasticity and Total Revenue

If your business holds a 70-percent-off sale, customers will be happy, but will the business be better off? Whether a business will be better off from raising prices or cutting prices depends on the elasticity of demand for its product or service. Elasticity of demand is the most important concept for determining if lower prices will lead your business to take in more or less money.

Explain how the relationship between elasticity of demand and total revenue determines business pricing strategies.

Total Revenue

"Better off," in this chapter, means your business will bring in more money. **Total revenue** is all of the money received from sales, and is equal to the price per unit (P) multiplied by the quantity sold (Q).

$$\text{Total revenue} = P \times Q$$

total revenue all money a business receives from sales, equal to price per unit (P) multiplied by quantity sold (Q)

A wonderfully simple relationship exists between elasticity and total revenue. When a business cuts prices,

- if demand for its product or service is *elastic,* the percentage increase in quantity is greater than the percentage decrease in price, so *total revenue ($P \times Q$) increases.*

- if demand for its product or service is *inelastic,* the percentage increase in quantity is less than the percentage decrease in price, so *total revenue ($P \times Q$) decreases.*

For the sake of completeness, when demand is unit elastic (= 1), the percentage increase in quantity equals the percentage decrease in price, so total revenue remains the same.

Figure 5.3 summarizes the relationship between elasticity and total revenue for a price cut.

Figure 5.3   Elasticity and Total Revenue

When Demand Is:		Price Cut Causes:
Elastic (> 1)	% change in Q > % change in P	Increased total revenue
Inelastic (< 1)	% change in Q < % change in P	Decreased total revenue
Unit Elastic (= 1)	% change in Q = % change in P	Unchanged total revenue

---

▲ Can this salesperson expect to make profits?

Price Cuts Are Smart Facing Elastic Demand

So a price cut is a smart decision when your business faces elastic demand. You receive a lower price on each unit sold, but you do make it up on volume! The percentage increase in quantity outweighs the percentage decrease in price, so total revenue increases.

If you are selling blue earbuds, consumers' demand for your product is elastic, which means that if they don't get a low price, they are very willing and able to shop elsewhere because good substitutes are available. When you cut the price of blue earbuds even a little, you attract all of the bargain-hunters. Your total revenue increases because the large increase in quantity outweighs the small decrease in price.

NOTE
For businesses facing elastic demand, price cuts are the smart choice and increase total revenue.

Price Rises Are Smart Facing Inelastic Demand

The smart decision when your business faces inelastic demand is to raise prices. You receive a higher price on each unit sold, and while you lose some sales, the percentage increase in price is greater than the percentage decrease in quantity, so total revenue increases.

If you are selling insulin, consumers' demand is inelastic, which means that they will not easily shop elsewhere because there are no good substitutes. When you raise the price of insulin, you don't lose many customers. Your total revenue increases because the percentage increase in price outweighs the small percentage decrease in quantity.

NOTE
For businesses facing inelastic demand, price rises are the smart choice and increase total revenue.

Smart Pricing Decisions Depend on Elasticity of Demand

Price elasticity of demand is important for any business pricing decision, even the price you get in bargaining with a car dealer. Most consumers hate bargaining over price because the dealer has better information about costs and knows how low he is willing to go on price. Your best strategy as a buyer is to try to convince the dealer that you will walk out if you don't get a low enough price, that you don't like this particular car that much and are considering alternative models from other manufacturers, or that you cannot afford the price. In other words, *you want the dealer to believe that your demand is elastic,* that you are willing to shop elsewhere if you don't get a low enough price because good substitutes are available. If you convince the dealer, then his best pricing decision is to offer you a very low price, because he believes that if he doesn't he will lose the sale entirely.

On the other hand, if the dealer thinks that you are not likely to walk out, that you love this particular car much more than any alternatives, or that you are wealthy and not price conscious, he will take these as signals that your demand is inelastic. His best pricing decision, because he believes this is a pretty sure sale, is to try to convince you to take expensive options that will actually increase the price.

All businesses have to live by the law of demand — a rise in price causes a decrease in quantity demanded. Smart businesses choose their price points depending on how much consumers' quantity demanded responds to a change in price — in other words, on price elasticity of demand.

Economics *Out There*

When It Comes to Reservations, Time Is Money

For restaurants, empty tables are lost revenues. While airlines and hotels have long been varying prices "to fill flights and rooms, restaurants' methods have largely remained in the icebox age." Restaurants are finally experimenting with "charging different prices for meals at different times" based on elasticity of demand.

How badly do diners want dinner reservations? Most prefer a 7 or 8 p.m. weekend reservation to a 5:30 Monday reservation. Demand is more inelastic for prime dining times and more elastic for off-peak times. Because of these differences, restaurants are thinking "that a dinner at 8 p.m. on Saturday should simply cost more than one at 5:30 on a Monday."

The Groupon-owned Savored website (http://savored.com) offers discounts for meals based on reservation time. "The challenge that every single restaurant is faced with is the elasticity of demand from consumers," said Ben McKean, Savored's co-founder. "In an off-peak hour, you might get only a couple of people who want to go to the restaurant, and in a peak hour you might get people out the door." Restaurants are "leaving so much on the table," he said.

So restaurants are charging more for peak hour meals (raising prices with inelastic demand increases total revenue) and less for off-peak meals (cutting prices with elastic demand increases total revenues).

How would you feel knowing the exact same meal would cost you less on a different night? Savored's market research showed that "People were O.K. with different prices . . . if you said it's 20 percent cheaper . . . during the week than on the weekend." People were not pleased "if you said it's 20 percent more expensive on the weekend."

By understanding and using elasticity of demand, many restaurateurs have increased their total revenue and bottom line.

Source: Stephanie Clifford, "When It Comes to Reservations, Time is Money," *The New York Times*, September 4, 2012, p. D5, http://www.nytimes.com/2012/09/05/dining/restaurant-prices-can-vary-by-reservation-time.html?_r=0

Calculating Elasticity and Total Revenue

Even if you were not looking forward to using the midpoint formula for price elasticity of demand (is there *anybody* who was looking forward to it?), I hope to convince you that a detailed numerical example is worth a few minutes of your time. Here are three reasons why.

1. You get to practise the detailed midpoint formula for calculating elasticity. Really. Don't forget that a nice thing about math is that there is a definite answer to a problem, and you have calculators to help with the ugly parts of finding it.

2. The example reveals that *elasticity changes depending on where you are along a demand curve*. Simple statements like "the demand for blue earbuds is elastic" have to be quantified to prevent your business from making a pricing mistake based only on the elasticity between two points on the demand curve.

3. The example creates a beautiful, clear set of graphs showing the relationship between elasticity and total revenue. The visual will help you understand this relationship that businesses, making pricing decisions, are obsessed with.

Elasticity Along a Straight Line Demand Curve   Figure 5.4 shows calculations for midpoint elasticity and total revenue for points *A – F* along a straight line demand curve.

Figure 5.4   Midpoint Elasticity and Total Revenue Calculations

Point	Price ($)	Quantity Demanded	Elasticity	Total Revenue ($)
A	50	0	$\dfrac{(15-0)}{(15+0)/2} = 9$	0
B	40	15	$\dfrac{(40-50)}{(40+50)/2}$ = 2.33	600
C	30	30	$\dfrac{(45-30)}{(45+30)/2} = 1$	900
D	20	45	$\dfrac{(20-30)}{(20+30)/2}$ = 0.43	900
E	10	60	$\dfrac{(75-60)}{(75+60)/2} = 0.11$	600
F	0	75	$\dfrac{(0-10)}{(0+10)/2}$	0

NOTE

Between points *B/C* and *D/E* in Figure 5.4, only elasticity numbers are shown, not calculations.

Columns 2 and 3 give the price (*P*) and quantity (*Q*) coordinates for each point on the demand curve. That is all you need to calculate elasticity using the midpoint formula.

Column 4 shows the elasticity between each set of points. For example, the elasticity between points *A* and *B* is 9, between points *B* and *C* is 2.33, and so on. Because elasticity is calculated *between* two points, the numbers for elasticity appear *halfway* between the rows for the two points. (See why it is called the midpoint formula?) Using the midpoint formula for column 4 has detailed calculations between 3 of the 5 sets of points – *A* to *B*, *C* to *D*, and *E* to *F*. For now, ignore the last column of Total Revenue.

Let's go through just one detailed calculation, between points *A* and *B*. The midpoint formula compares any two points labelled (P_0, Q_0) and (P_1, Q_1). The coordinates for (P_0, Q_0) are (*P* = 50, *Q* = 0) for point *A*. The coordinates for (P_1, Q_1) are (*P* = 40, *Q* = 15) for point *B*. Substituting into the formula gives

$$\frac{\dfrac{Q_1-Q_0}{\left(\dfrac{Q_1+Q_0}{2}\right)}}{\dfrac{P_1-P_0}{\left(\dfrac{P_1+P_0}{2}\right)}} = \frac{\dfrac{15-0}{\left(\dfrac{15+0}{2}\right)}}{\dfrac{40-50}{\left(\dfrac{40+50}{2}\right)}} = \frac{\dfrac{15}{7.5}}{\dfrac{-10}{45}} = 9$$

Even though the math gives an answer of –9, you can again ignore the minus sign. Elasticity equals 9 between points *A* and *B* along this demand curve. That takes care of my first reason for going through this detailed numerical example.

As you look at the other elasticity calculations notice that elasticity changes between different points along the straight line demand curve, from 9 to 2.33 to 1 to 0.43 to 0.11. Between *A* and *B* and between *B* and *C* demand is elastic (greater than 1). Between *C* and *D* demand is unit elastic (equal to 1). Between *D* and *E* and between *E* and *F* demand is inelastic (less than 1).

Along a straight line, slope is constant — it does not change. In contrast, elasticity changes along a straight line demand curve. *Elasticity is not the same as slope.* That is why it is incorrect to describe an entire demand curve as elastic or inelastic. There, that's reason two taken care of.

Calculating Total Revenue The last column in Figure 5.4 shows total revenue for each point on the demand curve. Total revenue is price times quantity, or *P* × *Q*. For point *A*, total revenue is $50 × 0 = $0. For point *B*, total revenue is $40 × 15 = $600. To understand the pattern of total revenue and its connection to elasticity, look at Figure 5.5a.

Figure 5.5a shows the different values for elasticity along the different parts of the demand curve. The top part of the demand curve is elastic, the middle part is unit elastic, and the lower part is inelastic.

Now look at the graph of total revenue in Figure 5.5b. The horizontal axis measures quantity, the same as the horizontal axis of Figure 5.5a. The vertical axis measures total revenue, *P* × *Q*. Calculating total revenue for every quantity between 0 and 75 gives a symmetrical, mountain-shaped curve. As quantity increases, total revenue rises, reaches a peak, and then falls.

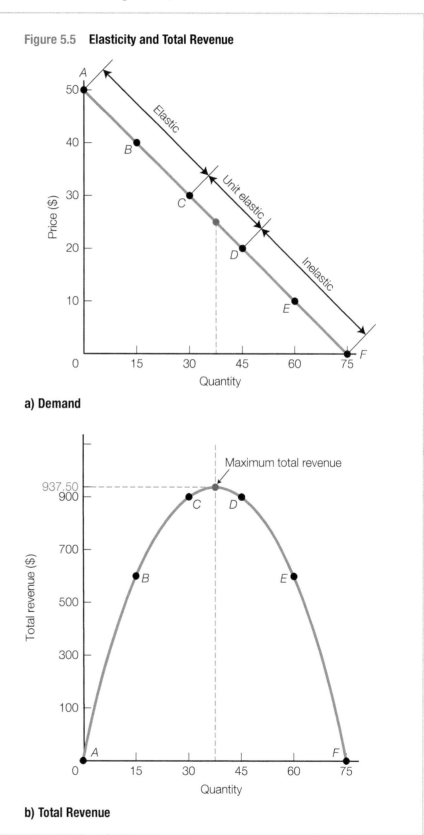

Figure 5.5 **Elasticity and Total Revenue**

a) Demand

b) Total Revenue

Price Cuts and Total Revenue Start at point *A* on the demand curve (corresponding to zero quantity and zero total revenue on the total revenue curve in Figure 5.5b). Price cuts move us down along the demand curve. What happens to total revenue? As price falls along the elastic part of the demand curve, from points *A* to *B* to *C*, total revenue on the bottom graph increases from 0 to $600 to $900. Halfway between points *C* and *D*, at a quantity of 37.5 and a price of $25, total revenue reaches a maximum of $937.50. Looking between points *C* and *D*, where demand is unit elastic, as price falls from $30 to $20, total revenue stays constant at $900. Finally, between points *D* and *E* and *F*, as price falls and we move further down along the inelastic part of the demand curve, total revenue decreases from $900 to $600 to 0.

The combination of the top demand graph (with the different elasticities) and the bottom total revenue graph tells the story behind business pricing strategies. If your business is facing elastic demand along the upper portion of the demand curve, cutting your price increases total revenue, and moves you up the total revenue mountain (which is smart). If your business is facing inelastic demand along the lower portion of the demand curve, cutting your price decreases total revenue, and moves you down the other side of the total revenue mountain (which is not smart).

That takes care of reason three — a beautiful, clear set of graphs showing the relationship between price elasticity of demand and total revenue.

Refresh 5.2

MyEconLab

For answers to these Refresh Questions, visit MyEconLab.

1. Explain the relationship between price cuts, elasticity, and total revenue.

2. In Figure 5.4, use point *B* as (P_0, Q_0) and point *C* as (P_1, Q_1). Use the midpoint formula to calculate the elasticity of 2.33. Now reverse the points, using point *C* as (P_0, Q_0) and point *B* as (P_1, Q_1) and redo the calculation. What is the difference between the two results?

3. Concession stands at movie theatres charge high prices for popcorn, drinks, and other refreshments. This pricing strategy increases total revenue. What does that imply about the price elasticity of demand for refreshments in movie theatres? What theatre policy helps make this demand elastic or inelastic?

How Far Will You Jump for the Money? Price Elasticity of Supply

The Magic Christian, a 1969 movie written in part by Monty Python and starring Peter Sellers and Ringo Starr (of the Beatles), is a satire on greed. A wealthy man with a perverse sense of humour performs bizarre social experiments to see what respectable people will do for money. In a memorable scene, people dive into a pool of excrement because they can keep any of the gold coins they find at the bottom.

What would it take to get you to dive into that pool? In pondering your answer (and please do forgive me for placing this image in your head), you might also be wondering what on earth this has to do with smart supply decisions.

We know from the law of supply that (all other things unchanged), a rise in price causes an increase in quantity supplied. A smart business supply decision depends on *by how much* you increase quantity supplied when the price rises.

What price would it take for you to "supply" a dive into that pool? By how much will you increase your work hours in response to your boss's higher wage offer? What determines by how much Paola increases her quantity supplied of piercings as the price of piercings rises?

The law of supply tells us that price and quantity supplied increase together and decrease together. We will look at the question: What changes more, the price or the quantity supplied? This *responsiveness* of quantity supplied to a change in price is related to greed and the quest for profits, but mostly it has to do with how easy or costly it is to increase production.

Bryan Bedder/Getty Images, Inc.

▲ What might you do to earn a dollar? A thousand dollars? A million? What makes the difference?

Responsiveness Again   I am hoping that by now the word "responsiveness" is connected for you with elasticity. Price elasticity of demand measures the responsiveness of the quantity demanded by consumers to a change in price. **Elasticity of supply** measures by how much the quantity supplied by businesses responds to a change in price.

Just like for demand, the quantity supplied can be inelastic (unresponsive to a change in price) or elastic (very responsive). Let's look at some examples.

You are standing by the pool in *The Magic Christian,* but simply cannot bring yourself to jump. Even with an astronomical increase in the price — from a loonie to a million gold coins at the bottom — you stay put. Your "supply" of jumps is totally unresponsive to even a 1 million percent increase in price. This is inelastic supply in the extreme.

More realistically, consider an industry like gold mining. When the world price of gold rises, what happens to the quantity of gold supplied? Not much, and certainly not much quickly. Gold is hard to find, and opening new gold mines is very expensive and takes years, even decades. The supply of new gold nuggets is *inelastic,* because quantity supplied is relatively unresponsive to even large rises in price. For **inelastic supply**, there is a small response in quantity supplied when the price rises.

Toward the other extreme, the supply of snow-shovelling services in most Canadian towns is relatively elastic. If the price offered rises even modestly, there is a willing supply of kids with shovels who don't have many other equally well-paying chances to work. And for anyone with a truck, it's not difficult or expensive to attach a plow and clear driveways in your spare time, before or after your regular job. Even a small rise in price causes a large increase in the quantity supplied of shovelling services, so supply is elastic. For **elastic supply**, there is a large response in quantity supplied when the price rises.

Perfect Elasticities of Supply   Figure 5.6 shows the extreme cases of elasticity of supply, which are similar to the extreme cases of elasticity of demand.

> **elasticity of supply**   measures by how much quantity supplied responds to a change in price

> **inelastic supply**   small response in quantity supplied when price rises

> **elastic supply**   large response in quantity supplied when price rises

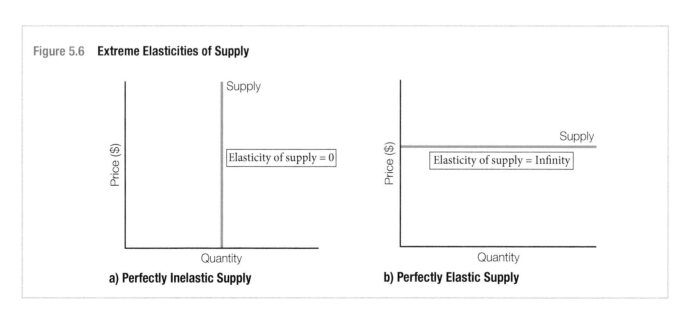

Figure 5.6   Extreme Elasticities of Supply

a) Perfectly Inelastic Supply

b) Perfectly Elastic Supply

The most extreme inelastic supply is elasticity of supply equal to zero. The vertical supply curve in Figure 5.6a has zero elasticity of supply. This shows your supply of jumps into the pool as totally unresponsive to any percentage change in price. It is called **perfectly inelastic supply**.

The most extreme elastic supply is elasticity of supply equal to infinity. The horizontal supply curve in Figure 5.6b has infinite elasticity of supply. This is the snow-shovelling example. If there were millions of kids desperate for even a penny more, a tiny increase in the price for snow-shovelling services would cause the percentage increase in quantity supplied to explode. Responsiveness is massive, approaching infinity. It is called **perfectly elastic supply**.

The basic idea is more important than the extreme cases. Elasticity of supply is about business responsiveness of quantity supplied to a change in price.

Measuring Business Responsiveness

This is the simple formula for calculating elasticity of supply:

$$\text{Elasticity of supply} = \frac{\text{Percentage change in quantity supplied}}{\text{Percentage change in price}}$$

The formula assumes that all of the other six factors that can affect supply are unchanged, so this is a controlled experiment measuring just the relationship (in the law of supply) between quantity supplied and price.

If the percentage change in quantity supplied is less than the percentage change in price, elasticity of supply is less than 1 and is inelastic. Quantity supplied is relatively unresponsive to a change in price.

If the percentage change in quantity supplied is greater than the percentage change in price, elasticity of supply is greater than 1 and is elastic. Quantity supplied is relatively responsive to a change in price.

Calculating Elasticity of Supply   Let's substitute some numbers into the formula, going back to your decision to work more hours for your boss. First she asked if you were willing to work 20 hours at $15/hour and you refused. When she then offered you $30/hour (a 100-percent increase), you agreed to supply 15 additional hours, for a total of 35 hours. If we convert the increase in quantity into a percentage (15 additional hours ÷ 20 original hours = 75 percent), your elasticity of supply is

$$\text{Elasticity of supply} = \frac{75 \text{ percent}}{100 \text{ percent}} = 0.75$$

That is a relatively inelastic response on your part (and your boss was disappointed!). A 100-percent increase in pay led you to increase your supply of hours by only 75 percent.

As a comparison, imagine that the same offer of a 100% pay increase had gone to one of your co-workers who was not in school, was working 10 hours a week, and had just received a massive credit card bill. He offers to supply 50 more hours, for a total of 60 hours. His increase in quantity of hours supplied is 500 percent (50 additional hours ÷ 10 original hours), so his elasticity of supply is

$$\text{Elasticity of supply} = \frac{500 \text{ percent}}{100 \text{ percent}} = 5$$

He has a relatively elastic response, so you are fortunate that your boss agreed to your triple-time hours before asking your co-worker.

NOTE
When supply is inelastic the number from the calculation is less than 1.

NOTE
When supply is elastic the number from the calculation is greater than 1.

The Midpoint Formula for Measuring Elasticity of Supply   The midpoint formula for calculating elasticity of supply is similar to the midpoint formula for elasticity of demand on page 111. The only difference is that Q_0, Q_1, P_0, and P_1 refer to points on a supply curve instead of on a demand curve.

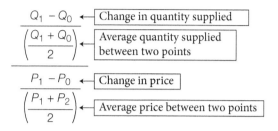

$$\frac{\dfrac{Q_1 - Q_0}{\left(\dfrac{Q_1 + Q_0}{2}\right)}}{\dfrac{P_1 - P_0}{\left(\dfrac{P_1 + P_2}{2}\right)}}$$

- $Q_1 - Q_0$ ← Change in quantity supplied
- $\left(\dfrac{Q_1 + Q_0}{2}\right)$ ← Average quantity supplied between two points
- $P_1 - P_0$ ← Change in price
- $\left(\dfrac{P_1 + P_2}{2}\right)$ ← Average price between two points

Gearing Up (Production) Can Be Hard to Do: Factors Determining Elasticity of Supply

What causes supply to be inelastic for some individuals and businesses and elastic for others? Two important causes are the availability of additional inputs and the time it takes to produce the product or service.

If Paola can easily hire more employees and buy more studs, all at the same prices, then her supply of piercings will be elastic. Even a small percentage rise in the price of piercings will cause her to increase her quantity supplied because her profits will increase. But if, as she tries to increase her quantity supplied, she faces higher opportunity costs and has to pay more for her inputs, it will take a bigger percentage rise in the price of piercings to get her to provide even a small increase in quantity. In that case, her supply is inelastic.

Availability of Inputs   The availability of inputs also helps explain the difference between supply elasticities for gold mining and snow shovelling. It is difficult to find new inputs for mining (gold deposits and gold mines), while it is easy to attract new workers to snow shovelling. Easy availability of new inputs makes for more elastic supply, while difficult and costly availability of new inputs makes for more inelastic supply.

Time   To see the importance of time, compare Paola's supply with the supply in the gold-mining industry. When the price of piercings rises, Paola can quickly adjust her quantity supplied. When gold prices rise, it can take years or even decades for the quantity supplied to adjust, because it takes time to discover and exploit new mines. Industries with quick time to production tend to have more elastic supplies. Industries with slow time to production tend to have more inelastic supplies.

Why Do We Care about Elasticity of Supply?

In 2007, the Alberta housing market was booming. Oil revenues were raising incomes for everyone in the industry and beyond, and new workers were moving into the province to take well-paying jobs. New-home builders were expanding the quantity supplied of housing as fast as they could, but ended up disappointing many customers when they couldn't deliver the quantities or at the prices promised. It is never good business to promise more than you can profitably deliver, and understanding elasticity of supply is important for avoiding broken promises. Shortages and higher wages in the building trades limited the profitable availability of inputs. Housing construction, although not as time-consuming as mining, does take time to adjust to new price conditions. A smart entrepreneur can't change these business conditions, but he or she can use elasticity of supply to make more accurate predictions of outputs and prices, and avoid disappointing customers.

It is always a smart business decision to pay no more for an input than you have to. Your boss, in her desperate triple-time wage offer to you, might have paid more than necessary for the extra work hours, compared to what she might have paid your co-worker who had a more elastic supply of labour. Knowing about elasticity of supply enables smart, informed choices, and can only help a business's bottom line.

NOTE
Elasticity of supply allows more accurate predictions of future outputs and prices (smart choices), helping businesses avoid disappointing customers.

Refresh 5.3

1. In your own words, explain the relationship between price and quantity supplied for inelastic supply and for elastic supply.

2. If your boss offers you a 20-percent raise, and in response you work 10 percent more hours, how would you describe your price elasticity of labour supply? Are these smart choices for both of you? Explain your answer.

3. Your business is about to launch an advertising campaign announcing your new low prices. You hope the ads will bring in many more customers. Explain why you need to be concerned about your elasticity of supply.

MyEconLab

For answers to these Refresh Questions, visit MyEconLab.

Can You Measure Substitutes?
More Elasticities of Demand

5.4

Define cross elasticity and income elasticity of demand, and explain how they measure substitutes and normal goods.

Elasticity is all about measuring responsiveness — *by how much* does quantity (demanded or supplied) *respond* to a change in price. Measurement of real events connect our simplified economic models of demand and supply to the real world. By comparing the models with measured facts, we can evaluate how well the models work to help us understand and predict what is going on out there.

Instead of measuring by how much a product's quantity demanded or supplied responds to a change in its price, we can also look at how quantity demanded *responds to changes in other variables* — changes in the prices of related products and changes in income. In this section, we'll look at other elasticities that allow us to measure some familiar economic concepts like substitutes, complements, necessities, and luxuries. The sizes of these elasticity measures have practical implications for business decisions.

Cross Elasticity of Demand

Remember the important distinction between a change in quantity demanded and a change in demand? (If not, do a quick review on page 46.) The quantity demanded of a product or service changes with a change in its price, while changes in any of the other factors affect demand. One of the factors held constant for the law of demand is the price of related products and services — substitutes and complements.

The **cross elasticity of demand** connects two *different* products or services. It measures the responsiveness of the demand for one product or service to a change in the price of another — a substitute or complement — other things unchanged. This is the simple formula for calculating the cross elasticity of demand:

$$\text{Cross elasticity of demand} = \frac{\text{Percentage change in quantity demanded}}{\text{Percentage change in price of a substitute or complement}}$$

The cross elasticity of demand can be a positive number or a negative number. We can't avoid negative numbers this time because this elasticity measure provides information about the *direction,* as well as size, of a response. The cross elasticity of demand is positive for a substitute and negative for a complement. To better understand why, we'll focus first on the direction of the response and then on the size.

Substitutes   Let's go back to Chapter 2 and the brooms that people use to sweep their sidewalks. Water, sprayed with a hose, is a substitute for brooms. Dustpans, for collecting the dirt and leaves, are a complement for brooms.

What happens to the demand for brooms when the price of water rises? People economize on their use of water for sweeping and substitute brooms instead. The demand for brooms increases — the demand curve for brooms shifts rightward.

In the denominator of the formula for the cross elasticity of demand for brooms, the percentage change in the price of water (a substitute for brooms) is positive. The price of water goes up. In the numerator, the percentage change in the quantity demanded of brooms is also positive. People demand more brooms.

A rise in the price of water increases in demand for brooms. A fall in the price of water decreases the demand for brooms. The price (of water) and the demand (for brooms) both change in the same direction. The cross elasticity of demand for substitutes is a positive number.

Complements   What happens to the demand for brooms when the price of dustpans rises? The combined cost of using a broom with a dustpan is now higher, so people economize on their use of both brooms and dustpans. The demand for brooms decreases — the demand curve for brooms shifts leftward.

In the denominator of the formula for the cross elasticity of demand for brooms, the percentage change in the price of dustpans (a complement for brooms) is positive. The price of dustpans goes up. In the numerator, the percentage change in the quantity demanded of brooms is negative. People demand fewer brooms.

A rise in the price of dustpans decreases the demand for brooms. A fall in the price of dustpans increase the demand for brooms. The price (of dustpans) and the demand (for brooms) change in opposite directions. The cross elasticity of demand for complements is a negative number.

By How Much? Calculating the cross elasticity of demand using the simple formula gives you a sign — positive or negative — that tells you if you are analyzing substitutes or complements. The calculation also gives a number — the *size* of the cross elasticity of demand.

NOTE
Larger numbers for cross elasticity of demand mean more perfect substitutes (negative cross elasticity) or more perfect complements (positive cross elasticity).

What does a number like +3.0 mean for cross elasticity of demand compared to a number like +0.5? The number measures the size of the shift of the demand curve. A large positive number (like +3.0) indicates a large rightward shift of the demand curve. A large negative number (like –3.0) indicates a large leftward shift of the demand curve. A smaller number indicates a small shift of the demand curve — rightward for a positive number and leftward for a negative number.

For substitutes (with a positive sign), the closer the products or services are to perfect substitutes for each other (blue and black earbuds), the larger the number for cross elasticity of demand will be. A change in the price of blue earbuds has a big impact on the demand for black earbuds. Water and brooms are probably not as good substitutes for each other, so the number for their cross elasticity of demand is smaller.

For complements (with a negative sign), the closer the products are to perfect complements for each other, the larger the number for cross elasticity of demand will be. Perfect complements are products or services that are always used together. Imagine if you had to buy left shoes separately from right shoes. (Since most people have one foot slightly larger than the other, why aren't shoes sold that way so you can buy different sizes? Perhaps a business opportunity for an entrepreneur?) Left and right shoes are almost perfect complements. Whenever you buy one, you also buy the other. French fries and gravy are not such close complements. Many would rather eat their fries with ketchup or vinegar or just salt, so their cross elasticity of demand will be smaller.

Measuring the cross elasticity of demand gives more precise information about the size of shifts of demand curves. When both demand and supply shift together, the models in Chapter 4 cannot predict what happens to the equilibrium price (when demand and supply both increase or decrease) or to the equilibrium quantity (when demand and supply change in opposite directions). The outcomes depend on how large or small the shifts of the demand and supply curves are. The cross elasticity of demand provides that shift size information and improves our understanding of how markets work.

Cross elasticity of demand also provides practical information for businesses. If you are selling cars, and gasoline prices rise, cross elasticity gives you an idea of the (negative) impact on your car sales.

Income Elasticity of Demand

Income is another factor that changes demand and shifts the demand curve.

The **income elasticity of demand** measures the responsiveness of the demand for a product or service to a change in income, other things unchanged. This is the simple formula for calculating the income elasticity of demand.

income elasticity of demand measures the responsiveness of the demand for a product or service to a change in income

$$\text{Income elasticity of demand} = \frac{\text{Percentage change in quantity demanded}}{\text{Percentage change in income}}$$

Income elasticity of demand can also be a positive or negative number — positive for a normal good and negative for an inferior good. Again, let's focus first on the direction of the response and then on the size.

Normal Goods

Airline travel is a normal good. An increase in income, all other things unchanged, increases the demand for airline travel. With more income, you are more likely to fly than to travel by car or train. The demand curve for airline travel shifts rightward.

Income elasticity of demand for normal goods is a positive number. Income and demand both change in the same direction. An increase in income increases the demand for airline travel, while a decrease in income decreases the demand for airline travel.

Inferior Goods

Kraft Dinner (now known as KD) is an inferior good. Many people eat Kraft Dinner because they can't afford the food they really want. When income increases, people can better afford higher-priced foods and restaurant meals, so the demand for Kraft Dinner decreases. The demand curve shifts leftward.

Income elasticity of demand for inferior goods is a negative number. Income and demand change in opposite directions. An increase in income decreases the demand for Kraft Dinner while a decrease in income increases the demand for KD.

Necessities and Luxuries

Normal goods can be described as necessities or luxuries by their income elasticities of demand, as well as by their price elasticities of demand (see section 5.1). Necessities and luxuries tend to have different price elasticities of demand because of different availability of substitutes. Normal goods with positive income elasticities can be described as necessities or luxuries, depending on the *size* of the number for income elasticity of demand.

income inelastic demand for normal goods that are necessities, the percentage change in quantity is less than the percentage change in income

Necessities tend to have **income inelastic demand** — income elasticities of demand less than one (but greater than zero). The percentage change in quantity demanded is less than the percentage change in income. Products with income inelastic demand include beer, furniture, and salt. When your income goes up, you buy more, but not much more, of products and services with income inelastic demand.

income elastic demand for normal goods that are luxuries, the percentage change in quantity is greater than the percentage change in income

Luxuries tend to have **income elastic demand** — income elasticities of demand greater than one. The percentage change in quantity demanded is greater than the percentage change in income. Examples of income elastic demand include airline travel, jewellery, and movies. When your income goes up, you buy a lot more of products and services with income elastic demand.

For businesses, it is useful to know your product's income elasticity of demand, whether it is negative (inferior good), positive but less than one (necessity), or positive and greater than one (luxury). If the economy is going into a recession and incomes are falling, you can predict increases in demand and sales for Kraft Dinner, large decreases in demand for luxury items, and more modest decreases in demand for necessities. Your plans for future supply will be more accurate with good information about income elasticity of demand.

Quick Guide to Elasticity Measures

Figure 5.7 is a good study device for reviewing all elasticity concepts.

Figure 5.7 Measures of Elasticity

Price Elasticity of Demand			
Simple Formula	**Description**	**Measures**	**Necessities or Luxuries**
Percentage change in quantity demanded ÷ Percentage change in price	Perfectly Inelastic	Zero	
	Inelastic	Greater than zero, but less than 1	Necessities
	Unit Elastic	1	
	Elastic	Greater than 1	Luxuries
	Perfectly Elastic	Infinity	

Elasticity of Supply			
Simple Formula	**Description**	**Measures**	
Percentage change in quantity supplied ÷ Percentage change in price	Perfectly Inelastic	Zero	
	Inelastic	Greater than zero, but less than 1	
	Unit Elastic	1	
	Elastic	Greater than 1	
	Perfectly Elastic	Infinity	

Cross Elasticity of Demand			
Simple Formula	**Description**	**Measures**	
Percentage change in quantity demanded ÷ Percentage change in price of a substitute or complement	Substitutes	Negative	
	Complements	Positive	

Income Elasticity of Demand			
Simple Formula	**Description**	**Measures**	**Necessities or Luxuries**
Percentage change in quantity demanded ÷ Percentage change in income	Normal Good	Positive	
	Inferior Good	Negative	
	Income Inelastic Demand	Positive and less than 1	Necess
	Income Elastic Demand	Positive and greater than 1	

Refresh 5.4

1. Choose two related products or services and use them to explain the simple formula for the cross elasticity of demand.

2. What do you think the number would be (positive or negative? size?) for the cross-elasticity of demand of two products that seem totally unrelated to each other? Explain your answer.

3. Evidence suggests that babies are a *normal good* for lower income earners and an *inferior good* for higher income earners. Use the income elasticity of demand to explain what this means, using the definitions of "normal" and "inferior" goods.

MyEconLab

For answers to these Refresh Questions, visit MyEconLab.

Use elasticity to explain who pays sales taxes and government tax choices.

▲ In British Columbia, tens of thousands of people protested the introduction of the HST. They believed it would increase their cost of living. The government argued it would lower the average cost of all products and services. How much of the HST do consumers actually pay?

tax incidence   the division of a tax between buyers and sellers

One reason Canadians love to cross the border to shop is what *doesn't* happen at cash registers in U.S. stores. The sales taxes that governments collect on purchases are much lower in the U.S. The states of Oregon, Montana, and New Hampshire have no sales taxes, and most states have sales taxes that are much lower than in Canada.

In Canada, the federal government sales tax is called the Goods and Services Tax (GST), and in many provinces it is combined with provincial sales taxes as the Harmonized Sales Tax (HST). Sales taxes are charged as a percentage of the price of what you buy. In 2014, in Ontario, New Brunswick, and Newfoundland the HST was 13%. It was as low as 5% in Alberta, and as high as 15% in Nova Scotia.

Canadian consumers love to complain about having to pay high sales taxes. But do consumers pay the tax? And how do governments decide which products and services to tax? Elasticity helps answer those questions.

Tax Incidence

The question of who pays the tax is called **tax incidence**. Tax incidence is the division of a tax between buyers and sellers, and depends on the elasticities of demand and supply.

Let's use a simple example where instead of a percentage like 10 percent, the tax is a fixed dollar amount of $20 per unit. The math is simpler that way. Many actual sales taxes, like those on cigarettes and gasoline, are a fixed dollar amount.

Figure 5.8 shows the (made-up) market for exercycles (exercise bicycles). The market is initially in equilibrium at the intersection of the demand (*D*) and supply (*S*) curves. The market-clearing price is $200 per exercycle and the market-clearing quantity is 50.

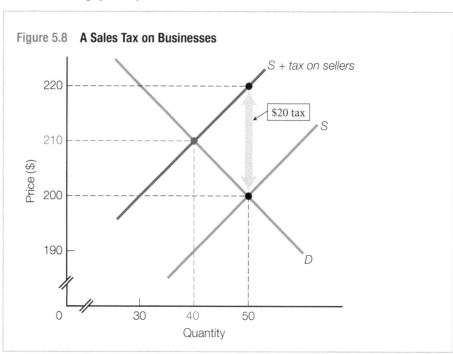

Figure 5.8   **A Sales Tax on Businesses**

The government decides to place a $20 tax on every exercycle sold. Governments collect sales taxes monthly from the sellers — the exercycle businesses have to send in $20 for each unit they sell. The tax increases the sellers' costs by $20 per exercycle, just as if inputs prices had go up by $20 per unit (section 3.4). The tax shifts the supply curve leftward to the supply curve labelled *S + tax on sellers*.

NOTE
A tax on sellers shifts up the supply curve by a vertical distance equal to the amount of the tax.

This is one of those graphs that makes more sense when you read the supply curve up and over as a marginal cost curve, because the tax shifts the supply curve up by a distance equal to the amount of the tax. The pink vertical arrow indicates the $20 tax. For the 50th exercycle, going up to the original supply curve and over to the price axis shows a marginal cost of $200. Going up from the 50th exercycle to the new *S + tax on sellers* curve and over shows a marginal cost of $220. Sellers have to pay the original $200 marginal costs per exercycle, and now have to pay an additional $20 tax, for a total of $220 per exercycle.

The sellers are paying the tax to the government, but your receipt for exercycles will show the $20 tax at the bottom that you, as the consumer or buyer, are paying. So who is paying the tax?

The answer, in this case, is that the buyer and the seller each pay part of the tax. Look at the new equilibrium price in this market after the tax. The unchanged demand curve and the new supply curve (*S + tax on sellers*) intersect at a price of $210 per exercycle and quantity of 40 exercycles. So buyers are paying $10 more per exercycle. The sellers are receiving that extra $10 per exercycle, but then have to pay $20 per exercycle to the government. So the sellers are also paying $10 per exercycle. The tax incidence of the $20 per exercycle tax is split evenly between buyers and sellers.

Taxes are not always split evenly between buyers and sellers. The division depends on the elasticities of demand and supply. Once again, the extreme values of elasticity give the clearest insight into how elasticity affects tax incidence.

Tax Incidence with Extreme Demand Elasticities   Figure 5.9 shows who pays the sales tax when demand is perfectly inelastic and perfectly elastic.

Figure 5.9   Tax Incidence with Extreme Demand Elasticities

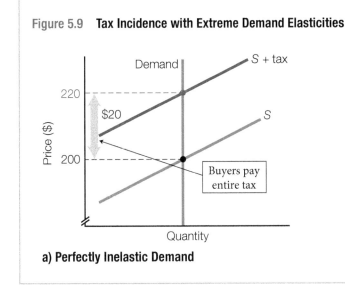

a) **Perfectly Inelastic Demand**

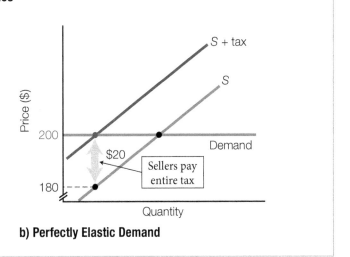

b) **Perfectly Elastic Demand**

When demand is perfectly inelastic — the vertical demand curve in Figure 5.9a — the supply curve shifts up by the amount of the tax of $20. The equilibrium price rises by the full amount of the tax, from $200 to $220. Buyers or consumers pay the entire tax. Inelastic demand means a low willingness to shop elsewhere, so consumers pay whatever price is set.

When demand is perfectly elastic — the horizontal demand curve in Figure 5.9b — the supply curve again shifts up by the amount of the tax of $20. But with perfectly elastic demand, buyers are not willing to pay even a penny more for the exercycles. They have a high willingness to shop elsewhere. The equilibrium price remains at $200, and sellers have to absorb the entire $20 tax. Sellers receive $200 per unit from buyers, but have to send the government $20 for each exercycle sold, ending up with only $180 per sale.

These extreme demand elasticities almost never happen in the real world. But they provide the basis for general rules about tax incidence that apply to all real world situations:

- The more inelastic demand is, the more buyers pay of a tax.
- The more elastic demand is, the more sellers pay of a tax.

Tax Incidence with Extreme Supply Elasticities   Figure 5.10 shows who pays the sales tax when supply is perfectly inelastic and perfectly elastic.

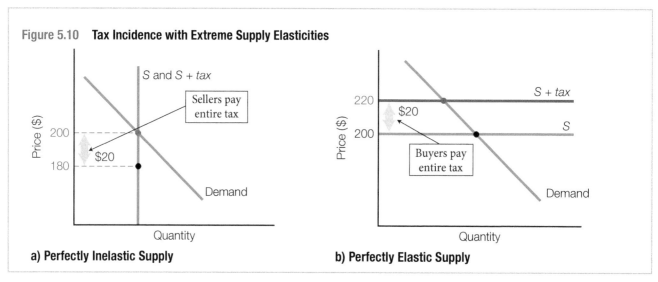

Figure 5.10   **Tax Incidence with Extreme Supply Elasticities**

a) Perfectly Inelastic Supply

b) Perfectly Elastic Supply

When supply is perfectly inelastic — the vertical supply curve in Figure 5.10a — the tax does not shift the supply curve. Suppliers will accept any price for the given quantity, which means they will accept the loss of $20 and still supply the same quantity. The equilibrium price remains at $200, and sellers absorb the entire $20 tax. Sellers receive $200 per exercycle from buyers, but have to send the government $20 per sale, ending up with $180.

When supply is perfectly elastic — the horizontal supply curve in Figure 5.10b — the tax shifts the supply curve up vertically by the $20 amount of the tax. The equilibrium price rises from $200 to $220, so buyers pay the entire tax.

Like the extreme demand elasticities, these extreme supply elasticities provide the basis for general rules about tax incidence:

- The more inelastic supply is, the more sellers pay of a tax.
- The more elastic supply is, the more buyers pay of a tax.

Figure 5.11 summarizes the general rules about tax incidence.

What's in Taxes for Government?

No matter who pays the tax, the tax money goes to the government. Figure 5.12 shows how governments estimate the tax revenues they collect from a sales tax.

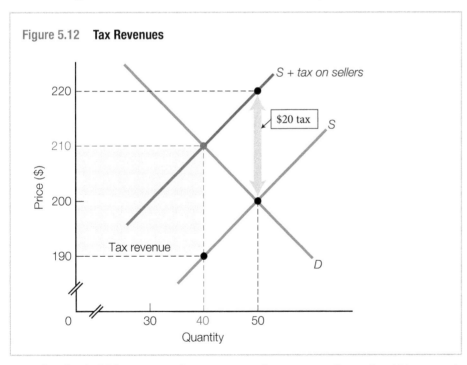

Figure 5.12   **Tax Revenues**

The shaded blue rectangle represents the revenue from the $20 per unit sales tax on exercycles. The height of the rectangle is the $20 tax per unit, and the width is the quantity, or number of units sold: 40 exercycles. The tax revenue formula is

tax per unit $\times$ units sold

or

$20 $\times$ 40 = $800.

Tax revenue depends on the elasticities of demand and supply. In general, the more inelastic demand and supply are, the greater the tax revenue for government. Why? Sales taxes decrease supply and therefore decrease the equilibrium quantity in a market. Elasticities determine *by how much* quantity decreases because of the tax. The more inelastic demand and supply are, the smaller the decreases in quantity, keeping the tax revenue larger.

For this reason, governments try to tax products and services with inelastic demands or supplies. Commonly taxed products like alcohol, cigarettes, and gasoline all have inelastic demands. While there are many reasons why governments choose to tax specific products and services, smart government choices for sales tax revenue depend on elasticities.

Measurement Stretches Understanding

Elasticity is a concept that can be stretched (that's economist humour) to measure the responsiveness of quantity demanded to changes in other variables besides price — changes in the prices of related products and changes in income. These elasticity measures help connect simple demand and supply models to real-world concepts like substitutes, complements, necessities, and luxuries, and help governments make smart tax policy choices.

Your opportunity cost of using elasticity concepts is doing a little math, but your benefit is a better understanding of how markets work and *by how much* consumers and businesses respond to changes in incentives, whether in the form of prices, incomes, or taxes.

Refresh 5.5

MyEconLab

For answers to these Refresh Questions, visit MyEconLab.

1. In your own words, explain the relationships between who pays a sales tax and elasticities of demand and supply.

2. Governments use sales taxes both to collect revenue and to change behaviour. If cigarette taxes are intended to discourage smoking rather than raise revenue, what elasticities of supply and demand for cigarettes will help governments achieve this policy objective? How do those elasticities compare to the elasticities that give government the most tax revenue?

3. Governments could collect sales taxes from sellers or from buyers. Explain why governments collect almost all sales taxes from sellers.

5.1 Measuring Your Responsiveness: Price Elasticity of Demand

Elasticity measures how responsive quantity demanded is to a change in price.

- The tool that businesses use to measure consumer responsiveness when making pricing decisions is **elasticity** (or **price elasticity of demand**), which measures by how much quantity demanded responds to a change in price.

- The simple formula is:

$$\text{Price elasticity of demand} = \frac{\text{Percentage change in quantity demanded}}{\text{Percentage change in price}}$$

- The midpoint formula between any two points on a demand curve like (Q_0, P_0) and (Q_1, P_1) is:

$$\frac{\dfrac{Q_1 - Q_0}{\left(\dfrac{Q_1 + Q_0}{2}\right)}}{\dfrac{P_1 - P_0}{\left(\dfrac{P_1 + P_0}{2}\right)}}$$

- **Inelastic demand** — small response in quantity demanded when price rises.
  - Example: Demand for insulin by a diabetic.
  - Value for formula is less than one.
  - Low willingness to shop elsewhere.
  - **Perfectly inelastic demand** — price elasticity of demand equals zero; quantity demanded does not respond to a change in price.

- **Elastic demand** — large response in quantity demanded when price rises.
  - Example: Demand for bluc earbuds.
  - Value for formula is greater than one.
  - High willingness to shop elsewhere.
  - **Perfectly elastic demand** — price elasticity of demand equals infinity; quantity demanded has an infinite response to a change in price.

- The price elasticity of demand of a product or service is influenced by:
  - available substitutes — more substitutes mean more elastic demand.
  - time to adjust — longer time to adjust means more elastic demand.
  - proportion of income spent — greater proportion of income spent on a product or service means more elastic demand.

5.2 Will You Make It Up in Volume? Elasticity and Total Revenue

Elasticity determines business pricing strategies to earn maximum total revenue — cut prices when demand is elastic and raise prices when demand is inelastic.

- **Total revenue** — all money a business receives from sales = price per unit *(P)* multiplied by quantity sold *(Q)*.
  - For businesses facing elastic demand, price cuts are the smart choice and increase total revenue.
  - For businesses facing inelastic demand, price rises are the smart choice and increase total revenue.

- As you move down a straight line demand curve, elasticity changes and is *not* the same as slope.
  - Elasticity goes from elastic, to unit elastic, to inelastic.
  - Total revenue increases, reaches a maximum when elasticity equals 1, and then decreases.

5.3 How Far Will You Jump for the Money? Price Elasticity of Supply

Elasticity of supply measures the responsiveness of quantity supplied to a change in price, and depends on the difficulty, expense, and time involved in increasing production.

- **Elasticity of supply** measures by how much quantity supplied responds to a change in price.

- The formula is:

$$\text{Elasticity of supply} = \frac{\text{Percentage change in quantity supplied}}{\text{Percentage change in price}}$$

  - The midpoint formula between any two points on a supply curve like (Q_0, P_0) and (Q_1, P_1) is similar to formula for price elasticity of demand.

$$\frac{\dfrac{Q_1 - Q_0}{\left(\dfrac{Q_1 + Q_0}{2}\right)}}{\dfrac{P_1 - P_0}{\left(\dfrac{P_1 + P_0}{2}\right)}}$$

- **Inelastic** — For inelastic supply, small response in quantity supplied when price rises. Difficult and expensive to increase production.
  - Example: supply of mined gold.
  - Value for formula is less than 1.
  - **Perfectly inelastic supply** — price elasticity of supply equals zero; quantity supplied does not respond to a change in price.

- **Elastic** — For elastic supply, large response in quantity supplied when price rises. Easy and inexpensive to increase production.
  - Example: snow-shovelling services.
  - Value for formula is greater than 1.
  - **Perfectly elastic supply** — price elasticity of supply equals infinity; quantity supplied has infinite response to a change in price.

- Elasticity of supply of a product or service is influenced by:
  - availability of additional inputs — more available inputs means more elastic supply.
  - time production takes — less time means more elastic supply.

- Elasticity of supply allows more accurate predictions of future outputs and prices, helping businesses avoid disappointing customers.

5.4 Can You Measure Substitutes? More Elasticities of Demand

Elasticity measures explain the responsiveness of quantity demanded to changes in prices of related products and income, and the division of a tax between buyers and sellers.

- **Cross elasticity of demand** — measures the responsiveness of the demand for a product or service to a change in the price of a substitute or complement.
  - The simple formula is:

$$\text{Cross elasticity of demand} = \frac{\text{Percentage change in quantity demanded}}{\text{Percentage change in price of a substitute or complement}}$$

- Cross elasticity of demand is a positive number for substitutes. The larger the number:
  - the larger the change in demand.
  - the larger the shift of the demand curve.
  - the closer the products or services are to being perfect substitutes.

- Cross elasticity of demand is a negative number for complements. The larger the number:
  - the larger the change in demand.
  - the larger the shift of the demand curve.
  - the closer the products or services are to being perfect complements.

- **Income elasticity of demand** — measures the responsiveness of the demand for a product or service to a change in income.
  - The simple formula is:

$$\text{Income elasticity of demand} = \frac{\text{Percentage change in quantity demanded}}{\text{Percentage change in income}}$$

  - Positive for normal goods; increase in income increases demand for normal goods.
  - Negative for inferior goods; increase in income decreases demand for inferior goods.

- **Income inelastic demand** —
  - income elasticity greater than 0 but less than 1
  - percentage change in quantity is less than the percentage change in price
  - normal goods that are necessities

- **Income elastic demand** —
  - income elasticity greater than 1
  - percentage change in quantity is greater than the percentage change in price
  - normal goods that are luxuries

5.5 Who Pays the HST?
Tax Incidence and Government Tax Choices

- **Tax incidence** — the division of a tax between buyers and sellers; depends on elasticities of demand and supply

- Elasticity of demand and tax incidence:
  - perfectly inelastic demand — buyers pay all
  - more inelastic demand — buyers pay more
  - more elastic demand — sellers pay more
  - perfectly elastic demand — sellers pay all

- Elasticity of supply and tax incidence:
  - perfectly inelastic supply — sellers pay all
  - more inelastic supply — sellers pay more
  - more elastic supply — buyers pay more
  - perfectly elastic supply — buyers pay all

- The more inelastic demand and supply are, the greater the tax revenue for government. For maximum revenue, governments try to tax products and services with inelastic demands and supplies.

TRUE/FALSE

Circle the correct answer. Solutions to these questions are available at the end of the book and on MyEconLab. You can also visit the MyEconLab Study Plan to access additional questions that will help you master the concepts covered in this chapter.

5.1 Price Elasticity of Demand

1. If you like Pepsi and Coke about the same, your demand for Pepsi is likely to be elastic. T F

2. Any elasticity value less than 1 is inelastic. T F

3. The fewer substitutes available, the more elastic demand is. T F

4. When negotiating a price on an expensive purchase, you want the dealer to believe that your demand is elastic — that is, you are willing to shop elsewhere if you don't get a low price because good substitutes are available. T F

5.2 Elasticity and Total Revenue

5. Total revenue ($P \times Q$) decreases when a business lowers the price of an inelastic good. T F

6. Price elasticity of demand is constant along a straight-line demand curve. T F

7. If a decrease in supply increases total revenue, demand must be inelastic. T F

8. Price cuts are smart when facing inelastic demand. T F

5.3 Price Elasticity of Supply

9. A horizontal supply curve is perfectly elastic. T F

10. The federal government of Canada introduced a Working Income Tax Benefit. This policy increases the return from working because it reduces the tax paid on earnings. Women's work-supply decision is more "elastic" to wages than men's, so women are more likely to benefit from this policy than are men. T F

11. If a 10-percent rise in price increases quantity supplied by 40 percent, supply is elastic. T F

5.4 More Elasticities of Demand

12. We would expect a negative cross elasticity of demand between hamburgers and hamburger buns. T F

13. An inferior good has a negative cross elasticity of demand. T F

14. Necessities have negative income elasticities of demand. T F

5.5 Tax Incidence and Government Tax Choices

15. The more elastic demand is for a service, the more consumers pay of the sales tax. T F

Circle the best answer. Solutions to these questions are available at the end of the book and on MyEconLab. You can also visit the MyEconLab Study Plan to access similar questions that will help you master the concepts covered in this chapter.

5.1 Price Elasticity of Demand

1. The fact that butter and margarine are close substitutes makes
   a) demand for butter more elastic.
   b) demand for butter more inelastic.
   c) butter an inferior good.
   d) margarine an inferior good.

2. Two points on the demand curve for volleyballs are

Price	Quantity Demanded
$19	55
$21	45

   What is the midpoint elasticity of demand between these two points?
   a) 2.5
   b) 2.0
   c) 0.5
   d) 0.4

3. If the price elasticity of demand is 2, a 1 percent fall in price will
   a) double the quantity demanded.
   b) decrease the quantity demanded by half.
   c) increase the quantity demanded by 2 percent.
   d) decrease the quantity demanded by 2 percent.

4. Price elasticity of demand will be larger,
   a) the shorter the time to adjust.
   b) the greater the proportion of income spent on the product.
   c) the harder it is to find good substitutes.
   d) when all of the above are true.

5.2 Elasticity and Total Revenue

5. A fall in tuition fees decreases a college's total revenue if the price elasticity of demand for college education is
   a) negative.
   b) greater than zero but less than one.
   c) equal to one.
   d) greater than one.

6. After visiting restaurants in Paris with fee-for-service toilets, a Canadian restaurant owner decides to charge customers a fee for bathroom use. How will bathroom use inside the owner's restaurant most likely change?
   a) Quantity demanded decreases; total revenue falls.
   b) Quantity demanded increases; total revenue rises.
   c) Quantity demanded decreases; total revenue rises.
   d) Quantity demanded increases; total revenue falls.

7. If the Jets cut ticket prices and find that total revenue does not change, the price elasticity of demand for tickets is
   a) zero.
   b) greater than zero but less than one.
   c) equal to one.
   d) greater than one.

8. A new technology lowers the cost of photocopiers. If the demand for photocopiers is price inelastic, photocopier sales
   a) decrease and total revenue increases.
   b) decrease and total revenue decreases.
   c) increase and total revenue increases.
   d) increase and total revenue decreases.

5.3 Price Elasticity of Supply

9. The statement "Even after the reward was doubled, nobody volunteered for the mission" illustrates
   a) the law of supply.
   b) elastic supply.
   c) inelastic supply.
   d) inelastic demand.

10. There would be a high elasticity of supply for a business
    a) in a small town with no available workers.
    b) in a large town with many available workers.
    c) with workers who are lazy and unwilling to work additional hours.
    d) with workers who threaten to quit if their hours are reduced.

11. Since real trees take a very long time to grow, this year's supply of real Christmas trees is
    a) low.
    b) high.
    c) elastic.
    d) inelastic.

5.4 More Elasticities of Demand

12. The cross elasticity of the demand for white tennis balls with respect to the price of yellow tennis balls is probably
    a) negative and high.
    b) negative and low.
    c) positive and high.
    d) positive and low.

13. If a 10 percent increase in income causes a 5 percent increase in quantity demanded, what is the income elasticity of demand?
    a) 0.5
    b) −0.5
    c) 2.0
    d) −2.0

14. Luxuries tend to have income elasticities of demand that are
    a) greater than one.
    b) greater than zero but less than one.
    c) positive.
    d) negative.

5.5 Tax Incidence and Government Tax Choices

15. If the price of a product is not affected by a sales tax
    a) supply is perfectly elastic.
    b) demand is perfectly elastic.
    c) elasticity of supply is greater than elasticity of demand.
    d) demand is perfectly inelastic.

6

What Gives When Prices Don't?

Government Policy Choices

LEARNING OBJECTIVES

After reading this chapter, you should be able to:

6.1 Explain how government-fixed prices cause quantities to adjust and market coordination to fail.

6.2 Describe price ceilings and explain the unintended consequences of government rent-control policies.

6.3 Describe price floors and explain the unintended consequences of government minimum wage laws.

6.4 Explain government policy trade-offs between efficient and equitable outcomes.

6.5 Describe two equity concepts and how to use positive economic thinking to achieve a normative policy goal.

EVERY TIME GAS PRICES JUMP by 20 cents per

litre, the complaints begin — oil companies are price gouging, gas taxes should be lowered, governments should do something. When drivers (who are also voters) complain about prices, politicians notice. Parliament holds hearings, and sometimes — like Canada's New Energy Program in 1974 — governments actually fix gas prices, making it illegal for suppliers to charge higher prices. The pattern is similar when tenants (voters) complain that rents are too high, or workers (voters) complain that wages are too low. Governments respond with rent control policies or minimum wage laws.

When high (or low) prices cause voters pain, governments are tempted to fix prices. Despite good intentions, the consequences are usually not what governments intended. Prices are signals that coordinate the smart decisions of consumers and businesses. Fixed prices cripple the flow of information and the incentives that make markets effective at producing what we want. In this chapter, we look at what happens when prices can't adjust.

Government policy choices, like consumer and business choices, involve trade-offs. When governments act to correct problems of affordability and fairness that markets create, there are often better solutions than fixed prices. But sometimes governments *might* still make smart policy choices that give up the market's benefits of flexible prices to promote more equitable outcomes.

Do Prices or Quantities Adjust? Unintended Consequences of Government Policies

When governments fix prices, markets try to coordinate those policy choices with choices by consumers and by businesses. The coordinated outcomes are often not what policymakers intended. But we can still use the Three Keys, comparing marginal benefits and marginal costs, to judge if government policies are smart choices.

When Price Is Fixed Too Low, Quantities Adjust

Suppose gas has been regularly selling for $1 per litre. That is a market-clearing price, matching the quantity of gas demanded and quantity of gas supplied at 85 million litres per month. Then, to no one's great surprise, a Middle East conflict destroys some oil refineries, and supply decreases.

The graph in Figure 6.1 shows the unchanged market demand (D_0), the original market supply (the dashed S_0 line), and the new market supply for gasoline (S_1) after the supply decrease. The table shows, for every price, the quantities behind the demand curve (column 2) and the new market supply curve (column 3). The last column shows, for every price, the difference between quantity demanded and quantity supplied.

Figure 6.1 **Market for Gasoline with Shortage**

Price per Litre	Quantity Demanded (millions of litres per month)	Quantity Supplied (millions of litres per month)	Shortage (−) or Surplus (+) (millions of litres per month)
$0.80	95	35	−60
$1.00	**85**	**55**	**−30**
$1.20	75	75	0
$1.40	65	95	+30
$1.60	55	115	+60

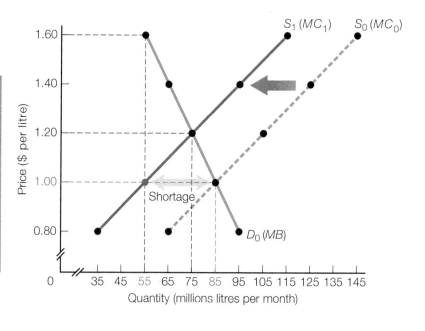

Prices Adjust   After the shift to the new market supply, if the price remains at $1 per litre there is a shortage. The unchanged quantity demanded (85 million litres per month) faces a reduced supply. At the price of $1 per litre (row 2 in the table in Figure 6.1), gasoline suppliers, now paying higher oil prices, are only willing to supply 55 million litres per month. There is a shortage of 30 million litres per month, indicated by the beige horizontal arrow on the graph.

So begins the classic Chapter 4 shortage story of frustrated buyers. Consumers compete against each other for the now hard-to-find gasoline, and bid up prices. Gasoline suppliers respond to the rising prices by supplying increased quantities. Rising prices also decrease quantity demanded, as consumers substitute away from more expensive gas, which fewer can afford (good thing you bought headphones for those additional transit rides). With flexible prices, adjustments continue until the price reaches the new equilibrium price of $1.20 per litre. At that market-clearing price, the shortage is eliminated and the quantity of gas demanded again matches the quantity supplied (75 million litres per month). This is how well-functioning markets coordinate smart choices for both consumers and businesses.

Quantities Adjust   What if the government, facing an election and worried about driver/voter complaints, fixes gas prices at $1 per litre? A new law makes it illegal for anyone to sell gasoline for more than $1 per litre. Governments have the power to fix prices, but they can't force businesses to produce if that price is not profitable.

The fixed-price story does not have a happy ending. At a price of $1 per litre, suppliers are only willing to supply 55 million litres per month. Now that prices can't adjust, buyers will continue to be frustrated. If you read the demand curve as a marginal benefit curve (up and over), the 55th million litre of gas is worth $1.60 to some consumer drivers. Drivers will try very hard to find gasoline; available gasoline is worth much more to them than the fixed $1 price. Consumers who are lucky enough to get gas at the fixed price will either spend hours driving around looking for stations that still have some gas, wait in long line-ups, or try to bribe gas station owners to supply them first. Most will have to give up some driving — there is a shortage of 30 million litres per month (85 million litres demanded – 55 million litres supplied). *Quantities adjust.*

Fixing prices does not change the voluntary quality of market exchanges. Businesses supply only if price covers all opportunity costs of production. Consumers demand only if they are willing and able to pay for the product or service at that price. For any price, set by the market or set by governments, businesses can reduce output or shut down factories or move their inputs elsewhere. Consumers can reduce their purchases or keep their wallets shut or buy something else. There are always substitutes.

Governments can legally fix prices, but consumers and businesses will *adjust quantities* to make their respective smart choices at the fixed price. The smart choices of consumers and the smart choices of businesses will not be coordinated when prices can't adjust. Both groups will be unhappy, which is neither what the policymakers wanted nor intended.

NOTE
When price is fixed below market-clearing, shortages develop (quantity demanded greater than quantity supplied) and consumers are frustrated. Quantity sold = quantity supplied only.

When Price Is Fixed Too High, Quantities Adjust

Chapter 4 also explained what happens in a well-functioning market when price is set too high. There would be a . . . [*Hint:* It's an *s*-word.] . . . *surplus.* The story is of frustrated suppliers who can't find willing buyers. Look at Figure 6.2, which repeats the information for the gasoline market in Figure 6.1 after supply decreases.

Figure 6.2   Market for Gasoline with Surplus

Price per Litre	Quantity Demanded (millions of litres per month)	Quantity Supplied (millions of litres per month)	Shortage (−) or Surplus (+) (millions of litres per month)
$0.80	95	35	−60
$1.00	85	55	−30
$1.20	75	75	0
$1.40	**65**	**95**	**+30**
$1.60	55	115	+60

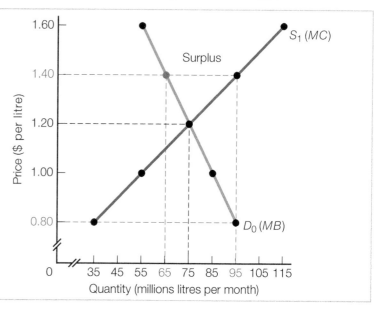

Prices Adjust   Suppose the price of gas is $1.40 per litre, *above* the market-clearing price. According to the table in Figure 6.2 (row 4), gasoline suppliers are happy to supply 95 million litres per month, but consumers will demand only 65 million litres per month. There is a monthly surplus of 30 million litres of gasoline, indicated by the blue horizontal arrow on the graph.

Businesses will compete against each other for hard-to-find customers, and cut prices. Falling prices increase quantity demanded, as consumers buy more of the now-cheaper gas. Gasoline suppliers respond to the falling prices with decreased quantities supplied. With flexible prices, adjustments continue until the price reaches the equilibrium price of $1.20 per litre. At that market-clearing price, the surplus is eliminated and the quantity of gas demanded again matches the quantity supplied (75 million litres per month).

Quantities Adjust   What if government stepped into the gasoline market and fixed a higher-than-market-clearing price of $1.40 per litre?

If you read the demand curve as a marginal benefit curve, the 95th million litre that suppliers would like to sell is worth only $0.80 to some consumers. Consumers won't pay $1.40 for a litre of gas that has a benefit of only $0.80. For all litres greater than 65 million, marginal benefit is less than the cost of $1.40. Without price cuts, consumers will buy only 65 million litres at the price of $1.40 per litre, so the quantity actually sold will be 65 million litres. The surplus of 30 million litres sits in storage tanks. Businesses cut back on the quantity of gasoline produced in future months, until the unsold surplus gasoline finally is sold. *Quantities adjust.*

The smart choices of consumers and the smart choices of businesses will not be coordinated when prices can't adjust. Businesses are willing to supply more gasoline, but are frustrated because they cannot sell it. And in a voluntary market system, neither businesses nor governments can force consumers to buy more at the higher price.

NOTE

When price is fixed above market-clearing, surpluses develop (quantity supplied greater than quantity demanded) and businesses are frustrated. Quantity sold = quantity demanded only.

Fixed Prices Prevent Markets from Functioning Well

When governments fix prices, either below or above the market-clearing price, the smart choices of consumers and businesses are not coordinated. The only way shortages or surpluses disappear is by quantities adjusting to whichever is less — to quantity supplied (with a shortage), or to quantity demanded (with a surplus).

NOTE
When prices are fixed, quantities adjust to whichever is less — quantity supplied or quantity demanded.

Economics *Out There*

Price Controls Keep Venezuelan Cupboards Bare

Venezuela, one of the world's top oil-producing countries, ran out of toilet paper in 2012. Despite steady revenues from its oil, shortages of basic items like milk, meat, and toilet paper are part of daily life there. Grocery shopping for most Venezuelans is "a hit or miss proposition."

Shoppers arrange their schedules around the once-a-week deliveries made to government-subsidized stores, often lining up before dawn to buy a single frozen chicken before the stock runs out. Or a bag of flour. Or a bottle of cooking oil.

President Hugo Chávez's socialist government imposed strict price controls intended to make basic foods and products more affordable for the poor. The unintended consequence is that "They are often the very products that are the hardest to find."

This is "a classic case of a government causing a problem rather than solving it. Prices are set so low...that companies and producers cannot make a profit. So farmers grow less food, manufacturers cut back production and retailers stock less inventory."

You don't have to be pro-capitalist to understand that when there is no possibility of profit from producing a product, the market stops providing it.

When governments fix prices, quantities adjust.

Sources: William Neuman, "With Venezuelan Food Shortages, Some Blame Price Controls," *The New York Times*, April 20, 2012, http://www.nytimes.com/2012/04/21/world/americas/venezuela-faces-shortages-in-grocery-staples.html?; Daniel Gross, "The Crappiest Economy?" The Daily Beast, May 16, 2013, http://www.thedailybeast.com/articles/2013/05/16/the-crappiest-economy.html

Refresh 6.1

1. If government makes it illegal for businesses to lower their prices, and there is a surplus of products and services in the market, explain how consumers and businesses will react.

2. You own a flower shop and usually sell roses for $25 a dozen. In the month before Valentine's Day, your suppliers charge you a higher price for roses. A politician, who has many romantics in his riding, gets Parliament to pass a private member's bill making it illegal to charge more than $25 for a dozen roses. Other flower prices are not fixed. What will be your smart business choice for Valentine's Day?

3. Tim Hortons charges the same price for coffee no matter what time of day it is. At your local Tims, there are times of the day you walk right up to the counter and order, and other times when you have to wait in line. Explain how quantities supplied and quantities demanded are being coordinated. If you were the CEO of Tims, would you change Tims's fixed-pricing policy? Explain your answer.

MyEconLab

For answers to these Refresh Questions, visit MyEconLab.

6.2

Do Rent Controls Help the Homeless? Price Ceilings

Describe price ceilings and explain the unintended consequences of government rent-control policies.

rent controls (example of a price ceiling) maximum price set by government, making it illegal to charge higher price

Not many citizens feel good seeing people sleeping out on the streets on a freezing winter night. Homelessness and a lack of affordable housing are serious problems in most big Canadian cities. To help solve these problems, compassionate and well-intentioned individuals, charitable organizations, and religious groups often ask governments to *do something* by controlling rents. **Rent controls** are a form of price fixing (rents are the monthly "price" of apartments). Governments set a maximum rent (called a **price ceiling**) that limits how high rents can be raised, while allowing rents to be flexible downward. (The government-fixed price of $1 per litre of gasoline in the previous section is another example of a price ceiling.)

Governments introduce rent-control policies in response to concerns of many groups. Rent controls obviously have benefits for renters (in Toronto, 40 percent of voters are renters), but also appeal to citizens who believe government should help those who are less fortunate, simply because it is the right, or ethical, thing to do. Religious groups also share a belief in helping the poor. Social activists argue that in a relatively wealthy and enlightened society like Canada, governments should ensure that essential services like affordable housing, education, and health care are available to all citizens. These services are too important, they argue, to be left to impersonal, profit-oriented markets alone to provide.

Benefits and Costs of Rent Control Policies

Like any choice, a government policy choice to do something about homelessness must weigh benefits and costs.

Benefits What are the perceived benefits of rent controls that lead governments to introduce them? A political benefit to governments (not to renters) is that the government does not have to spend any money (which building shelters or affordable apartments would require), yet voters perceive that the government is doing something to help.

For those who can find apartments, rent controls reduce the amount of money they have to pay for housing, leaving them more money for food, clothing, and other necessities. Some citizens and politicians who believe in the "Robin Hood principle" — named after the famous character from medieval folklore who robbed the rich and gave to the poor — see rent controls as a way of redistributing income from (relatively) rich landlords to (relatively) poor tenants.

NOTE
The "Robin Hood principle" is to take from the rich and give to the poor.

Costs Every choice has an opportunity cost. What are the costs that must be weighed against the benefits to decide whether rent controls are a smart policy choice for helping the homeless?

While rent controls are introduced with good intentions, they have some undesirable and unintended consequences. Like any fixed price, rent controls cripple the coordinating forces of well-functioning markets. Rent ceilings are always set *below* the market-clearing rent, creating a classic shortage. (A rent ceiling above the market-clearing rent would be irrelevant. When apartments are readily available at $1500 per month, what good does it do to have a law preventing rents from rising above $1600?)

Figure 6.3 shows a market for two-bedroom apartments without rent controls (Figure 6.3a) and with rent controls (Figure 6.3b). Let's focus first on the prices (rents) and quantities in the demand and supply curve reading of the graph. At the intersection of the demand and supply curves in Figure 6.3a, the market-clearing rent is $1500, and the market-clearing quantity is 6000 apartments.

With a price ceiling for rents set at $1000 in Figure 6.3b, landlords are only willing to supply 4000 apartments. The quantity of housing supplied is less than the 6000 apartments that would be supplied at the market-clearing rent. So while those who find apartments will be better off, there will be *fewer apartments available*. Quantities adjust.

With a shortage of 5000 apartments at the rent ceiling (the difference between the 9000 apartments demanded and the 4000 supplied), consumers who can no longer find apartments will be frustrated and worse off.

Inefficiency of Rent Controls

The marginal benefit and marginal cost reading of the demand and supply curves in Figure 6.3 allows us to compare the efficiency of the market-clearing outcome with the rent-controlled outcome. Recall from Chapter 4 that total surplus (consumer surplus plus producer surplus) is at a maximum for an efficient market outcome. All mutually beneficial trades happen, and marginal benefit equals marginal cost for the last (6000th) apartment rented in Figure 6.3a.

Because rent controls restrict the supply of housing, consumer surplus (green), producer surplus (blue), and total surplus in Figure 6.3b are less than for the efficient market outcome in Figure 6.3a. The grey area of deadweight loss in Figure 6.3b represents the mutually beneficial trades between consumers and landlords that are *not* happening with rent controls. With marginal benefits greater than marginal costs between 4000 and 6000 apartments, each of those additional 2000 apartments would make both consumers and landlords better off. But quantity supplied stops at 4000 apartments, where the marginal benefit of the 4000th apartment is far greater than the marginal cost. There are consumers out there who are willing and able to pay much more than $1000 if only they could find an apartment.

NOTE
Rent controls are inefficient and reduce total surplus.

Figure 6.3   Market for Two-Bedroom Apartments

Rent (per month)	Quantity Demanded (apartments per month)	Quantity Supplied (apartments per month)	Shortage (−) or Surplus (+) (apartments per month)
$2500	0	10 000	+10 000
$2000	3 000	8 000	+5 000
$1500	6 000	6 000	0
$1000	9 000	4 000	−5 000
$ 500	12 000	2 000	−10 000

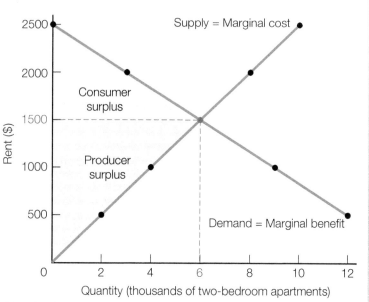

a) Market for Two-Bedroom Apartments

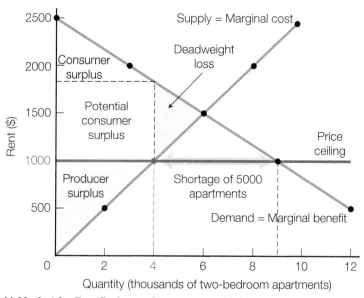

b) Market for Two-Bedroom Apartments with Rent Controls

Unintended Consequences of Rent Controls

Reducing Supply   While governments can fix rents, they cannot force landlords to supply apartments if the rent does not cover all opportunity costs of "producing" or supplying housing. Remember, the opportunity cost of any input is its *best alternative use.* At the controlled rents, some landlords may make more money by turning their building into condominiums, again reducing the supply of apartments. A homeowner who rents out a basement apartment in her house may decide it's not worth it at the lower rent ceiling and convert that space back to her own family's use. Smart choices change with changes in prices. With more time to adjust to the lower rent ceiling, fewer apartment buildings may be built (still more condos instead).

Landlord Power   With tenants competing for scarce apartments and willing to pay more than the controlled rent, landlords have the upper hand. Landlords may allow the physical condition of their properties to deteriorate, since they can be sure of finding tenants. Spending less on maintenance improves their profits in the short run. Let the tenants pay for painting and repairs! Landlords may also charge a potential tenant "key money," which is a polite term for a bribe, in exchange for giving that tenant (as opposed to the many other willing tenants) the key to the scarce apartment. Landlords are also in a position to discriminate against renting to tenants they don't like, both for legitimate reasons (are college students more likely to do property damage?) and illegitimate reasons (on the basis of race or religion).

Subsidizing the Rich   One final and clearly unintended consequence is that rent controls also subsidize the (relatively) rich! Rent controls apply to all apartments, not just apartments rented by those who have difficulty affording housing. Existing high-income tenants, who are both willing and able to pay more for their apartments, pay only the controlled rent.

Alternatives to Rent Controls

So, are rent control policies a smart choice for governments trying to ensure more affordable housing for the homeless? Almost every economist out there would give an emphatic *no* for an answer, and I hope I have convinced you, too. Rent controls, like any fixed price, sacrifice all the flexibility and advantages of well-functioning markets in producing the products and services we want, and directing them to those most willing and able to pay. As a way of trying to improve the supply of affordable housing, rent controls have many drawbacks, including the perverse, unintended results of reducing the total quantity of apartments on the market, and subsidizing housing for those who can afford it.

If, as a society, we want to help the homeless, much better choices are available. In a market economy, demand depends on willingness and ability to pay. No one has a greater willingness or desire for a service as basic as housing than someone who has none. The problem is ability to pay. Alternative policies to help the homeless would provide low-income consumers with government subsidies that could be applied to any housing they might find in the market. Or governments could build affordable housing and make sure it is available only to those who need it the most. While every government policy choice, including these, has opportunity costs that must be considered (will government bureaucrats do a better job of running a housing development than a private business?), these policies allow markets to flexibly coordinate the smart decisions of consumers and business, and result in more rental units, without subsidizing well-off tenants who do not need support.

A bigger policy question lurks behind this discussion of rent controls. Should governments make policy choices based on ethical concerns, even if those choices limit the ability of markets to function well? We will address that important question at the end of this chapter, but only after looking at another form of government price fixing — minimum wage laws.

Refresh 6.2

MyEconLab

For answers to these Refresh Questions, visit MyEconLab.

1. In your own words, define rent controls.

2. Explain the unintended consequences of rent controls for the choices of tenants and of landlords.

3. Many people argue that education, like housing, is an essential service that should be affordable — perhaps even free — for all citizens. Describe a set of policies that accomplishes the goal of education affordability for all, but avoids the problems of price controls that you have learned about in this section.

6.3 Do Minimum Wages Help the Working Poor? Price Floors

Describe price floors and explain the unintended consequences of government minimum wage laws.

minimum wage laws (example of a price floor) minimum price set by government, making it illegal to pay lower price

Have you ever worked at a minimum wage job? Any proposal to "raise the minimum wage" sure sounds good to someone in a minimum wage job. It means a raise, right? What's not to like about that?

Minimum Wage Laws Past and Present

Minimum wage laws arose to protect the less fortunate and most vulnerable members of society. Unskilled and uneducated workers in 19th-century Canada were on their own. Employers paid workers as little as they could. Dangerous working conditions and low wages led to the rise of unions and, in 1918, to the first minimum wage laws in British Columbia and Manitoba. These early laws applied only to women and to limited kinds of jobs. Over time, minimum wage laws were extended to men, to more job categories, and to other provinces. Minimum wages for men were usually higher than for women, on the belief that the male breadwinner of the family deserved more pay. It wasn't until 1974 that gender differences in minimum wages ended in all provinces!

2014 hourly minimum wages in Canada ranged from $10.00 in New Brunswick, Newfoundland, and Northwest Territories to $10.20 in Alberta, and Saskatchewan, and $11.00 in Ontario and Nunavut. Earning $11 per hour translates into a yearly income of about $22 000, which is impossible to live on in a Canadian city. Many charitable, religious, and social activist groups support increases in minimum wages to $20 per hour. Twenty dollars per hour

living wage $20 per hour, enough to allow an individual in a Canadian city to live above the poverty line

is called a **living wage** because it is high enough to allow an individual to live above what Statistics Canada defines as the poverty line. Roughly 15 percent of all Canadian families have incomes below the poverty line, and about 2 million Canadians aged 20 or older are in full-time, low-paying jobs that leave them below the poverty line. These are the working poor. There is a vigorous debate in Canada about the pros and cons of an increased minimum wage for helping the working poor.

The living wage proposal, like any minimum wage, is a fixed price for businesses hiring unskilled labour. It fixes a **price floor**, making it illegal for a business to hire anyone for a wage less than the minimum.

Benefits and Costs of Minimum Wage Laws

From the discussion of the unintended consequences of the other forms of price fixing by government (rent controls or price ceilings), and from your accumulating economics knowledge, you can probably guess that minimum wages are not all good news. There are both benefits and costs to minimum wage laws.

Labour Markets Are Input Markets Before looking at the benefits and costs of setting minimum wages in the labour market, I want to re-orient you by using the circular-flow model from Chapter 1 (Figure 1.5, page 14), reproduced in the illustration below. Labour markets have an important difference from housing or gasoline markets. Households and businesses interact in two sets of markets — input markets (on the right), where businesses buy the inputs they need from households to produce products and services, and output markets (on the left), where businesses sell their products and services to households.

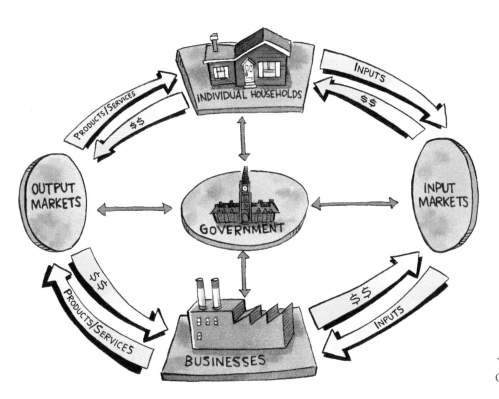

◀

Circular-Flow Model of Economic Life

Housing and gasoline are outputs, so businesses are the sellers and suppliers and households are the buyers and demanders. Labour is different. Labour is an input, so the roles are reversed. Households are the sellers and suppliers, and businesses are the buyers and demanders. Governments (in the middle) set the rules of the game and, in this chapter, choose to interact in both output markets (rent ceilings) and input markets (minimum wages).

Benefits   What are the perceived benefits of minimum wages? Like rent controls, a political benefit is that the government does not have to spend any money, yet voters perceive that the government is helping the working poor. More importantly, those workers who keep their jobs after the higher minimum wage becomes law are better off, earning closer to a living wage. They get a raise.

Costs   What are the costs that must be weighed against the benefits to decide whether minimum wage laws are a smart choice to help the working poor?

Figure 6.4 shows an unskilled labour market without and with a minimum wage. Let's focus on the prices (wages) and quantities in the demand and supply curve reading of the graph. The market-clearing wage in Figure 6.4a is $9 per hour, and the market-clearing quantity is 34 000 hours of labour.

At a minimum wage of $10 per hour (Figure 6.4b), businesses will only demand, or hire, 32 000 hours of unskilled labour. At the wage of $10 per hour, workers will supply 36 000 hours of labour. The extra 4000 hours of labour (36 000 − 32 000 = 4000) is a *surplus* in the labour market.

If prices could adjust, competition between workers looking for jobs would put downward pressure on the wage, until the wage fell to the market-clearing wage and the quantity of labour hired increased to the market-clearing quantity of 34 000 hours. But the price (wage) is fixed at the minimum wage. When prices can't adjust, quantities will.

Figure 6.4   Market for Unskilled Labour

Wage ($ per hour)	Quantity Demanded (thousands of hours per year)	Quantity Supplied (thousands of hours per year)	Shortage (−) or Surplus (+) (thousands of hours per year)
$11	30 000	38 000	+ 8000
$10	32 000	36 000	+ 4000
$ 9	34 000	34 000	0
$ 8	36 000	32 000	− 4000
$ 7	38 000	30 000	− 8000

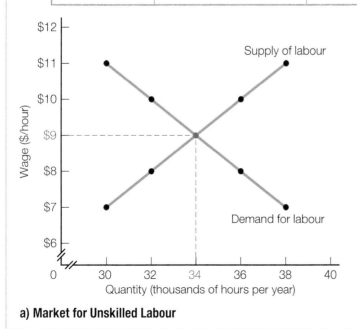

a) Market for Unskilled Labour

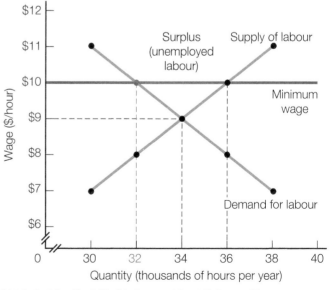

b) Market for Unskilled Labour with a Minimum Wage

Unintended Consequences of Minimum Wages

Every minimum wage law sets a wage *above* the current market-clearing price in the labour market. At the fixed minimum wage, like at any price above the market-clearing price, the quantity of labour demanded (by businesses) is less than it would be at the market-clearing wage. When any input to production, including labour, becomes more expensive, businesses reduce the input — hire fewer people and search for cheaper substitutes. If wages for janitors rise, businesses may switch from paper towels in washrooms to air dryers so they need fewer janitors. Businesses buying labour (in input markets) act like any smart consumer buying products and services (in output markets) — when the price rises, the quantity demanded decreases and the search is on for cheaper substitutes.

Unemployment   Chapter 3 showed that if wages or other input costs go up, market supply of the output decreases (review Figure 3.9 on page 70). When supply decreases, the price of output rises and quantity demanded decreases (see section 4.4). Businesses will sell less output, which is why they cut back on employment. Consumers will pay higher prices for products and services.

When the government raises the market-clearing wage to the minimum legal wage, those workers who are still hired at the new $10 minimum wage will be better off, but there will be *fewer jobs available*. Quantities adjust.

As wages rise, workers are willing to supply more labour. Chapter 3 explored how the hours you were willing to work increased as the boss offered you double time and then triple time. With a minimum wage above the market-clearing wage, there is a surplus of workers willing to work. The quantity of labour supplied is greater than the quantity demanded by employers. Workers who can no longer find jobs will spend more time and resources job searching, and will be frustrated and worse off. Statistics Canada defines workers who are willing to work but who cannot find jobs as "unemployed." Raising the minimum wage tends to increase unemployment.

While governments can fix minimum wages, they cannot force employers to hire workers.

Inefficiency   Minimum wage laws create inefficiency in the labour market, much like rent controls create inefficiency in the housing market. As we did for Figure 6.3, reading the demand and supply curves in Figure 6.4 as marginal benefit and marginal cost curves shows the inefficiency. On your own, identify the areas of consumer surplus, producer surplus, and deadweight loss in a labour market without (Figure 6.4a) and with (Figure 6.4b) a minimum wage. If you shade those areas, consumer surplus, producer surplus, and total surplus in Figure 6.4b are less than the efficient labour market outcome in Figure 6.4a.

NOTE
When governments set minimum wages above market-clearing wage, the quantity of labour supplied by households is greater than quantity of labour demanded by businesses, creating unemployment.

Economics *Out There*

Hundreds of Economists Say Raise the Minimum Wage

Many economists believe the benefits of a minimum wage outweigh the costs. In a high-profile ad signed by 650 economists — including five Nobel Prize winners — the economists argued that:

- A modest increase in the minimum wage would improve the well-being of low-wage workers and would not have the adverse effects that critics have claimed.

- The weight of evidence suggests modest increases in the minimum wage have had very little or no effect on employment.

- While controversy about the employment effects of the minimum wage continues, research shows that most beneficiaries are adult, female, and members of low-income working families.

Weighing the Benefits and Costs of Minimum Wages

So, are minimum wage laws a smart policy choice for governments trying to help the working poor? Many economists would say no, but not as strongly as to rent controls. Workers who get or keep jobs at the higher minimum wage will be better off. On the other hand, like any fixed price, minimum wages sacrifice the flexibility and advantages of well-functioning markets in coordinating the smart choices of consumers and workers and businesses. Minimum wages cause some unemployment because, when prices are fixed, quantities adjust.

How many workers will lose their jobs when minimum wages rise? Economists call this a factual or *empirical* question — the answer comes from real-world data. Those data are inconclusive. In some cases where minimum wages were introduced or increased, there were significant job losses. In others, there was not much change in employment among unskilled workers.

Elasticity of Demand for Unskilled Labour   The number of jobs lost when the minimum wage increases depends on the *elasticity of demand* for labour. When demand for unskilled labour is inelastic and businesses have few substitutes, a rise in the wage produces only a small response in decreased quantity demanded. The case is stronger for a living wage. But if demand for labour is elastic and businesses can easily substitute machines for people, a rise in the minimum wage produces a large decrease in the quantity of labour demanded. The living wage policy is less beneficial. Elasticity is important not just for businesses deciding on sale prices, but also for social activists making the case for a living wage and for governments making smart policy choices.

Whatever the data show, a full answer to the question, "Do minimum wages help the working poor," requires us to compare the gains from workers who remain employed and whose incomes go up with the lost income of workers who lose their jobs.

Alternatives to Minimum Wage Laws

Most economists believe better policy choices than minimum wage laws are available to help the working poor; policy choices that do not sacrifice a market's flexibility to coordinate smart decisions of consumers, workers, and businesses. For example, governments can provide training to unskilled workers so they become eligible for higher-paying jobs, or give direct wage supplements to raise their standard of living without risking higher unemployment. Like all choices, these policy alternatives have opportunity costs — they are more expensive than minimum wages in helping the working poor, so governments must decide where the money will come from.

David A. Barnes / Alamy

▲ This woman is protesting for a higher minimum wage. She is inferring that politicians do not know what living on minimum wage is really like. Do you agree with her viewpoint?

NOTE
The quantity of unemployment created by an increased minimum wage depends on the elasticity of business demand for unskilled labour.

NOTE
Alternative policies to help working poor are training programs and wage supplements. But all policies have opportunity costs to consider.

1. Explain what a "living wage" is and how it works as a price floor.

2. Explain how a rise in the minimum wage affects job losses when the demand for labour is inelastic, and when the demand for labour is elastic.

3. A new government policy is being considered to raise the minimum wage. If you were a lobbyist supporting this policy, what argument would you make? What data would you include? If you were a lobbyist for business and against this policy, what argument would you make? What data would you provide to support your position?

MyEconLab

For answers to these Refresh Questions, visit MyEconLab.

When Markets Work Well, Are They Fair?
Trade-Offs between Efficiency and Equity

6.4

Explain government policy trade-offs between efficient and equitable outcomes.

As an economist, I believe that when prices and quantities are allowed to adjust, well-functioning markets create incentives that balance the forces of competition (between consumers and between businesses) and the forces of cooperation (voluntary, mutually beneficial exchanges). When each consumer and business makes smart choices based only on self-interest, the coordinated result is the output of all the products and services we value most. I hope to convince you of the usefulness of markets in helping us all get the most out of life.

That appreciation for what markets can do does *not* translate into the conclusion that "Governments should always keep their hands off markets." Allowing markets to operate without government interaction is still a choice, and every choice has an opportunity cost. I also believe, like some social activists, religious groups, and other economists, that the opportunity cost of allowing markets to work well is sometimes unfairness or inequality.

Let me explain. Living in Toronto, I can't help but know some hard-core (and need I say long-suffering) Maple Leafs fans. Joe (not his real name) watches every hockey game on TV, attends games at the Air Canada Centre when someone gives him a ticket he usually can't afford, and has blue maple leaf logos tattooed on his...you don't want to know. If miracles happen and the Leafs ever make it to the seventh game of the Stanley Cup finals, there is no one more desperate, more willing, and more deserving to see the game. But poor Joe (literally and figuratively) won't be there. Tickets will go to the highest bidders, including many corporate executives who will write them off as business expenses.

Efficient Market Outcomes

NOTE
To say that well-functioning markets produce products and services we value most means outputs go to those most willing and able to pay. An efficient market outcome may not be fair or equitable.

When we say markets produce the products and services we value the most, we mean that outputs go to those most *willing and able to pay*. Joe is willing, but he is not able, so he gets no ticket. There is something about this outcome that does not seem fair. Economists use the word *efficient* to describe the outcome of a well-functioning market. An *efficient market outcome* (section 4.5 page 96), however, may not be fair or equitable.

The dictionary definition of *efficient* is "acting or producing effectively with a minimum of waste, expense, or unnecessary effort." When markets work well, businesses compete with each other, and successful, profitable businesses use inputs in the lowest cost combinations, and produce products and services that consumers demand. Businesses voluntarily produce the quantity of each product and service that consumers are willing and able to buy, and prices just cover all opportunity costs of production, including a normal profit.

Consumers compete with each other for the outputs of businesses, and products and services go to those most willing and able to pay. Consumers voluntarily buy the quantity of each product and service that businesses have produced. Because consumers buy only when marginal benefit is greater than the market-clearing price (marginal cost), they get the most "bang per buck," spending their income to get maximum possible satisfaction from every dollar. This coordination of smart choices by both businesses and consumers is an efficient market outcome. Total surplus, the sum of consumer surplus and producer surplus, is at a maximum.

Economics *Out There*

Is Price Gouging during a Disaster Wrong?

As Hurricane Sandy approached in October 2012, residents along the east cost of the U.S. and Canada rushed to stores to buy supplies that might not be available after the storm — gasoline, bottled water, flashlights, batteries, and canned soup.

With this unexpected surge in demand, products flew off the shelves, shortages occurred, and merchants raised prices. Outraged politicians warned that "price gouging during a state of emergency is illegal." Taking advantage of other's misfortune to make more profits also seems wrong to most people.

But using economic reasoning, *Slate Magazine* criticized anti-gouging laws that limit price increases during emergencies, and made a case for price gouging.

"Stopping price hikes during disasters may sound like a way to help people, but all it does is [worsen] shortages and complicate preparedness. The [need] to allocate goods efficiently doesn't vanish in a storm ... If anything, it becomes more important. And price controls in an emergency have the same results as they do any other time: They lead to shortages and overconsumption. Letting merchants raise

prices if they think customers will be willing to pay more isn't a concession to greed. Rather, it creates much-needed incentives for people to think harder about what they really need and appropriately rewards vendors who manage their inventories well."

They go on to argue that while customers won't like higher prices, they also are not going to like "running out of gasoline by 2 p.m. because it has all been bought up by earlier, stockpiling drivers." Anti-gouging laws don't create new supplies, they just "allocate them arbitrarily to whoever shows up first." And if customers knew that prices would rise, they would think twice about stockpiling products "just in case" and do less panic buying.

What do you think of these arguments? There is no single right answer because there are efficiency as well as equity considerations. Raising prices when there are shortages is a more efficient solution, but is it ethical or equitable? And which rule is more equitable, first-come first-served, or selling to those willing and able to pay higher prices?

Source: Matthew Yglesias, "The Case for Price Gouging," *Slate*, November 2012, http://www.slate.com/articles/business/moneybox/2012/10/sandy_price_gouging_anti_gouging_laws_make_natural_disasters_worse.html

Who Is Excluded from Efficient Market Outcomes?

Consumers who do not buy at equilibrium, market-clearing prices fall into two categories. The first doesn't find the product or service worth the price (marginal benefit is less than price) even though she can afford it. There are always substitutes. The second simply can't afford it, even though he wants it and finds the marginal benefit greater than the price. Joe, dejectedly watching the Stanley Cup on TV at home, is part of the second category.

Joe's misfortune is not a life-shattering tragedy. But what if, instead of the market for hockey tickets, we are talking about markets for what many consider to be essential services like housing, education, or health care? Are the benefits of an efficient market worth the sacrifice that might have to be made in terms of unfairness or inequality?

We have already seen the importance of ability to pay in setting an equitable housing policy that will still help the homeless in a cost-effective or efficient way. Let's look again at the potential trade-offs between efficiency and equity, but in the market for health care.

Health Care   Federal and provincial governments set the prices paid to the doctors, nurses, and hospitals who supply health-care services. The Canadian government also guarantees free access to most health-care services to all permanent residents and citizens, paying for those services through tax revenues. Governments fix the price of each health-care service (how much a doctor gets paid for an office visit, how much a hospital gets paid for providing a bed with nursing services, and so on), but governments cannot force doctors or nurses to work or force hospitals to admit patients. Each health-care practitioner can choose the quantity of services to provide at the fixed price. Some choose not to supply services in Canada at all, going instead to work in the United States, where prices are higher. There are alternatives for suppliers as well as for consumers.

Many dedicated and talented health-care workers in Canada work hard to provide fine medical care. But have you ever waited to get an appointment with a medical specialist in Canada? Do you know someone who is on a waiting list for a CAT scan or a surgical procedure? Of course the answer to these questions is "yes." When prices can't adjust, quantities will, and waiting lists are the most visible form of a quantity adjustment.

At the fixed price to consumers of zero, and a government-set price to suppliers, it is no surprise that the quantity demanded of medical services is far greater than the quantity supplied. As with any shortage, the market will produce only the quantity that suppliers are willing to provide, and frustrated consumers demanding medical care end up on waiting lists. This is one inefficiency that exists in the health-care system in Canada.

NOTE
In the Canadian public health-care system, everyone has relatively equal access to health-care services. Prices paid by consumers (zero) and to suppliers are fixed by governments, resulting in shortages and inefficiencies because quantity demanded exceeds quantity supplied.

▲ When prices can't adjust, quantities will, and waiting lists become the norm.

NOTE

In a private health-care system, anyone willing and able to pay gets health-care services. Prices are set efficiently in markets. Price adjustments match quantities demanded and supplied. Those unable to pay do not get health-care services, resulting in inequality.

Is Inefficient Health Care All Bad?   Does having an efficient market for health care mean that Canadian governments have made a not-smart policy choice? Not necessarily.

Consider the alternative of allowing a private market for health-care services, where consumers pay the bills; doctors, nurses, and hospitals set prices; and governments do nothing more than set the rules of the game and enforce property rights. The United States health-care system has many of these qualities. With shortages, prices rise, quantities demanded decrease, quantities supplied increase, and waiting lists disappear. The fortunate people who receive health-care services are those most willing and able to pay. Anyone not able to afford the equilibrium price does not receive medical care. They are in the same category as Joe. But since these consumers include families desperate for life-saving surgeries who simply cannot afford to pay, their tragedies are real. There are about 40 million people in the United States who do not have health-care benefits from an insurance company, which means they must pay all their medical bills themselves.

A switch in Canada to a private market in health-care services would add flexibility and incentives, and end waiting lists. Doctors, nurses, and health-care services would flow to where they are most valued, which means to those consumers most willing and able to pay. Many doctors would return to Canada from the United States. Market-driven health care would likely be more efficient, but the "haves" will get excellent care, and the "have-nots" may get no care at all. A private market outcome may be efficient, but at the cost of being less equitable. The Canadian-style outcome is more equitable, but at the cost of being less efficient.

NOTE

This simplified comparison of health care in Canada and the United States leaves out many details to highlight the trade-off between efficiency and equity.

In making these comparisons between health care in Canada and the United States, I am leaving out many details of both systems. The Canadian system has some market-based incentives and flexibility, and the U.S. system has some role for government through the Medicare and Medicaid programs. Private insurance companies also set many prices and limit quantities of services. But, as we learned in Chapter 1, a useful map or model must leave out less important details to focus attention on the most important information. I believe my simplifications help to show the key issue, which everyone acknowledges — the trade-off between efficiency and equity.

So how do governments, or you as a citizen voting for governments, choose between efficiency and equity? Both are desirable outcomes. Economics alone does not provide the answer.

Refresh 6.4

MyEconLab

For answers to these Refresh Questions, visit MyEconLab.

1. In your own words, describe what an "efficient market outcome" means for businesses and for consumers.

2. What are the trade-offs between efficiency and equity in comparing a private market for health-care services with government provision of health-care services?

3. If you had to choose between a health-care system run by the market or run by government, which would you prefer? Explain the reasoning behind your choice. What changes in your life might make you change your choice?

Choosing between Efficiency and Equity: What Economics Can and Cannot Do for You

6.5

Who is the greatest hockey player of all time? My wife, who is a bigger fan than I am, claims it is Bobby Orr. My buddy claims it is Wayne Gretzky. I have heard them argue for hours about this. Do you think it's someone else? Will it eventually be Sidney Crosby? Who is right? How do you choose?

Let's take a different perspective. Who scored more lifetime points, Bobby Orr or Wayne Gretzky? That question is easier to evaluate. It is an empirical question — you can check the facts. The facts show that Bobby Orr scored 915 points over 14 seasons; Wayne Gretzky scored 2857 points over 20 seasons. Those facts certainly support my buddy's claim.

But facts alone will not conclusively answer the greatest player question. That's because greatness has many different dimensions — points, goals versus assists, offensive versus defensive contributions, leadership, sportsmanship, toughness, and so on. Bobby Orr and Wayne Gretzky had different strengths and weaknesses, and played in different eras in the NHL. To come to a summary judgment requires placing a relative *value* on each dimension, and those values are a matter of opinion. There is no universally agreed upon definition of "greatness" in a hockey player.

Describe two equity concepts and how to use positive economic thinking to achieve a normative policy goal.

NOTE

If you are not a hockey fan, pick any sport or profession — writer, artist, filmmaker, actor, band — and make the case for who is or was the greatest.

Efficiency or Equity?

Empirical claims or statements are *positive statements* (section 1.4 page 13). Positive statements (like lifetime points scored) can be evaluated as true or false by checking the facts.

Claims or statements that involve value judgments or opinions are *normative statements*. A norm is a standard — a normative statement depends on which value or standard or ethic you believe is most important. If you place the highest value or weight on the scoring dimension, Wayne Gretzky might be the greatest. If you place the highest value on defensive contributions, it might be Number 4, Bobby Orr.

Economics *Out There*

Can We Eliminate the Trade-Off between Efficiency and Equity?

James Heckman is a Nobel Prize–winning economist who argues passionately that governments *should* pay for early childhood education (ECE). But his passion is more than a normative value judgment.

Here is his argument.

"Traditionally, equity and efficiency are viewed as competing goals.... What is remarkable is that there are some policies that both are fair — i.e., promote equity — and promote economic efficiency. Investing in the early years of disadvantaged children's lives is one such policy."

Heckman's research shows that inequality in early childhood produces inequality in a person's adult ability, educational achievement, health, and success. The disadvantages that arise later in life because of a child's genetic background, lack of parental involvement, or social environment can be overturned through investing in early childhood education.

Investment in ECE for disadvantaged children from birth to five years reduces achievement gaps, reduces the need for special education, increases the likelihood of healthier lifestyles, lowers crime rates, and reduces overall social costs from dealing with the problems of the adults these disadvantaged children become. Heckman estimates that every dollar invested in ECE yields a 7–10 percent per year return, higher than most investments.

"We can invest early to close disparities . . . or we can pay to remediate disparities when they are harder and more expensive to close."

So using tax dollars to pay for ECE not only reduces inequality, it also increases efficiency, by saving more money for society than the costs of ECE.

Source: James Heckman, "The Economics of Inequality: The Value of Early Childhood Education," *American Educator,* Spring 2011, pp. 31-47.

What is the connection to government policy choices about rent controls, minimum wages, price-gouging laws, or health care? Glad you asked. *Should* the government implement rent controls to help the homeless? *Should* the government pass minimum wage laws to help the working poor? *Should* the government make "price gouging" illegal during a natural disaster? *Should* the government push a health-care system that emphasizes equity over efficiency (Canadian style), or one that emphasizes efficiency over equity (U.S. style)? All these policy choices involve trade-offs between efficiency and equity. Your answer to these questions, or any politician's answer, depends on the *relative value* or weight placed on efficiency versus equity.

Equal Outcomes or Equal Opportunity?

In choosing between efficiency and equity, it is important to be careful about what those words mean. Economists agree on the definition of an efficient market outcome. But there is far less agreement — among economists or citizens — on what *equity* means. The two most common definitions of equity emphasize equal outcomes or equal opportunities.

Equal Outcomes   When everyone ends up with the same result, that is an equal outcome. The outcomes can be children getting identical slices of birthday cake, individuals earning the same income, citizens each getting one vote, or everyone getting access to the same level of health-care services. The end result is the same for all.

Equal Opportunities   An alternative definition of equity emphasizes starting conditions instead of end results. A game — including the "game of life" — is equitable if everyone has equal opportunities at the start. The same rules apply to everyone, and no one has any unfair advantages. With equal opportunities, each individual can end up with a different-sized piece of cake, a different income, or different health-care services, based on her choices, effort, and luck. There will be winners and losers, but there is equity in the form of equal opportunities.

The Politics of Equity   Here is an example of how these definitions of efficiency and equity matter for policy choices. Politicians running for government jobs will compete for your vote by proposing policies that they hope you agree with.

A conservative politician on the right of the political spectrum might oppose minimum wage laws because she believes the efficiency of markets is most important for generating the economic prosperity that will ultimately help people who are poor. She also might believe that markets are already equitable because they provide everyone with *equal opportunities*. She fully expects that each person's income and accomplishments in life will differ with differences in talents, initiative, and luck.

A left-leaning politician might favour minimum wage laws because he believes equity is more important than efficiency. He would accept some inefficiency and less economic prosperity for all if it improves the *equality of income*s. He does not believe that poor children have the same opportunities as rich children.

You cannot decide that one politician is wrong and the other right just on the basis of facts. You can decide which politician's *values* best match your own values.

What Economics Can and Cannot Do for You

Economic thinking alone won't allow you to judge government policy choices. You must choose which policies to support based on your own values and opinions. But once you decide on a particular policy choice or "end" you support, economic thinking is all about finding the most effective and efficient means to that end.

Economists excel (if I may say so) at evaluating empirical, or positive, claims. Economic thinking allows you to find right and wrong answers to questions like "Will a low fixed gasoline price create shortages and line-ups at the pumps?" We can observe what actually happened in Canada in 1974 when governments fixed prices. Or take the law of demand — the claim that a rise in price decreases quantity demanded. That is an empirical claim, and we can discover whether it is true or false by looking at factual evidence of prices and quantities.

Smart Government Policy Choices What is the most efficient policy for helping the homeless find housing? That is actually a positive, or empirical, question. Once you or the government have decided that equity is an important "end," economic thinking can help in picking the policy "means" that provides the most bang for the buck or that involves the least amount of waste.

On the other hand, "Should the government develop policies to help the homeless?" is a normative question involving value judgments. Normative questions and claims often use the word *should*. Watch for it to help distinguish positive from normative claims.

Economic thinking will help you intelligently evaluate claims you hear from politicians or administrators or bosses. Most politicians make claims about what they will do if elected, but leave out the opportunity costs of their plans. Every plan, every policy, every choice has an opportunity cost. Figure out what that is before passing judgment. And when a politician's policy claim does make clear the opportunity cost or sacrifice (often, tax increases are the opportunity cost of government spending programs), look to see if there is a better, more efficient way to achieve the same end.

Governments, when they function well, should be making smart choices. Government policy objectives, or ends, may be efficient markets, affordable housing, equitable incomes, environmental sustainability, or minimal taxes. Citizens' opinions will differ reasonably about those normative, value-based ends that are properly set for a society by democratically elected politicians. Those are not the smart choices. Once an end is chosen, economic thinking can help with the smart choices — finding the most efficient and effective means to the end. Being an informed, economically literate citizen will help you help governments make smart policy choices.

NOTE
Once you pick a political position or social goal to support based on your values, economic thinking helps identify the smartest choice of action to efficiently achieve that goal. Always weigh benefits against opportunity costs.

Refresh 6.5

1. Explain the difference between a positive statement and a normative statement. Give an example of each.

2. Pick a political party in Canada. Based on the policy statements on the party's website, how would you describe its positions on issues of efficiency versus equity?

3. Arguments often end with someone saying, "Everyone is entitled to an opinion." Does that mean that all opinions are equally valid? (The positive/normative distinction can help answer this question.)

MyEconLab

For answers to these Refresh Questions, visit MyEconLab.

Study Guide

6.1 Do Prices or Quantities Adjust?
Unintended Consequences of Government Policies

When government fixes prices, the smart choices of consumers and businesses are not coordinated. Quantities adjust to whichever is less — quantity supplied or quantity demanded.

- When price is fixed below market-clearing:
  - shortages develop (quantity demanded greater than quantity supplied) and consumers are frustrated.
  - quantity sold = quantity supplied only.

- When price is fixed above market-clearing:
  - surpluses develop (quantity supplied greater than quantity demanded) and businesses are frustrated.
  - quantity sold = quantity demanded only.

- When prices are fixed, quantities adjust to whichever is *less* — quantity supplied or quantity demanded.

- Governments can fix prices, but can't force businesses (or consumers) to produce (or buy) at the fixed price.
  - Businesses can reduce output or move resources elsewhere.
  - Consumers can reduce purchases or buy something else (there are always substitutes).

6.2 Do Rent Controls Help the Homeless?
Price Ceilings

Rent controls fix rents below market-clearing levels, and quantity adjustment takes the unintended form of apartment shortages.

- **Rent controls:** example of **price ceiling** — maximum price set by government, making it illegal to charge higher price.

- Rent controls sometimes justified by *Robin Hood principle* — take from the rich (landlords) and give to the poor (tenants).

- Rent controls have unintended and undesirable consequences:
  - create housing shortages, giving landlords the upper hand over tenants.
  - subsidize well-off tenants willing and able to pay market-clearing rents.
  - inefficiency, reducing total surplus below market-clearing amounts.

- Alternative policies to help the homeless that do not sacrifice market flexibility are
  - government subsidies to help those who are poor pay rent.
  - government-supplied housing.

- All policies have opportunity costs.

6.3 Do Minimum Wages Help the Working Poor?
Price Floors

Minimum wage laws fix wages above market-clearing levels, and quantity adjustment takes the unintended form of unemployment.

- **Minimum wage laws:** example of **price floor** — minimum price set by government, making it illegal to pay a lower price.
  - **Living wage** — estimated at $20 per hour, enough to allow an individual in a Canadian city to live above the poverty line.

- Minimum wage laws create unintended consequences.
  - When governments set minimum wages above the market-clearing wage, the quantity of labour supplied by households will be greater than the quantity of labour demanded by businesses, creating unemployment.
  - Inefficiency, reducing total surplus.

- Quantity of unemployment created by raising minimum wage depends on elasticity of business demand for unskilled labour.
  - When demand for unskilled labour is inelastic and businesses have few substitutes, rise in minimum wage produces *small* response in decreased quantity demanded.
  - When demand for unskilled labour is elastic and businesses can easily substitute machines for people, rise in minimum wage produces *large* response in decreased quantity demanded.
  - Minimum wages help the working poor if gains from workers who remain employed and whose incomes go up are greater than losses of incomes of workers who lose their jobs.
- Alternative policies to help the working poor that do not sacrifice market flexibility are:
  - training programs to help unskilled workers get higher-paying jobs.
  - wage supplements.
- All policies have opportunity costs.

6.4 When Markets Work Well, Are They Fair? Trade-Offs between Efficiency and Equity

Well-functioning markets are efficient, but not always equitable. Government may smartly choose policies that create more equitable outcomes, even though the trade-off is less efficiency.

- To say that well-functioning markets produce the products and services we value most means outputs go to those most willing and able to pay.
  - Efficient market outcomes may not be fair or equitable.
  - *Efficient market outcome* — coordinates smart choices of businesses and consumers so outputs are produced at lowest cost (prices just cover all opportunity costs of production), and consumers buy products and services providing the most bang per buck (marginal benefit greater than price).
- Consumers who do not buy at equilibrium, market-clearing prices are:
  - unwilling because marginal benefit is less than price (even though could afford to buy), and/or
  - unable to afford to buy, even though they are willing (marginal benefit is greater than price).

- Allowing markets to operate without government interaction is a choice with an opportunity cost — unfairness or inequality. There is a trade-off between efficiency and equity. In comparing U.S. market-driven health care with Canadian universal, government-run health care:
  - Canadian-style government outcome is more equitable, but at the cost of being less efficient.
  - U.S.-style private market outcome may be efficient, but at the cost of being less equitable.
  - Health-care waiting lists are a quantity adjustment when prices . . . are fixed too low.

6.5 Choosing between Efficiency and Equity: What Economics Can and Cannot Do for You

Once you choose to support a political position or social goal based on your values, positive economic thinking helps identify the smartest choices to efficiently achieve that goal.

- *Positive* (or empirical) *statements* — about what is.
  - Can be evaluated as true or false by checking the facts.
- *Normative statements* — about what you believe *should* be; involve value judgments.
  - Cannot be evaluated as true or false by checking the facts.
- Two definitions of equity:
  - Equal outcomes — at the end, everyone gets the same amount.
  - Equal opportunities — at the start, everyone has the same opportunities, but the outcomes can be different.
- For any policy choice, always weigh benefits against opportunity costs.

TRUE/FALSE

Circle the correct answer. Solutions to these questions are available at the end of the book and on MyEconLab. You can also visit the MyEconLab Study Plan to access additional questions that will help you master the concepts covered in this chapter.

6.1 Unintended Consequences of Government Policies

1. Fifty-six percent of young workers in Canada live at home with their parents. More young adults are remaining home or are "doubling up" in apartments. Doubling up is a quantity adjustment by tenants in the rental house market. T F

6.2 Price Ceilings

2. The following statement — with which 93 percent of economists from the American Economic Association were in agreement — is a positive statement. T F

A ceiling on rents reduces the quality and quantity of housing.

3. The following statement by the Sheldon Chumir Foundation for Ethics in Leadership is a positive statement. T F

Calgary's homeless population grew 740 percent between 1994 and 2006.

4. The following statement by the Manhattan Institute is a positive statement. T F

Examining investment in previously rent-controlled buildings, we find that the removal of rent controls increased the construction of new units and the renovation and repair of existing ones by approximately 20 percent over what would have been the case in the absence of decontrol.

5. Rent ceilings are usually applied to only part of the market. Tenants in the controlled market hold on to their apartments, forcing everyone else to shop in the more expensive uncontrolled market. In New York, 88 percent of tenants living in rent-controlled apartments have not moved in more than 25 years. According to demand and supply analysis, rental prices in the uncontrolled market will be lower as a result of a rent ceiling in the controlled market. T F

6.3 Price Floors

6. The following statement by the Organisation for Economic Co-operation and Development (OECD) is a positive statement. T F

A moderate minimum wage is generally not a problem.

7. The following statement by the Arthurs Commission on Canadian federal labour standards is a positive statement. T F

The government should accept the principle that no Canadian worker should work full time for a year and still live in poverty.

8. The following statement — with which 46 percent of economists from the American Economic Association were in agreement (27 percent disagreed) — is a positive statement. T F

A minimum wage increases unemployment among young and unskilled workers.

9. There is evidence that minimum wage laws significantly increase teen unemployment, slightly increase young adults' unemployment, and have no impact on employment for workers aged 25 or older. This suggests that elasticity of demand for labour is highest for workers aged 25 or older. T F

10. Canadian researchers found that the benefits of minimum wages go primarily to individuals in families that are less well off than the average. This suggests a minimum wage would reduce wage inequality and increase equity. T F

11. Suppose you just graduated and your provincial government has raised its minimum wage from $11 to $13. Assuming you were not working before, this would increase your incentive to look for work. However, you may be less likely to find work because businesses are now more likely to cut back on hiring workers in this wage range. T F

6.4 Trade-Offs between Efficiency and Equity

12. The Canadian Medical Association found 40 percent of Canadians grade their health-care system as a "C" or worse, partly due to unhappiness with long waiting times. Therefore, longer waiting times are a trade-off that Canadians make in order to have a more *efficient* health-care system. T F

13. The following statement by The Center for American Progress is a positive statement.　　T　F

Americans who were poor as children — and there are now 37 million of them — are much more likely than other citizens to commit crimes, to need more health care, and to be less productive in the workforce.

6.5　What Economics Can and Cannot Do for You

14. The following statement by many student associations across Canada is a positive statement.　　T　**F**

Tuition fees should be reduced.

15. Canada's progressive income tax system, which requires those who earn more to pay a higher percentage of their income to taxes, is based on a principle of equity.　　T　F

MULTIPLE CHOICE

Circle the best answer. Solutions to these questions are available at the end of the book and on MyEconLab. You can also visit the MyEconLab Study Plan to access similar questions that will help you master the concepts covered in this chapter.

6.1　Unintended Consequences of Government Policies

1. In 1973, oil price controls led to long gas lines and rationing at the pumps. The price controls were a
　a)　price ceiling, set above the market-clearing price.
　b)　price ceiling, set below the market-clearing price.
　c)　price floor, set above the market-clearing price.
　d)　price floor, set below the market-clearing price.

2. If the government set gas prices above the market-clearing price,
　a)　this would be a price floor.
　b)　gasoline suppliers would respond to the lower-than-market-clearing price by decreasing quantity supplied.
　c)　gasoline consumers would respond to the lower-than-market-clearing price by increasing quantity demanded.
　d)　this would result in long line-ups at the pumps.

3. Most of the employment impact of minimum wages does not come from businesses terminating workers whose wages now rise. Rather, the impact is businesses hiring fewer low-wage workers in the future. This response, or quantity adjustment, occurs because when wages rise, businesses
　a)　increase supply.
　b)　decrease quantity supplied.
　c)　go out of business.
　d)　search for cheaper input substitutes.

6.2　Price Ceilings

4. Rent ceilings imposed by governments
　a)　keep rental prices below the market-clearing price.
　b)　keep rental prices above the market-clearing price.
　c)　keep rental prices equal to the market-clearing price.
　d)　increase the quantity of rental housing.

5. Rent ceilings will
　a)　reduce the quantity of private rental construction.
　b)　reduce the quantity of existing rental units.
　c)　lower the quality of existing rental units.
　d)　all of the above.

6. After rent controls were imposed, the supply of apartments in Winnipeg declined between 1998 and 2005 from 54 924 units to 53 046. Which of the following effects on Winnipeg's rental housing market are consistent with economic thinking?
　a)　No affordable units were added by the private sector for years, and many existing units were withdrawn from the market.
　b)　Subsidized public housing programs have been the only source of new units in the low-to-medium price range.
　c)　Maintenance expenses fell, decreasing the quality of rental housing.
　d)　All of the above.

7. According to the Frontier Centre for Public Policy, "The most recent information on apartment rents and vacancy rates on the Prairies provides sufficient evidence that the best friend of tenants is the free market: Saskatchewan, with no controls, enjoys lower rents and substantially more supply. It is time to learn from Saskatchewan and end rent control in Manitoba." If rent controls were removed, which of the following would occur?
　a)　Prices would fall.
　b)　Shortages would increase.
　c)　Supply would increase.
　d)　All of the above.

8. In Canada, some provinces relaxed rent controls by permitting landlords to charge market rents *when the original occupants move out*. This provides
   a) tenants with an incentive to stay in their apartments as long as possible.
   b) landlords with an incentive to let the quality of existing apartments deteriorate.
   c) governments with an incentive to pass strong anti-eviction laws so that landlords cannot remove current tenants without justified cause.
   d) all of the above.

9. Ontario built about 27 000 apartment units per year in the six years before rent ceilings were introduced in 1974, and that dropped to around 4200 units per year after rent ceilings were introduced. Before rent ceilings were introduced in Ontario, the provincial government helped subsidize 27 percent of all rental units; by the early 1990s, it was more than 75 percent. This demonstrates that rent ceilings
   a) create shortages of housing.
   b) are costly for governments.
   c) reduce incentives for private-sector investment.
   d) do all of the above.

6.3 Price Floors

10. A price floor set below the equilibrium price results in
    a) excess supply.
    b) excess demand.
    c) the equilibrium price.
    d) an increase in supply.

11. Raising the minimum wage may have limited impact on reducing overall poverty rates because
    a) many minimum-wage workers are young people or earners who live in families that do not fall below the poverty line.
    b) many individuals who are in poverty are not working.
    c) raising the minimum wage is still not enough to help workers working part-year or part-time out of poverty.
    d) all of the above.

6.4 Trade-Offs between Efficiency and Equity

12. In markets without any government interaction, the question of who gets an apartment is decided by who is
    a) most willing to pay.
    b) most able to pay.
    c) most willing and able to pay.
    d) most willing and able to dance.

13. Which is a positive (empirical) statement?
    a) People who work for minimum wage should be able to feed their families.
    b) The minimum wage level should meet standards where, in a just society, individuals working full time are not in poverty.
    c) Minimum wage increases can significantly improve the lives of low-income workers and their families, without the adverse effects that critics claim.
    d) All of the above.

6.5 What Economics Can and Cannot Do for You

14. Which statement is *not* normative?
    a) Something should be done about the homeless.
    b) Rent ceilings would reduce the number of homeless people.
    c) Rent ceilings should be introduced to reduce the number of homeless people.
    d) All of the above.

15. In 1997, Canadian family incomes near the top of the income distribution were four times higher than family incomes near the bottom of the distribution. In the United States, the ratio is about five to one, while in Sweden and Finland the ratio is about three to one. The country with the most unequal distribution of income is
    a) Canada.
    b) the United States.
    c) Sweden.
    d) Finland.

7 Finding the Bottom Line

Opportunity Costs, Economic Profits and Losses, and the Miracle of Markets

HAVE YOU EVER HAD a teacher or a boss who acted like a little

dictator? Have you ever fantasized about life without a boss and opening your own business? ("Yes" to the first question often leads to "yes" to the second question.)

Once school and part-time jobs are distant memories, your success in life will depend largely on how you spend your time and your money. Business success has a clear and simple measure — the bottom line, or the profits that remain once you subtract all costs from your revenues.

But finding the bottom line and making smart business choices are not as simple as hiring an accountant to crunch the numbers. It turns out that economists have something valuable to add to the accountant's calculation of profits. Our old friend "opportunity cost" is the hidden key to smart choices about spending your time and money, whether you are running your own business, working for others, or even investing your lottery winnings — the other (fantasy) way to avoid having a boss.

In this chapter, we will revisit Keys 1 and 3 of the Three Keys to Smart Choices. Key 1 says "Choose only when additional benefits are greater than additional opportunity costs." Here you will see the importance of adding *implicit (hidden) costs* in Key 3: "Be sure to count *all* additional benefits and costs, including *implicit costs* and externalities." Key 3 not only will help you make smart business choices, but also will expose the importance of economic profits in directing markets to produce the products and services we value most.

What Accountants Miss: Accounting Profits and Hidden Opportunity Costs

Describe accounting profits, and explain how they miss hidden opportunity costs.

After suffering too many bosses, Wahid listens to the entrepreneurial voice inside his head and decides to set up his own web design business. He has been saving for a while, and a small inheritance from his grandfather brings his total ($40 000) high enough to get started. Trying to make smart choices, he develops a business plan for Wahid's Web Wonders (www.www.com). Let's see what the plan looks like to an accountant.

Obvious Costs and Accounting Profits

The details of Wahid's business plan for his first year appear in Figure 7.1. With the contacts he has made from part-time web design jobs, he *expects* (this word will be important later on) that he can generate $60 000 in revenues in his first year.

Figure 7.1 **Accountant's One-Year Business Plan for Wahid's Web Wonders**

Total Expected Revenues		**$60 000**
Obvious Costs	Depreciation	$ 5 000
	Rent	$14 000
	Web Hosting	$ 3 000
	Phone	$ 1 000
	Advertising	$ 2 000
Total Obvious Costs		**$25 000**
Accounting Profits		**$35 000**

depreciation decrease in the value of equipment over time because of wear and tear and because it becomes obsolete

Depreciation   To start his business, Wahid has to buy computer hardware and software that costs $20 000. He has to pay for that equipment all at once, which takes $20 000 of his $40 000 in savings. The equipment will last four years before it wears out. **Depreciation** is the decrease in value of equipment over time because of wear and tear and because it becomes obsolete.

When equipment lasts many years, Canada Revenue Agency (Canada's tax department) does not allow accountants to treat it all as a cost in the first year. Businesses must spread the cost out over the lifetime of long-lasting equipment. If the equipment lasts four years, then the allowable depreciation cost is $5000 per year ($20 000 divided by four years).

obvious costs (explicit costs) costs a business pays directly

Obvious Costs   Wahid found an office to rent in the design district for $14 000 per year and has a web hosting package for $3000 per year. He figures yearly phone expenses will be $1000 and advertising will cost $2000. These total costs (not counting depreciation) are $20 000 per year, which takes the rest of Wahid's savings. These are "**obvious costs**" in the sense they are plain to see. Economists also call these obvious costs **explicit costs**. Accountants include depreciation as part of obvious costs, so adding the $5000 depreciation cost Wahid is allowed to count, obvious costs for Wahid's first year total $25 000.

Accounting Profits   To calculate profits, accountants subtract obvious costs from revenues:

> **Accounting Profits** = Revenues − Obvious Costs (including depreciation)

So, for Wahid,

> Accounting Profits = $ 60 000   − $ 25 000 = $ 35 000

If things go according to plan, Wahid will end the first year with $35 000 in his pocket. Not bad for a first year in business. Or is it?

Your Time's Opportunity Cost

Accountants do not count the hidden opportunity costs of what the business owner could earn elsewhere with the time and money invested in the business. Economists call these hidden opportunity costs **implicit costs**.

The obvious, or out-of-pocket, cost of Wahid's time in his new business is zero — he is working for himself and not paying himself money. But in working for himself, he is giving up the best alternative use of his time. If the best job he could have (working for a boss) pays $38 000 per year, that is the hidden opportunity cost, or implicit cost, of Wahid's time invested in his own business.

Your Money's Opportunity Cost

If Wahid had borrowed money to start up the business, the interest he would have to pay to the bank would be an obvious cost to subtract from his revenues. But the $40 000 Wahid invests in his business has no obvious cost. Since he did not have to borrow the money, the obvious cost of borrowing is zero — he is loaning the money to himself.

IMPLICIT
COSTS &
EXTERNALITIES

Nonetheless, by investing his money in his business, he is giving up the best alternative use of the money. Wahid could have put the money in the bank and earned interest for a year, or invested it elsewhere. The interest, or return on investing elsewhere, that Wahid gives up is the hidden opportunity cost — the implicit cost — of using his own money. He cannot use the same money in two different places at the same time.

Calculating the precise opportunity cost of investing your own money is tricky because returns from business investing are *risky,* while returns from the bank are *guaranteed*. Let me explain this unequal comparison of returns.

Consider the numbers in the following choice. If you (or Wahid) invest $40 000 in a bank GIC (guaranteed investment certificate) that pays 5-percent interest, at the end of the year you get your $40 000 back and a guaranteed 5-percent return of $2000 ($40 000 × 0.05 = $2000) for a total of $42 000. You could instead invest $40 000 in your own business (or any other business), with the *expected* return also of 5 percent ($2000) if things go according to plan. But, if there is only an 80-percent chance that things will go well, which alternative would you choose? You probably choose the safe 5-percent return from the bank instead of the risky 5-percent return from the business.

Big gamblers are *risk-loving* and don't require much risk compensation when facing the uncertainty of a card game or a slot machine. Reluctant gamblers are *risk-averse* and want a high probability of winning before risking their money. Which kind of gambler are the casinos in Las Vegas looking for as customers? How big a gambler are you?

NOTE

Wahid's hidden opportunity cost (implicit cost) of investing his own $40 000 in his risky business is a 20 percent expected return, or $8000 — the guaranteed bank return of 5 percent plus an extra premium of 15 percent to compensate for risk.

Risky Business   A more important question for calculating your money's opportunity cost is: What *expected* return would it take for you to go for the risky business investment? You need to *expect more* than the safe 5 percent you will get from the bank in order to compensate for the risk of the business investment. Your personal risk compensation depends on your personality and your assessment of just how risky the investment is.

If you are a gambler at heart, economists call you *risk-loving*. You might not require much risk compensation to go for the uncertain investment as long as the returns are just a bit higher than the guaranteed return. (Did you ever think economists would have a technical term that includes the word love?) If you are more cautious, economists call you *risk-averse*. It would take a very high risk compensation to get you to go for the uncertain investment over the guaranteed bank investment.

Let's say you (and Wahid) believe an *extra, expected* 15-percent return would just compensate for the risk. You want an extra 15% risk premium, above the guaranteed 5%, to compensate for risk. Then you and Wahid would be equally pleased with the two paths, one with a *guaranteed* 5-percent return, the other with an *expected* 20-percent return (the same 5 percent from the bank plus 15 percent more to compensate for the risk of the uncertain return).

In investing his own money, Wahid would be equally pleased with a *guaranteed* 5-percent return of $2000 on his initial investment of $40 000, or an *expected* 20-percent return of $8000. He would give up the guaranteed $2000 to try for an *expected* $8000 return, and he would give up the expected $8000 return in exchange for the guaranteed $2000. Either option can measure the hidden opportunity cost of investing his $40 000.

Since Wahid's business plan *expects* (I told you this word would be important) revenues of $60 000 in the first year, the return is not guaranteed. So the number to use for the hidden opportunity cost of using and risking his own money is not the bank return of 5 percent; it is the 20-percent return that adds a premium of 15 percent for risk compensation. The total *expected* return needs to be $8000 on his $40 000 risky investment ($40 000 × 0.20 = $8000).

Wahid's risk premium of 15 percent is personal to him. A different investor who is risk-loving would have a smaller risk premium. A more risk-averse investor would have a larger risk premium.

In section 7.2, let's look at Wahid's "profits" once we consider these hidden opportunity costs of his time and money — the implicit costs of investing his time and money.

◄ To get the best mortgage for her income and views on risk, this woman is doing her homework. Her time researching mortgage options and weighing them against her needs and personality will pay huge dividends.

Mark Baigent/Alamy

Economics *Out There*

Which Mortgage Is Right for You?

If you own a home, should you pick a variable-rate mortgage or a fixed-rate mortgage? The answer has much to do with your attitude toward risk.

- The interest rate on a variable-rate mortgage varies as market interest rates change. The interest rate on a fixed-rate mortgage is fixed for the entire term.

- Historical data show that a variable-rate mortgage is cheaper — you almost always pay less interest over the full term of your mortgage if you go with a variable rate. But there is a

risk involved as rates go up and down. If rates go down, you benefit and pay less, if rates go up, you lose and pay more. Your total interest cost is uncertain — it varies as rates vary.

- Financial advisers suggest a variable-rate mortgage *if* your personality or wealth can handle the uncertainty and risk. But if the risk will keep you awake at night, they advise you to go for a fixed rate. You will pay for that certainty, but you get peace of mind.

- People who are risk-averse need to be paid more to take risk — or will pay more to avoid risk — than risk-loving individuals.

Refresh 7.1

1. Your sister is thinking about investing in a new business venture. Define the concept of implicit costs (hidden opportunity costs) for her and explain to her why it is important to understand these costs before she invests.

2. The current bank interest rate is 5 percent. You borrow $10 000 from the bank as well as invest $20 000 of your own money in a new business for a year. Detail the obvious costs and the implicit costs (hidden opportunity costs) for both amounts of money you are investing.

3. You are deciding whether to safely invest your lottery winnings in the bank or to risk investing them in a friend's start-up business. What factors, including your own attitude toward risk, would lead you to choose to invest in your friend's business rather than take the safe path with the bank?

MyEconLab

For answers to these Refresh Questions, visit MyEconLab.

7.2 What Economists Find: Normal Profits and Economic Profits

Define normal profits and economic profits, and explain their differences.

Accountants, economists, and ordinary people all think of profits as revenues minus costs. Profits are what's left over when all costs have been paid. And if costs are greater than revenues, there's a loss. But a more precise definition of profits and losses depends on what gets included in costs. And a precise definition is important for making smart business decisions.

Recall the accountant's definition of profits:

Accounting Profits = Revenues − Obvious Costs (including depreciation)

Economists have two more-precise definitions: normal profits and economic profits.

Normal Profits

normal profits
- compensation for business owner's time and money
- sum of hidden opportunity costs (implicit costs)
- what business owner must earn to do as well as best alternative use of time and money
- average profits in other industries

Normal profits are compensation for the use of a business owner's time and money, the sum of the hidden opportunity costs. Normal profits are what a business owner must earn to do as well as he could have done in the best alternative uses of his time and money. In other words, normal profits are the average profits in other industries.

The *time component* of normal profits is the value of the best alternative use of the owner's time. For Wahid, that is the $38 000 he could have earned by using his time working for another company. The *money component* of normal profits is the best alternative return on investment, including risk compensation. For Wahid, that is the $8000 he *expects* on his $40 000 investment. So, normal profits for the first year of Wahid's Web Wonders business are $46 000 ($38 000 + $8000).

Economic Profits

The economist's definition of profits is "revenues minus *all opportunity costs*." Like accountants, economists subtract all obvious costs from revenues. These out-of-pocket, explicit costs are also opportunity costs. The best alternative use of the $25 000 Wahid spends on the obvious things like rent, phone expenses, and so on is still $25 000 worth of different business-related items he could have bought instead.

The key difference between economists and accountants is that economists also subtract hidden opportunity costs from revenues:

economic profits revenues minus all opportunity costs (obvious costs plus hidden opportunity costs)

Economic Profits = Revenues − All Opportunity Costs

= Revenues − (Obvious Costs + Hidden Opportunity Costs)

Since the sum of hidden opportunity costs is defined as normal profits, the definition of economic profits can also be written as

Economic Profits = Revenues − (Obvious Costs + Normal Profits)

With all these definitions and equations, you are no doubt thinking, "Why is he bothering with these tiny details? Are these details really all that important?" No one should be subjected to tiny details *unless those details are important for understanding*. Let me show you why the definition of economic profits matters for making smart business choices.

Figure 7.2 revisits Wahid's business plan, but as it would look to an economist.

Figure 7.2   Economist's One-Year Business Plan for Wahid

Total Expected Revenues			$60 000
Obvious Costs	Depreciation	$ 5 000	
	Rent	$14 000	
	Web Hosting	$ 3 000	
	Phone	$ 1 000	
	Advertising	$ 2 000	
Total Obvious Costs			$25 000
Accounting Profits			$35 000
Hidden Opportunity Costs	Wahid's Time	$38 000	
	Wahid's Money	$ 8 000	
Total Hidden Costs			$46 000
Economic Profits			($11 000)*

*On business plans and balance sheets, losses are indicated with parentheses:
($11 000) is an eleven thousand dollar loss.

According to the economist's calculation, when you subtract all of Wahid's opportunity costs ($25 000 in obvious costs and $46 000 in hidden opportunity costs) from his expected revenues ($60 000), Wahid is suffering **economic losses** of $11 000! What this means is that Wahid is *not* covering all of his opportunity costs.

economic losses negative economic profits

What Economists Find   Wahid's accounting profits are $35 000. But if, instead of working and investing in his business, he had worked elsewhere and invested his money either in the bank or in an investment equally as risky as his business, he would have earned between $40 000 (guaranteed) and $46 000 (expected). The amount of $35 000 in accounting profits might sound attractive, but it is not as good as Wahid's best alternative uses of his time and money. With these numbers, *Wahid has not made a smart choice* (other than avoiding having a boss). He is worse off financially after a year of running his business than he would have been working and investing his money elsewhere.

NOTE
If revenues are less than all opportunity costs, a business owner has not made a smart decision. He would be better off if he had invested in alternative uses of his time and money. With economic losses, a business owner earns less than normal profits, less than average profits in other industries.

Refresh 7.2

1. If your business earns accounting profits of $50 000 and economic profits of $20 000, what are your hidden opportunity costs?

2. You earn a good salary, but you hate your boss. You develop a plan to start your own business that projects economic profits of $5000 at the end of the first year. But just as you are about to go ahead with your new business, you are offered a job for $15 000 *more* than you were earning before. How does that change your projected economic profits? Would it change your decision to start your new business? Why or why not?

3. Do you think it correct to use economic profits as opposed to accounting profits when judging the success or failure of a business? Explain your reasons.

MyEconLab

For answers to these Refresh Questions, visit MyEconLab.

7.3

Red Light, Green Light: How Economic Profits Direct the Invisible Hand

Explain how economic profits signal smart business decisions and coordinate consumer and business choices.

Economic profits are the most important signal — the key bottom line — for judging smart business decisions. Accounting profits provide some useful information, but not enough. To illustrate, let's look at three alternative end-of-year scenarios for Wahid. While his business plan was based on *expected* revenues, what happens if his *actual* revenues turn out to be $60 000, $71 000, or $80 000? In each of the three scenarios, his obvious costs and hidden opportunity costs (normal profits) are the same as before (see Figure 7.2).

In each of the three scenarios in Figure 7.3, Wahid has positive accounting profits, seeming to indicate that he is doing well. But the economic profit calculations tell a different story.

Figure 7.3 Alternative Profit Scenarios for Wahid's Web Wonders

Scenario	One	Two	Three
Revenues	$ 60 000	$ 71 000	$ 80 000
Total Obvious Costs	$ 25 000	$ 25 000	$ 25 000
Total Hidden Opportunity Costs	$ 46 000	$ 46 000	$ 46 000
Accounting Profits	$ 35 000	$ 46 000	$ 55 000
Economic Profits	($ 11 000)	$ 0	$ 9 000

In scenario one, with revenues of $60 000, Wahid's economic profits are negative — economic losses of $11 000. Wahid is kicking himself because he is worse off than if he had chosen the best alternative uses of his time and money — he is not even earning normal profits. His profits are less than average profits in other industries.

In scenario two, with revenues of $71 000, Wahid's economic profits are zero. That doesn't sound good, but it means that Wahid's revenues are just covering all of his opportunity costs of production (obvious costs and hidden opportunity costs). Wahid will be content. He did as well as he could have done with the best alternative uses of his time and money (and he was his own boss!). He is not kicking himself.

In scenario three, with revenues of $80 000, Wahid's economic profits are positive, $9000 *above normal profits*. Wahid is one happy web designer. Positive economic profits indicate he is doing better than the best alternative uses of his time and money. His profits are greater than average profits in other industries. Wahid has made a smart choice for his first year.

Wahid's smart choice combines Keys 1 and 3 of the Three Keys to Smart Choices. Key 1 says, "Choose only when additional benefits are greater than additional *opportunity costs*." Key 3 says, "Be sure to count *all* additional benefits and costs, including *implicit costs* and externalities." "Additional benefits" are Wahid's revenues. His business's additional opportunity costs include obvious costs as well as Key 3's implicit costs, or hidden opportunity costs. (Externalities, which are not important here, are discussed in Chapter 11.)

The combination of Keys for business decisions can be written as "Choose only when revenues are greater than all opportunity costs," or, even more simply,

ADDITIONAL BENEFITS VS. OPPORTUNITY COSTS

IMPLICIT COSTS & EXTERNALITIES

Choose only when economic profits are positive.

Economic Profits Signal the Way

More than just a signal for smart business decisions, economic profits create the incentive for businesses to supply the products and services that consumers demand.

In Chapter 4, we saw how markets coordinate the smart choices of consumers and businesses. Markets form prices — through the interaction of demand and supply — which provide signals and incentives that affect everyone's smart choices. When there are imbalances between demand and supply, prices adjust to coordinate smart choices.

In this chapter, we add economic profits to the description of the equilibrium price. For a business, changing prices affect both revenues (prices of products or services sold) and costs (prices of inputs bought). While well-run businesses try to keep track of all of that changing information, if they just focus on the bottom line — on pursuing economic profits — they produce the products and services consumers want.

Just like traffic signals keep drivers moving smoothly to their different destinations quickly and safely, economic profits direct businesses to produce what consumers want. To see this more clearly, let's examine Wahid's three alternative scenarios for economic profits shown in Figure 7.3.

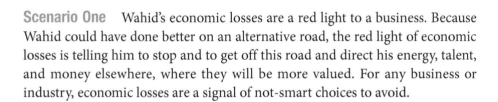

Scenario One   Wahid's economic losses are a red light to a business. Because Wahid could have done better on an alternative road, the red light of economic losses is telling him to stop and to get off this road and direct his energy, talent, and money elsewhere, where they will be more valued. For any business or industry, economic losses are a signal of not-smart choices to avoid.

Scenario Two   With zero economic profits, Wahid is just covering all of his opportunity costs, including earning normal profits. This is a yellow light — proceed with caution. Wahid has no incentive to get off the road, and no incentive to move to a different road. His profits are the same as average profits on other roads, in other industries. Yellow is an "equilibrium" signal — no reason to change. Economists call this a business's **breakeven point**.

breakeven point   business just earning normal profits — no economic profits, no economic losses

NOTE
Economic profits are green lights
signalling smart business decisions —
stay or get on that road.

Scenario Three

Scenario Three Wahid's economic profits are *over and above* normal profits — *over and above* the best alternative uses of his time and money. This is a green light. It says Wahid made a smart choice and should continue on this road, investing more time and money in expanding his business. When outsiders see economic profits in a particular line of business, they shift their time and money out of industries that are suffering economic losses or just breaking even, and into green-light industries.

Market Equilibrium

Economic profits add another time dimension to the market price adjustments discussed in Chapter 4.

Short-Run Market Equilibrium

short-run market equilibrium
quantity demanded equals quantity
supplied, but economic losses or
profits lead to changes in supply

Short-Run Market Equilibrium If there are mismatches between quantity demanded and quantity supplied in a market, the resulting shortages or surpluses create pressure for prices to rise or fall. When prices finally adjust to the market-clearing price, quantity demanded equals quantity supplied.

Economists use the term **short-run market equilibrium** to describe a market where quantity demanded equals quantity supplied (section 4.3). But what about economic profits? In Chapter 4, before discussing economic profits, we could not know if there were economic losses, economic profits, or zero economic profits at the short-run market equilibrium price.

The short-run market equilibrium price in Chapter 4 sits still, but only if economic profits are zero. Economic losses or economic profits signal additional adjustments in supply. With more time to adjust, business owners will follow the signals of economic losses and profits to move their abilities and money into different industries.

Economic Losses and Exit

Economic Losses and Exit When there are economic losses, prices are not covering all of the business's opportunity costs of production. Consumers don't value the product or service enough to pay the price that covers all business costs, including hidden opportunity costs, or normal profits. Smart businesses get off that road, leave the industry, and move their time, money, and inputs elsewhere — to a promise of economic profits.

Figure 7.4a tells the story of economic losses and exit. The original demand and supply curves are D_0 and S_0. The short-run market equilibrium is at price P_S (the subscript S stands for *short-run*) and quantity Q_S. But at price P_S and quantity Q_S, businesses are suffering economic losses. (The losses do not appear directly on the graph, they are a result of the combination of the price P_S, quantity Q_S, and costs.)

When businesses exit the industry, supply decreases (Chapter 3). The supply curve shifts leftward toward S_1, which pushes prices up. The decrease in supply moves the market price up along the unchanged demand curve D_0. Businesses keep exiting, supply keeps decreasing, prices keep rising, and losses keep decreasing, until the price rises to P_L (the subscript L stands for *long-run*) and the equilibrium quantity falls to Q_L.

The yellow horizontal line at P_L represents the price at which economic profits are zero. At price P_L and quantity Q_L, revenues just cover all opportunity costs of production (including normal profits), and economic profits are zero.

Long-Run Market Equilibrium   When businesses are breaking even, and economic profits are zero, there is no strong incentive for any change. Businesses are doing as well as they could elsewhere. Economists describe an industry where businesses have zero economic profits as being in **long-run market equilibrium**. Business owners in this industry are not jumping for joy, but they are also not jumping out of windows because of financial ruin. They are not kicking themselves.

A long-run market equilibrium exists when all of the forces of demand and supply are in balance *and economic profits are zero*. The difference between short-run and long-run market equilibrium is the additional time it takes for supply changes to adjust economic profits to zero.

In long-run market equilibrium, the price consumers are willing to pay just covers businesses' opportunity costs of production, including normal profits. Businesses are supplying the quantity of products or services that consumers are willing and able to buy at that price.

long-run market equilibrium
quantity demanded equals quantity supplied, economic profits are zero, no tendency for change

NOTE
The difference between short-run and long-run market equilibrium is the additional time it takes for supply changes to adjust economic profits to zero.

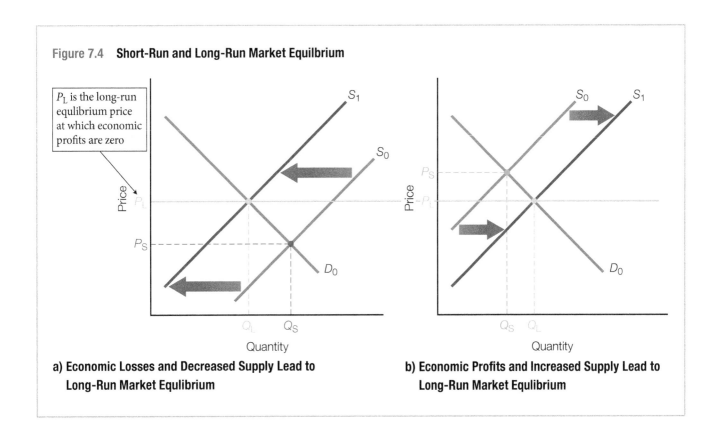

Figure 7.4   **Short-Run and Long-Run Market Equilbrium**

P_L is the long-run equilibrium price at which economic profits are zero

a) **Economic Losses and Decreased Supply Lead to Long-Run Market Equlibrium**

b) **Economic Profits and Increased Supply Lead to Long-Run Market Equlibrium**

NOTE

When businesses focus on the bottom line — pursuing economic profits — markets produce what consumers want.

Economic Profits Signal a "Go"   The graph in Figure 7.4b tells the story of economic profits and new business entry. The original demand and supply curves are D_0 and S_0. The short-run market equilibrium is at price P_S and quantity Q_S. But at price P_S and quantity Q_S, businesses are making economic profits. (The profits do not appear directly on the graph, they are a result of the combination of the price P_S, quantity Q_S, and costs.)

As new businesses enter the industry, supply increases. The supply curve shifts rightward toward S_1, which pushes prices down. The increase in supply moves the market price down along the unchanged demand curve D_0. But as long as economic profits remain, businesses keep entering, supply keeps increasing, prices keep falling, and profits keep decreasing until the price falls to P_L and the equilibrium quantity falls to Q_L. Traffic stabilizes only once prices have fallen enough to just cover all opportunity costs of production, and economic profits have fallen to zero. At the long-run equilibrium price P_L and quantity Q_L, revenues just cover all opportunity costs of production (including normal profits), and economic profits are zero.

Economic Profits Are Supply Signals   On the supply side of markets, economic profits are the key signal directing the self-interest of businesses to produce the products and services that consumers want. Changes in economic profits trigger changes in supply, which change prices, moving an industry from a short-run market equilibrium to a long-run market equilibrium.

Long-run market equilibrium price is the price markets move toward. Economic profits are the signals for moving, and supply shifts are the mechanism for moving. By finding the real bottom line of economic profits, we reveal Adam Smith's invisible hand directing business owners' self-interest to produce the miracle of markets.

Refresh 7.3

MyEconLab

For answers to these Refresh Questions, visit MyEconLab.

1. State the main difference between economic and accounting profits. What signal does it send to new businesses considering entering an industry when economic profits are negative? Zero? Positive?

2. Explain how the rule "Choose only when additional benefits are greater than additional opportunity costs" is the same as "Choose when economic profits are positive."

3. Businesses in the beachball market are currently earning zero economic profits. A heat wave strikes and demand for beachballs skyrockets, so a shortage develops, driving up beachball prices. Using economic profits as the key, use a demand and supply graph to explain all the choices that will be made before the beachball market once again returns to long-run market equilibrium with zero economic profits.

Study Guide

7.1 What Accountants Miss: Accounting Profits and Hidden Opportunity Costs

Accounting profits equal revenues minus all obvious costs, including depreciation. But accounting profits miss the hidden, implicit opportunity costs of a business owner's time and money.

- **Obvious costs (explicit costs)** — costs a business pays directly. Accountants count all obvious business costs and include **depreciation:**
  - decrease in the value of equipment over time because of wear and tear and because it becomes obsolete.
  - allowable yearly depreciation cost is the price of equipment divided by number of years it lasts.
- **Accounting profits** —
  Revenues – Obvious Costs (including depreciation).
- **Implicit costs** — hidden opportunity costs of what business owner could earn elsewhere with time and money invested.
  - Opportunity cost of time — best alternative use of business owner's time.
  - Opportunity cost of money — best alternative use of business owner's money invested in the business; must include compensation for risk.
- Risk compensation depends on attitudes toward risk.
  - A risk-loving investor does not require much compensation for taking risks.
  - A risk-averse (risk-avoiding) investor requires a high compensation for taking risks.

7.2 What Economists Find: Normal Profits and Economic Profits

Smart business decisions return at least normal profits — what a business owner could earn from the best alternative uses of her time and money. There are economic profits over and above normal profits when revenues are greater than all opportunity costs of production, including hidden opportunity costs.

- **Normal profits:**
  - compensation for business owner's time and money
  - sum of hidden opportunity costs (implicit costs)
  - what business owner must earn to do as well as best alternative use of time and money
  - average profits in other industries

- **Economic profits** equal
  - Revenues minus all Opportunity Costs
  - Revenues − (Obvious Costs + Hidden Opportunity Costs)
  - Revenues − (Obvious Costs + Implicit Costs)
  - Revenues − (Obvious Costs + Normal Profits)
- Key difference between economists and accountants is that economists subtract *hidden opportunity costs* when calculating profits.
  - Economic profits are less than accounting profits.
- **Economic losses** — negative economic profits.
  - If revenues are less than all opportunity costs, business owner has not made a smart decision and would be better off in alternative uses of time and money.
  - With economic losses, business owner is earning less than normal profits, less than average profits in other industries.

7.3 Red Light, Green Light: How Economic Profits Direct the Invisible Hand

The simplest rule for smart business decisions is "Choose only when economic profits are positive." When businesses pursue economic profits, markets produce the products and services consumers want.

- Economic profits (and losses) serve as signal for smart business decisions.
  - With economic losses (red light): businesses leave industry, supply decreases, pushing prices up, until prices just cover all opportunity costs of production and economic profits are zero.
  - With **breakeven point** (yellow light): businesses just earning normal profits. Market equilibrium with zero economic profits or losses. No tendency for change.
  - With economic profits (green light): businesses expand and enter industry, supply increases, pushing prices down, until prices just cover all opportunity costs of production and economic profits are zero.
- **Short-run market equilibrium** — quantity demanded equals quantity supplied, but economic losses or profits lead to changes in supply.

- **Long-run market equilibrium** — quantity demanded equals quantity supplied, economic profits are zero, no tendency for change.
  - The price consumers are willing and able to pay just covers businesses' opportunity costs of production, including normal profits.
  - The difference between short-run and long-run market equilibrium is the additional time it takes for supply changes to adjust economic profits to zero.

- On the supply side of markets, economic profits are the key signal directing businesses to produce the products and services that consumers want. Changes in economic profits trigger changes in supply, which changes prices, moving an industry from a short-run market equilibrium to a long-run market equilibrium.

TRUE/FALSE

Circle the correct answer. Solutions to these questions are available at the end of the book and on MyEconLab. You can also visit the MyEconLab Study Plan to access additional questions that will help you master the concepts covered in this chapter.

7.1 Accounting Profits and Hidden Opportunity Costs

1. Appreciation is the decrease in value of equipment over time because of wear and tear and because it becomes obsolete.   T **F**

2. The opportunity cost of a self-employed worker's time is zero.   T **F**

3. If you borrow money from your parents for free, the opportunity cost of using that money to start a business is zero.   T **F**

4. Returns from investing in stocks are *guaranteed,* while returns from saving money in the bank are *risky.*   T **F**

5. Individuals who are risk averse need to be paid more to take a risk than risk-loving individuals would.   **T** F

6. The best alternative use of your money could be the interest earned if you put the borrowed money in a savings account.   **T** F

7.2 Normal Profits and Economic Profits

7. The time component of normal profits is the value of the best alternative use of the owner's money.   T **F**

8. The money component of normal profits is the best alternative return on investment, including risk compensation.   **T** F

9. The interest rate is 10 percent per year. You invest $50 000 of your own money in a business and earn accounting profits of $20 000 after one year. If the opportunity cost of time is zero, economic profits are $30 000.   T F

10. It is a smart choice to remain in business if accounting profits are greater than zero.   T **F**

7.3 How Economic Profits Direct the Invisible Hand

11. If revenues increase, business owners will be more likely to stay in the industry.   **T** F

12. The difference between short-run and long-run equilibrium is the additional time it takes for supply changes to adjust normal profits to zero.   T F

13. Economic profits cause an increase in industry supply and a fall in price.   T F

14. Businesses are at the breakeven point when revenues equal hidden opportunity costs.   T **F**

15. Businesses will leave an industry when economic profits are zero.   T **F**

MULTIPLE CHOICE

Circle the best answer. Solutions to these questions are available at the end of the book and on MyEconLab. You can also visit the MyEconLab Study Plan to access similar questions that will help you master the concepts covered in this chapter.

7.1 Accounting Profits and Hidden Opportunity Costs

1. **What do accountants miss?**
   - a) opportunity costs
   - b) obvious opportunity costs
   - **c) hidden opportunity costs**
   - d) everything

2. **Success should be measured by**
   - a) revenues.
   - b) costs.
   - c) accounting profits.
   - **d) economic profits.**

3. Abdul operates his own business and pays himself a salary of $20 000 per year. He refused a job that pays $30 000 per year. What is the opportunity cost of Abdul's time in the business?
   a) $10 000
   b) $20 000
   c) $30 000
   d) $50 000

4. If you borrow money from the bank to start a business, the interest you pay to the bank is
   a) an obvious cost.
   b) subtracted from revenues.
   c) included in the calculation of accounting profits.
   d) all of the above.

5. An economist considers someone who is a gambler and does not need much compensation to go for an uncertain investment to be
   a) crazy.
   b) risk loving.
   c) risk averse.
   d) all of the above.

7.2 Normal Profits and Economic Profits

6. Normal profits include
   a) compensation for the use of a business owner's time and money.
   b) the sum of hidden opportunity costs.
   c) what a business owner could have earned elsewhere.
   d) all of the above.

7. Which of the following is *not* another way of saying "hidden opportunity costs"?
   a) explicit costs
   b) implicit costs
   c) normal profits
   d) the sum of the opportunity costs of time and money

8. The key difference between economists and accountants is that economists
   a) are always smarter.
   b) are always better looking.
   c) subtract hidden opportunity costs when calculating profits.
   d) add opportunity costs when calculating profits.

9. The definition of economic profits can also be written as
   a) Economic Profits = Revenues − (Obvious Opportunity Costs + Normal Profits).
   b) Economic Profits = Revenues − (Obvious Opportunity Costs + Hidden Opportunity Costs).
   c) Economic Profits = Accounting Profits − Hidden Opportunity Costs.
   d) All of the above.

10. If your business earns accounting profits of $50 000 and economic profits of $20 000, what are your hidden opportunity costs?
    a) $20 000
    b) $30 000
    c) $60 000
    d) $70 000

11. If your business earns accounting profits of $50 000 and economic losses of $20 000, what are your hidden opportunity costs?
    a) $20 000
    b) $30 000
    c) $60 000
    d) $70 000

7.3 How Economic Profits Direct the Invisible Hand

12. A business owner should enter an industry when
    a) economic profits are positive.
    b) additional benefits are greater than additional opportunity costs.
    c) revenues are greater than all opportunity costs.
    d) all of the above.

13. Which of the following "signals the way" when making decisions to enter or exit an industry?
    a) revenues
    b) normal profits
    c) economic profits
    d) yield signs

14. When economic profits are zero, businesses are
    a) breaking even.
    b) not kicking themselves.
    c) likely to remain in the industry.
    d) all of the above.

15. When there are economic losses in an industry,
    a) price falls.
    b) supply decreases.
    c) quantity supplied decreases.
    d) demand decreases.

8

Pricing Power

Monopoly to Competition and In Between

DO YOU PREFER LOW OR HIGH PRICES?

This is a trick question. If you answered "low prices," you were thinking as a consumer who buys Gatorade or headphones or doughnuts. If you answered "high prices," you were thinking as a business person who sells piercings, or web services, or your own hours of labour. In Canada's market economy, we each play dual roles — as buyers (of the products and services we need) and as sellers (of inputs earning income).

As consumers or businesses, we rarely get to choose prices. Prices are determined through the interaction of demand and supply in markets. Prices settle somewhere between the maximum consumers are willing to pay (marginal benefit) and the minimum businesses are willing to accept (covering all marginal opportunity costs of production). Businesses generally seek higher prices, aiming for economic profits. Consumers seek lower prices, bargains that leave zero economic profits for businesses.

What determines exactly where market prices end up between the two extremes? Why are economic profits high in some markets and non-existent in others? The short answer is competition. This chapter explores how competition influences a business's power to price its products and services. And that *pricing power* depends on what substitutes (competing products or services) are available to consumers and on the elasticity of demand.

Since we all sell something to earn income, whether as a business or a worker, knowing about competition helps you make smart choices in pricing your products and services, negotiating a salary, or competing with other sellers in your market.

Dreams of Monopoly and Nightmares of Competition: Price Makers and Price Takers

Differentiate between monopoly and perfect competition, and explain what businesses aim for and what businesses fear.

monopoly only seller of a product or service; no close substitutes available

market power business's ability to set prices

price maker pure monopoly with maximum power to set prices

Think of yourself as a seller hoping to set high and profitable prices. Let's look at the competitive situations you might face, starting with the extremes of your best case and worst case. Then we'll look at the situations in between.

Monopoly

For a seller's best case, let's go back to the example in Chapter 3, where it's Sunday night and your boss calls in a panic, begging you to work as many hours as possible next week. All your co-workers are sick and you are the only person who knows how to run the store. As the *only seller* of labour trained for that store, an economist would say you have a **monopoly**. The word *monopoly* comes from the Greek words *mono* (meaning "one") and *poly* (meaning "seller"). A monopoly is the *only seller* of a product or service — *no close substitutes are available.*

Price Maker Instead of asking how many hours you will work at different wages, suppose your boss says, "I desperately need you to work 60 hours next week. I have no one else. Name your price." (Don't you wish life were always like that?) That power to set prices is called **market power**. A monopoly has maximum power to set prices. The only seller of a product or service that has no close substitutes is a **price maker**. You can name your price.

When Xerox Corporation developed the first photocopy machine in 1959, it had a monopoly. There were no other quick and inexpensive ways to copy a document. The only (and they were poor) substitutes available involved copying by hand, using carbon paper between two sheets of paper on a typewriter (when the typewriter keys pounded the first sheet, they also created a carbon copy on the paper behind), or going to a printing company. The original Xerox 914 machine leased for $95 per month (about $800 in today's dollars) and made enormous profits for Xerox. During the years before other photocopy machines appeared, Xerox earned profits at rates of 1000 percent — for every dollar you invested in Xerox, you got back $1000! Xerox was a highly profitable price maker with maximum pricing power.

These office workers were using the Xerox 914 photocopier — this a breakthrough technology in 1959. The name Xerox 914 came from the ability to copy document sizes up to 9 × 14 inches. As the first to develop and market this technology, Xerox was a price maker. What new products have you seen introduced that allowed the business to be a price maker?

Can't Force Buyers to Buy While price makers have maximum power to set prices, their market power is still limited by what buyers are willing and able to pay. The law of demand always operates — higher prices mean lower quantity demanded. So the trade-off of setting a higher price is lower sales. The price maker's goal is to find the price and quantity combination that yields the greatest profits. When your boss asks you to name your selling price for working, you could answer "one million dollars." It's a free country, and you can charge any price you want. But freedom exists for buyers, too — no one can be forced to buy. Your boss would likely laugh and close the store for the week because she would lose less by closing than by paying you $1 million. If Xerox set the price of its photocopiers much higher, customers might find it cheaper to go to printing companies or to pay for handwritten copies, or even to do without copies. The lower sales from higher prices might more than offset the higher price, so profits could be lower. Even monopoly price makers must live by the law of demand.

Heritage Image Partnership Ltd / Alamy

Inelastic Demand For Monopoly   The demand curve that a monopolist faces looks like Figure 8.1. The demand curve is steep and inelastic because there are no close substitutes. The law of demand applies — as the monopolist raises prices, quantity demanded decreases. When demand is inelastic, even a large percentage increase in price (from P_0 to P_1) causes only a small percentage decrease in quantity demanded (from Q_0 to Q_1). Because the increase in price is greater than the decrease in quantity demanded, higher prices increase total revenue (price × quantity) as long as demand is inelastic.

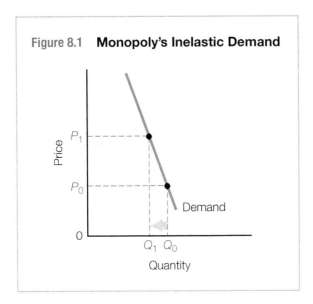

Figure 8.1   **Monopoly's Inelastic Demand**

But if the price is set too high — $1 million — even a monopolist with maximum market power will have no buyers, no revenues, and no profits.

Perfect Competition

A small wheat farmer in Saskatchewan is a worst-case example of a seller's market power. Although the farmer is proud of the #1 quality wheat he grows, thousands of other farmers in Canada and around the world are selling the identical product. Perfect substitutes for the farmer's wheat are instantly available.

Price Taker   If the market price of #1 quality wheat is $4 per bushel, what chance does this farmer have of setting and getting a price higher than that? Even $4.01? The answer is zero. No buyer will pay even a penny more because he can easily get the identical product for $4. The farmer is a **price taker**, with no market power. This is a case of **perfect competition**, where many sellers are producing identical products (perfect substitutes). Profits are limited to normal profits. The best this farmer, or any business in perfect competition, can hope for is to recover all of his opportunity costs of production, which include normal profits. Economic profits are zero. This is the long-run market equilibrium scenario of Chapter 6. With no ability to raise prices, his only hope for economic profits is to produce at a lower cost than his competitors.

price taker   business with zero power to set prices

perfect competition   many sellers producing identical products or services

Demand Is Perfectly Elastic for Perfect Competition   A single small farmer or business in perfect competition faces a demand curve that looks like Figure 8.2. The demand curve is horizontal at the market price of $4 per bushel.

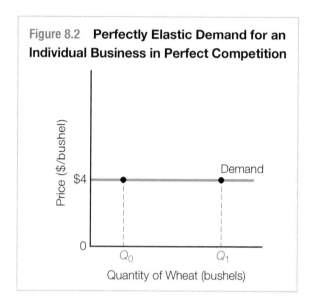

Figure 8.2   **Perfectly Elastic Demand for an Individual Business in Perfect Competition**

The bad news about being a small supplier in perfect competition is that you have no price-making power — you are a price taker. The good news is that no matter how much you supply (Q_0 or Q_1), the market will demand it. You will find buyers for any quantity you can produce, and you don't have to lower your price to sell more.

Because economic profits are zero, there is not much incentive to increase your capacity to produce output unless you can create a competitive advantage through lower costs, product differentiation, or innovation — strategies we will examine in section 8.4.

Every business, or seller, dreams of being a price maker like a monopoly and dreads the prospect of perfect competition, where it is a passive price taker. Most business decisions are motivated by the desire for the economic profits and market power of a monopoly, yet the forces of competition are usually pushing businesses back toward their nightmare of perfect competition.

Refresh 8.1

MyEconLab

For answers to these Refresh Questions, visit MyEconLab.

1. In your own words, define "perfect competition" and "monopoly." Besides wheat, list three other products or services that have markets like perfect competition. List three products or services that have markets like a monopoly.

2. Explain how the forces of competition and the law of demand still operate even in the market structure of monopoly.

3. To increase revenues, a business may lower rather than raise its prices. Use the concept of elasticity of demand to explain how this business strategy would work.

How Much Competition Is Going On? Market Structure

The markets for newly invented products (photocopiers in 1959, Apple's iPhone in 2007) and wheat are extreme cases. Most businesses are in between the extremes of all-powerful price makers and passive price takers. What factors common to all markets affect businesses' power to price? The answer is **market structure** — the characteristics that affect competition and a businesses's pricing power. Market structure has three main characteristics: available substitutes, number of competitors, and barriers preventing new competitors from entering the market. Let's look at each of these before re-examining the concept that sums up a business's pricing power — elasticity of demand.

market structure characteristics that affect competition and pricing power — available substitutes, number of competitors, barriers to entry of new competitors

"What's a Market" Depends on "What's a Substitute"

A market is not a place or a thing, it's a process — the interaction between buyers and sellers. A market brings together buyers and sellers of a *particular* product or service. *Particular* is an important word.

Broad Markets, More Substitutes, Less Pricing Power   How we define a market depends on how we define a *particular* product or service. In 2007, the iPhone was unique because of Apple's touchscreen software and distinctive design. There were other products combining cell phones, music players, and web browsers — the RIM BlackBerry and the Palm Treo. (Do any of you remember Palm Pilots? Google them.) If we shift from a narrow definition of the market for iPhones to a broader definition of the market for smartphones — mobile cell/music/web devices — then Apple was no longer the single seller, and buyers had a wider set of choices. There are always substitutes. The more broadly we define a market the more substitutes there are — and the more competitors there are. If you wanted only an iPhone (that's particular!), Apple had a monopoly and was a price maker. But if you wanted a mobile cell/music/web device, there were more substitutes — meaning more elastic demand — and more sellers with less pricing power. We expect lower prices for mobile cell/music/web devices than for iPhones alone.

NOTE
Markets can be defined broadly or narrowly. More broadly — more substitutes and competitors. More narrowly — fewer substitutes and competitors.

Narrow Markets, Fewer Substitutes, More Pricing Power   The reverse is also true. The more narrowly we define a market, the fewer substitutes there are — and the fewer competitors. For the broadly defined wheat market, our Saskatchewan farmer has thousands of competitors, and consumers can choose among thousands of identical bushels of wheat. But the definition of the market gets narrower if the "buy and eat local" movement (eat only foods grown within 200 kilometres of where you live) becomes fashionable in Saskatoon and Regina. Then farmers within a 200-kilometre radius of those cities have far fewer competitors, and "buy local" consumers in those cities have fewer substitutes — meaning more inelastic demand. Local farmers gain market power, and we expect higher prices for locally grown wheat.

If your boss will hire only workers specifically trained for her store, you are the only seller. But if she defines the labour market more broadly, she might bring in workers from similar chain stores elsewhere in the city, or go to a temporary agency, hire workers with some retail experience, and spend a day training them. The more broadly she defines the labour market, the more substitutes she has, the more competitors you face, and the lower is your price power as a seller.

One more example for you coffee addicts out there. Do you have a favourite brand: Tim Hortons, Second Cup, or Starbucks? If you are a die-hard Tims addict, then you don't consider other brands as substitutes, and there is a limited number of sellers you'll buy from (probably only one or two Tims in your neighbourhood). But if all you want is hot caffeine, there are many substitutes and many sellers with less price power.

Product Differentiation, Fewer Substitutes, More Pricing Power

Businesses or sellers are always trying to develop brand loyalty among customers, because when customers rule out other substitutes, the seller has fewer competitors and greater ability to raise prices. Any attempt by a business to distinguish its product or service from those of competitors is called **product differentiation**. If the wheat farmer tried raising prices to (non-local) customers, his sales would fall to zero. But Tims can charge a higher price than 7-Eleven can for coffee, and Apple can charge a higher price than generic phone manufacturers like Huawei can. The more you, as a seller, can convince potential buyers that there are fewer substitutes out there, the more likely it is that you will be a price maker rather than a price taker.

Product differentiation may come from actual product differences (smartphones may have different features, styles, pricing plans) or from advertising that attempts to convince you that one coffee brand is better, even though the coffee tastes pretty much the same. (See Economics Out There.)

product differentiation attempt to distinguish product or service from those of competitors

Counting Competitors:
How Many Competing Businesses?

Once you define your market and identify which products or services are substitutes, the second characteristic affecting competition and pricing power is the number of other businesses selling similar products or services. For all market structures, the general rule is: *the fewer competitors, the more pricing power; the more competitors, the less pricing power.*

Counting your competitors is not always as easy as it seems. Some markets are mostly local. If you are a business selling piercings, dry cleaning, or fruits and vegetables, most of your customers and competitors are in a limited geographical area around you. You can easily identify them.

NOTE
Fewer competitors = more pricing power.
More competitors = less pricing power.

Economics *Out There*

What's Your Favourite Beer — and Why?

Molson's Canadian or Labatt's Blue? Beer companies spend millions in advertising to convince you that their particular beer tastes better than the competition, and many consumers do prefer one brand to the other. But why?

In tests, where beer drinkers were given different beers to try, most could not taste or tell the difference between brands. They could not pick out their favourite beer from the competition's brands.

That's product differentiation without any actual product differences! Advertising can be an effective competitive strategy to create product loyalty which gives a business greater pricing power.

But other markets are not bound by geography, and counting competitors is hard. Wahid, in Chapter 7, located his web design business in the design district of the city because that's where most of his city customers expect to find design services. It's also where most of Wahid's local competitors are. But the internet, digital technologies, video conferencing, and inexpensive airfares have exploded the geographical boundaries of competition.

This explosion of competition is good and bad for businesses. The good news for Wahid is that he can extend his market, sell his services anywhere in the world, and increase his sales. The bad news is that design companies anywhere in the world can compete for Wahid's customers, which limits his pricing power. If you are selling design services, books, or movies, your competitors are not just local businesses, but also Chapters, Amazon, and sellers anywhere in the world connected through eBay or craigslist or other websites. Counting competitors is hard!

For consumers, the internet's explosion of competition is generally good news — more choices and lower prices. When consumers can easily compare restaurants or hotels on *Yelp!* or *Trip Advisor*, businesses must keep prices down and quality up close to those of competitors, reducing business pricing power.

Keeping Competitors Out and Profits In: Barriers to Entry

Competitors may be *actual* businesses already selling in your market, or they may be *potential* sellers who are looking to enter your market because they are attracted to your high economic profits. When Xerox was earning profits at rates of 1000 percent per year, you can bet other businesses were very interested in figuring out a way to start producing photocopy machines and getting a piece of that hugely profitable action. This is the green-light scenario from Chapter 7.

As new businesses enter a market, supply increases and prices and economic profits fall. For a monopoly to continue to earn economic profits over many years, it must find ways to keep out potential competitors. Economists call the ways to keep out competitors **barriers to entry**. There are two main types of barriers — legal barriers and economic barriers.

barriers to entry legal or economic barriers preventing new competitors from entering a market

Legal Barriers to Entry New inventions, like Xerox's photocopy machine or Apple's iPhone, or new methods of production can be protected against competition by legal patents. A **patent** gives an inventor the exclusive right to supply his new product or service, or to license it to other businesses in exchange for royalty payments for 20 years in Canada. Apple took out more than 200 patents on the iPhone before the product appeared. Similarly, a legal **copyright** gives exclusive rights to the creator of a literary, musical, dramatic, or artistic work. Patents and copyrights give inventors property rights over what they have produced, one of the rules of the game that is necessary for markets to work well.

patents and copyrights exclusive property rights to sell or license creations, protecting against competition

So, governments keep new competitors out of a market by passing laws giving a business the exclusive right to supply a product or service. Why, I hope you are wondering, would the government restrict competition and help guarantee economic profits for certain businesses and artists? Patents and copyrights are necessary to create incentives encouraging the research, development, and creation of inventions and art that improve our standard of living and quality of life.

To better see the role of patents and copyrights, imagine what might happen if they did not exist. Pharmaceutical companies can spend decades and invest tens of millions of dollars developing and producing new lifesaving drugs, like antibiotics, or costly drugs that end up failing. Without patents, competitors could buy the successful drugs, analyze their chemical composition, and create comparable drugs to sell at a much lower price. Competition would drive drug prices down to the cost of production, and the inventing company would never recover the research and development investment. As a business, why would you ever again spend money on research and development?

The same incentives apply to artistic works. Without copyright, a studio would never recover the multi-million dollar investment in producing a film, and there would be no hope of profits. If anyone could legally copy the finished film, upload it, and stream it for free (making money from advertising on the download website), there would be no financial reason for a studio to ever start another movie.

Patents and copyrights attempt to balance businesses' and artists' need for "incentives to invent" with consumers' desires for reasonably priced innovative products and services. Once businesses and artists have had a reasonable chance to recover their investments and earn economic profits, patents and copyrights expire. The entry of competitors at that point forces down prices to where more consumers benefit. After patents expire, generic versions of drugs appear at much lower cost. For example, you can now buy no-name ibuprofen for much less money than Advil, which had the original, now-expired patent on the formula for ibuprophen. (Why are some consumers still willing to pay more for Advil, which is chemically identical to no-name ibuprophen? See Economics Out There.)

Economics *Out There*

Pricing Headaches and Sex

When their patents expired, allowing new competition from cheaper generic versions of their products to come on to the market, Advil and Viagra adopted different pricing strategies.

Advil continued to use a product differentiation strategy, with advertising that emphasized the quality of Advil (trusted, recommended by doctors, highest manufacturing standards, . . .). Consumers who believe the advertising claims are willing to pay a higher price for the perceived quality of Advil than for the no-name competition.

Following a 2012 Supreme Court of Canada ruling that ended its patent on Viagra, Pfizer Canada cut the price to match the generic versions of the erectile dysfunction drug. The ruling "wiped out Pfizer's market dominance." A Pfizer spokeswoman said they are "committed to ensuring that Viagra patients can continue to have access to the original brand at a competitive price."

Pfizer, counting on consumer loyalty, is hoping to retain a large share of the market. The company believes many consumers will prefer the original product to the generic equivalent, but decided that demand conditions would not allow them to maintain a higher price.

Two similar cases but two different marketing strategies.

Source: "Pfizer cuts costs of Viagra to compete with generic pills after court ruling," The Canadian Press, November 22, 2012.

One last example of a legal barrier to entry is Canada Post's exclusive right to deliver first-class mail. Did you ever wonder why competitors haven't tried to provide better daily mail delivery? They would be breaking the law, which exists to ensure that all Canadians have access to inexpensive mail service. Without the law, competitors would jump into the profitable locations — like densely populated cities — and abandon the rural and remote communities where delivery costs are high and potential profits are low.

Economic Barriers to Entry A business may be able to keep competitors out and economic profits high simply by being big. For most products, **average total cost** — the total cost per unit of output — decreases as the business produces larger quantities of output. Economists describe this benefit of being big as **economies of scale** — average total cost decreases as the scale of production increases. If a big business is already supplying most of a market, a new competitor trying to enter will start with lower sales and therefore higher average total cost. The new business simply can't compete on price.

average total cost total cost per unit of output

economies of scale average total costs of producing decreases as quantity (scale) of production increases

Average total cost is the most important cost concept for understanding economic barriers to entry. Business costs will be discussed in more detail in the next chapter.

How Do You Spell Competition?
E-L-A-S-T-I-C-I-T-Y of Demand

The three characteristics of market structure — available substitutes, number of businesses, and barriers to entry — make up the competitive environment for a business and determine its market power — its ability to be a price maker rather than a price taker. Market power determines where price settles, between the maximum consumers are willing to pay and the minimum businesses are willing to accept (covering all opportunity costs of production). All three characteristics of market structure relate to elasticity of demand, which gives us a shortcut for understanding market power.

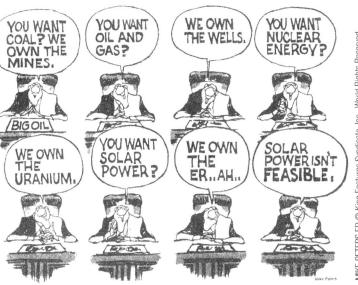

In this cartoon, pricing power comes from one company owning all the products (except the sun) — a monopoly. Consumers will have very little choice. Look back at Figure 8.1, Monopoly's Inelastic Demand.

High Pricing Power with Inelastic Demand
Businesses with the highest pricing power tend to have the most inelastic demand. In 1959, Xerox had enormous power to set a high price for its photocopy machines. Like the extreme case of inelastic demand for insulin by diabetics, a rise in price caused almost no decrease in quantity demanded, because few good substitutes were available. Xerox was the only seller, and patents created barriers to the entry of new businesses.

With fewer substitutes, consumers have less choice and are in a weaker bargaining position. Businesses have more market power to be able to raise prices (that is, be more of a price maker) and still keep selling. Product differentiation can create the same pricing power and decrease the elasticity of demand. If a business can develop brand loyalty, it makes demand for its product more inelastic.

Low Pricing Power with Elastic Demand   Businesses with the lowest pricing power tend to have the most elastic demand. Take the extreme case of the demand for wheat. No supplier/farmer in perfect competition can raise its price without losing all sales because many perfect substitutes are available. There are many competing businesses and no barriers to entry.

With more substitutes, consumers have more choice and are in a stronger bargaining position. Businesses have no power to raise prices. With perfect substitutes there is no product differentiation or brand loyalty, so the demand for every supplier's particular bushel of wheat is perfectly elastic.

While the 1959 photocopy and current wheat markets are extremes, the rule applies to the entire continuum of market structures in between, which we will explore in the next section. *In general, the higher the pricing power, the more inelastic demand is. The lower the pricing power, the more elastic demand is.*

Figure 8.3 summarizes the relationships between market structure, competition, pricing power, and elasticity of demand for monopoly and perfect competition.

NOTE
Higher pricing power = more inelastic demand.
Lower pricing power = more elastic demand.

Figure 8.3   Market Structure and Pricing Power: Monopoly and Perfect Competition

Market Structure Characteristic	Monopoly	Perfect Competition
Pricing Power	Price Maker	Price Taker
Product Substitutes	No Close Substitutes	Many Perfect Substitutes
Number of Sellers	1	Many, Many
Barriers to Entry	High	None
Elasticity of Demand	Low/Inelastic	High/Elastic

Refresh 8.2

MyEconLab

For answers to these Refresh Questions, visit MyEconLab.

1. Write a definition of market structure that includes its three main characteristics.

2. Even after patents expire, brand-name drugs like Advil and Tylenol sell for more than chemically identical no-name generic drugs. Describe two strategies that the companies that produce the brand names can employ to keep existing customers and gain new ones. How can they get consumers to pay more for their brand names than for no-name generics?

3. What counts as a substitute product depends on how broadly or narrowly you define the market. Pick any specific product or service. Explain how it could be seen as a monopoly. Then present a position showing the opposite, that it is not really a monopoly.

Mash-Ups of Market Structure: Oligopoly and Monopolistic Competition

When my eight-year-old daughter saw black-and-white television for the first time (I didn't consider her education complete until she had seen *I Love Lucy*), she described it as "grey TV." She described it as it really was – many different shades of grey. If you think of monopoly as black and perfect competition as white, then most real-world market structures are in the many shades of grey between them. The markets in which you sell and buy as a business, worker, or consumer are almost all on the continuum between the end points of monopoly and perfect competition.

Figure 8.3 showed how the characteristics of market structure change in moving from monopoly to perfect competition. Pricing power moves from price maker to price taker, available substitutes go from none to many, the number of sellers goes from one to many, entry barriers go from high to low, and elasticity of demand goes from inelastic to elastic.

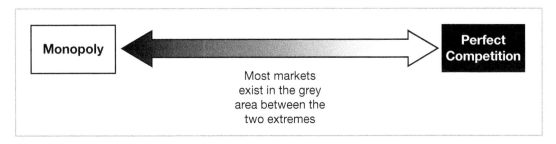

As with any continuum, it is helpful to group ranges together that have similar characteristics. Age is a continuum between birth and death. When you have to identify someone's age, you can try to be precise (she is 22 but acts like she's 15), or you can generalize by using an age group — she is 20-something, he is middle-aged, they are seniors. Economists find it helpful to bundle some of the market structures between the extremes into groups called oligopoly and monopolistic competition. Both groups are mash-ups in that they combine some characteristics of monopoly and some of perfect competition.

Oligopoly An **oligopoly** is a market structure with a few big businesses that control most of the market. The word *oligopoly* again comes from the Greek — *oligos* ("few") and *poly* ("sellers"). The gaming hardware market is an oligopoly, with Microsoft, Sony, and Nintendo as the major sellers. Oligopolists are price makers, but don't have as much pricing power as a monopolist. Any time one of the major sellers changes its price, the others usually make a similar change. While there is product differentiation (playing with a Wii wand is different from playing on a PlayStation), the products are often fairly close substitutes — a characteristic closer to perfect competition. The cola market (Pepsi and Coke) is another example of an oligopoly. With available substitutes, demand is more elastic than for monopoly, but more inelastic than perfect competition. Finally, there are usually barriers to entry in an oligopolistic market. The sellers are usually big, with economies of scale that make it hard for new competitors to enter. These characteristics of oligopoly are summarized in Figure 8.4 on page 194.

oligopoly few big sellers control most of the market

monopolistic competition many small businesses make similar but slightly differentiated products or services

Monopolistic Competition   **Monopolistic competition** is, by name, a mash-up of monopoly and perfect competition. Restaurants, piercing parlours, dry cleaners, and hair salons are all examples of monopolistic competition. Many small businesses are making similar but slightly differentiated products or services. Like perfect competition, there are no barriers to entry, so the only hope for economic profits comes from the product differentiation that gives each business some slight pricing power, or from producing at lower cost. Businesses might differentiate their products or services to compete on quality, service, marketing, or price. Pricing power and elasticity of demand for monopolistic competition are closer to perfect competition than to monopoly.

Figure 8.4   Market Structure and Pricing Power

Market Structure Characteristic	Monopoly	Oligopoly	Monopolistic Competition	Perfect Competition
Pricing Power	Price Maker (maximum pricing power)	Price Maker (much pricing power)	Price Maker (limited pricing power)	Price Taker (no pricing power)
Product Substitutes	No Close Substitutes	Differentiated Substitutes	Differentiated Substitutes	Many Perfect Substitutes
Number of Sellers	1	Few	Many	Great Many
Barriers to Entry	High	Medium	None	None
Elasticity of Demand	Inelastic	Inelastic	Elastic	Elastic

NOTE
Figure 8.4 is a great study tool. Keep in mind a particular real-world industry for each structure (gaming hardware sellers for oligopoly, restaurants for monopolistic competition).

Figure 8.4 gives you the different characteristics of the full range of market structures, from the extremes of monopoly and perfect competition to the mash-ups in the middle of the continuum of oligopoly and monopolistic competition. These groupings of market structure are often used in media reporting of economic events, and we will use them again in Chapter 10 to talk about government policies to deal with abuses of competition and monopoly.

Refresh 8.3

MyEconLab

For answers to these Refresh Questions, visit MyEconLab.

1.   Describe the differences between oligopoly and monopolistic competition. Between monopolistic competition and perfect competition.

2.   Use your answer to question 1 to explain why oligopoly and monopolistic competition can best be described as mash-ups.

3.   You are thinking of opening a gardening business during the summer — you will cut, weed, rake, and water lawns. What market structure would you be competing in? Describe your pricing strategy using the term "elasticity of demand."

To Compete Is a Verb: How Do Businesses Compete?

8.4

Explain how businesses compete, and why the process of creative destruction improves productivity and living standards.

The 1980 Wimbledon Men's Final is considered by many to be one of the greatest tennis matches in history. Bjorn Borg, the icy, methodical, four-time reigning champion from Sweden, defeated the brash young American challenger John McEnroe in five sets to win his fifth consecutive Wimbledon title. This was a classic competitive battle, with each player using every shot in his arsenal, matching winning shot for winning shot in a heroic quest for victory. TV coverage of subsequent Borg/McEnroe matches often played the then-popular Police song "Every Breath You Take," emphasizing the words in the song that say I will be watching every move that you make and every step that you take.

Competition among sellers in markets is much like sports competitions — take any shot or action to gain a competitive advantage. Every business, or seller, dreams of winning the market power and economic profits of monopoly. The businesses and individuals that succeed do more than dream — they *take actions* (make smart choices) to make those dreams come true. What do businesses and individuals do to compete? Competition is an active process of trying to find an advantage over your competitors, to capture more sales in the market, to beat out other candidates for a job. But (sing along here) *every choice you make, every action you take* happens in the context of a market, where all your competitors have the same dream of winning and all are taking similar actions while watching yours. The consequences for the market and the economy as a whole are not necessarily what the competitors hoped for.

What Do Businesses Do to Compete?

Competition in business takes many forms, but it is always an active attempt to increase profits and gain the market power of monopoly.

competition active attempt to increase profits and gain the market power of monopoly

Cutting Costs Cutting costs is a key competitive weapon. If your business can reduce waste, find lower-cost raw materials, or develop new technologies that save money, you gain competitive options. With its ruthless efficiency, size, and buying power, Walmart is famous for forcing suppliers to cut "to the bone" — that is, forcing their suppliers to cut the prices of products they provide to Walmart to the lowest point possible. By cutting your costs, you can earn higher profits while matching your competitors' prices, or you can profitably cut your prices to get new sales and attract customers away from your competitors. Attracting customers is especially effective when demand is price elastic.

Improving Quality and Product Innovation Instead of competing on price, you may want to compete by providing a higher *quality* product or service ("Paola's Piercing uses only platinum studs") or by offering better service or warranty protection. It's just like how your taking this course and getting a post-secondary education differentiates you from high-school graduates and earns you more pricing power in labour markets.

Improved quality also takes the form of new products. "To compete" may mean developing innovative new products like the photocopy machine or the iPhone. Innovation creates a product or service not available to your competition. These actions differentiate your product or service from those of your competitors, earning you some pricing power and inelasticity of demand.

Advertising and Brand Loyalty   Advertising can expand your market and establish brand loyalty that gives you some pricing power. Does your tablet have "Intel Inside"? Would you ever wear a pair of Gap jeans instead of Tommy Hilfiger? Advertising not only can make your demand more inelastic, but also can increase the demand for your product or service by stealing customers from competitors, or by finding new consumers who just didn't know about your product or service.

Eliminating Competition   Businesses also compete by buying out or merging with competitors to reduce substitutes and gain economies of scale. In 2012 Leon's Furniture bought out its rival The Brick to reduce Canadian competition. The buyout also gave the combined businesses economies of scale by creating a single national distribution network and online shopping service. Eliminating the competition reduces the number of available substitutes and increases your pricing power.

Economics *Out There*

Where's the Real Competition ?

Leon's takeover of The Brick was prompted by the entry of new U.S. competitors — Target and Walmart. To compete with the economies of scale of the U.S. retail giants, the friendly merger created a bigger, more efficient national distribution network and online shopping service.

By retaining the separate Leon's and The Brick brands, the company can differentiate its products and prices in different markets. This strategy also helps prevent any new entries into the furniture market.

This strategy of creating "fake" competition is also used by Luxottica corporation, a maker and marketer of eye glasses and eye glass frames. They own LensCrafters, Pearle Vision, Sears Optical, and Sunglass Hut outlets. As well, they design and manufacture almost all of the specialty frames such as Ray-Ban, Oakley, Prada, and Versace. The different outlets and specialty frames are presented as competition to each other when, in reality, they are all owned by the same huge multi-national company.

Source: Canadian Press, "Leon's buys domestic rival The Brick in $700M deal" *National Post,* November 11, 2012; "High prescription eyeglass costs vex consumers," CBC news website, December 2012.

▲ This cartoon is making fun of Starbucks for being in so many locations that the only place left for new outlets is in people's homes.

Building Barriers to Entry   Businesses can also gain market power by building barriers to entry. Have you ever wondered why there seems to be a Starbucks on every corner in some neighbourhoods? Is there really enough coffee business to go around? Don't more sales at one Starbucks come from fewer sales at the Starbucks down the block? Maybe. But the Starbucks business strategy is to *take as many good locations as possible to prevent competitors from setting up at those locations.* Densely spaced locations serve as a barrier to entry for other coffee competitors — there's just nowhere for them to open.

Here's another surprising example of a barrier to entry. The market for laundry detergent seems very competitive, with many, many substitute products — Tide, Ivory, Gain, Downy, Cheer. But all these products are made by the same company, Procter & Gamble (P&G). What about Wisk and All? Both made by Unilever. While the detergent market appears to be highly competitive, it is in fact an oligopoly, with just a few major players producing all the different products.

Why does P&G make so many competing brands? The variety serves as a barrier to entry to new businesses. If P&G made only one brand, a new supplier could target its advertising against a single competitive product and get noticed. But with five P&G products, each with advertising and brand loyalty, the chances of success for a new detergent are much lower, so most businesses don't even try.

What is common to all these competitive actions is the attempt to beat your rivals using every tactic in your business arsenal to increase your profits.

The Invisible Hand, Like Gravity, Is Unforgiving: Freedom Meets Competition

Unlike sports, business competition is not always "winner takes all." Many businesses in a market can make profits, but to do so each must at least match — or in some way better — the actions of all other competitors. As a result of pressure to match the competition, most businesses in a market adopt similar tactics.

Business and sports competition have many parallels. If the best players develop new physical conditioning routines that give them an advantage (Borg outlasted McEnroe in the fifth set largely because of superior conditioning), or adopt new technologies like carbon fibre racquets that are superior to wooden versions, all players have to follow suit to survive at that competitive level. (I will be watching every move that you make and every step that you take.) Individual competitive actions by businesses spread quickly throughout a market, unless there are barriers like patents. Businesses that don't keep up with the competition suffer economic losses and eventually go bankrupt or out of business — they cease to be players. Only businesses that stay competitive survive.

Economic Freedom   One of the great ironies of the market economy is that it provides all of us with extraordinary economic freedom — freedom to make business decisions, to invest and spend our money as we please, to choose our occupations, to pursue our own self-interest. These freedoms are greater than in any other economic system in history. But because we all, whether as businesses or individuals, play the role of sellers who depend on the market to earn a living, we must play by the market's competitive rules. Not every choice is really available to us all the time.

Competitive Pressure   The competitive pressure of the market limits the choices we can make if we want to succeed as a seller. For example, Wahid may believe advertising for his web design business is a waste of money. But if all his competitors advertise, and his sales suffer, he will be forced to advertise. As a caring boss, Paola may want to pay her piercing employees generous wages. But if her competitors pay less and can undercut her piercing prices and take all her customers, she must pay lower wages, cut other costs, or risk going out of business. After the successful introduction of Apple's iPhone, imagine the "choice" that competitors had about whether or not to innovate and attempt to match the iPhone's features — no choice at all. And even if you don't expect to run a business but dream of being a writer or an artist, if you can't sell your work you'll continue to be a restaurant server who does some art in your spare time. The market economy gives us tremendous freedom of choice, but the pressure of competition is relentless.

Matching competitors' actions usually means matching price cuts on existing products or services. Once a business serves up a competitive action or tactic that generates economic profits, the forces of competition pull those profits back down to earth. Just like gravity pulls everything down to the ground, competitive forces are always pulling prices down toward the level of perfect competition, where businesses earn only normal profits. The only resistance to the downward pull of competitive prices comes from the pricing power your business develops because of product differentiation or barriers to entry. If prices are not forced down by the actions of competitors within your market, economic profits will attract new competitors, and the increased supply will pull down prices and profits. The market, like gravity, constantly puts downward pressure on prices.

Economics Out There

Higher Wages = Lower Costs?

There are different ways to achieve low costs. One Deutsche Bank business analyst looked at the high wages and generous benefits Costco pays it employees, and claimed there is no way Costco can compete with Walmart, which pays much less, offers fewer benefits, and vigorously opposes attempts at unionization, which would increase its labour costs. "At Costco, it's better to be an employee or a customer than a shareholder," he said.

But *Business Week* magazine found that "by compensating employees generously to motivate and retain good workers, one-fifth of whom are unionized, Costco gets lower turnover and higher productivity." Costco also has less "shrinkage" (the polite term for employee theft) and lower training costs from lower turnover, which reduces total labour costs.

The bottom line: Costco has lower labour costs and higher productivity than Walmart, even though Costco pays its employees much more. There are different strategies for cutting costs.

Source: Based on "Commentary: The Costco Way," *BusinessWeek*, April 12, 2004.

NOTE
Once a business takes an action producing economic profits, competition pulls profits back toward normal profits and pulls prices back toward perfect competition.

Back to Equilibrium   The price toward which competition continually pulls businesses is the market-clearing price of Chapter 4, which balances quantity demanded and quantity supplied. This equilibrium price coordinates the smart choices of consumers and businesses. No consumer is kicking himself for paying too much, and each business is earning the average rate of profits being earned in any other market (adjusted for risk and other market structure differences).

Paradoxically, the competitive actions businesses take pursuing the economic profits of monopoly pull each market back to a long-run equilibrium situation, where most businesses and products and prices are similar, prices just cover all opportunity costs of production, and businesses earn only normal profits as in perfect competition. Competition is the force behind Adam Smith's invisible hand, channelling business self-interest — the dream of monopoly profits — to yield the unintended consequence of the production of all the products and services consumers want, at the lowest possible costs.

Competition as Creative Destruction: Breaking Free of Equilibrium

When markets work well, businesses supply the products and services that consumers most want, and do so efficiently, at lowest cost. Not surprisingly, business leaders and wealthy individuals who benefit from markets make this claim all of the time. Even Karl Marx (1818–1883), the famous communist thinker and revolutionary, was a great admirer of the productivity of the market economy!

Why Marx Admired Capitalism   Marx was a severe critic of the market economy due to the inequalities in wealth he observed. He called it the capitalist system, referring to the capitalists who ran it as "the bourgeoisie" (the ruling class) and the workers he observed being exploited as "the proletariat" (wage labourers). At the same time, though, he recognized the market's great strength. In his call to revolution in *The Communist Manifesto* (1848, co-authored with Friedrich Engels), Marx wrote that "The bourgeoisie, during its rule of scarce one hundred years, has created more massive and more colossal productive forces than have all preceding generations together."

What makes market economies so enormously productive? Why are we so much better off than our great-grandparents were? What accounts for these continual increases in our ability to produce products and services and the impressive increases in standards of living (whether those increases are spread equitably or inequitably across the population)? The answers lie in the same competitive forces of Adam Smith's invisible hand that channel the restless energy of profit-seeking self-interest into the public good.

The competitive actions that businesses take do much more than pull prices back to competitive levels, pull economic profits back to zero, and bring demand and supply into equilibrium. Over a longer period of time, these competitive innovations make businesses more productive and improve living standards and product choices for consumers.

Schumpeter's Creative Destruction   Joseph Schumpeter (1883–1950) was a brilliant economist who recognized that competition drove the ever-changing and ever-more-productive market economy. Business's competitive actions "incessantly revolutionize the economic structure from within, incessantly destroying the old one, incessantly creating a new one. This process of **creative destruction** is the essential fact about capitalism." (Is that not a great phrase — *creative destruction*?) Competitive innovations not only generate economic profits for the winners, but also destroy the losers while making the world better for consumers. Computers made typewriters and carbon paper obsolete — have you ever used a typewriter at all, let alone to make carbon copies? DVDs destroyed VHS tapes, digital downloads and mobile music players destroyed CDs, LED lights are eliminating incandescent bulbs, robotic assembly lines replaced the jobs of craftsmen and craftswomen who used to make cars and clothing and bread. All these innovations and more were introduced in the competitive quest for monopoly profits, but ended up improving living standards while destroying the less productive or less desirable products and services and production methods. The resources that used to make now obsolete products and services moved into new, more productive industries.

This incessant process of change is behind many of the controversial competitive trends we see today. Jobs in Canada are being destroyed as corporations move manufacturing to Asia and "off-shore" their computer programming and call centre jobs to India. We will discuss these trends more fully in macroeconomics when we examine the pros and cons of globalization. But there is no denying that the outcome is more efficient businesses, with cheaper products and services for most of us (understanding that a win for consumers as a whole can still have individual losers — sellers and workers in the destroyed markets).

The bourgeoisie, during its rule of scarce one hundred years, has created more massive and more colossal productive forces than have all preceding generations together.

—*Karl Marx and Friedrich Engels,* The Communist Manifesto *(1848)*

creative destruction   competitive business innovations generate economic profits for winners, improve living standards for all, but destroy less productive or less desirable products and production methods

The innovations of the Canadian business BlackBerry revolutionized business communication, making it faster and more efficient, while earning handsome profits for shareholders. But BlackBerry's success destroyed jobs among competitors (what ever happened to Palm?), reduced business profits in competing forms of communication, and eliminated jobs for secretaries who used to handle business correspondence. Then BlackBerry itself was attacked by those same continuous forces of creative destruction.

The inherent and incessant change and growth of the market economy comes from unleashing the power of self-interest in all humans, but channelling it through competition and the invisible hand to improve living standards. This strength of a market economy is also a weakness. Sometimes the quest for monopoly power is so excessive and successful that it is not in the public interest. When competition fails, governments step in with competition laws, which we will examine in Chapter 10. Constant change can also contribute to "boom and bust" cycles of economic activity (which economists call *business cycles*), which are the focus of much of macroeconomics.

But before we get to all of that, we will look more closely in the next chapter at how businesses that have at least some price-making power (the majority of "grey" markets) make smart choices of the precise combination of price and quantity that yields maximum profits.

Refresh 8.4

MyEconLab

For answers to these Refresh Questions, visit MyEconLab.

1. Describe in your own words two actions a business can take to compete. Give a real-world example of each.

2. Explain, in your own words, Schumpeter's process of creative destruction. Explain how creative destruction is good for the majority but harmful to some minorities.

3. Markets combine freedom of choice with tremendous competitive pressure to supply products and services the markets value. This combination is connected to the age-old philosophical question about whether humans have free will, or whether our choices are all determined by other forces in society. Argue that your choice of "what you want to be when you grow up" is an example of free will. Then argue that the freedom of your choice is an illusion and that your choice is determined by economic forces in society.

Study Guide

CHAPTER 8 SUMMARY

8.1 Dreams of Monopoly and Nightmares of Competition: Price Makers and Price Takers

Businesses aim for monopoly's economic profits and price-making power. Competitors usually push businesses toward the normal profits and price taking of perfect competition.

- **Monopoly** — only seller of a product or service; no close substitutes are available.
  - demand curve is steep and inelastic
- **Market power** — business's ability to set prices.
- **Price maker** — monopoly with maximum power to set prices.
- Businesses can set any price they choose, but cannot force consumers to buy. Even monopoly price makers must live by law of demand.
- **Perfect competition** — many sellers producing identical products or services.
  - demand curve is horizontal and perfectly elastic at the market price
- **Price taker** — business with zero power to set prices.

8.2 How Much Competition Is Going on? Market Structure

Pricing power depends on the competitiveness of a business's market structure — available substitutes, number of competitors, barriers to the entry of new competitors — and on elasticity of demand.

- **Market structure** — characteristics that affect competition and a business's pricing power:
  - available substitutes
  - number of competitors
  - barriers to entry of new competitors
- Broader definition of market = more substitutes and competitors = more elastic demand = less pricing power.
- Narrower definition of market = fewer substitutes and competitors = more inelastic demand = more pricing power.

- **Product differentiation** — attempt to distinguish product or service from those of competitors:
  - allows seller to reduce competition and substitutes and increase pricing power
  - can take the form of actual differences or perceived differences
- Pricing power and number of competitors
  - fewer competitors = more price power
  - more competitors = less price power
- **Barriers to entry** — legal or economic barriers preventing new competitors from entering a market.
- **Patents** and **copyrights** are legal barriers — exclusive property rights to sell or license creations, protecting against competition.
  - give businesses short-term monopoly power as an incentive for invention, but eventually expire to give consumers reasonably priced products and services
- **Economies of scale** are economic barriers — average total cost of producing decreases as quantity (scale) of production increases.
  - **Average Total Cost** = Total cost per unit of output
- Higher pricing power = more inelastic demand
  - consumers have few substitutes or strong brand loyalty
- Lower pricing power = more elastic demand
  - consumers have many substitutes or no brand loyalty

8.3 Mash-Ups of Market Structure: Oligopoly and Monopolistic Competition

The four main market structures are monopoly, oligopoly, monopolistic competition, and perfect competition.

- **Oligopoly** — few big sellers control most of the market.
- **Monopolistic competition** — many small businesses make similar but slightly differentiated products or services.

- In moving across the continuum of market structures from monopoly to perfect competition:
  - pricing power moves from price maker to price taker
  - available substitutes go from none to many
  - number of sellers goes from one to many, many
  - entry barriers go from high to low
  - elasticity of demand goes from low/inelastic to high/elastic

8.4 To Compete Is a Verb: How Do Businesses Compete?

Businesses actively compete for monopoly's economic profits and pricing power. This process of creative destruction drives competitors who do not adequately respond out of business, while unintentionally improving productivity and living standards for all.

- **Competition** — active attempt to increase profits and gain the market power of monopoly.
  - cutting costs
  - improving quality and product innovation
  - advertising and brand loyalty
  - eliminating competition
  - building barriers to entry

- While a market economy provides extraordinary economic freedom
  - to make business decisions, to invest and spend as we please, to choose our occupations — as sellers who depend on markets to earn a living we must play by the market's competitive rules.

- **Creative destruction** — competitive business innovations generate economic profits for winners, improve living standards for all, but destroy less productive or less desirable products and production methods.

- Competitive actions by businesses can have the unintended consequence of *business cycles* — up and down fluctuations of overall economic activity.

TRUE/FALSE

Circle the correct answer. Solutions to these questions are available at the end of the book and on MyEconLab. You can also visit the MyEconLab Study Plan to access additional questions that will help you master the concepts covered in this chapter.

8.1 Price Makers and Price Takers

1. Monopolists have market power and do not have to live by the law of demand. T **F**

2. A worker who is the only one with a particular skill in her community has a monopoly over that skilled labour in her community. **T** F

3. The only seller of a product or service with no close substitutes is a price maker. **T** F

4. Sellers always prefer selling at higher prices. T **F**

5. Businesses prefer to have a monopoly over perfect competition. **T** F

8.2 Market Structure

6. Of all market structures, barriers to entry are highest for monopoly. **T** F

7. If McDonald's were to buy Wendy's, this would reduce McDonald's economies of scale. T **F**

8. The higher the market power, the lower the elasticity of demand. **T** F

8.3 Oligopoly and Monopolistic Competition

9. In monopolistic competition there are many perfect substitutes. T **F**

10. Businesses in monopolistic competition have some pricing power. **T** F

11. The elasticity of demand is higher for oligopoly than for monopolistic competition. T **F**

12. The gaming hardware industry is an example of monopolistic competition. T F

8.4 How Do Businesses Compete?

13. Dreams of monopoly market power and profits generate competitive actions that produce outcomes resembling perfect competition. **T** F

14. Competition is about figuring out ways to match your rival suppliers in the market. T F

15. Every choice you make, every action you take happens in the context of a market. **T** F

MULTIPLE CHOICE

Circle the best answer. Solutions to these questions are available at the end of the book and on MyEconLab. You can also visit the MyEconLab Study Plan to access similar questions that will help you master the concepts covered in this chapter.

8.1 Price Makers and Price Takers

1. A monopolist
- a) is the only seller of a product or service.
- b) is a price maker.
- c) has no close substitutes.
- d) is all of the above. ✓

2. The trade-off to setting a higher price is
- a) higher sales.
- b) lower sales. ✓
- c) higher revenues.
- d) nothing — there is no trade-off.

3. The effect on the nearby farming industry of the "buy and eat local" movement will
- a) make it more competitive.
- b) increase the number of substitutes available.
- c) reduce the number of substitutes available. ✓
- d) all of the above.

8.2 Market Structure

4. Monopolies can exist even though economic profits are supposed to attract entry from new businesses, if there are
- a) economies of scale.
- b) legal barriers that prevent new businesses from entering.
- c) economic barriers that prevent new businesses from entering.
- d) all of the above. ✓

5. Patents and copyrights increase market power by
- a) increasing the number of buyers.
- b) increasing the number of sellers.
- c) preventing other businesses from competing. ✓
- d) making it easier for other businesses to compete.

6. Which of the following could receive a patent?
- a) a song
- b) a poem
- c) an iPhone ✓
- d) all of the above

8.3 Oligopoly and Monopolistic Competition

7. Which of the following is *not* a market structure?
- a) monopoly
- b) oligopoly
- c) competitopoly ✓
- d) perfect competition

8. Which market structure has the lowest barriers to entry?
- a) monopoly
- b) oligopoly
- c) monopolistic competition
- d) perfect competition ✓

9. Which market structure has the highest elasticity of demand?
- a) monopoly
- b) oligopoly
- c) monopolistic competition
- d) perfect competition ✓

10. Which market structure has the most number of sellers?
- a) monopoly
- b) oligopoly
- c) monopolistic competition
- d) perfect competition ✓

11. Which market structure does *not* have pricing power?
- a) monopoly
- b) oligopoly
- c) monopolistic competition
- d) perfect competition ✓

12. Which market structure does *not* have close substitutes?
- a) monopoly ✓
- b) oligopoly
- c) monopolistic competition
- d) perfect competition

8.4 How Do Businesses Compete?

13. How do businesses compete?
- a) lower prices
- b) better product quality
- c) better service quality
- d) all of the above ✓

14. Advertising
- a) makes demand more elastic. ✗
- b) makes demand more inelastic. ✓
- c) reduces demand for a product or service.
- d) does all of the above.

15. Robotic assembly lines reduce the jobs available for assembly-line workers. This phenomenon is called
- a) karma.
- b) destructive creationism.
- c) creative destruction. ✓
- d) the handmaid's tale.

Pricing for Profits

Marginal Revenue and Marginal Cost

IMAGINE YOU RUN A BUSINESS and have

some pricing power. How do you find the combination of price and quantity sold that yields the greatest profits? There are so many variables to consider. On the demand side, how much are your customers willing to pay, and how much will your sales decrease as you raise prices? On the supply side, what are your costs, and are they increasing, decreasing, or constant as you increase quantity? And what about the competition — what substitutes are available, how many other businesses are you competing against, and what barriers are keeping out new competitors?

Making a smart business choice about price and quantity sounds complicated. Do you need to hire an economist? Actually, you don't — business owners make these decisions on their own all the time. In business, as in cooking, if you're not sure what to do, follow a recipe. In this chapter you will learn the recipe for pricing for profits. It's simple enough to state in one sentence, and it yields smart choices no matter how much or how little pricing power a business has. In the rest of this chapter, I will explain each "ingredient" and how to combine them.

The basic ingredients are marginal revenue and marginal cost, and they are combined in the recipe for pricing for profits. Because *marginal* means "additional," Key 2 of the Three Keys for Smart Choices plays a starring role: "Count only *additional* benefits and *additional* opportunity costs."

9.1 Is the Price You See the Revenue You Get?
Marginal Revenue

Define marginal revenue, and explain how it depends on market structure and when it differs from price.

Here is the business recipe for maximum profits: Estimate marginal revenues and marginal costs, and then set the highest price that allows you to sell the highest quantity for which marginal revenue is greater than marginal cost.

The recipe sounds more complicated than it really is. Cookbooks often provide a photo of the completed dish to give you a feel for what you are about to make. Let's look at a simple business decision to get a feel for the basic ingredients of marginal revenue and marginal cost.

Basic Ingredients

Suppose Paola's Parlour for Piercing and Nails is open weekdays from 11 a.m. to 7 p.m. Some of Paola's customers tell her it would be more convenient for them if the shop stayed open later, until 10 p.m. Is it smart for Paola to stay open later?

Marginal Revenues How would you make that decision? Well, a smart business decision will increase Paola's profits, and profits increase when revenues are greater than costs. To determine if Paola increases her profits by staying open later, you need to know her *additional revenues* and her *additional costs*. Additional revenues are how much additional money she will take in selling piercings and nail sets during those three extra hours. Economists call additional revenues **marginal revenue**. Marginal revenue can be calculated as the change in total revenue — revenue from additional sales between 7 p.m. and 10 p.m. — or as the revenue from selling one more unit of a product or service.

marginal revenue additional revenue from more sales or from selling one more unit

Marginal Costs Be careful about estimating additional costs. The additional three hours of wages Paola must pay her employees clearly count, as do costs of additional studs, nail polish, and extra electricity from operating lights and equipment. Additional costs Paola must pay as a result of staying open later are *marginal costs*. But fixed costs (also called sunk costs in section 3.2), like rent or insurance, do not change with the decision to stay open later. Fixed costs do not change (they are fixed) with changes in the quantity of output a business produces. Fixed costs do not affect smart decisions — only marginal costs do.

Choose When Marginal Revenues Are Greater Than Marginal Costs If Paola's estimated marginal revenues are greater than her marginal costs, her profits increase by staying open later. It's a smart decision and she and her customers will be happy. But if her estimated marginal costs are greater than her marginal revenues, her profits decrease. If marginal costs are greater than marginal revenues, she should continue to close at 7 p.m., even though it means a few disappointed evening customers.

Whether it's extending hours, introducing a new product or service, opening a new location, launching an advertising campaign, or hiring new employees (more on this in Chapter 12) — any of these decisions are smart as long as estimated marginal revenues are greater than marginal costs. Businesses always compare marginal revenues and marginal costs in making smart decisions.

With that simple snapshot of the basic ingredients of any smart business decision, let's look in more detail at a business's pricing decision.

NOTE
The simple rule for smart business decisions is "Choose when marginal revenues are greater than marginal costs." Marginal revenues are a business's "additional benefits" in Key 1.

ADDITIONAL
BENEFITS
VS.
OPPORTUNITY
COSTS

One Price Rules When Buyers Can Resell

You walk into Tim Hortons, order a medium double-double, and pay the usual $1.50. How would you feel if the next customer ordered the same coffee and were charged only 75 cents?

Most products and services have one price, not a different price for each customer. Why is that? First, it's not a good idea to make your customers angry and resentful. Second, competitive economic forces tend to equalize prices. Tims customers like you, who paid $1.50, would save money by not buying at the counter, but instead by offering to buy coffee from the low-price customers for less than $1.50. Low-price customers would make easy money by reselling their coffees to customers like you for more than 75 cents. Self-interest and competition between coffee drinkers would push the price toward a single price.

Most products that are easily resold tend to have a single price. But as you will see in section 9.4, sometimes businesses can charge different customers different prices for the same product or service to increase profits. Here, we are going to stick to examples where a business has to charge all customers the same price for the same product or service. The one-price rule has a big impact on a business's marginal revenue.

Economics *Out There*

iResentment

Less than three months after introducing the iPhone in 2007 at US$599, Apple cut the price by more than 25 percent, to $399. This was an attempt to increase sales to those not willing to pay the original price.

This caused so much resentment among original customers that Apple was forced to back-pedal. Steve Jobs quickly apologized and offered original customers a US$100 credit.

- This is the kind of resentment that enforces the one-price rule among products that can be easily resold like iPhones.

NOTE
Products easily resold tend to have a single price in the market.

Marginal Revenue

Marginal revenue also depends on *market structure* — how competitive your industry is, and whether your business is a price taker or a price maker.

After drinking his coffee, suppose a farmer sells wheat in a market structure of perfect competition. The market price of a bushel of wheat is $4 and he is a price taker. As one of many small farmers, he can sell as much as he can produce at that $4 price. He can't charge a higher price, or he will lose all of his customers. And he has no reason to charge a lower price if he can get $4 per bushel.

Last year, he planted and harvested 10 000 bushels of wheat and sold his crop for $40 000. That $40 000 was his total revenue — price × quantity. This year he plants more wheat, harvests 11 000 bushels and sells his crop at $4 a bushel for $44 000. His total revenue increased from $40 000 to $44 000.

The farmer's decision to plant more wheat is like Paola's decision to keep her shop open later. Both decisions increase total revenue.

Marginal revenue can be defined and calculated two ways.

Change in Total Revenue The farmer's total revenue increases by $4000, from $40 000 to $44 000. This is the marginal revenue from the farmer's decision to plant more wheat. Marginal revenue is the change in total revenue.

Revenue from Selling One More Unit   Marginal revenue can also be defined and calculated as the *additional revenue from selling one more unit of your product or service*. The farmer gets additional revenue of $4000 from selling an additional 1000 bushels of wheat. So his additional revenue per bushel is $4000 divided by 1000 bushels — $4 per bushel.

You might be wondering why I am wasting so many words explaining the marginal revenue of $4 per bushel. The farmer can sell each bushel for $4, so of course the marginal revenue per bushel is $4. Duh! But that's not always the case.

When Marginal Revenue Equals Price

The calculation of marginal revenue per unit is obvious when a business is a price taker in perfect competition. The wheat farmer's decision to produce more wheat has no effect on the market because as a small producer — one of thousands of suppliers — his increase in supply does not affect market supply or market price. Each small business in perfect competition can sell as many units as it can produce at the market price, so the marginal revenue for each additional unit sold *is* the price.

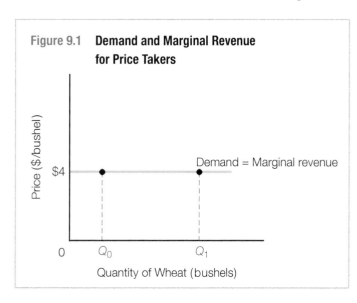

Figure 9.1   Demand and Marginal Revenue for Price Takers

Marginal Revenue Curve for Price Takers   As discussed in section 8.1, the demand curve facing an individual business in perfect competition looks like Figure 9.1. And since marginal revenue equals price, this demand curve is also a marginal revenue curve.

To read Figure 9.1 as a demand curve, start at the price and go over and down to the quantity. At the market price of $4 per bushel, the market will demand any quantity that you can produce (for example, Q_0 or Q_1). You don't have to lower your price to sell more in perfect competition.

This demand curve is also a marginal revenue curve. (Yes, I am repeating myself, on purpose.) You read a marginal revenue curve the same way you read a marginal benefit curve (section 2.3) or marginal cost curve (section 3.3). Start at the quantity, and go up and over to the marginal revenue. Whether the farmer is selling his 10th bushel (suppose $Q_0 = 10$) or his 10 000th bushel (suppose $Q_1 = 10\,000$), going up and over to the price axis, the marginal revenue is $4. Each bushel brings the farmer a marginal revenue equal to the price of a bushel of wheat.

What seems so obvious for price takers turns out *not* to be true for price makers. Not all demand curves double as marginal revenue curves.

NOTE
For price takers, the demand curve is also a marginal revenue curve. Marginal revenue equals price.

When Marginal Revenue Is Less Than Price

What about businesses with some pricing power? Price makers — whether monopolies, oligopolies, or small monopolistic competitors like Paola's Parlour for Piercing and Nails — can raise prices without losing all of their sales to competitors. Barriers to entry, brand loyalty, or advertising all can create pricing power. But price makers still face the law of demand. They will sell less if they raise their prices. And *to sell more, they must lower their prices*. The demand curve for price makers is downward-sloping.

Calculating Marginal Revenue for Price Makers　This is where the one-price rule becomes important. As long as a product can be resold and a business does not want to anger its customers, to sell more price makers must lower the price *on all units,* not just on new sales. The result is that *for price makers marginal revenue per unit is less than price.* Let's look at a simple example with made-up numbers.

NOTE
For price-making businesses in monopoly, oligopoly, and monopolistic competition, marginal revenue per unit is less than price. Because of the one-price rule, businesses must lower price on all units, not just new sales.

Figure 9.2　**Demand and Marginal Revenue for Price Makers with One-Price Rule**

Row	Price ($)	Quantity Demanded	Total Revenue (price × quantity)	Marginal Revenue (change in total revenue)
A	$20	0	$ 0	
				▸ $18
B	$18	1	$18	
				▸ $14
C	$16	2	$32	
				▸ $10
D	$14	3	$42	
				▸ $ 6
E	$12	4	$48	
				▸ $ 2
F	$10	5	$50	

Figure 9.2 shows how many piercings Paola expects her customers to demand at different prices, and her revenues. (We will add costs in section 9.2.) These numbers are for each hour her parlour is open. The second column shows the different prices Paola is *thinking* about setting for a single nose piercing. The third column shows how many piercings she estimates her customers will demand at each price. The fourth column calculates her total revenues (price multiplied by quantity). If Paola charges $20 (row *A*), she will have no customers and no revenues. If instead she sets a price of $18 (row *B*), she will sell one piercing and get total revenues of $18 ($18 × 1). If she sets a price of $16 (row *C*), she will sell two piercings and get total revenues of $32 ($16 × 2). Paola must lower her price to sell more piercings — that is the law of demand.

To understand marginal revenue — the last column in Figure 9.2 — let's compare two prices that Paola is considering in rows *B* and *C*. In *planning* her price-making strategy, if she wants to increase her sales from one to two piercings, she must drop the price from $18 to $16. If she does so, total revenues increase from $18 to $32. So what is Paola's additional, or marginal, revenue from selling the second piercing? It is the change in total revenue from $18 for one piercing to $32 for two piercings, or $14 ($32 − $18). The $14 appears *between* rows *B* and *C* because marginal revenue is the change in moving *between* the total revenues of rows *B* and *C*.

Are you surprised by the $14? If Paola sells the second piercing in row *C* for $16, why is her marginal revenue only $14, and not the $16 price?

The answer lies in the one-price rule. To sell the second piercing at the lower price of $16, Paola must also drop the price of the first piercing from $18 to $16. So *while Paola gets an additional $16 from the second piercing, she has to subtract the $2 less she gets on the first piercing*: $16 − $2 = $14. That is why Paola's marginal revenue from selling the second piercing is only $14, not $16.

NOTE
Even when price cuts increase total revenue, marginal revenue from each additional unit sold decreases as sales increase.

Time Machine Explanation Why Marginal Revenue Is Less Than Price

Still not clear? This is where a time machine is helpful. Paola, like most business owners, has to make a price-making decision *before* sales start. Customers want to know the prices when they walk into the store.

Suppose she chooses the row *B* price of $18 for a piercing. After one hour, she has sold one piercing, for total revenue of $18. Now take the time machine back to before Paola decides on a price. This time, she chooses the row *C* price of $16 for a piercing. After one hour, she has sold two piercings for a total revenue of $32. Both piercings had to sell for the same price of $16 because of the one-price rule. One more trip back in the time machine. Paola chooses the row *D* price of $14. After one hour, she has sold three piercings for a total revenue of $42.

The marginal revenue *between* the decisions of an $18 price in row *B* and a $16 price in row *C* is $14 ($32 – $18). The marginal revenue *between* the decisions of a $16 price in row *C* and a $14 price in row *D* is $10 ($42 – $32). Does that make more sense — not the time machine, but the calculations of marginal revenue as the change in total revenue *between* pricing decisions?

In reality, there is no time machine, and Paola only gets to choose one price, and must sell all piercings at that price. Think about the pricing decision as being *planned* — on paper, or in discussions, *before the selling begins*. Which time-machine scenario price will be most profitable for Paola?

▲ Paola must plan her pricing decisions before the selling actually begins. She must choose a pricing strategy that she thinks will maximize her profits, and hope that it works.

Marginal Revenue Curve for Price Makers Figure 9.3 graphs the information from Figure 9.2. Points *A* – *F* on the demand curve correspond to rows *A* – *F* in the table. This is a typical downward-sloping shaped demand curve for any price-making business. To keep the table of numbers from getting too long, I omitted the points on the demand curve below *F*.

Figure 9.3 Demand and Marginal Revenue for Price Makers

Row	Price ($)	Quantity Demanded	Total Revenue (price × quantity)	Marginal Revenue (change in total revenue)
A	$20	0	$ 0	
				$18
B	$18	1	$18	
				$14
C	$16	2	$32	
				$10
D	$14	3	$42	
				$ 6
E	$12	4	$48	
				$ 2
F	$10	5	$50	

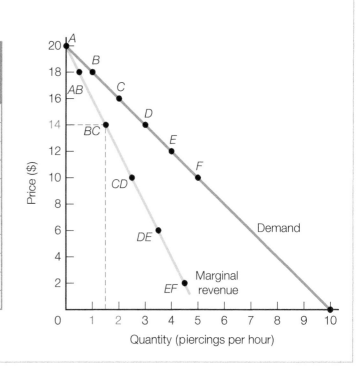

What's new on the graph is the marginal revenue curve (actually a straight line). The points on the marginal revenue curve come from the marginal revenue column in the table of numbers.

You draw a marginal revenue curve the same way you read it — start at the quantity and go up and over to the marginal revenue. But we calculate marginal revenue *between* quantities. For example, *between* rows *B* and *C*, quantity demanded goes from one to two piercings. Since we are moving *between* quantity 1 and quantity 2, we split the difference and use the quantity 1½ to plot the value for marginal revenue — point *BC* on the marginal revenue curve. All of the other points on the marginal revenue curve are plotted the same way, halfway *between* the quantities used for the marginal revenue calculations.

Notice that *the marginal revenue curve for price makers is not the same as the demand curve.* For any quantity, marginal revenue is less than price for price makers.

NOTE
For price makers, the marginal revenue curve is *different* from the demand curve. Marginal revenue is less than price.

What about Total Revenue?   Marginal revenue is one basic ingredient in the recipe for maximum profits — choose when marginal revenues are greater than marginal costs. But even as marginal revenue is falling, total revenue is still increasing. Look again at the table. Total revenue increases from $0 in row *A*, to $18, to $32, . . . to $50 in row *F*. For the same rows, marginal revenue is falling from $18, to $14, . . . to $2. Even though marginal revenue is falling, as long as it is greater than zero, it is adding to total revenue.

As the growth in your height slowed down in your late teens, each year you grew a little less. But as long as you kept growing, you kept getting taller. Your marginal growth (additional growth per year) was falling, but your total height kept increasing.

You might think that a price-making business will keep cutting its price to increase total revenue. But you would be wrong. There is a reason why the ingredients in the recipe for maximum profits are *marginal* revenue and *marginal* cost. Smart choices are made at the margin — Key 2 of the Three Keys to Smart Choices. But before I can explain why marginal revenue is more important than total revenue, we must first examine the marginal cost ingredient.

ADDITIONAL
BENEFITS
& COSTS

Refresh 9.1

1. In your own words, define marginal revenue.

2. The connection between marginal revenue and price depends on a business's competitive environment. Why are marginal revenue and price the same for a business that is a price taker in perfect competition? Why is marginal revenue less than price for a business that is a price maker?

3. You own a business that personalizes smartphone covers. Explain to your investors how lowering your price may actually increase your total revenue.

MyEconLab

For answers to these Refresh Questions, visit MyEconLab.

9.2 Increasing or Constant? Marginal Cost

Explain when marginal cost increases and when it is constant as a business increases output.

The profits from any business decision depend upon marginal revenue being greater than marginal cost. A price-taking business in perfect competition can sell as much as it can produce without lowering price. Marginal revenue equals the price of output, and both are constant as the quantity produced increases. For a price-making business facing the one-price rule, marginal revenue is less than the price of output, and falls as the business cuts prices to increase its quantity of sales. What happens to marginal cost as quantity increases?

Different businesses have different marginal cost patterns. To answer the question of what happens to marginal cost as quantity increases, we have to shift our focus from the demand side, which determines revenues, to the supply side, which depends on costs. Let's look at the two most likely patterns of what happens to marginal cost as quantity increases — increasing marginal cost and constant marginal cost.

Figure 9.4 shows increasing (a) and constant (b) marginal costs.

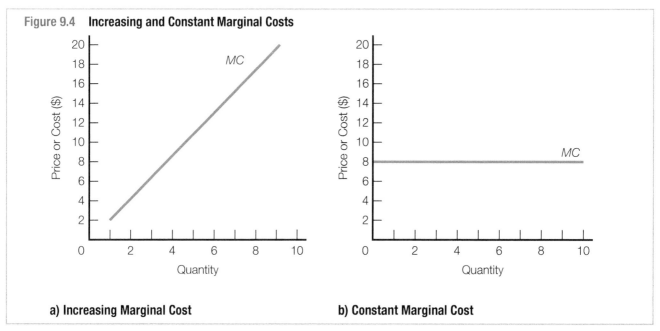

Figure 9.4 Increasing and Constant Marginal Costs

a) Increasing Marginal Cost

b) Constant Marginal Cost

Increasing Marginal Cost

Paola's shop is busy, with all her employees either piercing or nail painting. If a busload of tourists shows up all wanting piercings, what happens to Paola's marginal costs as she tries to increase piercing output?

There is not enough time to call in additional employees, so the only way for Paola to supply more piercings is to shift employees away from nail painting. Chapter 3 illustrated that as she switches employees from nail painting to piercing her marginal opportunity costs increase. She switches her worst nail painters first and doesn't lose much, but eventually she has to switch her best nail painters and loses more nail revenues. Of course, she is earning more revenues on the piercing side to offset the reduced revenues on the nail side. Her ultimate choice, as we will see, depends on a comparison of marginal revenues and marginal costs. But for now, we are just looking at the cost side, and Paola has increasing marginal costs as she increases her output of piercings.

Diminishing Returns   The wheat farmer in perfect competition provides a different example of increasing marginal costs. A smart wheat farmer will first plant his best, most productive land before planting less productive land.

Suppose it costs the farmer $500 in variable costs (for seeds, labour, fertilizer) to plant the best plot of land, which grows 500 bushels of wheat. The marginal cost per bushel of wheat is $500 divided by 500 bushels of wheat equals $1 per bushel of wheat. If the farmer wants to increase his quantity of wheat, he plants the next best plot of land. With the same $500 in variable costs, this less productive land grows only 250 bushels of wheat. The marginal cost per bushel of wheat is now $500 divided by 250 bushels equals $2 per bushel of wheat. Further increases in wheat output grown on even less productive land have even higher marginal costs.

As output increases, this pattern of decreasing productivity and increasing marginal costs is called **diminishing returns**. When increases in output lead to lower (or diminishing) productivity, then marginal costs increase. There is another example of diminishing returns in the appendix to this chapter.

diminishing returns   as output increases, decreasing productivity increases marginal costs

Most businesses operating close to capacity have increasing marginal costs as they try to increase output. Increasing output can mean adding more employees, or more employee hours, often at more expensive overtime rates. In some businesses, like oil drilling, to increase output they must shift to more expensive sources of inputs, like going from easily drilled oil wells to more difficult and costly oil sands extraction. There are businesses in all market structures — perfect competition, monopolistic competition, oligopoly, and monopoly — that have increasing marginal costs. Their marginal cost curves look like Figure 9.4a, sloping up to the right. As quantity increases, marginal cost also increases.

NOTE
Businesses operating near capacity, or shifting to more expensive inputs, have increasing marginal costs to increase output.

Constant Marginal Cost

If Paola's shop is not very busy when the busload of piercing-seeking tourists arrives, what happens to her marginal costs?

If Paola is already paying her employees for being at work, those wages are a sunk cost. What are Paola's *additional costs* in increasing her output of piercings? Remember, fixed costs like rent and insurance do not change with increases in output. Paola's additional costs, or the marginal cost of one more piercing, is just the cost of the stud and the additional electricity used by the piercing gun. That is a small, constant amount for each additional piercing.

Most businesses that are *not* operating near capacity have constant marginal costs as they increase output. For example, if a plane is not full, what is the marginal cost of adding one more passenger? A very small amount — the cost of snacks served (if any, these days!), and the tiny increase in fuel consumption for the extra weight of the passenger and luggage. All other costs of flying this extra passenger (salaries, airport landing fees, advertising, cost of buying new airplanes) are fixed costs — they do not change with one additional ticket. The same goes for the constant marginal cost of a seat in a movie theatre. Many price makers in the market structures of monopolistic competition, oligopoly, and monopoly have constant marginal costs. Their marginal cost curves look like the horizontal line in Figure 9.4b — as quantity increases, marginal cost stays constant.

In making a smart business decision, you need to identify if your business has increasing marginal costs or constant marginal costs. But no matter whether your marginal costs are increasing or constant, the same recipe applies for pricing for maximum profits.

NOTE
Businesses not operating near capacity have constant marginal costs to increase output.

Refresh 9.2

1. Define marginal cost in a way that someone who has never taken an economics course will understand it.

2. What if, when the busload of piercing-seeking tourists arrives at Paola's busy shop, she has employees on standby who she could bring in very quickly, and who would be paid their regular hourly wage? What difference, if any, would that make to Paola's marginal cost of increasing piercing output?

3. Pick one business where you think marginal costs are increasing and one where they are constant. Explain your choices showing why in each case marginal costs are increasing or constant.

9.3 Recipe for Profits: Marginal Revenue Greater Than Marginal Cost

Explain quantity and price decisions in the recipe for maximum profits, and show the importance of marginal revenue and marginal cost.

Now that we have looked at the basic ingredients of marginal revenue and marginal cost, it's time to combine them using the recipe of pricing for profits.

The recipe is: **Estimate marginal revenues and marginal costs and then set the highest price that allows you to sell the highest quantity for which marginal revenue is greater than marginal cost.**

Once we have estimated marginal revenues and marginal costs, a smart business "cook" needs to make two related decisions about quantity and price:

- Find the highest quantity for which marginal revenue is greater than marginal cost.
- Set the highest price that still allows you to sell that quantity.

NOTE
Recipe for maximum profits is easiest to follow by first looking at the quantity decision, then the price decision.

It is easiest to follow the recipe if we make the quantity decision first, and follow it with the price-setting decision.

Recipe for Profits in Numbers

Let's continue using the simple numbers from Figure 9.2. Figure 9.5 reproduces those numbers, showing how many nose piercings Paola estimates her customers will demand at different prices, and the revenues she will collect. Like any business with pricing power, Paola must lower her price to sell more. Because the one-price rule applies, that means Paola's marginal revenue falls with each increase in piercings sold, and marginal revenue falls faster than the falling price — compare columns 2 (Price) and 5 (Marginal Revenue).

Marginal revenue is listed *between* quantities of output (for example, between quantity 1 in row *B* and quantity 2 in row *C*) because marginal revenue is the change in moving *between* the total revenues from selling different quantities ($18 for 1 unit in row *B* and $32 for 2 units in row *C*).

Marginal cost may be increasing or constant. Let's start with constant marginal cost, because the numbers are simpler. But the recipe is the same even if marginal cost is increasing with increased output. (There is an example with increasing marginal costs in the appendix to this chapter.)

Column 6, Marginal Cost, shows Paola's marginal cost for each additional nose piercing is constant at $8, no matter what the quantity. This is the case where Paola is not operating near capacity, and is already paying her employees for being at work. The only additional costs for a nose piercing are the costs of the stud and the additional electricity used by the piercing gun. Paola estimates those marginal costs are $8 per piercing. Like marginal revenue, marginal cost is listed *between* quantities because it is the additional cost in moving *between* different quantities of output.

Figure 9.5 Paola's Marginal Revenues and Marginal Costs for Nose Piercings

				Column			
1	2	3	4	5	6	7	
Row	Price	Quantity Demanded	Total Revenue	Marginal Revenue	Marginal Cost	Change in Total Profit	
A	$20	0	$ 0			$ 0	
				➤$18	$8		
B	$18	1	$18			+$10	
				➤$14	$8		
C	$16	2	$32			+$ 6	
				➤$10	$8		
D	$14	3	$42			+$ 2	
				➤$ 6	$8		
E	$12	4	$48			−$ 2	
				➤$ 2	$8		
F	$10	5	$50			−$ 6	
				➤−$ 2	$8		
G	$ 8	6	$48			−$10	

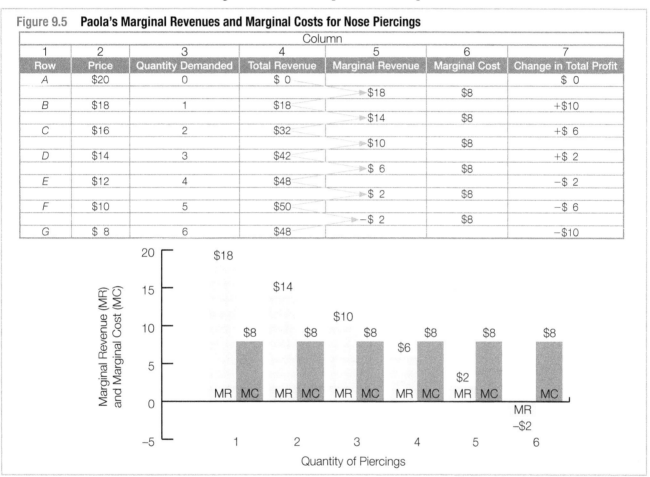

Quantity Decision What is Paola's smart quantity decision — how many nose piercings should she produce to get maximum profits? The recipe says to find the highest quantity for which marginal revenue is greater than marginal cost. Let's look at the quantities one by one, starting with the first piercing (row *B*).

If Paola produces one piercing, her marginal revenue is $18 and her marginal cost is $8. That is clearly a smart decision because marginal revenue is greater than marginal cost. The last column in Figure 9.5 shows the net impact on Paola's total profits from producing that first piercing. Total profits go up by $10, which is the amount by which marginal revenue ($18) exceeds marginal cost ($8).

Moving to row *C*, if Paola increases output to two piercings, her marginal revenue is $14 and her marginal cost is $8. Total profits increase by a further $6, so this is still a smart decision. Moving to row *D*, if Paola continues to increase output to three piercings, total profits increase by a further $2 — still smart.

NOTE
Look in sequence at each quantity — first piercing, second piercing, and so on. For each quantity, compare marginal revenue and marginal cost. If marginal revenue is greater than marginal cost, total profits will increase. Stop increasing quantity when marginal revenue is less than marginal cost.

Things change in moving to row *E*. If Paola increases output to four piercings, her marginal revenue is $6, which is less than her marginal cost of $8. Total profits *decrease by $2* if Paola produces the fourth piercing. Not a smart decision. Things get even worse if Paola produces a fifth or sixth piercing. After three piercings, profits fall as additional costs are greater than additional revenues.

Price-Making Decision   Once you have all the information for the quantity decision, the price-making decision is a piece of cake. Like any business, Paola wants to set the highest possible price that allows her to sell her target quantity of three nose piercings. Look at row *D* in Figure 9.5. The highest price Paola can charge and still sell three piercings is $14.

Recipe for Profits in Graphs

Figure 9.6 combines the demand and marginal revenue curves from Figure 9.3 with the constant marginal cost curve from Figure 9.4b.

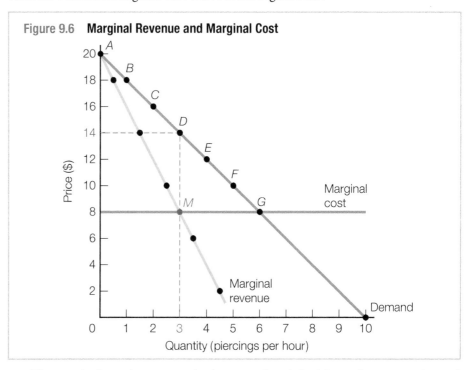

Figure 9.6   **Marginal Revenue and Marginal Cost**

The graph shows how to apply the two related decisions about quantity and price in the recipe for profits.

- Find the highest quantity for which marginal revenue is greater than marginal cost.
- Set the highest price that still allows you to sell that quantity.

Quantity Decision   To make the quantity decision first, look for where the marginal revenue and marginal cost curves intersect (point *M*). Go down from point *M* to read the number on the quantity axis — three piercings. Three is the highest quantity for which marginal revenue is greater than marginal cost. For all quantities less than three, marginal revenue is greater than marginal cost. Producing any of these quantities is a smart choice. For all quantities greater than three, marginal cost is greater than marginal revenue. Any quantity greater than three is *not* a smart choice. Three piercings is the dividing line between quantities that increase profits (up to three) and quantities that decrease profits (over three).

NOTE
Once you choose the (target) quantity with maximum profits, set the highest possible price allowing you to sell the target quantity.

Price-Making Decision   To set the highest price that still allows you to sell the highest quantity, start with three piercings on the quantity axis and go up to the demand curve (at *D*) and over to the price axis to find the price to charge — $14.

Where Marginal Revenue and Marginal Cost Intersect   The point (*M*) where the marginal revenue curve intersects the marginal cost curve is the key to the graphical version of the recipe for profits. Reading down from point *M* gives you the quantity (3) for maximum profits. Reading up from point *M* to the demand curve and over gives you the highest price the business can charge for those three units ($14). Sometimes a (graphical) picture is worth a thousand words or numbers!

NOTE
The intersection of the *MR* curve and *MC* curve is the key to the recipe for maximum profits.

Why Is This Recipe the Best?
Pricing for Maximum Economic Profits

When Paola applies the recipe for maximum profits, her smart business decision is to produce three nose piercings and to set her price at $14. How do we know *this* combination of price and quantity yields maximum *economic profits*? Businesses are ultimately interested in economic profits — revenues minus all opportunity costs (obvious costs plus normal profits). We looked at marginal revenues and marginal costs, and how Paola's decisions *change* total profits, but what about Paola's obvious fixed costs, like rent and insurance? **Fixed costs** are costs that do not change with the quantity of output produced — they are fixed. And what about the normal profits Paola needs to earn if she is to do as well as in any other business? While the success of a recipe is judged by how the dish tastes, the success of the recipe for profits is judged by whether *economic profits* are greatest, when *all costs* are taken into consideration.

fixed costs do not change with the quantity of output produced

NOTE
Economic profits
   = revenues − all opportunity costs
   = revenues − (obvious costs
     + normal profits)

Figure 9.7 reproduces all the information on revenues and costs from Figures 9.2 and 9.5 and adds two more columns. The Total Costs column adds Paola's fixed costs to the sum of all of her marginal costs. To keep the numbers very simple, assume that the portion of her fixed costs for nose piercings is $10. That number includes the normal profits she must earn on her investment to be doing as well as in any other line of business. The Economic Profits column subtracts Total Costs (which include fixed costs and normal profits) from Total Revenues.

Figure 9.7   Paola's Calculation of Economic Profits for Nose Piercings

					Column			
1	2	3	4	5	6	7	8	9
Row	Price	Quantity Demanded	Total Revenue	Marginal Revenue	Marginal Cost	Change in Total Profits	Total Costs (Fixed Costs + Sum of Marginal Costs)	Economic Profits (Total Revenue − Total Costs)
A	$20	0	$ 0			$ 0	$10 (Fixed Costs)	−$10 (Losses)
				$18	$8			
B	$18	1	$18			+$10	$18	$ 0
				$14	$8			
C	$16	2	$32			+$ 6	$26	$ 6
				$10	$8			
D	$14	3	$42			+$ 2	$34	$ 8
				$ 6	$8			
E	$12	4	$48			−$ 2	$42	$ 6
				$ 2	$8			
F	$10	5	$50			−$ 6	$50	$ 0
				−$ 2	$8			
G	$ 8	6	$48			−$10	$58	−$ 8 (Losses)

In row *A*, if Paola has no revenues and still has fixed costs of $10, her economic profits are a loss of $10. In row *B*, if Paola sells one piercing for $18, total revenues are $18 and total costs are $18 ($10 fixed costs plus $8 marginal cost for one piercing), so economic profits are $0. In row *C*, if Paola sells two piercings for $16 each, total revenues are $32, total costs are $26 ($10 fixed costs plus $8 marginal cost for the first piercing and $8 marginal cost for the second piercing), so economic profits are $6.

According to the recipe, row *D* has maximum profits. If Paola sells three nose piercings for $14 each, total revenues are $42 and total costs are $34, so economic profits are $8. What if Paola — thinking that more has been better so far — increases her output more?

Look at row *E* to see why that would be a mistake, like burning the cake by keeping it in the oven too long. If Paola sells four piercings for $12 each, total revenues are $48 and total costs are $42, so economic profits are $6. That is *less than* the smart choice of three piercings at a price of $14. Economic profits get even worse for five or six piercings.

It is important to understand the difference between the related columns Change in Total Profits and Economic Profits. Change in Total Profits tells you *by how much profits change* as a result of a decision, while Economic Profits are the *final outcomes* — what your business actually earns. Smart business decisions are based on economic profits.

Back to the Three Keys to Smart Choices

The original version of our recipe for maximum economic profits is: **Estimate marginal revenues and marginal costs and then set the highest price that allow you to sell the highest quantity for which marginal revenue is greater than marginal cost.**

When we arrange the steps in the order that businesses actually follow with the quantity decision first, the recipe looks like this:

- Find the highest quantity for which marginal revenue is greater than marginal cost.
- Set the highest possible price that allows you to sell all quantities for which marginal revenue is greater than marginal cost.

The quantity decision is much like the decision about whether Paola should keep her shop open in the evenings. In that decision, which did not involve setting prices, the only question was whether marginal revenues were greater than marginal costs.

In the quantity decision about how many nose piercings to produce, Paola compares marginal revenue and marginal cost for each additional piercing. If she makes a similar detailed decision about hours, it is like comparing marginal revenues and marginal costs for staying open one extra hour, from 7–8 p.m., then making the same comparison for an additional hour from 8–9 p.m., and finally comparing marginal revenues and marginal costs for the 9–10 p.m. hour. The principle is the same — keep increasing your quantity of output or extending your business as long as marginal revenue is greater than marginal cost. The principle applies to all business decisions.

I hope this recipe for pricing for profits reminds you of the map or model for smart choices from Chapter 1, which consists of Three Keys to Smart Choices:

1. Choose only when additional benefits are greater than additional *opportunity costs*.

2. Count only *additional* benefits and *additional* opportunity costs.

3. Be sure to count *all* additional benefits and additional opportunity costs, including *implicit costs* and *externalities*.

Our recipe for pricing for profits is much like Keys 1, 2, and 3. Paola's business "benefits" are her economic profits. A smart, profit-maximizing business decision is producing only when *marginal* revenues (*additional* benefits) are greater than *marginal* costs (*additional* opportunity costs). Differences in fixed costs (including *implicit costs* from Key 3) will not change Paola's decision.

As Key 2 says, focus only on *marginal* revenues (*additional* benefits) and *marginal* costs (*additional* costs). If Paola focused instead on *total* revenues, which are at a maximum ($50) in Figure 9.7 for five piercings, her economic profits are zero — not a smart decision. If Paola focused on *total* costs, which are at a minimum ($10) in Figure 9.7 for producing no piercings at all, her economic profits are a loss of $10 — again, not smart.

By producing the highest quantity for which marginal revenue is greater than marginal cost — three piercings — and then setting the highest possible price that allows her to sell all three piercings, Paola maximizes her economic profits ($8) and makes a smart choice. Judge the success of this recipe not by taste, but by maximum economic profits.

The recipe for pricing for profits works for any business that has to follow the one-price rule. But what happens if businesses can set different prices for different customers for the very same product or service? Check out section 9.4 to find out.

3 KEYS TO SMART CHOICES

1 CHOOSE ONLY WHEN ADDITIONAL BENEFITS ARE GREATER THAN ADDITIONAL OPPORTUNITY COSTS.

2 COUNT ONLY ADDITIONAL BENEFITS AND ADDITIONAL OPPORTUNITY COSTS.

3 BE SURE TO COUNT ALL ADDITIONAL BENEFITS AND COSTS, INCLUDING IMPLICIT COSTS AND EXTERNALITIES.

GeorgSV/Fotolia

Refresh 9.3

1. Rewrite the steps in the recipe for maximum economic profits in your own words, in the order that businesses actually do them.

2. Suppose Paola's marginal revenues and fixed costs are the same as in Figure 9.7, but her marginal costs are increasing: $1 for the first piercing, $2 for the second, $3 for the third, $4 for the fourth, $5 for the fifth, and $6 for the sixth piercing. What quantity and price will Paola choose if she is making a smart decision? [*Hint:* Create a table like Figure 9.7.]

3. You have been working too many hours at your part-time job (which pays $10 per hour), and your Economics marks are suffering. Your father, who wants you to do better in school but recognizes your desire for cash, offers you this deal. For every 1-percent increase in your mark on the next test, he will pay you $6. You estimate that one additional hour of studying will raise your mark 5 percent; a second hour of studying will raise your mark 4 percent; a third hour, 3 percent; a fourth hour, 2 percent; and a fifth hour, 1 percent. If all you are trying to do is make the most money, how many hours should you study?

MyEconLab

For answers to these Refresh Questions, visit MyEconLab.

9.4

Divide and Conquer: Price Discrimination Recipes for Higher Profits

Define price discrimination, and explain how it leads to higher profits by taking advantage of differences in elasticity of demand.

price discrimination charging different customers different prices for the same product or service

If businesses price for profits, why do they give some customers discounts for the same product or service? Seniors and children pay less for movies, even though the cost to the movie theatre of one more bum in one more seat (the marginal cost) is the same, regardless of age. For the same airline ticket from Vancouver to Montreal, you pay much less if you book at least two weeks in advance and stay over a Saturday. And your phone plan gives away evening and weekend minutes for free, when your provider's cost of delivering those phone calls is exactly the same as for daytime minutes.

Are these discounts really smart business pricing decisions, or are the businesses being charitable? How can a business be pricing for maximum profits if it is not charging the same high price to all customers? These differential prices are definitely smart and not at all charitable — they actually *increase a business's total profits*. Charging different customers different prices for the same product or service is called **price discrimination**.

Breaking the One-Price Rule

Price discrimination breaks the one-price rule, and is possible only when a business can:

- prevent low-price buyers from reselling to high-price buyers
- control resentment among high-price buyers

It's easy to resell a physical product like an iPad or a camera or a textbook — think eBay or craigslist. So it's not accidental that most examples of price discrimination involve services (getting pierced, viewing a movie, flying on an airline, using phone minutes) that cannot be easily resold. (Want to buy my nose piercing?) Ticket takers at movie theatres will not let in a 20-year-old holding a senior or child ticket. Airlines were checking ID long before the post-9/11 security concerns — you always had to prove you were the person named on the ticket. And while some phone plans allow you to share minutes with selected friends, you generally cannot resell your minutes to someone else.

How do businesses control resentment among the high-price buyers? It's all in the marketing, and the key word is *discount*. Businesses describe the higher price as the "regular" price, and the lower price as the "discounted" price. They could just as easily call the lower price the regular price, and the higher price a "premium" price. You don't need to be a marketing genius to understand why businesses choose the word *discount*!

Would it bother you to hear how little I paid for this flight?

William Hamilton

Discriminate (Cleverly) by Elasticity

So why charge lower prices to some customers? The answer goes back to elasticity of demand. In Chapter 5 we asked whether it is a smart choice for a business to hold a sale and cut prices. For revenues (price × quantity), it is a smart choice as long as the increase in quantity more than makes up for the decrease in price. Remember: "You make it up in volume." That happens when demand is elastic — even a small fall in price produces a large, responsive (elastic) increase in quantity demanded. Customers with elastic demands have a lower willingness to pay and respond well to discounts.

But if demand is inelastic — a change in price produces only a small, unresponsive (inelastic) change in quantity demanded — then the smart choice is to *raise* the price to increase revenues. The higher price more than makes up for the small decrease in quantity. Customers with inelastic demands have a higher willingness to pay and they won't all disappear if you raise prices.

So *if* you can break the one-price rule and set more than one price for your service, it is smart to set a lower price for the customers who have elastic demands, and a higher price for the customers with inelastic demands.

But how do you identify customers with different elasticities of demand, and get them to voluntarily pay different prices? This is where price discrimination schemes are so clever. Even if customers could describe their willingness to pay, none would volunteer their *high* willingness to pay if they knew you would then charge them a higher price. That would be as foolish as going to a car dealership dressed in a tuxedo and announcing how desperately you want the car whose price you are about to negotiate. The clever business strategy is to set conditions that divide customers into groups roughly approximating elastic demanders and inelastic demanders, and then charging the elastic demanders a lower price and the inelastic demanders a higher price. How do businesses accomplish what sounds like another complicated recipe for pricing for profits?

Price Discrimination at the Movies Let's start with movies. Seniors often have fixed incomes and are less willing or able to pay $13 for a movie. And parents, who pay for most of the children's tickets purchased, are less willing to pay for a child (especially if they have more than one!) than for themselves. This group (seniors and children) has, generally speaking, more elastic demand. A lower price will lead to a relatively large increase in quantity demanded, increasing total revenues. For other adults, especially the prime age group of 18- to 35-year-old moviegoers, movies are an important part of social life, and they (is this you?) are more willing and able to pay for a movie. You don't need to offer them a discount to get them into the seats. Society accepts these price differences, as it seems fair that people who are less able to pay get a lower price.

People accept price discrimination at the movies. Now that you know about price discrimination, how do you feel about different ticket prices for different groups of movie goers?

Price Discrimination on Airplanes For airlines and phone providers, the secret for successful price discrimination is to distinguish business customers from non-business customers, and set higher prices for the business customers (oops, I mean give discounted prices to non-business customers).

How do the airlines get away with that, since no customer will voluntarily tell you she is a business traveller if she knows it means you will charge a higher price? Airlines set restrictions (buy weeks in advance and stay over a Saturday) on the cheaper tickets, which makes them unattractive to business travellers but pose few problems for holiday travellers. Businesspeople often have to travel at the last minute — if the client is demanding, you usually have to go. Most business travellers, especially if they have families, do not want to be away for the weekend if they can help it (and they don't get paid for the weekend!). Businesses are also willing to pay more for tickets because they are a legitimate cost that can be charged back to the customer. For all these reasons, the airline restrictions identify the travellers whose demand is more inelastic, and who are more willing and able to pay.

On the other hand, if you are planning a holiday, buying an airline ticket in advance is no big deal. You have to ask your boss for the days off in advance anyway. You want to stay over the weekend because it adds days to your holiday beyond the workweek. And holiday travellers are very price sensitive. If an airline ticket is too expensive, they might take a driving vacation instead. Discounted tickets mean far more holiday trips, and higher revenues from non-business customers whose demand is more elastic, and who are less willing and able to pay.

NOTE
Price discrimination allows businesses to lower prices to attract price-sensitive customers (elastic demanders) without lowering prices to everyone else (inelastic demanders).

Anthony Lung, Pearson Education

Plan Name	Basic	Enhanced	Super Plus
Monthly fees	$17	$25	$35
Minutes (Billed by the second)	60	90	300
Text messages sent	70	200	Unlimited
Text Messages received	Free	Free	Free
Evenings & Weekends (Weeknights from 7 p.m. to 8 a.m. and weekends Friday 7 p.m. to Monday 8 a.m.)	n/a	n/a	n/a

▲ Price discrimination is all around us. Phone plans and airline ticket prices are two obvious examples. Where else do you see price discrimination? Do you agree with it?

Why Evening and Weekend Minutes Are Free How do Bell, Rogers, and Telus separate business customers from others, since customers will not voluntarily reveal that they want a business rate plan if they know that means a higher price? Phone providers charge "regular" prices for core business hours, and offer discounted prices for evenings and weekends. While business is increasingly becoming a 24-hour-a-day experience (ask anyone who has to carry a business phone), core business hours are still 9 a.m. to 5 p.m. Businesses must have phone service during the day, and are willing and able to pay for it. Phone bills, like airfares, are a legitimate business expense that can be recovered from customers. Businesses have a relatively inelastic demand, and a high willingness to pay for daytime minutes.

For many of us, it's no big deal to text during the day and make personal calls in the evening or on the weekend. Non-business consumers are less willing and able to pay, and have more elastic demand. Discounted plans with free evening and weekend minutes are a bargain that will lead us to use our phones more and lead to higher revenues for the phone companies.

Recipe for Price Discrimination The basic recipe for using price discrimination to increase profits is:

- prevent resale of the product or service
- charge a lower price to the elastic demand group (lower willingness to pay)
- charge a higher price to the inelastic demand group (higher willingness to pay)
- control resentment among higher price buyers

Price discrimination is a way of lowering the price to attract additional customers who are more sensitive to price (elastic demanders) without lowering the price to everyone else (inelastic demanders).

Doubling Up the Recipe for Profits

While I hope the basic recipe and examples of price discrimination make sense, they do not tell you *exactly* where a business should set its prices. A business that can prevent resale and control resentment should charge lower prices to elastic demanders and higher prices to inelastic demanders. *But exactly which higher price and exactly which lower price?*

Luckily, you already have the answers to those questions. Remember the business recipe for maximum profits? Estimate marginal revenues and marginal costs, and then set the highest price that allows the sale of the highest quantity for which marginal revenue is greater than marginal cost. That more precise recipe also applies to price-discriminating businesses.

To set exact prices *for each separate group,* the price-discriminating business estimates marginal revenues and marginal costs, and then sets the highest price that allows the sale of the highest quantity for which marginal revenue is greater than marginal cost. If a business correctly separates the groups according to elasticity, and applies the precise pricing recipe, the result is a lower price for the elastic group, a higher price for the inelastic group, and higher economic profits than the one-price strategy.

Economics *Out There*

Are You a Coupon Clipper?

Why do stores offer discounts for customers who have coupons, instead of just lowering prices for everyone?

Coupons are a form of price discrimination. Two customers (one with coupon, one without) pay different prices for the same product. Bargain-conscious customers with lower willingness and ability to pay will take the time and effort to find the coupons. Customers who are less price conscious will pay the full price rather than spend time clipping coupons. Coupons are the smarter, more profitable business strategy.

Because everyone has the option of using coupons, there is no resentment among the full-price customers.

Why Stop at Two? Price-discrimination strategies are not limited to only two groups. The more finely a business can successfully subdivide its customers by elasticity, the more profits it will earn. Airlines have different prices for 14-day advance purchase, 7-day advance purchase, 3-day advance purchase, and so on. Think about the huge number of different phone rate plans there are. All these clever price-discriminating strategies are finely tuned attempts by businesses to match prices with willingness to pay, lowering prices to attract additional customers who are more sensitive to price (elastic demanders) without lowering prices to everyone else (inelastic demanders).

Putting It All Together

Back in Chapter 5, I said, "All businesses have to live by the law of demand — a rise in price causes a decrease in quantity demanded. Smart businesses choose their price points depending on how much consumers' quantity demanded responds to a change in price — in other words, on price elasticity of demand."

In this chapter, I have combined that information about price elasticity of demand (which affects marginal revenue) with cost information (marginal cost) to find the recipe for pricing to get maximum economic profits: Estimate marginal revenues and marginal costs, and then set the highest price that allows you to sell the highest quantity for which marginal revenue is greater than marginal cost. For businesses with price-setting power, price discrimination fine-tunes that recipe, if they can get around the law of one price, prevent resale, and control resentment to set different price points for different subgroups of consumers. Pricing for profits can be as much of an art as cooking!

Economics *Out There*

Squeezing More Profits with Dynamic Pricing

Even traditional organizations like the Royal Winnipeg Ballet and Regina's Globe Theatre are following movie theatres and airlines and using price discrimination. How much does the same seat in the same row for the same show cost? It depends!

As shows become popular, prices go up for the "hottest seats on the hottest nights." This is called dynamic pricing. Using "heat maps" of seat popularity, the theatre sets continuously changing prices.

Price discrimination identifies elastic and inelastic demanders and prices accordingly. Dynamic pricing continuously adjusts the price discrimination strategy as new data become available.

Even ballet productions use elasticity of demand information to price for profits!

▲ Online shopping is a substitute for in-store shopping, making demand more elastic. As a result, businesses like this shoe store have little pricing power. And businesses selling online use dynamic pricing to identify elastic and inelastic demanders—increasing total revenue while allowing you to save money if you are willing to see a concert on an off-peak night or buy your airline tickets at the last minute.

Refresh 9.4

1. In your own words, write the basic recipe for successful price discrimination.

2. Compare the phone plan you have chosen with more expensive plans.
   What factors went into your decision to select your plan?
   What does your plan tell you about your price elasticity?

3. Explain the difference between dynamic pricing and price discrimination.
   State your opinion on the fairness of these pricing strategies.
   Should businesses be allowed to use them? Explain your answer.

Are Maximum Profits Good for All?
Market Structure and Efficiency

For maximum economic profits, the recipe for any business in any market structure is — **set the highest price that allows you to sell the highest quantity for which marginal revenue is greater than marginal cost.** Smart businesses produce all quantities up to where marginal revenue equals marginal cost, and then charge the highest possible price that allows them to sell all output.

But is what's good for business profits good for the economy as a whole? If all businesses follow the recipe for profits, does that produce an efficient outcome? It turns out the answers to these questions depend on market structure.

We will apply the Chapter 4 concepts of consumer surplus and producer surplus to the marginal revenue and marginal cost information to compare the efficiency of different market structures (section 4.4, page 87). The relationship between marginal revenue and price is different for different market structures. For price-taking businesses in perfect competition, marginal revenue equals price. For all other market structures where businesses have some price-making power, marginal revenue is less than price. These differences create different outcomes for the economy as a whole.

In all market structures, marginal cost may be increasing or constant as output increases. To simplify our efficiency comparisons and discover what's best for the economy as a whole, we will look only at examples of increasing marginal cost for all market structures. (The results would be similar with constant marginal costs.)

Efficiency of Perfect Competition and Price Takers

In perfect competition, many small sellers produce identical products or services. Each business is a price taker, but can sell as much output as it can produce at the market price. The price just covers all marginal opportunity costs of production. Because a business does not have to lower price to sell more quantity, price equals marginal revenue. Each identical business is following the recipe for profits, producing the quantity where marginal revenue equals marginal cost. Due to perfect competition, the maximum profits to be earned are just normal profits. Now let's check the efficiency of this outcome.

Perfect Competition Is Efficient   The market demand and supply curves for perfect competition are shown in Figure 9.8a, (which is similar to Figure 4.10a). The demand curve is the sum of all of the individual consumers' demand curves, and the supply curve is the sum of all of the individual businesses' marginal cost curves. The demand curve is also a marginal benefit curve; the supply curve is also a marginal cost curve. The equilibrium price where the curves intersect — in this case $60 — equals both the marginal benefit and the marginal cost of the 600th unit. For all quantities up to 600 units, marginal benefit is greater than marginal cost. Consumer surplus equals the shaded green area under the marginal benefit (demand) curve, but above the market price. Producer surplus equals the shaded blue area below the market price, but above the marginal cost (supply) curve. Total surplus, consumer surplus plus producer surplus, is maximum for perfect competition. This is an efficient market outcome, coordinating the smart choices of consumers and businesses.

Figure 9.8 Efficiency of Price Takers and Price Makers

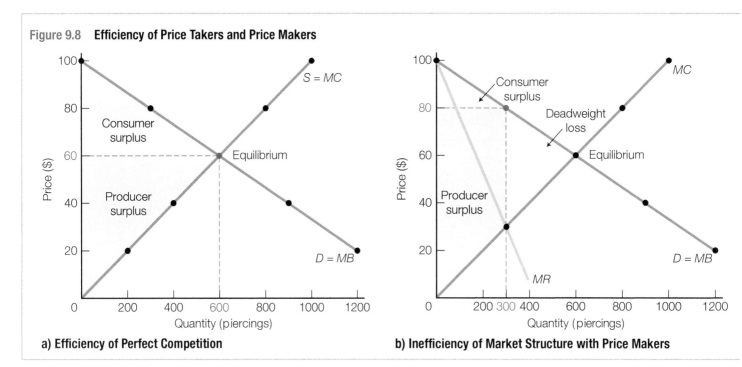

a) Efficiency of Perfect Competition

b) Inefficiency of Market Structure with Price Makers

Inefficiency of Market Structures with Price Makers

For the same demand curve and supply curves in Figure 9.8a, imagine the market is now supplied by one monopolist instead of many, many small businesses. The demand curve is now *the demand curve facing the monopolist.* The monopolist has price-making power, and must lower price to sell more. Because of the one-price rule, marginal revenue is less than price. To apply the recipe for maximum profits, we must also draw in the marginal revenue curve in Figure 9.8b.

The supply curve is now the monopolist's marginal cost curve, which is the same as the sum of all of the previous businesses' increasing marginal cost curves.

Price-Making Power Is Inefficient   Using the recipe for profits, the monopolist finds the quantity where the marginal revenue and marginal cost curves intersect, which in this case is 300. The highest possible price for selling 300 units is $80. Compare the price and quantity of monopoly with perfect competition. The monopolist restricts output from 600 units to 300 units, and raises price from $40 to $80. With the same inputs, the monopolist is producing less and charging a higher price — clearly inefficient for the economy as a whole!

We can also judge efficiency by comparing the consumer and producer surpluses of the monopolist with those of perfect competition. Compared to Figure 9.8a, the monopolist's consumer surplus in Figure 9.8b has shrunk to the green triangular area below the demand curve but above the price line of $80. The monopolist captures some of the lost consumer surplus as producer surplus.

The shaded grey area is deadweight loss (section 4.5) — potential consumer and producer surplus from the units between 300 and 600 that the monopolist does not produce. Deadweight loss reduces the total surplus for this price-making monopolist — consumer surplus plus producer surplus — to less than for perfect competition. Deadweight loss signals an inefficient market outcome.

Price-making power allows businesses to restrict output and raise prices to maximize their profits, but creates deadweight loss. The outcome is not as good for the economy as a whole as the efficiency of price-taking perfect competition.

Are Inefficient Price Makers All Bad?

The market structure of perfect competition is more *efficient* than any market structure with price makers — monopolistic competition, oligopoly, or monopoly. But there are reasons besides efficiency that might lead us to prefer price-making market structures.

Perfect competition has identical businesses producing identical products. There is no product differentiation. That would get boring very fast — "variety is the spice of life." Product differentiation creates price-making power and inefficiency, but the gains in variety may be worth the losses in efficiency.

New products are also inconsistent with perfect competition. New products come with some price-making power for their creators. While over time, competitors develop similar products — Apple's iPhone was followed pretty quickly by Samsung and other Android smartphones — new products are not usually created by price-taking businesses in perfect competition.

The economic profits of price makers, while inefficient, can finance innovation — research and development, new products, new cost-cutting techniques, new management structures, new low-cost sources of labour overseas. These competitive acts of creative destruction generate economic profits for the winners, while improving living standards for all.

Market structures with price-making power are inefficient, but have other benefits. In the next chapter we will look at some government policies aimed at fixing those inefficiencies and their outcomes.

Refresh 9.5

1. Explain in your own words why market structures with price-making power are inefficient.

2. Redraw Figure 9.8b but make the marginal revenue and marginal cost curves intersect at a quantity of 200 piercings. At that point, what are the output, price, consumer and producer surpluses, and deadweight loss?

3. If I claim that "efficient price-taking businesses are better for society than inefficient price-making businesses," is that a positive or a normative statement? Do you agree with the claim? What arguments would you make to support your position?

MyEconLab

For answers to these Refresh Questions, visit MyEconLab.

Study Guide

9.1 Is the Price You See the Revenue You Get? Marginal Revenue

Marginal revenue equals price for price takers and is less than price for price makers. Smart businesses choose actions when marginal revenue is greater than marginal cost.

- **Marginal revenue** — additional revenue from more sales or from selling one more unit.

- Marginal revenue depends on market structure (how competitive an industry is) and whether a business is a price taker or a price maker.
  - Marginal revenue *equals* price for price-taking businesses in perfect competition.
  - Marginal revenue *less than* price for price-making businesses in all other market structures.

- One-price rule — products easily resold tend to have a single price in the market.
  - When a price-making business lowers price, it must lower price *on all units* sold, not just new sales.
  - The one-price rule is why marginal revenue is less than price for price makers.

9.2 Increasing or Constant? Marginal Cost

As output increases, marginal cost increases for businesses operating near capacity or when businesses' additional inputs cost more. Marginal cost is usually constant for businesses not near capacity.

- **Diminishing returns** — as output increases, decreasing productivity increases marginal costs.

- Businesses operating near capacity, or shifting to more expensive inputs, have increasing marginal costs to increase output.

- Businesses not operating near capacity have constant marginal costs to increase output.

9.3 Recipe for Profits: Marginal Revenue Greater than Marginal Cost

A smart business decision for maximum economic profits involves both quantity and price decisions. The quantity decision is: Produce all quantities for which marginal revenue is greater than marginal cost. The price decision is: Set the highest possible price that allows you to sell that quantity. Key to maximum profits is to focus on marginal revenues and marginal costs, not on total revenues and total costs.

- Recipe for maximum profits is easiest to follow by first looking at the quantity decision, then the price decision.
  - Increase in quantity yields increase in profits if marginal revenue is greater than marginal cost.
  - Stop increasing quantity when marginal revenue is less than marginal cost.

- Once you choose the quantity with maximum economic profits (target quantity), the price part of recipe is to set the highest possible price that allows you to sell the target quantity.

- Intersection of the *MR* curve and *MC* curve is the key to the recipe for maximum profits.

- **Fixed costs** — do not change with the quantity of output produced.
  - Rent and insurance are examples of fixed costs.

- Economic profits = revenues – (obvious costs + normal profits)

9.4 Divide and Conquer: Price Discrimination Recipes for Higher Profits

Price discrimination is a business strategy that divides customers into groups. Businesses increase profits by lowering the price to attract additional price-sensitive customers (elastic demanders), without lowering the price to others (inelastic demanders).

- **Price discrimination** — charging different customers different prices for the same product or service.

- Price discrimination breaks the one-price rule. Possible only when business can:
  - prevent low-price buyers from reselling to high-price buyers
  - control resentment among high-price buyers
- Most examples of price discrimination involve *services,* which cannot easily be resold.
- Price discrimination increases profits by:
  - charging lower price to elastic demand group (lower willingness to pay)
  - charging higher price to inelastic demand group (higher willingness to pay)
- Price-discriminating business estimates marginal revenues and marginal costs for each separate group, then sets prices allowing the sale of all quantities for which marginal revenue is greater than marginal cost.

9.5 Are Maximum Profits Good for All? Market Structure and Efficiency

Maximum profits bring efficiency for perfect competition, but inefficiency for market structures with price-making power.

- Perfect competition, with price-taking businesses, is an efficient market structure.
  - Businesses just earn normal profits — economic profits are zero.
  - Maximum total surplus (consumer surplus plus producer surplus).
- All other market structures, with price-making businesses, are inefficient.
  - With same inputs, businesses reduce output and raise prices.
  - Businesses earn economic profits.
  - Total surplus is less than perfect competition because of deadweight loss from reduced output.
- There are benefits to market structures with price-making power and economic profits.
  - Product variety.
  - Economic profits finance innovations and creative destruction, improving living standards for all.

TRUE/FALSE

Circle the correct answer. Solutions to these questions are available at the end of the book and on MyEconLab. You can also visit the MyEconLab Study Plan to access additional questions that will help you master the concepts covered in this chapter.

9.1 Marginal Revenue

1. If your business decision results in marginal revenue being greater than zero, profits will increase. T **F**

2. Products that can easily be resold tend to have a single price. **T** F

3. To sell more, monopolists must lower the price on new sales only. T **F**

9.2 Marginal Cost

4. Marginal costs tend to be constant as output increases if the business is operating below capacity. T **F**

5. The marginal cost of adding passengers on a plane increases with every ticket sold. T **F**

6. Constant marginal cost means total costs are always the same. T **F**

9.3 Recipe for Profits

7. If marginal costs are greater than marginal revenues, then profits decrease. **T** F

8. An increase in the cost of rent will change the profit-maximizing quantity of output for a business. **T** F

9. The price your business chooses does not depend on the quantity you expect to sell. T **F**

9.4 Price Discrimination for Higher Profits

10. Price discrimination occurs when a business charges different customers different prices for the same product or service. **T** F

11. Price discrimination occurs more frequently among products than services. T **F**

12. Price discrimination increases profits when businesses can provide discounts to the inelastic demand group. T **F**

9.5 Market Structure and Efficiency

13. Economic profits are a sign of an efficient market structure. T F

14. Efficient market structures are always better than inefficient market structures. T F

15. Price-making power reduces consumer surplus and increases producer surplus. T F

MULTIPLE CHOICE

Circle the best answer. Solutions to these questions are available at the end of the book and on MyEconLab. You can also visit the MyEconLab Study Plan to access similar questions that will help you master the concepts covered in this chapter.

9.1 Marginal Revenue

1. Marginal revenue is the additional
   a) sales revenue from staying open later.
   b) profit from staying open later.
   c) cost from staying open later.
   d) all of the above.

2. Self-interest and competition will most likely push the price toward a single price for
   a) haircuts.
   b) coffee.
   c) tennis lessons.
   d) Broadway show tickets.

3. Which statement about prices and marginal revenues is *true*?
   a) Marginal revenue equals price for monopolists.
   b) Marginal revenue equals price for businesses in perfect competition.
   c) Marginal revenue is greater than price for monopolists.
   d) Marginal revenue is greater than price for businesses in perfect competition.

9.2 Marginal Cost

4. The marginal cost of staying open an extra hour includes
   a) additional wages.
   b) additional costs of hydro/electricity.
   c) additional costs of time.
   d) all of the above.

5. To increase output, marginal costs increase when a business must
   a) shift to more expensive sources of raw materials.
   b) switch workers from jobs they are good at to jobs they are not so good at.
   c) use more workers at overtime rates.
   d) do all of the above.

6. A business probably has constant marginal costs if
   a) workers are sending text messages and checking Facebook instead of working.
   b) customers are angry that wait times at the checkout are ridiculously long.
   c) it is offering workers increased overtime-pay rates.
   d) it is selling Christmas trees and it is the Christmas season.

9.3 Recipe for Profits

7. With each additional item sold by a monopolist under the one-price rule,
   a) total revenue falls.
   b) marginal revenue falls by less than price.
   c) marginal revenue falls by the same amount as the fall in price.
   d) marginal revenue falls by more than price.

Use the information from question 3 of the "Refresh" summary at the end of section 9.3 (repeated here) to answer questions 8 and 9.

You have been working too many hours at your part-time job (which pays $10 per hour), and your Economics marks are suffering. Your father, who wants you to do better in school but recognizes your desire for cash, offers you this deal. For every 1-percent increase in your mark on the next test, he will pay you $6. You estimate that one additional hour of studying will raise your mark 5 percent; a second hour of studying will raise your mark 4 percent; a third hour, 3 percent; a fourth hour, 2 percent; and a fifth hour, 1 percent. If all you are trying to do is make the most money, how many hours do you study?

8. If all you are trying to do is make the most money, and you have only five hours to divide between studying and working, how many hours should you *work*?
   a) 1
   b) 2
   c) 3
   d) 4

9. You have only five hours to divide between studying and working. Suppose your boss gets desperate and offers to pay you $15 an hour. How many hours will you now *work*?
   a) 1
   b) 2 ✓
   c) 3
   d) 4

9.4 Price Discrimination for Higher Profits

10. Price discrimination increases profits when businesses can
    a) charge lower prices to consumers with elastic demand.
    b) charge higher prices to consumers with inelastic demand.
    c) control resentment among higher-price buyers.
    d) do all of the above. ✓

11. The secret for successful price discrimination is to set
    a) higher prices for customers with elastic demand.
    b) higher prices for all customers.
    c) lower prices for customers with elastic demand. ✓
    d) lower prices for customers with inelastic demand.

12. The passenger next to you who paid more than you did for her airline ticket is probably
    a) smarter than you.
    b) older than you.
    c) travelling for business. ✓
    d) all of the above.

9.5 Market Structure and Efficiency

13. When businesses follow the recipe for maximum profits, the outcome is
    a) always efficient.
    b) efficient for price-taking market structures and inefficient for price-making market structures.
    c) efficient for price-making market structures and inefficient for price-taking market structures.
    d) also best for the economy.

14. Industries with perfect competition have
    a) maximum total surplus. ✓
    b) deadweight loss.
    c) the benefits of creative destruction.
    d) product variety.

15. Industries with price-making power have
    a) the benefits of creative destruction.
    b) deadweight loss.
    c) marginal revenue equal to marginal cost at the quantity of output with maximum total profits.
    d) all of the above.

hr studying	%0 T	$	OC	choice
1st	5	30	$10	study
2nd	4	24	$10	
3rd	3	18	$10	
4th	2	12	$10	
5th	1	6	$10	work

9 Appendix

Exploring Perfect Competition

Productivity, Costs, Quantities, and Profits

LEARNING OBJECTIVES

After reading this appendix, you should be able to:

9A.1 Explain why marginal revenue equals price for price-taking businesses in perfect competition.

9A.2 Describe how diminishing marginal productivity increases marginal costs and shapes the average total cost curve.

9A.3 Explain why the marginal cost curve determines the supply curve for businesses in perfect competition.

9A.4 Explain economic profits and losses as signals for businesses to exit or enter industries and change supply.

BUSINESSES DREAM of gaining monopoly's price-making power

and economic profits. But businesses have nightmares about competitive forces that push toward perfect competition's price-taking and normal profits. Those were the lessons of Chapters 7 and 8. Chapter 9 identified marginal revenues and marginal costs as the most important concepts for making smart business profit decisions.

If we combine the concepts in these three chapters and focus on the market structure of perfect competition, we can tell more detailed stories about real, not dreamed, business decisions: How do businesses decide on what quantity to supply? Where does the upward-sloping supply curve come from? How do marginal costs affect other business costs? Exactly how do economic profits direct the invisible hand?

This appendix explores the revenues and costs of perfect competition to find the answers to these questions.

9A.1
All Equal !
Marginal Revenue and Price

Explain why marginal revenue equals price for price-taking businesses in perfect competition.

The wheat industry is a good example of the market structure of perfect competition, where many identical small sellers produce an identical product or service. Each business is a price taker, but can sell as much output as it can produce at the market price.

Figure 9A.1a shows the market demand and supply curves for the wheat industry. At the intersection of the market demand and market supply curves, the equilibrium, market-clearing price for wheat is $4 per bushel.

The demand curve facing an individual wheat farmer in Figure 9A.1b is the horizontal line at a price of $4 per bushel. No buyer will pay even a penny more than $4 because he can easily get the identical product elsewhere for $4. Because the small farmer can sell as much wheat as he can grow at the market price of $4, there is no need to lower price to sell more. Marginal revenue equals price. This horizontal demand curve is also a marginal revenue curve for the farmer.

Figure 9A.1   Perfect Competition: Industry and Individual Business Demand and Price

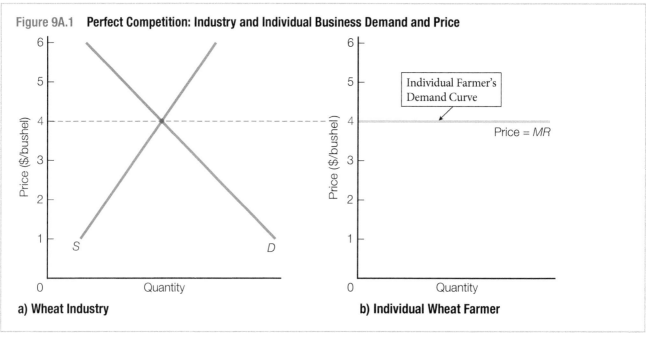

a) Wheat Industry

b) Individual Wheat Farmer

The market structure of perfect competition has a simple relationship between marginal revenue and price: They are the same. That's why this section is so short! (Section 9.1 explains in more detail why marginal revenue equals price for a business in perfect competition.)

Refresh 9A.1

MyEconLab
For answers to these Refresh Questions, visit MyEconLab.

1. Explain in your own words why marginal revenue and price are equal for a small business in perfect competition.

2. Identify another industry that fits the description of perfect competition. Explain your choice.

3. Starting from perfect competition, what changes in an industry would cause price to be *unequal* to marginal revenue?

More Gets You Less: Costs and Diminishing Marginal Productivity

Marginal costs are the most important costs for smart profit decisions, but other costs also play a role. Chapter 7 explained obvious or explicit costs like rent or wages, as well as hidden opportunity costs like normal profits. Let's look more closely at obvious costs, to better see where marginal costs come from, and how they determine a business's quantity supplied decision and the upward-sloping supply curve.

Fixed Costs and Variable Costs

Wheat farmers, like most businesses, have fixed costs and variable costs. *Fixed costs* (Chapter 9) are for inputs that do not change with the quantity of output produced. Fixed costs for the wheat farmer include land costs, property taxes, and insurance. To simplify the example, we will combine normal profits — compensation for a business owner's time and money — with fixed costs. **Variable costs** do change with output — they vary! Variable costs include the amount of water and fertilizer the farmer uses, and especially the number of labourers the farmer must hire to increase the quantity of wheat he grows. Adding together the fixed costs and the variable costs gives us the **total cost**.

variable costs change with changes in the quantity of output produced

Total Cost = Total Fixed Costs (including normal profits) + Total Variable Costs

total cost fixed costs plus variable costs

Diminishing Marginal Productivity

Let's use some easy, made-up numbers to illustrate these costs. To simplify even further, suppose that the farmer's only variable cost is what he pays for additional labourers.

Total Product and Marginal Product   Figure 9A.2 (on the next page) shows what happens to the farmer's total output of wheat as he hires more labourers. Column 2 lists the different number of labourers he could hire per year, from zero to five. Column 3 shows the total quantity of wheat produced per year when the labourers work with the fixed amount of land and other inputs. The total output that labourers produce when working with all fixed inputs is also called **total product**.

Column 4 lists each labourer's **marginal product** — the *additional* output gained from adding one more labourer. Marginal product is calculated as the change in total product from adding one more labourer. As you might guess from Key 2 (count only *additional* benefits and *additional* costs), marginal product is more important than total product. Ignore the last column — marginal cost — for now.

total product total output labour produces when working with all fixed inputs

marginal product additional output from hiring one more unit of labour

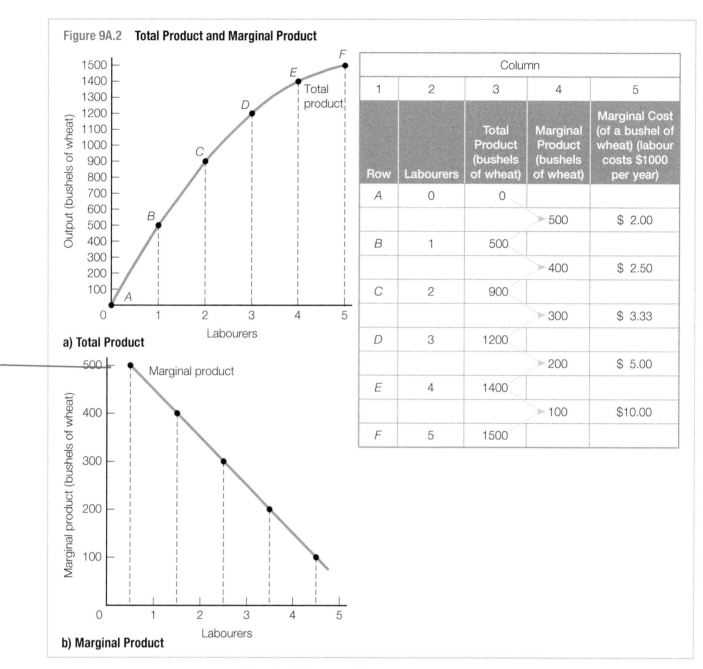

Figure 9A.2   Total Product and Marginal Product

a) Total Product

b) Marginal Product

	Column				
	1	2	3	4	5
Row	Labourers	Total Product (bushels of wheat)	Marginal Product (bushels of wheat)	Marginal Cost (of a bushel of wheat) (labour costs $1000 per year)	
A	0	0			
			500	$ 2.00	
B	1	500			
			400	$ 2.50	
C	2	900			
			300	$ 3.33	
D	3	1200			
			200	$ 5.00	
E	4	1400			
			100	$10.00	
F	5	1500			

Marginal Products Decrease   Marginal products are measured in bushel of wheat — we will add dollar costs shortly — and decrease with each additional labourer. The first labourer hired increases total product from zero to 500 bushels of wheat. The marginal product of the first labourer is 500 bushels of wheat. Because marginal product is the *change* in total product, it is listed halfway between total products of zero and 500. The second labourer hired increases total product from 500 bushels to 900 bushels. Her marginal product is 400 bushels of wheat. The third labourer hired increases total product from 900 bushels to 1200 bushels, a marginal product of 300 bushels of wheat.

The numbers in the table in Figure 9A.2 are shown in the graphs. Figure 9A.2a shows the total product produced by 1, 2, 3, 4, and 5 labourers. Because total product is the output of all labourers working with all fixed inputs, the numbers for total product appear directly above the total number of labourers. For example, 2 labourers produce an output of 900 bushels of wheat, so 900 bushels is plotted directly above 2 labourers.

Figure 9A.2b shows the marginal product of the 1st, 2nd, 3rd, 4th, and 5th labourers. Because marginal product measures the *change* in total product as you add more labourers, marginal product appears *halfway* between labourers. For example, the marginal product in changing from 1 labourer to 2 labourers — 400 bushels — is plotted halfway between 1 and 2 labourers.

Looking at column 4 of the table or at the Figure 9A.2b, the marginal product of each additional labourer decreases. Marginal product decreases because of **diminishing marginal productivity**. With fixed amounts of tools and other inputs, as you add more labourers, they have to share tools, and eventually may get in each others' way. Productivity diminishes. As you add more of a variable input to fixed inputs, the marginal product of the variable input eventually diminishes.

Measuring diminishing productivity and output in bushels of wheat or any product is a start, but businesses are interested in the bottom line of profits. To calculate profits, we have to turn these quantities of output into costs, and subtract costs from revenues.

diminishing marginal productivity as you add more of a variable input to fixed inputs, the marginal product of the variable input eventually diminishes

From Diminishing Marginal Productivity to Increasing Marginal Costs

The marginal cost of an additional bushel of wheat depends on how much the farmer pays for each labourer. Marginal cost can be calculated as the additional opportunity cost of increasing quantity supplied (section 3.1) or as the change in total costs from producing an additional bushel of wheat. How much does each additional bushel of wheat cost the farmer as he increases output by hiring more labourers?

NOTE
Marginal cost can be calculated as the change in total cost of producing an additional unit of output.

Increasing Marginal Costs Sticking with simple, made-up numbers, suppose each labourer can be hired for $1000 per year. The last column of the table in Figure 9A.2 shows the farmer's marginal cost calculations.

The first labourer the farmer hires has a marginal product of 500 bushels of wheat. It costs the farmer $1000 for that labourer, so the marginal cost of each bushel the labourer produces is

$$\frac{\$1000}{500 \text{ bushels}} = \$2 \text{ per bushel of wheat}$$

This $2 is the *additional* cost the farmer must pay per bushel to increase output from zero to 500 bushels. The marginal cost of $2 per bushel does not include fixed costs, which we will get to soon.

To further increase output, the farmer must hire a second labourer for a year and pay an additional $1000. The second labourer produces only 400 additional bushels of wheat. The marginal cost of each bushel the second labourer produces is

$$\frac{\$1000}{400 \text{ bushels}} = \$2.50 \text{ per bushel of wheat}$$

For the 3rd, 4th, and 5th labourers, marginal costs per bushel continue to increase from $3.33 to $5.00 to $10.00.

NOTE

As more labourers produce more
output, diminishing marginal
productivity increases marginal costs.

As more labourers are hired and output increases, diminishing marginal
productivity increases marginal costs.

Figure 9A.3 graphs the quantity of output (on the horizontal axis) and the
marginal cost (on the vertical axis) from the table of numbers in Figure 9A.2. As
with all marginal variables, marginal cost is plotted halfway between the relevant
quantities of output. For example, marginal cost of $2 per bushel is plotted above
250 bushels, halfway between the zero bushels produced with no labour and the
500 bushels produced by the first labourer hired.

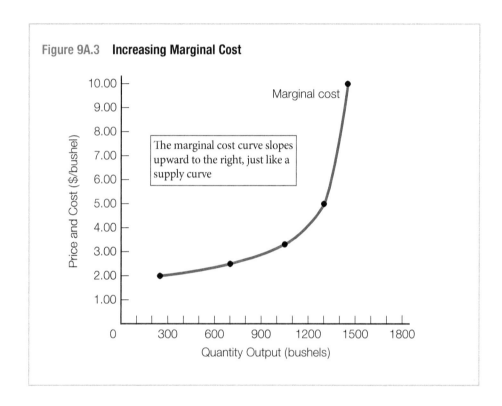

Figure 9A.3   Increasing Marginal Cost

The marginal cost curve slopes
upward to the right, just like a
supply curve

From Marginal Costs to Average Total Costs

To complete the picture of the farmer's costs, we only have to add information
about fixed costs. Let's say, for this example, total fixed costs (which include a
payment for normal profits) are $1800.

Figure 9A.4   Marginal Costs and Average Total Costs

		Column					
1	2	3	4	5	6	7	8
Row	Labourers	Output (Total Product bushels wheat)	TFC (Total Fixed Cost)	TVC (Total Variable Cost)	TC (Total Cost)	MC (Marginal Cost)	ATC (Average Total Cost)
A	0	0	$1800	0	$1800		— —
						$2.00	
B	1	500	$1800	$1000	$2800		$5.60
						$2.50	
C	2	900	$1800	$2000	$3800		$4.22
						$3.33	
D	3	1200	$1800	$3000	$4800		$4.00
						$5.00	
E	4	1400	$1800	$4000	$5800		$4.14
						$10.00	
F	5	1500	$1800	$5000	$6800		$4.53

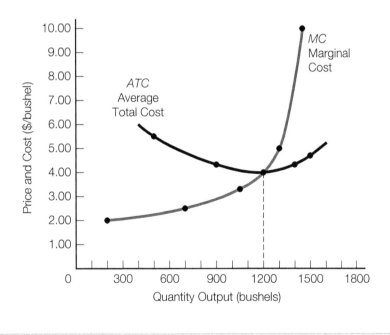

Total Costs and Marginal Cost   The table in Figure 9A.4 has the same columns as the table in Figure 9A.2, except Figure 9A.4 leaves out the Marginal Product column and adds cost columns. For each quantity of output in column 3, column 4 shows the total fixed cost (*TFC*). The $1800 is the same for every quantity of output, because fixed costs are fixed — they do not vary with output.

Column 5 shows the total variable cost (*TVC*) for hiring all labourers required to produce that quantity of output. A quantity of 900 bushels of output, for example, requires two labourers for a *TVC* of $2000.

Total cost (*TC*) in column 6 adds total fixed cost (*TFC*) and total variable cost (*TVC*).

The numbers in the marginal cost (*MC*) column are the same as in Figure 9A.2 on page 236, but they are calculated in a different way. Figure 9A.2 calculates marginal cost *between* rows by dividing an additional labourer's cost ($1000) by his or her marginal product measured in bushels of wheat. In Figure 9A.4, marginal cost is also calculated *between* rows, but by taking the change in total cost and dividing by the change in quantity of output. For example, between Rows *A* and *B*, total cost changes by $1000 (from $1800 to $2800) and the quantity of output changes by 500 bushels (from zero to 500). $1000 divided by 500 bushels equals $2 per bushel.

The two calculations give the same result because fixed costs do not change between rows *A* and *B*. The change in total cost ($1000) equals the additional labour cost ($1000) in Figure 9A.2. And the change in output (500 bushels) between rows *A* and *B* equals the marginal product of the first labourer (500 bushels) in Figure 9A.2.

average total cost   total cost per unit of output

Average Total Cost   The last column (8) in Figure 9A.4 shows the **average total cost** (*ATC*) of a bushel of wheat at each quantity of output. *ATC* is calculated for each row as total cost (*TC*) divided by quantity of output. For row *B*, the total cost (*TC*) is $2800 and the quantity of output is 500 bushels of wheat. So *ATC* equals $5.60 per bushel ($2800 divided by 500 bushels).

Marginal cost (*MC*) is the most important cost concept for business decisions, but average total cost (*ATC*) is a close second. All of the other cost concepts in Figure 9A.4 are much less important and are shown mainly because they are necessary for calculating average total cost (*ATC*).

The graph in Figure 9A.4 uses the numbers in the table to graph marginal cost and average total cost.

Marginal Cost and Average Total Cost   The average total cost curve has a U-shape. As output increases, *ATC* first decreases, reaches a minimum at 1200 bushels of output, and then increases. There is an important relationship between marginal cost and average total cost that explains the U-shape of the average total cost curve.

For any quantity between zero and 1200 bushels, marginal cost is less than average total cost — the marginal cost curve is *below* the average total cost curve. For any quantity greater than 1200 bushels, marginal cost is more than average total cost — the marginal cost curve is *above* the average total cost curve. The average total cost curve is *decreasing* for quantities up to 1200 bushels (downward sloping to the right), and *increasing* for quantities greater than 1200 bushels (upward sloping to the right). At the point where average total costs stop decreasing and start increasing, the average total cost curve is at its minimum — its lowest point — exactly at 1200 bushels of output.

NOTE
Where *MC* < *ATC*, *ATC* is decreasing. Where *MC* > *ATC*, *ATC* is increasing. Where *MC* = *ATC*, *ATC* is at its minimum.

Marginal and Average Again   The relationship between average total cost and marginal cost is very similar to your average marks in a class. Suppose you have had three quizzes with scores of 4, 5, and 6 marks. You calculate your average mark by adding the scores and dividing by the number of quizzes — (4 + 5 + 6) ÷ 3 = 15 ÷ 3 = 5 marks.

Now suppose you take an *additional* quiz (think additional = marginal) and do badly, getting only 1 mark. What does that do to your average? Your average is now 4 marks (4 + 5 + 6 + 1) ÷ 4 = 16 ÷ 4 = 4 marks. Because your additional quiz score is lower than your average, it pulls your average down. When marginal cost is less than average total cost, it pulls average total cost down. Like your marks, *ATC* is decreasing.

Then you take yet another quiz and get 19 marks. Good job! Your average is now 7 marks (4 + 5 + 6 + 1 + 19) ÷ 5 = 35 ÷ 5 = 7 marks. Because this additional (marginal) quiz score is higher than your average, it pulls your average up. When marginal cost is greater than average total cost, it pulls average total cost up. *ATC* is increasing.

Refresh 9A.2

1. In your own words, explain diminishing marginal productivity.

2. Explain how diminishing marginal productivity causes the average total cost curve to be U-shaped.
   [*Hint:* Your explanation needs to include marginal cost.]

3. How do you know that the marginal cost curve intersects the average total cost curve at the minimum point of the average total cost curve?

MyEconLab
For answers to these Refresh Questions, visit MyEconLab.

9A.3

Prices and the Recipe for Profits: Marginal Cost Curve Determines the Supply Curve

Explain why the marginal cost curve determines the supply curve for businesses in perfect competition.

NOTE

The recipe for profits has two steps:

1. Find the highest quantity for which marginal revenue is greater than marginal cost.

2. Set the highest price that still allows you to sell that quantity.

Perfect competition simplifies the recipe by skipping step 2 because businesses are price-takers.

Using just the marginal cost curve and the average total cost curve, we can now explain the wheat farmer's quantity decision, the upward-sloping supply curve, and how profits direct the invisible hand.

Every price-taking business in perfect competition must accept the market price. Without any pricing power, the only business decision is what quantity of output to produce.

To make a smart choice, our wheat farmer, like any business in any market structure, follows the recipe for profits.

Estimate marginal revenues and marginal costs, then set the highest price that allows you to sell the highest quantity for which marginal revenue is greater than marginal cost.

Marginal revenue equals the market price of $4 per bushel of wheat. Marginal costs appear on the marginal cost curve. The farmer's only decision is to find the highest quantity for which marginal revenue is greater than marginal cost.

Figure 9A.5   Smart Quantity Choice for Economics Profits with Different Prices

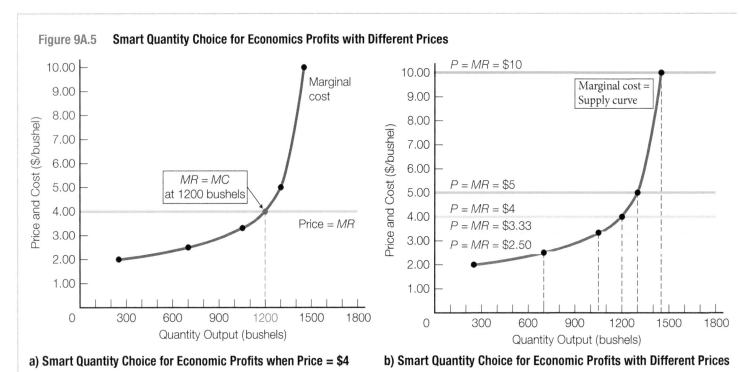

a) Smart Quantity Choice for Economic Profits when Price = $4

b) Smart Quantity Choice for Economic Profits with Different Prices

Maximum Economic Profits Where *MR* = *MC*

Applying the recipe for profits to Figure 9A.5a on page 242, the farmer's smart choice for the quantity of output is 1200 bushels of wheat. The horizontal marginal revenue curve and the upward sloping marginal cost curve intersect at the quantity 1200 bushels. If the farmer produces any less, marginal revenue is greater than marginal cost for each bushel, so the farmer misses out on profits. If the farmer produces more than 1200 bushels, marginal cost is greater than marginal revenue. The farmer loses money on every bushel above 1200. So 1200 bushels is the smart choice of quantity for maximum profits.

Figure 9A.5b shows the farmer's smart quantity decision for different prices that might be set in the wheat market. If the market price is $2.50, the marginal revenue and marginal cost curves intersect at 700 bushels, which is the quantity supplied yielding maximum profits at that price. At a market price of $5, the marginal revenue and marginal cost curves intersect at 1300 bushels, which is the quantity supplied yielding maximum profits at that price. Using this simple graph, the wheat farmer can easily choose the quantity of wheat to supply at any given price to earn maximum profit.

Marginal Cost Curve Determines the Supply Curve   The *law of supply* states that if the price of a product or service rises, the quantity supplied increases. An increase in price increases quantity supplied as you move up along the supply curve.

You have just traced the supply curve of the individual farmer! Look at Figure 9A.6, which pairs different market prices with the quantity supplied by the farmer at each price.

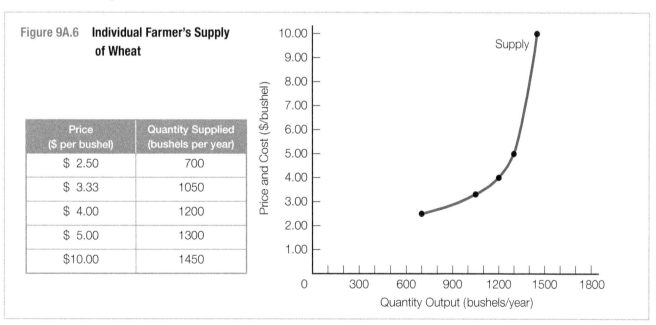

Figure 9A.6   Individual Farmer's Supply of Wheat

Price ($ per bushel)	Quantity Supplied (bushels per year)
$ 2.50	700
$ 3.33	1050
$ 4.00	1200
$ 5.00	1300
$10.00	1450

A supply curve shows, for any price, what the business's quantity supplied will be. For each price, there is a quantity supplied that is best for the farmer — the quantity that results in maximum profits. In general, the marginal cost curve is the supply curve for a business in perfect competition.

The marginal cost curve is a supply curve "in general" because businesses will not supply at prices that are so low they don't even cover variable costs. In the graph for Figure 9A.6, notice that the farmer does not supply any wheat below a market price of approximately $2. The supply curve does not go down to a zero price.

NOTE
In general, the marginal cost curve is the supply curve for a business in perfect competition.

Market Supply Curve   The market supply curve comes from adding up all individual business's supply curves. (Look back at section 3.3) For any price, the market supply curve shows the total quantity supplied from all businesses in the industry. If there are 1000 identical wheat farmers, the market supply curve for wheat is shown in Figure 9A.7.

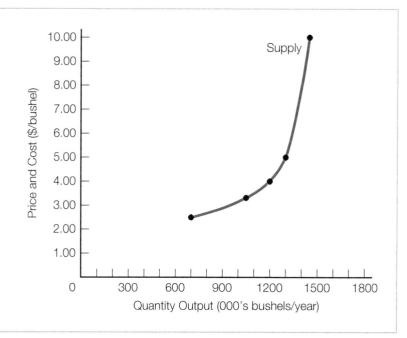

Figure 9A.7   Market Supply of Wheat with 1000 Farmers

Price ($ per bushel)	Quantity Supplied (bushels per year)
$ 2.50	700 000
$ 3.33	1 050 000
$ 4.00	1 200 000
$ 5.00	1 300 000
$10.00	1 450 000

The market supply curve also slopes upward to the right — as price increases, quantity supplied increases — since all identical businesses face diminishing marginal productivity. Diminishing marginal productivity — the source of increasing marginal costs as output increases — is the most important force determining the upward slope of individual business and market supply curves in perfect competition.

Add diminishing marginal productivity to the list of reasons you have learned for how higher prices create incentives for increased quantity supplied:

• Higher prices are necessary to cover increasing marginal opportunity costs that arise because inputs are not equally productive in all activities.

• Higher prices can bring higher profits, whether marginal costs are increasing or constant.

• Higher prices are necessary to cover increasing marginal costs that arise from diminishing marginal productivity.

The recipe for profits explains the smart decisions about quantity supplied for the wheat farmer in perfect competition — movement along a supply curve. The law of supply works as long as other factors besides price do not change.

The last section of this appendix uses the average total cost curve and economic profits to explore changes in supply — shifts of the supply curve — when one of those other factors does change.

1. In your own words, explain the three reasons why higher prices create incentives for businesses to increase quantity supplied.

2. Explain why the marginal cost curve is also the supply curve for businesses in perfect competition.

3. If the market price of wheat falls from $5 to $4 per bushel, calculate the change in the farmer's quantity supplied decision. Explain why the farmer makes that change.

MyEconLab
For answers to these Refresh Questions, visit MyEconLab.

Go or Stay?
Short-Run and Long-Run Equilibrium

9A.4

Explain economic losses and profits as signals for businesses to exit or enter industries and change supply.

There is one last smart choice for a business in perfect competition — whether to stay in its current industry or move to a different industry.

As discussed in Chapter 3, a change in the number of businesses is one of the six factors that can change supply — shift the supply curve. When businesses exit or enter an industry, the industry supply curve shifts.

To make the smart decision to go or to stay, the business needs to know about its economic losses or profits. That's where the average total cost curve — which includes normal profits — comes in.

Three Short-Run Economic Profit Scenarios

Figures 9A.8 – 9A.10 show three different short-run economic profit scenarios. These scenarios are similar to those Wahid's Web Wonders business faced in section 7.3. All businesses want maximum economic profits, which equal total revenues minus total costs. The graphs have information that allows you to see economic profits, even though total revenues and total costs don't appear directly.

From Economic Profits to Economic Profits per Unit   To connect the graphs to economic profits, follow these few steps.

$$\text{Economic Profits} = \underset{(\text{Price} \times \text{Quantity})}{\text{Total Revenue}} - \text{Total Costs}$$

If we divide by the number of units (Q), we get:

$$\frac{\text{Economic Profits}}{Q} = \frac{\text{Total Revenue}}{Q} - \frac{\text{Total Costs}}{Q}$$

So we end up with

$$\text{Economic profits per unit} = \text{Price} - ATC$$

NOTE
Economic profits per unit = Price − ATC

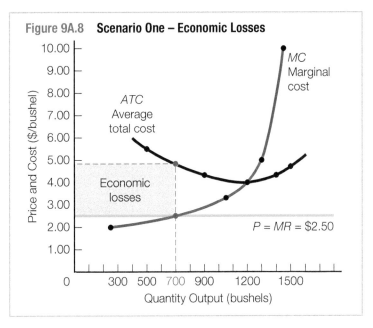

Figure 9A.8 **Scenario One – Economic Losses**

This formula for economic profits per unit allows us to calculate economic profits (or losses) in each scenario.

Scenario One — Economic Losses In Figure 9A.8, the market price is $2.50 per bushel. The recipe for profits says the farmer's smart quantity supplied choice is 700 bushels. At 700 bushels, the price of $2.50 equals the farmer's marginal costs, so the price is enough to pay the farmer's marginal cost. But there is not enough left over to pay all the other costs, including normal profits. At 700 bushels, the farmer's average total cost (*ATC*) is about $4.90, which includes all fixed costs (including normal profits) and variable costs.

The formula for economic profit per unit is

$$\text{Price} - ATC = \$2.50 - \$4.90 = -\$2.40 \text{ (economic loss)}$$

You can see the $2.40 economic loss per bushel as the vertical distance on the red rectangle labelled *Economic losses*. The horizontal distance on the red rectangle measures the number of bushels produced (700). Total economic losses is the area (height × width) of the red rectangle, which is $2.40 economic loss per bushel times 790 bushels = –$1896.

This quantity of 700 bushels is a short-run equilibrium output for the farmer, because he is making the smartest choice he can with the given price, his fixed inputs, and variable inputs. But the farmer is not happy — he is kicking himself. This is not a long-run equilibrium because the price does not cover all opportunity costs of production. Smart businesses exit the industry, and move their time, money, and inputs to where there is a promise of economic profits. Economic losses are a red light signalling smart businesses to get out of the industry.

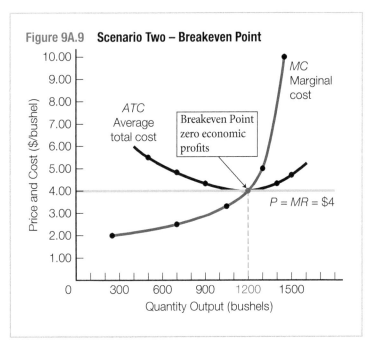

Figure 9A.9 **Scenario Two – Breakeven Point**

Scenario Two — Breakeven Point In Figure 9A.9, the market price is $4 per bushel. The farmer's smart quantity supplied choice is 1200 bushels. At 1200 bushels, average total cost (*ATC*) is also $4, because the *P* = *MR* curve intersects both the *MC* curve and the *ATC* curve at $4. The $4 market price just covers the farmer's average total costs, which include all costs, including normal profits. The farmer is making normal profits, but no more. His economic profits are zero.

Economic profit per unit is

$$\text{Price} - ATC = \$4 - \$4 = \$0 \text{ (zero economic profits)}$$

This is the *breakeven point* for the farmer. He is doing as well as the best alternative uses of his time and money. His profits are normal profits only — the same as average profits in other industries. This quantity of 1200 bushels is a short-run equilibrium output for the farmer because he is making the smartest choice he can with his fixed inputs and variable inputs. It is also a long-run equilibrium because economic profits are zero, and there is no incentive for the farmer to change industries.

Scenario Three — Economic Profits   In Figure 9A.10, the market price is $10 per bushel. The farmer's smart quantity supplied choice is 1450 bushels. At 1450 bushels, the farmer's average total cost *(ATC)* is about $4.50. The $10 market price not only covers the farmer's marginal costs, it more than covers his average total costs, which include all costs, including normal profits.

The formula for economic profit per unit is

$$Price - ATC = \$10.00 - \$4.50 = \$5.50 \text{ (economic profit)}$$

You can see the $5.50 economic profit per bushel as the vertical distance on the green rectangle labelled *Economic profits*. The horizontal distance on the green rectangle measures the number of bushels produced (1450). Total economic profits on all bushels produced is the area (height × width) of the green rectangle, which is $5.50 economic profit per bushel × 1450 bushels = $7975.

This quantity of 1450 bushels is a short-run equilibrium output for the farmer, because he is making the smartest choice he can with his fixed inputs and variable inputs. Even though the farmer is happy with this outcome, it is not a long-run equilibrium. Economic profits are a signal that consumers are willing to pay a price greater than businesses' opportunity costs of production. This green light directs the farmer to invest more time and money in the industry. It is also a signal for other businesses to enter.

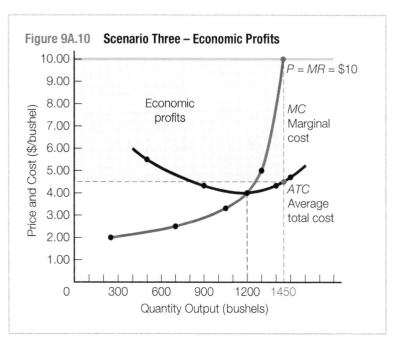

Figure 9A.10   Scenario Three – Economic Profits

Long-Run Economic Profit Adjustments

Figure 9A.11 shows what happens in the long run following each short-run economic profit scenario.

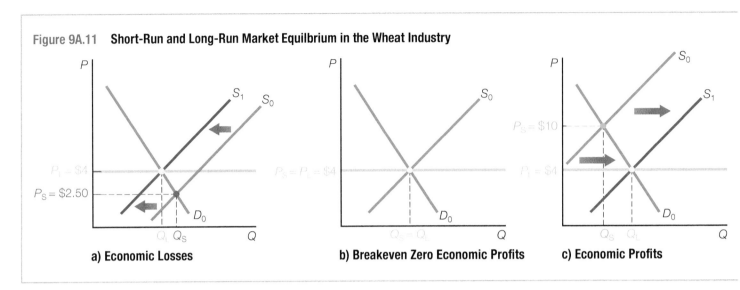

Figure 9A.11   Short-Run and Long-Run Market Equilbrium in the Wheat Industry

a) Economic Losses

b) Breakeven Zero Economic Profits

c) Economic Profits

Scenario One — Long Run Adjustments to Economic Losses   Figure 9A.11a
(similar to Figure 7.4a on page 177) tells the story of economic losses and exit.
The market supply curve for wheat associated with the short-run equilibrium
price (P_S) of $2.50 per bushel is S_0. With economic losses at the $2.50 price,
businesses exit the wheat industry, shifting the market supply curve leftward
towards S_1. The market price rises, businesses keep exiting, and supply keeps
shifting leftward until reaching S_1. Once at supply curve S_1, the new $4 market
price is high enough to just cover all opportunity costs of production. The $4 per
bushel price of wheat is a long-run equilibrium price (P_L). Businesses no longer
have any incentive to move and shift supply.

Scenario Two — Breakeven Point Is Long-Run Equilibrium   Figure 9A.11b
shows the wheat industry's market demand and supply curve when the price is
$4 per bushel. This is both a short-run equilibrium price and a long-run
equilibrium price. With zero economic profits, businesses stay where they are.
No one is kicking herself. There is no incentive for businesses to exit or enter the
wheat industry.
  Zero economic profits are a yellow light, signalling proceed with caution.
Yellow is an "equilibrium" signal — no reason to change. This industry
has average, or normal, profits. No economic profits, but no economic
losses either.

Scenario Three — Long-Run Adjustments to Economic Profits
Figure 9A.11c (similar to Figure 7.4b on page 177) tells the story of economic
profits and entry. The market supply curve for wheat associated with the
short-run equilibrium price (P_S) of $10 per bushel is S_0. With economic
profits available, businesses enter the wheat industry, shifting the market
supply curve rightward toward S_1. The market price falls, businesses keep
entering, and supply keeps shifting rightward until reaching S_1. Once at
supply curve S_1, the new $4 market price has fallen enough to just cover all
opportunity costs of production. That $4 per bushel price of wheat is a long
run equilibrium price (P_L). Businesses no longer have any incentive to move
and shift supply.

The Invisible Hand Again

Exploring the market structure of perfect competition gives more complete stories about an individual business's costs, economic profits, and quantity supplied decisions. Diminishing marginal productivity is the force behind increasing marginal costs and shapes the upward-sloping marginal cost curve, the individual business supply curve, and the market supply curve.

The detailed cost information makes it easier to see different economic loss and profit scenarios, which serve as signals for businesses to exit or enter industries. Economic losses and profits cause changes in supply, which change prices and quantities, moving an industry from a short-run equilibrium to a long-run equilibrium with zero economic profits.

In long-run equilibrium, each business in perfect competition is producing at the breakeven point, where average total costs are at a minimum. Each business is producing efficiently, at the lowest possible average total cost. This is one of the desirable outcomes from perfect competition. The other desirable outcome comes from economic losses and profits, signalling the invisible hand to direct business owners' self-interest to unintentionally produce the miracle of markets — the products and services that consumers most value.

NOTE

In long-run equilibrium, each business in perfect competition is producing at the lowest possible average total cost, and producing the products and services that consumers value the most.

Refresh 9A.4

1. Which of the three scenarios would cause businesses to enter an industry? Explain why that increase in the number of businesses in an industry causes the market supply curve to shift rightward.

2. In Figure 9A.9, explain why the breakeven point is a market price of $4 per bushel and an output of 1200 bushels.

3. The paper clip industry is perfectly competitive and is initially in long-run equilibrium. Then the demand for paper clips decreases because people are using tablets and less paper. Using one graph for the paper clip industry and one graph for an individual business like Figures 9A.11a and 9A.8, (remember to title your graphs), tell the story of what will happen to market price, economic profits or losses, and the adjustment to a new long-run equilibrium.

MyEconLab

For answers to these Refresh Questions, visit MyEconLab.

Study Guide

9A.1 All Equal ! Marginal Revenue and Price

The demand curve for an individual price-taking business in perfect competition is also a marginal revenue curve — a horizontal line at the market price.

- In the market structure of perfect competition, each small, identical business is a price-taker.
  - Because each business can sell as much output as it can produce at the market price, there is no need to lower price to sell more.
  - Marginal revenue equals price.
  - Each business's individual demand curve — a horizontal line at the market price — is also its marginal revenue curve.

9A.2 More Gets You Less: Costs and Diminishing Marginal Productivity

Because of diminishing marginal productivity, marginal costs increase as output increases, and the average total cost curve is U-shaped.

- A business's **Total Cost** = Total Fixed Costs + Total Variable Costs
  - *Fixed costs* — do not change with quantity of output produced; include *normal profits* (compensation for a business owner's time and money – average profits in all industries).
  - **Variable costs** — change with changes in the quantity of output produced.
- **Total Product** — total output labour produces when working with all fixed inputs.
  - **Marginal product** — additional output from hiring one more unit of labour.
  - **Diminishing marginal productivity** — as you add more of a variable input to fixed inputs, the marginal product of the variable input eventually diminishes.
- As more labourers produce more output, diminishing marginal productivity increases marginal costs (*MC*).
  - The marginal cost curve slopes upward to the right.
  - Marginal cost can be calculated as the change in total cost of producing an additional unit of output.

- **Average Total Cost** (*ATC*) — total costs per unit of output
  - Total costs divided by quantity
  - *ATC* curve is U-shaped — as output increases, *ATC* first decreases, then increases.
  - Where *MC* is less than *ATC*, *ATC* is decreasing.
  - Where *MC* is greater than *ATC*, *ATC* is increasing.
  - Where *MC* equals *ATC* (*MC* and *ATC* curve intersect), *ATC* is at its minimum.

9A.3 Prices and the Recipe for Profits: Marginal Cost Curve Determines the Supply Curve

The marginal cost curve determines the supply curve for businesses in perfect competition.

- Recipe for profits in perfect competition is to find the highest quantity for which marginal revenue (*MR*) is greater than marginal costs (*MC*).
  - If *MR* = *MC*, the business earns maximum total profits.
  - If *MR* > *MC*, the business increases quantity of output to increase profits.
  - If *MR* < *MC*, the business decreases quantity of output to increase profits.
- *Law of Supply* — if the price of a product or service rises, the quantity supplies increases. Three reasons why higher prices create incentives for increased quantity supplied:
  - Higher prices are necessary to cover increasing marginal opportunity costs that arise because inputs are not equally productive in all activities.
  - Higher prices can bring higher profits, whether marginal costs are increasing or constant.
  - Higher prices are necessary to cover increasing marginal costs that arise from diminishing marginal productivity.

9A.4 Go or Stay?
Short-Run and Long-Run Equilibrium

Economic losses and profits are signals for businesses to exit or enter an industry, shifting industry supply and returning the industry to long-run equilibrium, where economic profits are zero and average total costs are at a minimum.

- The marginal cost and marginal revenue curves are most important for finding a business's short-run equilibrium — the quantity of output yielding maximum total profits. Economic profits may be positive or negative (economic losses) in short-run equilibrium.

- The average total cost (*ATC*) curve is most important for finding a business's long-run equilibrium, where economic profits are zero.

- Economic profits (or losses) per unit = Price – *ATC*

- Three economic profit scenarios

  - **Scenario One** — Economic losses are red lights, signalling businesses to exit an industry, decreasing industry supply. Market price rises, businesses keep exiting, and industry supply keeps shifting leftward until price rises to equal *ATC*, covering all opportunity costs of production.

  - **Scenario Two** — The *breakeven point* for a business is the price and quantity combination with zero economic profits. This is a yellow light, signalling businesses are breaking even and just earning normal profits. The is no incentive for businesses to exit or enter the industry, and no change in industry supply.

  - **Scenario Three** — Economic profits are green lights, signalling businesses to enter an industry, increasing industry supply. Market price falls, businesses keep entering, and industry supply keeps shifting rightward until price falls to just equal *ATC*, covering all opportunity costs of production.

- In long-run equilibrium, each business is producing efficiently, at the lowest possible average total cost.

- Economic profits and losses act as an invisible hand, directing business owner's interest in profits so that the market produces the products and services that consumers value the most.

TRUE/FALSE

Circle the correct answer. Solutions to these questions are available at the end of the book and on MyEconLab. You can also visit the MyEconLab Study Plan to access additional questions that will help you master the concepts covered in this chapter.

9A.1 Marginal Revenue and Price

1. The market structure of perfect competition is also called imperfect competition. T F

2. The industry demand curve for perfect competition is a horizontal line at the market price. T F

3. Because an individual business in perfect competition can sell as much as it can produce at the market price, price equals marginal revenue. T F

4. The industry supply curve in perfect competition is upward sloping. T F

9A.2 Costs and Diminishing Marginal Productivity

5. Total costs equal marginal costs plus variable costs. T F

6. As you add more of a variable input to fixed inputs, the total product of the variable input eventually diminishes. T F

7. Diminishing marginal productivity increases marginal costs. T F

8. When marginal cost is greater than average total cost, average total cost is increasing. T F

9. When marginal cost is equal to average total cost, average total cost is at its maximum. T F

9A.3 Marginal Cost Curve Determines the Supply Curve

10. Perfect competition simplifies the recipe for profits because businesses are price takers. T F

11. In general, the average total cost curve is the supply curve for businesses in perfect competition. T F

12. When a business in perfect competition follows the recipe for profits, it chooses a quantity of output where marginal revenue equals marginal cost. T F

13. At the breakeven quantity of output for   T   F
a business in perfect competition, marginal
cost equals average total cost.

14. When businesses are suffering economic   T   F
losses, the market price eventually rises.

15. When businesses are breaking even,   T   F
normal profits are zero.

MULTIPLE CHOICE

Circle the best answer. Solutions to these questions are available at the end of the book and on MyEconLab. You can also visit the MyEconLab Study Plan to access similar questions that will help you master the concepts covered in this chapter.

9A.1   Marginal Revenue and Price

1. **Which of the following is *not* a characteristic of perfect competition?**
   a) downward-sloping industry demand curve
   b) horizontal demand curve facing each individual business
   c) each business decides its quantity of output
   d) slightly differentiated products

2. **A business facing a perfectly elastic demand curve for its product**
   a) is not a price-taker.
   b) wants to lower its price to increase sales.
   c) wants to raise its prices to increase total revenue.
   d) has a marginal revenue curve equal to the price of the product.

3. **The demand curve for an individual business in perfect competition is**
   a) perfectly elastic.
   b) perfectly inelastic.
   c) also the business's marginal cost curve.
   d) also the business's average total cost curve.

9A.2   Costs and Diminishing Marginal Productivity

4. **Which of the following statements by a restaurant owner refers to diminishing marginal productivity?**
   a) "The higher the quality of the ingredients we use, the higher the cost of producing each meal."
   b) "We can increase the number of meals we serve by just adding more kitchen staff, but each additional worker adds fewer meals than the previous worker because traffic in the kitchen will get worse."
   c) "We can serve the same number of meals with fewer kitchen staff, but we would have to buy more labour-saving kitchen equipment."
   d) "We can serve the same number of meals with less kitchen equipment, but we would have to hire more kitchen staff."

5. **Marginal cost is the amount that**
   a) total cost increases when one more labourer is hired.
   b) fixed cost increases when one more labourer is hired.
   c) total cost increases when one more unit of output is produced.
   d) fixed cost increases when one more unit of output is produced.

6. **A business's total fixed costs are $100. If total costs are $200 for one unit of output and $310 for two units, what is the marginal cost of the second unit?**
   a) $100
   b) $110
   c) $200
   d) $210

7. **If *ATC* is decreasing as output increases, *MC* must be**
   a) equal to *ATC*.
   b) less than *ATC*.
   c) greater than *ATC*.
   d) decreasing.

8. **According to the idea of diminishing marginal productivity,**
   1 marginal productivity eventually increases.
   2 marginal productivity eventually decreases.
   3 marginal cost eventually increases.
   4 marginal cost eventually decreases.
   a) 1 and 3
   b) 1 and 4
   c) 2 and 3
   d) 2 and 4

9A.3 Marginal Cost Curve Determines the Supply Curve

9. In perfect competition, each business
    a) chooses price but not quantity of output.
    b) chooses quantity of output but not price.
    c) chooses both price and quantity of output.
    d) cannot choose either price or quantity of output.

10. The supply curve for a business in perfect competition is generally its
    a) marginal cost curve.
    b) marginal revenue curve.
    c) average total cost curve.
    d) marginal product curve.

11. A business in perfect competition earns maximum total profits when it chooses the quantity of output where marginal revenue
    a) equals average total cost.
    b) is greater than price.
    c) equals marginal cost.
    d) is greater than marginal cost.

9A.4 Short-Run and Long-Run Equilibrium

12. A business in perfect competition will earn economic profits when
    a) marginal revenue is greater than average total cost.
    b) marginal revenue is less than average total cost.
    c) marginal revenue equals average total cost.
    d) price equals average total cost.

13. If a profit-maximizing business in perfect competition is earning economic profits, it must be producing a quantity of output where
    a) price is greater than marginal cost.
    b) price is greater than marginal revenue.
    c) marginal cost is greater than average total cost.
    d) marginal cost is less than marginal revenue.

14. When economic profits are zero in an industry of perfect competition,
    a) the product will not be produced in the short run.
    b) the product will not be produced in the long run.
    c) revenues are not covering implicit costs.
    d) none of the above are true.

15. An industry of perfect competition is in short-run equilibrium with price below average total cost. Which of the following is *not* a prediction of what will happen in long-run equilibrium?
    a) Price will increase.
    b) Industry output will increase.
    c) Economic profits will be zero.
    d) Businesses will exit the industry.

10 When Markets Fail

Natural Monopoly, Gaming, Competition, and Government

LEARNING OBJECTIVES

After reading this chapter, you should be able to:

10.1 Define market failure and explain the challenge for policymakers of a natural monopoly.

10.2 Explain how strategic interaction between competitors complicates business decisions, creating two smart choices.

10.3 Explain how governments use laws and regulations to promote competition, discourage cartels, and protect the public from dangerous business practices.

10.4 Differentiate between the public-interest view and the capture view of government regulation.

Mel Evans/Associated Press

ARE YOU HAPPY WITH your local cable TV company's
prices and service? Did you know that the Canadian Radio-television and Telecommunications Commission (CRTC) willingly gives your cable company a legal monopoly on providing services in your neighbourhood? Why would the CRTC *prevent* competition? Why not just allow the competitive market to operate?

Markets usually work to provide the products and services we value most. Adam Smith's invisible hand can channel smart choices for you into smart choices for all. But sometimes markets fail to produce outcomes that are in society's best interests. In the next three chapters we will explore *market failures* that result in problems, such as natural monopolies (like cable TV) and cartels (like the Organization of Oil Exporting Countries – OPEC), pollution (Chapter 11), and poverty and inequalities (Chapter 12). When markets fail, governments often step in to correct the failures. Regulations, Crown corporations, and competition laws are all attempts by governments to produce more efficient and desirable outcomes for society.

While well-intentioned, these government policies can sometimes do more harm than good, making the outcome *less* efficient and *less* desirable. Like rent controls, government regulations can have negative, unintended consequences. When that happens, we call it *government failure* rather than market failure. Sometimes policies designed to protect the public work well, but sometimes government policies end up promoting the special interests of the businesses being regulated.

In this chapter, we examine the trade-offs involved with government policies to deal with market failures. Understanding these trade-offs will help you make better choices as a citizen voting for politicians supporting regulation policies you approve — and may even reduce your frustration with your cable company!

NATURAL MONOPOLY, GAMING, COMPETITION, AND GOVERNMENT **255**

10.1 Size Matters: Market Failure and Natural Monopoly

Imagine a world where many cable TV companies compete for your business. Sounds like a consumer's dream come true, doesn't it? Competitors provide choices, which consumers value. And just like the downward pull of gravity, competitive forces pull prices down toward levels of perfect competition, where businesses cover all opportunity costs but earn only normal profits. While the dream of cable competitors sounds wonderful, be careful what you wish for. Let's describe what would happen if your dream came true.

By far the largest cost for cable companies is the network of thousands of kilometres of fibre-optic cable running under the streets or paralleling electricity wires above ground. Once the network is in place and the company has paid for programming, the marginal cost of supplying a signal to an additional subscriber is almost zero — the cost of flipping a switch. While the fixed costs of the network are high, the variable costs of adding subscribers are very low. The result is that *average total costs keep decreasing as the high fixed costs are spread over a larger number of subscribers.*

Right now in your neighbourhood, there is only one such cable network because the CRTC (Canadian Radio-television Telecommunications Commission) has granted a local monopoly to Rogers, Eastlink, Shaw, or whichever company is your provider. If there were competition in the cable TV industry, every entering competitor would have to dig or string a complete network. And every time you or a neighbour decided to switch providers, there would be digging or rewiring to hook you up to the other cable system. Besides those higher variable costs, each cable company would end up with fewer subscribers in your neighbourhood over which to spread costs, so average total costs would be higher for all. Competition forces prices down to levels just covering average total costs and normal profits. But if average total costs are higher with multiple competing cable companies, *prices will be higher compared to a single cable company.*

▶ Cable companies operate with a government-granted monopoly. Many consider this a natural monopoly. Do you think the government should force the cable companies to share their cables with potential rivals after their initial investment costs have been recovered?

Mel Evans/Associated Press

Economies of Scale   The cable TV business, like water and electricity utilities, has *economies of scale* (section 8.2) — as a business's scale of production increases, average total costs decrease with increasing quantities. Economists call these kinds of businesses **natural monopolies**. To achieve lowest average total cost, economies of scale allow only a single seller.

natural monopoly   economies of scale allow only a single seller to achieve lowest average total cost

Even if competitors were allowed in the cable TV industry, eventually the biggest company with economies of scale could under-price the smaller companies — forcing them out of business or into takeovers or mergers. The competitive forces that force down prices would result in a single seller with a monopoly's price-making power! This type of monopoly seems inevitable, like a force of nature. But is it really?

Market Failure

Sometimes the market's competitive forces fail to bring prices down to just cover all opportunity costs of production, and do not push costs down to minimum average total costs. **Market failure** happens when market outcomes are inefficient or inequitable. Instead of producing the miracle of markets, they fail and produce outcomes that are not in society's best interests.

market failure   when markets produce outcomes that are inefficient or inequitable

Efficiency and Equity Again   Market failure can be evaluated in terms of inefficiency: Does the market outcome have lowest average total cost, or maximum total surplus (consumer surplus plus producer surplus — shown in section 4.5)? But even an efficient market outcome — where products and services produced at lowest cost go to those most willing and able to pay — may not be fair or equitable (section 6.4).

Inequality and "society's best interests" are harder to evaluate than efficiency because they involve normative judgments (section 1.4). Evaluating the equity of market outcomes involves answering questions like, "Do you believe that markets should meet the equity standards of equal outcomes or equal opportunities (section 6.5)?" And, "If there is a trade-off between efficiency and equity, which one *should* the government, acting in 'society's best interests,' try and achieve?"

Government faces many challenges when designing policies to try to correct market failures.

The Government Policy Challenge

The only way to achieve the efficiency of lowest cost production in businesses with economies of scale is to have a single large business supply the entire market. Size matters. But, of course, that private business, for example your local cable provider, will act like any other profit-maximizing monopoly. While its costs may be low, no competitors are forcing it to pass on those cost savings to consumers through lower prices. The monopolist with economies of scale follows the same recipe for profits as any other business with pricing power: Estimate marginal revenues and marginal costs, and then set the highest price that still allows it to sell the highest quantity for which marginal revenue is greater than marginal cost. Compared to the competitive outcome, the monopolist will restrict output and raise prices, setting the price well above average total costs to earn the highest possible economic profits.

This is the challenge facing government policymakers: **How do you gain the low-cost efficiencies of economies of scale, but avoid the inefficiencies of monopoly's restricted output and higher price?**

The two major policies that governments around the world use to deal with this challenge are public ownership and regulation.

NOTE
With natural monopoly, the challenge for policymakers is to gain low-cost efficiencies of economies of scale but avoid inefficiencies of monopoly's restricted output and higher price.

Public Ownership: Crown Corporations

In Canada, public ownership of businesses with economies of scale takes the form of **Crown corporations**. Crown corporations are created by the federal or provincial governments, which own 100 percent of the corporation's assets. Crown corporations can be created by government, or from buying out the assets of private businesses. There are Crown corporations in electricity, water, and gas, as well as in industries that don't necessarily have economies of scale but are seen as publicly important for other economic, political, or social reasons (culture, alcohol, lotteries, agriculture, fisheries). Here are examples of Crown corporations in Canada:

- BC Hydro
- Canada Post
- Canadian Broadcasting Corporation (CBC)
- GO Transit
- Hydro-Quebec
- Saskatchewan Liquor and Gaming Authority
- VIA Rail Canada

While Crown corporations such as utilities (water, gas, electricity) achieve economies of scale, they are not a perfect solution to the policy challenge. The disadvantages come from the lack of competitive pressure. Incentives are weak for reducing costs or increasing efficiency or exploring innovative new technologies. And there are the usual risks of a large, bureaucratic organization — waste, lack of performance incentives, and too many rules.

Regulated Private Monopoly

The other government response to the policy challenge of economies of scale is to allow a single private business, but have the government regulate it. This is what the CRTC does in regulating the cable TV industry. Each cable provider is given a monopoly for its assigned neighbourhoods, but the price it can charge subscribers is regulated by the government. Here are examples of industries in Canada where private businesses are also regulated:

- banks
- air transportation, including airports
- railway and road transportation across borders
- telephone, telegraph, and cable systems
- uranium mining and processing
- fisheries as a natural resource

Rate of Return Legislation

In principle, government regulators try to set prices that just cover average total costs, including normal profits. In practice, regulators do not directly observe costs, and can't tell how hard the business is trying to keep costs low, so they use a technique called **rate of return regulation**. The regulated monopoly is allowed to charge a price that earns it the normal rate of return, or normal profits — the average rate of profits in other industries.

Rate of return regulation is not a perfect solution to the policy challenge either. The "normal rate of return" policy creates an incentive for managers of the regulated businesses to exaggerate their reported costs, since they are guaranteed a normal rate of return on all costs. "Costs" may include luxury consumption for management, such as a private box at the Air Canada Centre (justified in the name of entertaining clients), limousines, company jets, international travel, entertainment, and so on.

In the final section of this chapter, we will look again at the advantages and disadvantages of unregulated monopolies and at government alternatives for dealing with the challenges of natural monopolies.

What's So Natural about Natural Monopoly?

The term "natural monopoly" implies there is something inevitable about these technologies that will always produce a monopoly, like a law of nature that never changes. Natural monopolies arise when the technology has economies of scale that require a single supplier. But technologies change. Before 1990, the only way to place a long-distance call from Canada to Europe was through the single undersea cable that linked the continents. Phone companies had a natural monopoly. But the development of new technologies changed the industry to a more competitive market structure. Advances in fibre optics and VoIP (Voice over Internet Protocol) technologies meant that phone company cables could carry television signals, and cable companies could also provide phone services. Satellites provided yet another technology for delivering phone and television signals. So what had been a regulated monopoly changed. Natural monopolies are only as natural as the current technology.

Refresh 10.1

1. What is a natural monopoly, and how does it help consumers?

2. In your own words, explain the challenge facing government policymakers in dealing with natural monopolies.

3. Identify one regulated private monopoly you buy services from. Find out from its website everything you can about its costs and the regulations under which it operates. Do you think its services could be improved? Explain your answer.

MyEconLab

For answers to these Refresh Questions, visit MyEconLab.

Cooperate or Cheat?
Prisoners' Dilemma and Conspiracies

10.2

Almost every Thursday before a long weekend, prices seem to rise simultaneously at gasoline stations across Canadian cities. By Saturday or Sunday a few stations cut their prices, and within a few days, prices fall everywhere. This odd pricing behaviour repeats in regular cycles.

Explain how strategic interaction between competitors complicates business decisions, creating two smart choices.

Gasoline Price Wars and Conspiracies

Gasoline price-swings often cause motorists to complain so bitterly that governments form committees to investigate whether the oil companies are conspiring unfairly to raise prices. The investigations rarely find clear evidence of conspiracy (although gas station owners in Québec were convicted in 2012 of conspiring to fix gasoline prices).

My wife (who is not an economist, thank goodness) always asks, "So when it's not a conspiracy, and the price of oil certainly doesn't change that much over a weekend, why do gas prices rise and fall like that, and why don't the stations learn to keep prices steady?" I, the economist, actually have answers to her questions. (Why she never accepts or remembers my answers is another story, but I am counting on you to do better.)

Both simultaneous gasoline price rises *and* gas price wars result from strategic, competitive decisions by the stations and the oil companies that own them. Gas prices fluctuate wildly on long weekends not because of changes in the cost of oil used to produce gasoline, but because of a tension that exists between stations trying to agree to keep prices high, but being tempted to cheat on the agreement in order to sell more gas. Is this quick explanation as clear to you as it is to my wife? Let me explain using the unlikely example of police interrogation tactics.

The Prisoners' Dilemma: Game Theory and Strategic Behaviour

Strategic, competitive decisions, like gas pricing, can be better understood using **game theory**. Game theory began as an abstract mathematical tool developed in the 1940s by John von Neumann and Oskar Morgenstern. It was extended by John Nash, a Princeton professor who won the Nobel Prize in Economics in 1994 and was the subject of the 2001 movie *A Beautiful Mind*. The beauty of game theory is its simplicity in helping us understand any strategic situation where the players of the game have to make decisions while worrying about what their rivals will do. Game theory is used by economists and political scientists to understand the OPEC oil cartel, nuclear arms races between countries, and even gasoline price wars.

The simplest example of game theory is called the **prisoners' dilemma**, which describes a scenario you have seen on countless TV detective shows. Two criminals, let's say Bonnie and Clyde, are caught in the act of robbing a bank. They know the police have the evidence to convict them of bank robbery. The police suspect the pair murdered a bank teller in a previous robbery, but don't have the evidence to prove murder.

The detective in charge has a plan to get Bonnie *or* Clyde to confess to the murder. He places the prisoners in separate rooms, with no ability to communicate with each other. He then sets up rewards (reduced jail time) for cooperating with the police by confessing, and penalties (more jail time) for denying the murder charge if the other prisoner confesses. The detective's plan is to build up mistrust between Bonnie and Clyde, and to get each one to worry the other will confess.

Payoffs Depend on the Other's Choice The rewards and penalties are illustrated in Figure 10.1. Let me explain how to "read" the figure. The two players are Bonnie and Clyde. Each has a single strategic choice — either to *confess* to the murder, or to *deny* the murder. The payoff to each choice depends on the other prisoner's choice. Bonnie's payoffs are in beige: Clyde's payoffs are in dark orange. Look at payoff box *A*. If Bonnie and Clyde both confess to the murder, they each get 10 years in prison for both crimes — armed bank robbery and murder. Look at payoff box *B*. If Bonnie confesses but Clyde denies, Bonnie gets rewarded with only a 5-year sentence for both crimes, while Clyde gets hit with the maximum 25-year sentence. Payoff box *C* is the reverse of *B*. If Clyde confesses but Bonnie denies, Clyde gets the lower 5-year sentence and Bonnie gets 25 years. And if both deny the murder, they can be convicted only of bank robbery and get 7 years each (box *D*).

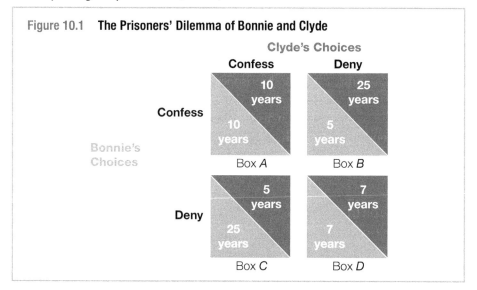

Figure 10.1   The Prisoners' Dilemma of Bonnie and Clyde

Nash Equilibrium What choices are Bonnie and Clyde likely to make? We need to figure out Bonnie's best choice *given Clyde's choice,* and Clyde's best choice *given Bonnie's choice.* This is called a **Nash equilibrium** (after John Nash), and tells us the outcome of the game.

Let's start with Bonnie (Bonnie's payoffs are in beige). If Clyde confesses, Bonnie's best choice is to confess, because 10 years in jail (box *A*) is better than 25 years (box *C*). If Clyde denies, Bonnie's best choice again is to confess, because 5 years in jail (box *B*) is better than 7 years (box *D*). No matter what choice Clyde makes, the detective has set up the outcomes so Bonnie's best choice is to confess.

Nash equilibrium   outcome of a game in which each player makes her own best choice given the choice of the other

What about Clyde (Clyde's payoffs are in orange)? If Bonnie confesses, Clyde's best choice is to confess, because 10 years in jail (box *A*) is better than 25 years (box *B*). If Bonnie denies, Clyde's best choice again is to confess, because 5 years in jail (box *C*) is better than 7 years (box *D*). No matter what choice Bonnie makes, the detective has set up the outcomes so Clyde's best choice is to confess.

So both Bonnie and Clyde confess, each gets a 10-year jail sentence, and the detective gets promoted. This outcome (except for the promotion) is the Nash equilibrium of the game.

The "dilemma" part of the prisoners' dilemma comes from the fact that each prisoner is motivated to confess, when each would be better off if they could trust each other to deny (7 years instead of 10 years). Game theory exposes a complication to our rule for smart choices — choose only when additional benefits are greater than additional opportunity costs. There seem to be *two* smart choices for the prisoners, hence the dilemma. The smart choice is to *confess if you don't trust the other*. But the other smart choice is to *deny if you can trust the other*. Smart choices are complicated by considering what your rivals will do, and whether or not you can trust them.

Game Theory and Gas Prices   So (my wife might ask), what does all this have to do with gas prices? Everything! Gas station owners face the same dilemma. Their strategic choice is not to deny or confess, but to *cooperate* with an implicit agreement to keep prices high, or to *cheat* on the agreement and cut prices. There is no need for a clever detective to set the incentives of the game. Self-interest, the quest for profits, and competition do the trick.

If station owners can trust each other to raise prices before the weekend and *cooperate* with the agreement to keep them high (this is the equivalent of box *D* in the prisoners' dilemma, where both prisoners deny and get their best outcome), profits will be maximized for all. But each owner has an incentive to *cheat* on this agreement (confess), hoping that if his is the only station to lower prices just a little, he will sell far more gasoline at what is still a relatively high price. But once cheating begins, trust breaks down and all owners are driven to the Nash equilibrium outcome, where everyone cheats (the equivalent of box *A*, where both prisoners confess). Prices fall and profits are reduced. Eventually, reduced profits lead owners to take a chance on trusting each other again, since they figure it couldn't be worse than the existing low prices and profits. All stations raise their prices, and the cycle of pricing behaviour begins again. But hopefully, now that you know some game theory, the pricing behaviour doesn't seem quite so odd — the instability of price and profit outcomes can be explained by the cycle of trust and non-trust.

Trust or No Trust?   The important insight of game theory is the *tension* between the Nash equilibrium outcome (where the best choice for players who can't trust each other is to confess or cheat) and the fact that both players could make themselves better off if they *could* trust each other (and deny or cooperate). With the complication of trust, there are now two smart choices. Keeping gas prices simultaneously high is one smart choice based on trust. Gas price wars, another smart choice, break out when there is no trust. Now, I hope, you understand it well enough to explain it to my wife or to your friends.

NOTE
Key insight of game theory is the tension between the Nash equilibrium outcome (players who can't trust each other's best choice is to cheat/confess) and the better outcome (if both players trust each other and cooperate/deny). With the complication of trust, there are two smart choices.

Refresh 10.2

MyEconLab

For answers to these Refresh Questions, visit MyEconLab.

1. In your own words, explain the idea of the prisoners' dilemma.

2. What is a Nash equilibrium?

3. Other than in setting gas prices, what is another competitive area where this situation might arise? Explain, using game theory, the two smart choices available to the players in the competitive area you selected.

C-Words Everywhere: Cartels, Collusion, Cheating, Competition Law, *Caveat Emptor*

There may be limited evidence of conspiracy in fixing gasoline prices, but economists, consumers, and governments have long worried about businesses secretly cooperating to improve profits by fixing prices, restricting output, or sacrificing safety to cut costs.

Well-Dressed Thieves

Cooperate is a polite, friendly sounding word. However, the other c-words generally used to describe businesses that cooperate are *collusion* by a *cartel*. The dictionary definition of **collusion** is "secret or illegal cooperation or conspiracy, especially in order to cheat or deceive others."* A **cartel** is an association of manufacturers or suppliers formed to maintain high prices and restrict competition.

collusion conspiracy to cheat or deceive others

cartel association of suppliers formed to maintain high prices and restrict competition

OPEC The best-known international cartel today is OPEC — the Organization of Petroleum Exporting Countries. OPEC formed in 1961 and gained world prominence in 1973, when the 12 member countries agreed to restrict their combined outputs, reducing the supply of oil and driving up the world price. The price of a barrel of oil shot up from $3 to $12 over just four months — a 300 percent increase! The collusive agreement set individual production quotas, so each country had to restrict its output below its previous production levels. By managing to trust each other to stick to the quotas in the agreement, OPEC acted like a single monopoly. The rise in oil prices transferred billions of dollars of wealth out of the pockets of consumers and businesses in oil-consuming countries and into OPEC's pockets.

But just like the prisoners or the gas station owners, OPEC members had — and continue to have — an ever-present temptation to cheat on their agreement. Over time, energy conservation efforts and new oil suppliers (attracted by the economic profits and not being part of OPEC) caused prices to fall. The recession of 1981–1983, which reduced economic activity and decreased demand for oil, caused a more dramatic fall in price. OPEC members began to cheat and increase output, causing oil prices to fall further. Since that time, OPEC has swung between periods of trust and high oil prices, and periods of mistrust, cheating, and lower oil prices. Just as game theory predicts!

There is great temptation for businesses to form cartels because the payoffs to collusion are high. Cartels generally transfer money from consumers to business profits. Collusive agreements to fix prices are a clear and knowing conspiracy against consumers. To put it bluntly, consumers get robbed. An Australian government official said it well: "Cartels are theft — usually by well-dressed thieves." See Economics Out There on page 265 about thievery in the Canadian chocolate industry.

People of the same trade seldom meet together, even for merriment and diversion, but the conversation ends in a conspiracy against the public, or in some contrivance to raise prices.

— Adam Smith

* New Oxford American Dictionary 3rd Edition edited by Stevenson and Lindberg (2010) Definition of "*collusion*". By permission of Oxford University Press, USA

Competition Law

The OPEC cartel does not break the law, but only because there is no international law prohibiting cartels. But almost every country, including Canada, has national laws prohibiting collusion among businesses to fix prices and restrict competition.

In the late 1800s, there were Canadian cartels in many industries, from biscuits to coal to coffins to fire insurance. These cartels (called *combines* or *trusts* at the time) attracted consumer and government concerns. Parliament passed the first anti-combines (also called anti-trust) act in 1889, making it illegal for businesses to combine to form monopolies or near-monopolies. The act also forbade collusion among businesses to raise prices or restrict supplies to customers, or to do anything that would "unduly lessen" competition.

Most industrialized countries passed similar laws as part of the legal *rules of the game* (along with property rights and the enforcement of contracts discussed in section 4.1) governing economic activity and markets. Such laws make it illegal for businesses to communicate about fixing prices, and prevent cartels from signing legal contracts to enforce cooperation. Anti-combines laws drive price-fixing agreements underground, making it harder for colluding businesses to see each other's actions, to trust each other, and to enforce their collusion. These laws, like the detective putting prisoners in separate rooms, prevent communication and cooperation among companies. The goal is to encourage each business to compete and act only in its individual self-interest in order to get invisible hand outcomes that are better for consumers and society as a whole.

NOTE
The 1986 *Competition Act* aims "to maintain and encourage competition in Canada in order to promote the efficiency and adaptability of the Canadian economy."

The Competition Act   Today's anti-combines law is called the *Competition Act*, passed by Parliament in 1986. Its purpose is "to maintain and encourage competition in Canada in order to promote the efficiency and adaptability of the Canadian economy."

This purpose sounds clear, but it is often hard to distinguish *competitive* business behaviour from *collusive* behaviour. Competition takes many forms, but it is (as we saw in section 8.4) always an active attempt to increase profits and gain the market power of monopoly. When businesses buy or merge with other competitors in their markets, they increase their profits and pricing power by eliminating competitors and substitute products.

But if the merger also provides economies of scale that lower costs or allow the business to better compete internationally, the merger promotes "efficiency and adaptability."

The *Competition Act* distinguishes two kinds of anti-competitive offences with different legal penalties.

NOTE
Desirable competitive behaviour — always an active attempt to increase profits and gain the market power of monopoly — is hard to distinguish from undesirable collusive behaviour.

- *Criminal offences* include price fixing, bid rigging (see Economics Out There, page 265), and false or misleading advertising. Trials are held by the courts, and penalties include prison sentences and fines.

- *Civil offences* are less serious, and include mergers, abusing a business's dominant market position, and other actions that lessen competition. Charges are heard by a quasi-judicial Competition Tribunal composed of federal judges and business experts. Penalties include fines and legal prohibitions of mergers and anti-competitive business practices.

Criminal Offences   Canada, along with Australia, Britain, France, Germany, Ireland, Japan, and the United States, uses prison time to penalize business executives convicted of price fixing. When large, sophisticated businesses make secret agreements to fix prices, they are conspiring against consumers. These underground agreements are highly profitable and hard to discover, so tough penalties like prison terms help discourage collusive agreements.

The *Competition Act* raises the expected costs (prison time) to businesses of price-fixing compared to the expected benefits (profits). Fines do the same, but a fine alone that is large enough to discourage price fixing could financially ruin a business, reduce competition and unintentionally penalize innocent players like suppliers to the company (who might lose sales) and workers (who might lose their jobs).

The threat of prison terms also helps governments uncover secret cartels. Like the detective in the Bonnie and Clyde case, government officials can offer deals — reduced sentences or amnesty — to whistle-blowers who reveal the cartel agreement. This sets up a Nash equilibrium similar to the prisoners' dilemma because each conspirator can make herself better off by confessing to the agreement and escaping punishment. The tougher the prison penalties, the greater the incentive to be the first to confess.

Economics *Out There*

Hershey Guilty of Price-Fixing in Canadian Chocolate Cartel

Hershey Canada Inc. pleaded guilty in June 2013 for its role in fixing the price of chocolate products, violating the criminal conspiracy provision in the *Competition Act*. Hershey was fined $4 million.

The conspiracy involved Hershey, Nestlé Canada, Mars Canada, and ITWAL Limited, a national network of wholesale distributors. The Competition Bureau learned about the conspiracy through its Immunity Program, which gives the first conspirator to reveal an offence immunity from prosecution.

Recently, the Competition Bureau toughened the prison penalties for criminal offences under the *Competition Act*. The prison sentences, of up to 14 years, can no longer be served outside a prison. The penalty of real jail time for non-cooperating conspirators increases the incentives for price-fixers to "confess" and cooperate.

To learn more about competition law and Competition Bureau Canada, go to www.competitionbureau.gc.ca. For the federal Competition Tribunal, see www.ct-tc.gc.ca.

Civil Offences   Civil, or non-criminal, offences like mergers are reviewed by a Competition Tribunal. The Tribunal first determines if the merger will lessen competition in that market. The Tribunal then *also* must determine if the merger will create any increased efficiencies. The decision must weigh the costs of the merger (decreased competition) with the benefits (increased efficiencies). Does this sound familiar? It is Key 1 of the Three Keys to Smart Choices! The Competition Tribunal prohibits the merger if expected costs are greater than expected benefits, and allows the merger if expected benefits are greater than expected costs.

ADDITIONAL
BENEFITS
VS.
OPPORTUNITY
COSTS

Should the Buyer Alone Beware?
Regulatory Agencies in Canada

In recent years in Canada, hundreds of dogs and cats died from eating tainted pet food that contained the poison polyvinyl. Mattel and Hasbro recalled thousands of toys because they contained lead paint that was potentially poisonous for children. And inexpensive toothpastes imported from China contained a toxic ingredient that was cheaper than the proper ingredient. It was discovered only when the few unfortunate people who were the first to use the toothpaste died.

In pursuing lower costs, competitive advantage, and higher profits, private businesses may use cheaper, even dangerous, materials and compromise workers' and consumers' health and safety. The same economic forces behind the invisible hand may produce deadly results when used by reckless and unethical businesses and individuals.

Competition ensures that, *eventually,* as word gets around, consumers will stop buying from businesses that produce harmful products and turn to safe competitors. But few citizens want to be the laboratory mice who serve as the signal to future consumers to beware, so they call on their elected representatives in government to do something. That usually takes the form of regulating the questionable industry.

Paul Poplis/Photolibrary/Getty Images

▶ Sometimes, in the pursuit of profit, businesses may put the public at risk. How closely should governments monitor private companies?

Let the Buyer Beware?   *Should* the government play the role of regulator for products and services? If so, how effective will that regulation be? The debate over this question goes back centuries, to the beginning of trade. You can tell the debate is ancient because the phrase used to describe it — *caveat emptor* — is from Latin. **Caveat emptor** means "Let the buyer beware."

One answer to the question is that it is the responsibility of consumers, not government, to monitor the quality of what they buy. Far too many products and services exist for government to be able to monitor them all. Even if the government were capable of such an enormous task, the required bureaucracy would cost far more than the benefits of screening out the minority of products that are dangerous (additional costs of regulation greater than additional benefits — Key 1 for smart choices).

caveat emptor   "let the buyer beware" — the buyer alone is responsible for checking the quality of products before buying

ADDITIONAL
BENEFITS
VS.
OPPORTUNITY
COSTS

Another answer is that there are certain products — nuclear power, medicines, poisonous insecticides, and so on — that the average consumer is simply not capable of evaluating. Similarly, there are professional services — from doctors, lawyers, accountants, tradespeople — for which most of us will not know whether those professionals are doing a good job or whether they are quacks pretending to do a good job. As a consumer, you don't want to be the one to be deceived, especially if the deception costs you your health, your fortune, or even your life (additional benefits of regulation greater than additional costs).

Forms of Regulation There is no single right answer to the regulation question. As a result, some products and services are regulated, and many others are not. There are three major forms of government regulation in Canada.

Federal and provincial *government departments* regulate certain industries or roles. For example, the Department of Labour enforces regulations designed to prevent businesses from compromising worker safety when trying to keep costs down.

Governments appoint independent *agencies and boards*, usually called commissions, to regulate another type of industry. Examples include the Public Service Commission, the Canadian Dairy Commission, the Nova Scotia Board of Public Utility Commissioners, the Canadian Wheat Board, and the Atomic Energy Control Board. Senior government bureaucrats at these agencies and boards are usually experts in the industry, and often are recruited from the regulated businesses. The guiding principles the government legislation provides — that businesses act "in the public interest," or allow only "just and reasonable rates" — are sufficiently vague that regulators have considerable freedom in setting and enforcing regulations.

Because professions like medicine or law or trades involve specialized training, they can be knowledgeably regulated only by a member of that profession or trade. Governments give *professional associations*, like the Canadian Medical Association, the Canadian Bar Association, and the International Brotherhood of Electrical Workers, the authority to regulate themselves. The associations decide who is qualified to practise, and discipline members who don't live up to their professional standards.

But there is a fine line between ensuring quality service and ensuring the self-interest of the profession. For example, rules that guarantee a certain type of training for doctors or engineers also prevent professionals who have trained in different countries from practising here. This restricts the supply of doctors, lawyers, engineers, and tradespeople, which, as you read in Chapter 4, restricts competition and raises the price consumers pay for these services.

All of these regulations are intended to serve the public interest. But do they? The guiding principles are vague, and there are close relationships between the regulatory bodies and the industries they regulate. It is also possible that the regulators serve the interests of businesses in the industry at the public's expense — the subject of the final section of this chapter.

Refresh 10.3

MyEconLab

For answers to these Refresh Questions, visit MyEconLab.

1. Outline the two kinds of anti-competitive offences in the 1986 *Competition Act*, and explain the basic difference between them.

2. Do you agree with the principle of *caveat emptor*? Explain your answer, providing details from both sides of the argument.

3. Construct a payoff matrix (similar to Figure 10.1) for two oil companies forming a cartel, where the single strategic choice is to *collude* (stick to an agreement to restrict output and raise prices) or to *cheat* on the agreement. Your payoffs should be made-up, reasonable numbers of the expected financial profits of each combination of player choices. Explain the difference between the Nash equilibrium of the game and the outcome that would be best for the two oil companies.

10.4 Pick Your Poison: Market Failure or Government Failure?

Differentiate between the public-interest view and the capture view of government regulation.

In most situations, market outcomes serve society's best interest — the public interest. Thanks to the competitive pressures of the invisible hand, markets provide the products and services we value most, do so efficiently, and at the lowest possible cost. But markets can fail when there are natural monopolies with economies of scale, when there is monopolistic collusion among competitors, and from unethical behaviour among profit-seeking businesses. When markets fail, consumers call on governments for action, believing that government regulation will improve the outcome. Consumers-as-citizens speak up to say, "Government *should* regulate industries where there is market failure."

Should Governments Regulate? Public-Interest View or Capture View

The positive/normative distinction from section 1.5 indicates that the word *should* signals that the statement "Government *should* regulate industries where there is market failure" is normative. Normative statements involve value judgments or opinions — as opposed to positive statements, which can be evaluated as true or false by checking the facts.

Even the most careful economic thinking cannot answer the *normative* question, "*Should* government regulate industries where there is market failure?" That answer will be different for different individuals, and depends on the values they hold. Economic thinking *is* helpful in answering a related *positive* question — "When will government action improve market failure outcomes, and when will government action produce an outcome that is actually worse than market failure?"

Public-Interest View of Government Regulation   When government actions improve on market (failure) outcomes, they contribute to the public interest. Economists call this the **public-interest view** of government regulation. According to this view, government regulations act to eliminate waste, achieve efficiency, and promote the public interest, just like the invisible hand of markets usually does when markets work well.

Capture View of Government Regulation   When government actions turn out to be worse than the market (failure) outcomes, it is often because industry interests turn the regulatory process to their own advantage. Economists call this the **capture view** of government regulation. The regulators have been "captured" by the industry they are supposed to regulate. The regulations are set and enforced in ways that promote the interests of businesses in the industry instead of promoting the public interest.

Evidence and Explanations

Which view of government regulation is correct? The available evidence is mixed — some supports the public-interest view, some supports the capture view. Let's look at a few examples of the evidence. And since the evidence necessary to evaluate these views as true or false is not always available or clear, it is also useful to look at the explanations behind the two views.

Evidence   Regulated natural monopolies tend to earn higher rates of return than the average rate of profits in the economy. For example, the regulated cable TV industry earns more than a 10-percent rate of return per year, almost double the economy average. The fact that the rate of return is greater than the economy average supports the capture view. On the other hand, the public-interest view gets some support as long as the 10-percent rate of return is less than what a private monopolist would earn running the industry. We don't know what the private returns would be, since there are no private cable TV businesses operating outside of the regulations.

Do Crown corporations operate as efficiently as private businesses? Research studies have tried to answer this question by comparing two similar businesses, where one is run publicly and one privately. Comparisons include a Canadian public railway (Canadian National — CN) with a private railway (Canadian Pacific — CP), and an Australian public domestic airline (Trans Australia Airlines — TAA) with a private domestic airline (Ansett Australia). The studies found that costs for the Crown corporations were significantly higher than for the private businesses. For example. CN's costs were 14 percent higher than CP's costs. But it is not clear if the results of these studies can be generalized and used to judge other industries.

WE SHOULD HAVE READ THE FINE PRINT MORE CAREFULLY BEFORE PURCHASING THESE REALLY CHEAP AIRFARES!!

▲ Deregulation sometimes brings unintended results. Do you think this cartoonist is for or against deregulation of the airline industry?

Another way to evaluate the competing views of government regulation is to look at what happens to regulated industries when they are deregulated — when government regulations are removed. If the public-interest view is true, we expect prices and profits to rise after deregulation. If the capture view is true, we expect prices and profits to fall. The airline and trucking industries used to be heavily regulated by Transport Canada, and long-distance phone industries (among others) were regulated by the CRTC. In the 1980s, many governments around the world removed regulations and allowed businesses to compete in the marketplace.

This small pizzeria owner buys over $100 000 in cheese every year. His pizza prices must cover this cost. Without supply management by the government, he would save over half that cost and sell cheaper pizzas to his customers. While cheese producers are happy with this situation, what do you think about it?

Mixed Results   The evidence is mixed over all industries, but for the airline, trucking, and long-distance industries, prices fell and outputs increased after deregulation. This supports the capture view, suggesting that the regulated industries were operating like a cartel, restricting output and raising prices.

Much of the strongest evidence supporting the capture view comes from the Canadian agricultural sector. The National Farm Products Council (NFPC) regulates the production of eggs, chickens, and turkeys, much like a cartel, establishing production quotas for each producer and setting prices. These regulations are justified in terms of promoting "efficient, competitive Canadian agriculture," "a stable supply of poultry and eggs for Canadian consumers," and "stable farm incomes." One study estimated that the regulated prices of the NFPC transferred over $100 million a year from Canadian consumers to 4600 individual chicken producers, in much the same way that OPEC transfers money from consumers and businesses in oil-consuming countries into OPEC's pockets. See Economics Out There (page 271) for a similar story from the Canadian dairy industry.

The evidence on the effectiveness of the *Canadian Competition Act* is much more uniform. Most economists agree that legislation has served the public interest well.

For many regulated industries, there simply isn't conclusive evidence that allows us to evaluate whether the public-interest view or the capture view more accurately describes the outcomes. For that reason, it is also helpful to understand the explanations behind each view, so you can at least think a bit more carefully about whatever information is available.

Explanations   There is a straightforward explanation behind the public-interest view of government regulation. Government regulators have the public's interest in mind, and make decisions on the basis of what is best for society.

The explanation behind the capture view of government regulation is more complicated. The capture view seems to imply that government regulators collude with those in the industry being regulated, and conspire against the public interest. The actual explanation is not so sinister. It is basically a cost–benefit explanation applied to politics.

According to the capture view, even if government regulators begin with the public interest in mind, the decisions they end up making are influenced by the lack of competitive incentives, vague regulation guidelines, and necessarily close relations between the regulators and the industry being regulated.

Economics *Out There*

Cheese Smuggling? Only in Canada

Two Niagara police officers were arrested in 2012 for smuggling U.S. cheese into Canada to sell to pizzerias and restaurants. Why smuggle cheese? It's supply and demand plus regulation.

On the supply side, the Canadian dairy industry is heavily regulated by the federal government. The Canadian Dairy Board sets production quotas and prices for all dairy products, and protects those prices by restricting dairy imports into Canada. A recent study found that Torontonians and Montrealers pay about 77% more for 2 percent milk than do consumers in upstate New York. Another study estimates that the higher Canadian dairy prices are equivalent to a $175 000 transfer from Canadian consumers to each of the roughly 12 000 dairy suppliers. Besides restricting supply and raising prices, the Canadian Dairy Board protects dairy producers from competitive pressures of creative destruction that would lead to greater efficiencies, economies of scale, and innovation.

Demand for smuggled cheese comes from restaurant owners. Even a small pizzeria buys over $100 000 worth of cheese a year. Smuggled U.S. cheese could save a Canadian pizzeria at least $50 000 a year, while still leaving a profit for the smugglers.

While the "supply management" policies of the Canadian Dairy Board are intended to provide dairy producers with a fair return on their investments and to provide consumers with a continuous supply of quality products, the regulators seem to have been "captured" by dairy interests.

Political Pressures   It's not just the regulators who are influenced. Regulations that favour industry producer interests over the public interest are passed and supported by elected politicians who can be influenced by lobbying, campaign contributions, and political pressure to act in the interests of businesses, labour organizations, or other special interest groups. When the Canadian Dairy Commission is considering a rise in the regulated price of cheese, think about the potential political reactions. If you are a consumer, how important is the extra 25 cents per kilogram that you will have to pay? If you even hear about the price rise, will it cause you to change your vote for your member of parliament or make a large campaign contribution to make sure your interests are represented? Not likely.

But if you are one of the average B.C. dairy farmers with net assets of $5.6 million and average net cash income of $155 000, that 25 cents per kilogram means tens of thousands of dollars every year, and even more in terms of the value of your assets. As a producer in the industry, you have a very, very strong incentive to be politically active when regulations are discussed.

The political pressures from the unequal distribution of costs and benefits tempt politicians to support regulations that favour producers. The tiny cost to many consumers creates only weak political pressure to lower prices. The huge benefits for the relatively few producers in the regulated industry make it worth their while to apply enormous political pressure (votes, political actions, campaign contributions) to "capture" the interests of the politicians to raise prices.

Those same unequal costs and benefits lead "captured" politicians to support regulations, like those in the dairy industry, that enforce cartel-style collusion within the industry, keep out new (and lower-cost) potential competitors, and monitor prices to avoid cheating on quotas. All these regulations are passed in the name of protecting quality or safety or promoting a "stable supply" in the public interest. But the businesses in the industry benefit the most.

NOTE
According to the capture view, concentrated benefits to businesses make regulations worth lobbying for, while small costs to individual consumers do not create political pressure for regulators to serve the public interest.

Trade-Offs: Market Failure or Government Failure?

We began this chapter by identifying a key market-failure challenge facing government policymakers: How do you gain the low-cost efficiencies of economies of scale, but avoid the inefficiencies of monopoly's restricted output and higher price? The policy responses to that challenge include regulated natural monopolies, Crown corporations, and competition laws to discourage collusion and cartels.

All these government attempts to deal with market failure involve trade-offs. It's important for you, as a citizen who elects the politicians who create these policies, to understand the trade-offs. As you know only too well (I hope!), every choice, even a policy choice to leave the market alone, has an opportunity cost. This chapter exposes those opportunity costs so that you can make smart political choices based on the values you hold.

What are the trade-offs? First, you want to compare any choice with the next best alternative. It is not useful to compare a market failure outcome with an ideal but unattainable government policy outcome. Keep it real!

When comparing a market-failure outcome with a government-regulation outcome, weigh the costs and benefits of the actual outcomes. That means evaluating whether the government outcome is better or worse than the market failure outcome. If the public-interest view applies to that industry, the government outcome may be superior to the market failure outcome.

Government Failure? If the capture view applies, it is more difficult to tell. It may be a case of comparing market failure with what economists call **government failure**. Government failure occurs when regulations fail to serve the public interest. Even when aiming for the public interest, government policymakers sometimes lack timely and accurate information for making smart policy decisions. Add in the complexity of the economy, and government policymakers can make "honest mistakes" when trying to solve complex problems. Policymakers can also be influenced to support the industry being regulated.

> **government failure** when regulations fail to serve public interest

- Sometimes the market outcome, even with monopoly power, is better than the government regulation outcome if there is significant government failure.

- Sometimes the government outcome, especially with public-interest regulations, is better than the market outcome if there is significant market failure.

In comparing industry outcomes, we can often make positive statements about which is better for consumers in terms of efficiency, and lowest costs of production, prices, and rates of return.

But there are other aspects of the outcomes that are not so easy to compare. What is the value of public safety? How much is it worth to you to know that you will not be poisoned by the toothpaste you buy, or that nuclear power plants are operated safely, or that your doctor is well-trained and not a quack? If governments step in and regulate those industries, and the prices of the products or services goes up, is that a worthwhile trade-off? That is a normative question — it depends on how you value low prices relative to the risk of the occasional dangerous product (one nuclear accident sure can ruin your day) or the wrong medical advice.

Economic thinking cannot make those normative choices for you. As a citizen, your views on regulation will depend on the relative values you place on many outcomes, including efficiency, equity, low prices for consumers, public safety, and quality control. Economic thinking can help answer the related *positive* question, "When will government action improve market failure outcomes, and when will government action fail and actually produce an outcome that is worse than market failure?" The answer to that positive question depends on available evidence. Which failure is worse — market failure or government failure? No option is perfect; each has an opportunity cost. Pick your poison.

NOTE
Economic thinking cannot make normative policy choices for you, but can help answer the positive question, "Will government action improve market failure outcomes, or will government action fail and produce a worse outcome than market failure?"

Refresh 10.4

1. Explain the public-interest and capture views of government regulation.

2. If a previously regulated industry is deregulated, and we observe that prices rise and output falls, which view of government regulation does that evidence support? Explain why.

3. In Chapter 5, we observed that a conservative politician might value efficiency more than equity, while a left-leaning politician might value equity more than efficiency. Which of the two views on government regulation — public-interest or capture — do you think a conservative politician is more likely to hold? Which view is a left-leaning politician more likely to hold? Explain your answers.

MyEconLab

For answers to these Refresh Questions, visit MyEconLab.

Study Guide

10.1 Size Matters: Market Failure and Natural Monopoly

Natural monopolies are a market-failure challenge for policymakers — gain the low-cost efficiencies of economies of scale, but avoid the inefficiencies of monopoly's restricted output and higher price.

- **Market failure** — when markets produce outcomes that are inefficient or inequitable.

- *Economies of scale* — average total costs decrease as quantity of output increases.

- **Natural monopoly** — economies of scale allows only a single seller to achieve lowest average total cost.
  - Natural monopolies are an example of market failure.
  - Natural monopolies are based on current technology. When technology changes, natural monopoly may change to more competitive market structures.

- The two major policies governments use to deal with challenge of natural monopoly are public ownership and regulation.
  - **Crown corporations** — publicly owned businesses in Canada. Achieve economies of scale, but lack of competition weakens incentives to reduce costs or innovate.
  - **Rate of return regulation** — set price allowing regulated monopoly to just cover average total costs and normal profits.

10.2 Cooperate or Cheat? Prisoners' Dilemma and Cartels

Strategic interaction among competitors complicates business decisions, creating two smart choices — one based on trust and the other based on lack of trust.

- **Game theory** — a mathematical tool for understanding how players make decisions, taking into account what they expect rivals to do.
  - Gasoline pricing is a strategic decision that can be understood using game theory.

- **Prisoners' dilemma** — a game with two players who must each make a strategic choice, where results depend on the other player's choice.

- **Nash equilibrium** — outcome of a game in which each player makes her own best choice given the choice of the other.

- Two smart choices exist in a prisoners' dilemma game: one based on *lack of trust* and one based on *trust*.
  - If the other player cannot be trusted, the smart choice is to cheat/confess; all players are driven to the Nash equilibrium outcome where everyone cheats/confesses.
  - If the other player can be trusted, the smart choice is to cooperate/deny; all players are driven to the equilibrium outcome where everyone cooperates/denies.
  - The prisoners' "dilemma" is that each player (prisoner) is motivated to cheat (confess), yet both would be better off if they could trust each other to cooperate (deny).

10.3 *C*-Words Everywhere: Cartels, Collusion, Cheating, Competition Law, *Caveat Emptor*

Governments use laws and regulations to try to promote competition, discourage cartels, and protect the public from dangerous business practices.

- **Collusion** — conspiracy to cheat or deceive others.

- **Cartel** — association of suppliers formed to maintain high prices and restrict competition.
  - OPEC (Organization of Petroleum Exporting Countries) is an international cartel that acts like a monopoly.

- Desirable competitive behaviour — always an active attempt to increase profits and gain the market power of monopoly — is hard to distinguish from undesirable collusive behaviour.

- The *Competition Act* attempts to prevent anti-competitive business behaviour and raises the expected costs to business of price fixing (through prison time, fines, legal prohibition) relative to the expected benefits (profits).
  - Criminal offences (punished by prison time, fines): price fixing, bid rigging, false/misleading advertising.
  - Civil offences (punished by fines, legal prohibitions): mergers, abusing dominant market position, lessening competition.
  - The Competition Tribunal weighs the costs of lessening competition against the benefits of any increased efficiencies.

- *Caveat emptor* ("let the buyer beware") — the buyer alone is responsible for checking the quality of products before buying.

- Certain products — nuclear power, medicines, poisonous insecticides — arc regulated by government because the average consumer cannot know the product's quality.

- Major forms of government regulation in Canada: government departments, agencies and boards, professional associations.

10.4 Pick Your Poison: Market Failure or Government Failure?

The public-interest view of government regulation suggests government actions improve market-failure outcomes, while the capture view suggests government actions produce government failure.

- **Public-interest view** — government regulation eliminates waste, achieves efficiency, and promotes the public interest.

- **Capture view** — government regulation benefits the regulated businesses, not the public interest.

- Evidence is mixed on government regulation — some supports the public-interest view, some supports the capture view.
  - Most economists agree that the *Competition Act* serves the public interest well.

- **Government failure** — when regulations fail to serve public interest.
  - Sometimes the market outcome, even with monopoly power, is better than the government regulation outcome if there is significant government failure.
  - Sometimes the government outcome, especially with public interest regulations, is better than the market outcome if there is significant market failure.

- Economic thinking cannot make normative policy choices for you, but can help answer the positive question, "Will government action improve market failure outcomes, or will government action fail and produce a worse outcome than market failure?"

TRUE/FALSE

Circle the correct answer. Solutions to these questions are available at the end of the book and on MyEconLab. You can also visit the MyEconLab Study Plan to access additional questions that will help you master the concepts covered in this chapter.

10.1 Market Failure and Natural Monopoly

1. An outcome that is inefficient and inequitable is a market failure. T F

2. Natural monopolies occur in industries with high fixed costs. T F

3. Crown corporations occur only in industries with economies of scale. T F

10.2 Prisoners' Dilemma and Cartels

4. The payoffs to each choice in a prisoners' dilemma game do *not* depend on the other prisoner's choice. T F

5. The Nash equilibrium outcome in the prisoners' dilemma game is that both players confess. T F

6. In the prisoners' dilemma game, each player is better off confessing. T F

10.3 Cartels, Collusion, Cheating, Competition Law, *Caveat Emptor*

7. The *Competition Act* attempts to prevent anti-competitive business behaviour, such as the collusion to raise prices and restrict output in cartels. T F

8. Competition Tribunals will prevent a merger if the benefits of increased efficiencies exceed the costs of decreased competition. T F

9. *Competition Act* penalties for civil offences include prison sentences. T F

10. The principle of *caveat emptor* means that government is responsible for monitoring the quality of products and services. T F

11. The discipline of market competition ensures that, *eventually*, consumers will stop buying from businesses that produce harmful products. T F

12. The additional costs of regulation always exceed the additional benefits of regulation. T F

10.4 Market Failure or Government Failure

13. If the public-interest view is true, prices and profits will rise after deregulation. If the capture view is true, prices and profits will fall. T F

14. For the airline and trucking industries, prices fell and outputs increased after deregulation. This supports the public-interest view. T F

15. Evidence supporting the public-interest view of government regulation would show that profit rates in regulated industries are higher than profit rates in non-regulated industries. T F

MULTIPLE CHOICE

Circle the best answer. Solutions to these questions are available at the end of the book and on MyEconLab. You can also visit the MyEconLab Study Plan to access similar questions that will help you master the concepts covered in this chapter.

10.1 Market Failure and Natural Monopoly

1. Market failure can happen when there are
a) inequalities.
b) economies of scale.
c) inefficiencies.
d) all of the above.

2. A natural monopoly is likely to have
a) low fixed cost and low marginal cost.
b) low fixed cost and high marginal cost.
c) high fixed cost and low marginal cost.
d) high fixed cost and high marginal cost.

3. Which of the following is *least* likely to be a natural monopoly?
a) electric utility
b) taxi service
c) water and sewer service
d) cable TV service

4. The challenge facing government policymakers is
a) who will be the next *Canadian Idol*.
b) how to gain the low-cost efficiencies of economies of scale, but avoid the inefficiencies of monopoly's restricted output and rise in price.
c) how to avoid the low-cost efficiencies of economies of scale, but gain the inefficiencies of monopoly's increased output and lower price.
d) how to gain the low-cost efficiencies of economies of scale, but avoid the inefficiencies of monopoly's increased output and lower price.

5. An industry with high _____ is likely to have economies of scale.
a) average total costs
b) marginal costs
c) opportunity costs
d) fixed costs

10.2 Prisoners' Dilemma and Cartels

6. John Nash, who extended the idea of game theory, was the subject of what Academy Award–winning movie?
a) *Beauty and the Beast*
b) *A Beautiful Economist*
c) *A Beautiful Mind*
D) *A Beautiful Body*

7. In the prisoners' dilemma with Bonnie and Clyde, each prisoner will be best off if
a) both prisoners confess.
b) both prisoners deny.
c) Bonnie denies and Clyde confesses.
d) Clyde denies and Bonnie confesses.

10.3 Cartels, Collusion, Cheating, Competition Law, *Caveat Emptor*

8. Gas prices fluctuate wildly on long weekends because of
a) changes in the cost of oil used to produce gasoline.
b) changes in the cost of gasoline.
c) the cycle of trust and lack of trust among gasoline station owners.
d) the cycle of trust and lack of trust between parents and teenagers.

9. According to game theory,
   a) businesses within cartels are tempted to cheat.
   b) businesses within cartels have incentives to cooperate.
   c) prison penalties help governments uncover secret cartels.
   d) all of the above are true.

10. Anti-combines (or anti-trust) laws attempt to
   a) support prices.
   b) establish Crown corporations.
   c) prevent monopoly practices.
   d) regulate monopolies.

11. Criminal offences in the *Competition Act* include
   a) price fixing.
   b) bid rigging.
   c) false advertising.
   d) all of the above.

12. The Canadian Radio-television and Telecommunications Commission (CRTC) is an example of regulation through
   a) public ownership.
   b) government departments.
   c) government-appointed agencies.
   d) self-governing bodies.

10.4 Market Failure or Government Failure

13. Which of the following is an example of a *government failure*?
   a) Deregulation in the airline industry resulted in lower prices and changed the price–quality mix in a pro-consumer way.
   b) Previous regulations in the airline industry led airlines to provide more luxuries than consumers would choose to pay for.
   c) Routes that airlines were once required to service are no longer served under deregulation because they are unprofitable.
   d) Competition in the telecommunications sector moved prices closer to marginal cost.

14. Which of the following statements about government regulation is/are *true*?
   a) The public-interest view suggests government actions improve market failure outcomes.
   b) The capture view suggests government actions produce government failure.
   c) Government failure can be worse than market failure because regulators act for the regulated industry instead of consumers.
   d) All of the above.

15. Economic thinking can be helpful in answering the following question(s):
   a) "When will government action improve market failure outcomes?"
   b) "When will government action fail?"
   c) "When will government action produce an outcome that is worse than market failure?"
   d) All of the above.

11 Acid Rain on Others' Parades

Externalities, Carbon Taxes, Free Riders, and Public Goods

LEARNING OBJECTIVES

After reading this chapter, you should be able to:

11.1 Describe how externalities cause market failure, so smart private choices differ from smart social choices.

11.2 Explain the rule for coordinating private choices with smart social choices when there are negative externalities.

11.3 Identify how government policies for polluters can internalize externalities to create smart social choices.

11.4 Explain how positive externalities create the free-rider problem of public goods and cause markets to fail.

11.5 Identify how government subsidies can internalize positive externalities to create smart social choices.

EVERYONE SEEMS TO BE an environmentalist today,

and for good reason. We clearly understand environmental problems like pollution, global warming, and the damage from second-hand smoke. But acceptable solutions are less clear. I'll bet money that you — and most people — would answer "yes" if I asked, "Do you want a world without pollution?" Well, we could have a world without pollution — all we have to do is eliminate all internal combustion engines and most other power sources, reduce our standard of living, and go back to living in caves. When described this way, most people do not want a world without pollution. While the environmental benefits are appealing, the opportunity costs (in reduced standard of living) are enormous. All choices, including environmentally sound choices, have opportunity costs.

So how do we, individually and collectively, make smart choices about how much pollution to tolerate? Economists have a concept called *externalities* that brings clarity to making smart choices about pollution. When your cigarette smoke causes your non-smoking housemate to develop cancer in 20 years, the cost of treating that cancer is a *negative externality* you don't consider in your decision to smoke. *Positive externalities* exist when others benefit from your actions without paying. For example, if most people get flu shots, even those who don't get shots benefit from the reduced likelihood of catching the flu.

Markets fail when externalities exist, producing too many of the things we don't want (like pollution, traffic jams, and second-hand smoke) and too few of the things we do want (like vaccinations, education, and good public transit). In this chapter, you will learn how to clear the confusion and, as a voter, identify the costs and benefits of smart policy choices for dealing with externality-based market failures.

11.1 Handcuffing the Invisible Hand: Market Failure with Externalities

Describe how externalities cause market failure, so smart private choices differ from smart social choices.

Chapter 4 described how market-clearing prices coordinate the smart choices of consumers and of businesses. Here's a sentence from that chapter to refresh your memory: "Price signals in markets create incentives so that while each person acts only in her own self-interest, the unintended consequence is the coordinated production of all the products and services we want."

But if markets are so good at producing the "goods" (products and services) we want, why does market coordination of economic activity also produce "bads" like pollution and traffic jams? The answer, in a word, is externalities. Externalities cause market failure by disconnecting smart choices for individuals from smart choices for society as a whole.

How Much Does That Honda Civic Really Cost?

After years of riding the bus, even with the comfort of headphones to block out others' mind-numbing cell phone conversations, you are ready to buy a car. You've had your eye on a blue Honda Civic, and are crunching the numbers to see if you can afford it. Your private additional costs include monthly payments, insurance, gas, repairs, and maybe parking. If you can afford it, and if the additional benefits of driving versus taking transit make you willing to pay those costs, then buying the car is a smart choice for you.

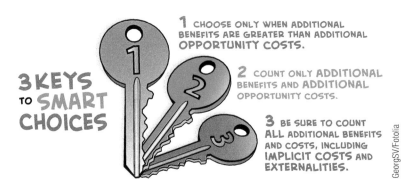

3 KEYS TO SMART CHOICES

1 CHOOSE ONLY WHEN ADDITIONAL BENEFITS ARE GREATER THAN ADDITIONAL OPPORTUNITY COSTS.

2 COUNT ONLY ADDITIONAL BENEFITS AND ADDITIONAL OPPORTUNITY COSTS.

3 BE SURE TO COUNT ALL ADDITIONAL BENEFITS AND COSTS, INCLUDING IMPLICIT COSTS AND EXTERNALITIES.

GeorgSV/Fotolia

Your decision is based mostly on Key 1 of the Three Keys to Smart Choices: Choose only when additional benefits are greater than additional *opportunity costs*. The money you pay represents *opportunity costs* because that money could have been spent on other things. Key 2 enters with the emphasis on *additional* benefits and costs. (The cost of the driver's education course you took years ago is a *sunk cost* and doesn't influence your smart choice.)

There are also social costs you don't have to consider when choosing your Honda Civic. The exhaust from your driving will contribute to air pollution, to global warming, and — depending on your choice of muffler or sound system — to noise pollution that might drive your neighbours crazy. By adding one more car to the roads, you will (marginally) worsen traffic jams and increase other drivers' commute times. Your choice creates these real costs to others and to society as a whole, *but you don't have to directly pay for them.*

Negative Externalities   Economists call these additional social costs **negative externalities**, or **external costs**. They are costs to society from your private choice that affect others, but that you do not pay. External costs affect people *external to* the original activity — others not involved in the exchange between you and the Honda dealer.

This brings us at last to Key 3 for smart choices (which we haven't discussed except for implicit costs in Chapter 7), which emphasizes the word *all*: Be sure to count *all* additional benefits and additional opportunity costs, including *implicit costs* and *externalities*.

When there are negative externalities, opportunity costs include both private costs and external costs. So the costs to society — social costs — are greater than just private costs.

Social Costs = Private (Opportunity) Costs + External (Opportunity) Costs

Phone conversations you are trying to avoid overhearing on the bus are an example of a negative externality. While she is not out to irritate you, an unintended consequence of that private conversation is what you experience as "noise pollution" — an external cost. A last example is an electrical utility using a coal-burning generator that emits sulphur dioxide as a byproduct. The utility does not have to pay for the external costs from the damage caused by the resulting global warming, air pollution, and acid rain. Economists also refer to negative externalities as "spillover effects".

▲ Unintended costs often attach to events. Producing much-needed energy, living in a car-oriented society, or communicating with friends creates negative externalities. Should those costs be built into the products and services we use?

The Invisible Hand Fails   Based only on your private costs, buying the Honda may be a smart choice for you. But adding in the external costs, it may not be a smart choice for society. When there are negative externalities, smart private choices (using Keys 1 and 2) are different from smart social choices (Keys 1, 2, and 3). There is *market failure* — the outcome is inefficient and not in society's best interests. The invisible hand fails to coordinate smart individual choices with smart social choices — those that balance social benefits with social costs.

If we had to pay the external costs as well as the usual private costs of our choices, then we would probably buy fewer cars, have fewer public phone conversations, and produce less coal-generated electricity. But because we generally do *not* pay external costs, consumers buy, and businesses produce, too many products and services with negative externalities.

Was It Good Just for You?

IMPLICIT COSTS & EXTERNALITIES

Externalities come in two flavours — negative and positive. While negative externalities involve external costs, *positive* externalities involve external *benefits*. Key 3 says to be sure to count *all* additional benefits as well as additional opportunity costs.

Positive externalities happen on the *benefits* side. For example, think about your decision to go to college or university. Your additional private benefits include your significantly higher lifetime income compared to high school graduates (a topic in Chapter 12), and the satisfaction you get from acquiring more knowledge. You obviously estimated that those additional private benefits to you were greater than your additional opportunity costs of attending school.

There are also social benefits you probably did *not* consider when choosing to go to school. With the skills you gain in school, employers will not have to spend as much money and time training you. Educated citizens, who can make informed political choices and participate in public debate and election campaigns, also improve the functioning of our democracy, to the benefit of all citizens. And evidence shows that citizens with more education are less likely to commit crimes or depend on social assistance payments. Your smart decision saves industry and the government money as well as aiding our democratic institutions.

positive externalities (external benefits) benefits to society from your private choice that affect others, but that others do not pay you for

Positive Externalities Economists call these additional social benefits **positive externalities** or **external benefits**. They are benefits to society from your private choice that affect others, but that others do not pay (you) for. External benefits go to people *external to* the original activity — others not involved in the exchange between you and your school.

When there are positive externalities, benefits include both private benefits and external benefits. So, when positive externalities are factored in, social benefits are greater than private benefits.

$$\text{Social Benefits} = \text{Private Benefits} + \text{External Benefits}$$

Public transit is another example of a positive externality. If you decide against the Honda Civic and continue to take public transit, your private benefits include the ability to get around inexpensively, without car expenses. But by keeping one more car *off* the roads, you unintentionally reduce pollution for everyone, reduce traffic jams, and decrease other drivers' commute times. Do you get any thanks or reward from others who benefit from your choice? No. In fact, economists have a term for people who benefit from the positive externalities of other people's actions — *free riders*.

Free Riders Economists call people who consume products or service without paying *free riders*. Based only on your private benefits and costs, choosing school over work may be a smart choice for you. But many workers would switch their choices to school *if only they were paid for the external benefits of that choice*. Similarly, taking public transit may be a smart choice for you. But many drivers would switch to public transit *if only they were paid for the external benefits of that choice*. When there are positive externalities, smart private choices (using Keys 1 and 2) are different from smart social choices (Keys 1, 2, and 3). External benefits allow others to "free ride" on our private choices. There again is *market failure* — the outcome is inefficient and not in society's best interests.

If there were some way to force the free riders to pay students and transit riders for the benefits the free riders receive, then there would be more education and more public transit. But because free riders do not have incentives to pay us for the external benefits that our choices produce, consumers buy, and businesses produce, too few products and services with positive externalities.

No Ownership, No Incentives, No Coordinated Choices

What is it about externalities, both negative and positive, that causes market failure and problems for the invisible hand? The answer is *lack of clear property rights*. Property rights — government's legal protection of property and enforcement of contracts (section 4.1) — are a necessary part of the "rules of the game" for markets to work. Without property rights, you have no incentive to produce for exchange because customers could take your work for free. Property rights give us the incentive to make smart choices because we have to pay for costs and because we are legally entitled to receive benefits and rewards for producing products and services others value.

Clear property rights are missing for negative or positive externalities. Who has rights to the atmosphere, where pollution is dumped and global warming occurs? Individuals and businesses own legal title to pieces of land, but that doesn't prevent others from pumping pollution into the air above, which then spills over into all of the atmosphere. There is no easy way to charge for the costs imposed on others by the pollution. And when you *reduce* pollution by taking public transit instead of driving, you don't get rewarded for the benefits you provide to others.

Tragedy of the Commons   The lack of clear property rights causes another common environmental problem with the dramatic name "the tragedy of the commons." The name comes from grassland outside of villages called "the commons" in 16th century England. No one owned the land. It was held in common among all villagers, who used it to graze their privately owned cows and sheep. With no price for grazing, everyone overused the free resource to feed their animals for private use or sale. The animals ate all of grass, which could not regrow. The "tragedy" was the overuse and depletion of the resource — the destruction of a common good.

The overuse of a free resource is partially a free-rider problem, because no one could be excluded from the commons, just like no ship can be excluded from seeing the warning light from a lighthouse. But the commons also has a negative externality problem because adding your cow or sheep to the commons to eat the grass makes it harder for other animals to find grass to eat. This negative externality is just like your decision to add your car to the roads, which worsens traffic jams and increases other drivers' commute times.

A modern version of the tragedy of the commons is the depletion of the east-coast cod fishery in Canada. There are no property rights to fish swimming in international waters, and the use of sophisticated, massive fishing ships from many countries led to overfishing and the depletion of the fish stocks. A total ban on cod fishing in the North Atlantic in 1992 prevented the total destruction of the fishery, but it is not clear if the fish population will ever recover to previous levels.

Therein is the tragedy. Each man is locked into a system that compels him to increase his herd without limit — in a world that is limited. Ruin is the destination toward which all men rush, each pursuing his own best interest in a society that believes in the freedom of the commons.

—Garrett Hardin (1968), "The Tragedy of the Commons"

No Incentives   Whether as an individual or a business, if you don't pay a cost or receive a payment because no property rights exist, you don't consider those costs or payments in your choices. External costs are someone else's problem, and external benefits are someone else's gain. So you, quite reasonably, ignore them all.

As a result, you do more activities (driving) that produce external costs (pollution) than if you had to pay those costs. Without clear property rights, you do fewer activities (taking transit) that generate external benefits (reduced pollution) than if you were paid for those benefits.

Wrong Prices   Without clear ownership and legally enforceable property rights, there's no payment of costs or collection of revenues. Those missing costs and revenues affect prices, which are the incentives we all respond to in making smart choices. When there are negative externalities, prices are too low because of missing costs. Prices do not cover all opportunity costs of production, including social costs. When there are positive externalities, prices are too high because of missing benefits and revenues. Transit prices would be lower for everyone if free riders paid for the benefits of cleaner air and reduced traffic. And in the case of common resources, there are no prices at all.

The invisible hand helps markets coordinate private smart choices to be smart choices for society as a whole *when prices adjust to reflect all costs and all benefits*. Without ownership and property rights, externalities arise, and prices don't accurately reflect all social costs and benefits. Markets fail because the invisible hand is handcuffed.

Refresh 11.1

1. Explain why economists also call negative externalities "spillover" effects.

2. Talking in large lecture halls is a problem, both for instructors who can't concentrate and attentive students who can't hear. Can you explain this problem in terms of externalities? Why is this problem hard to solve?

3. Many condominiums have strict rules about the colour of window coverings. Explain this rule in terms of externalities. Is it fair to restrict the owners' choices in this way? Explain your answer.

11.2 Why Radical Environmentalists Dislike Economists: Efficient Pollution

Explain the rule for coordinating private choices with smart social choices when there are negative externalities.

Economists — including me — argue that a smart society should choose an "efficient" amount of pollution. This position angers many environmentalists. These environmentalists take the position that *any* amount of pollution is too much — zero pollution is their goal.

The Price (Opportunity Cost) of Pollution

Here's a good illustration of the economist's argument. Suppose I offered you $1 to drink a tall glass consisting of rats that had been liquefied in a blender. Would you? I'm guessing not. But what if you were a contestant on a television show where contestants are offered large sums of money to do unimaginably horrible and frightening tasks? Suppose you are offered $1 million? People on those shows say yes to offers like this all the time. A choice about an action that in principle is disgusting or wrong often turns out to depend on the price.

Instead of asking what you need to be paid to do something disgusting, what price would you pay *to get rid of* something disgusting and wrong? A world that has eliminated pollution sounds good in principle, but most of us are unwilling to pay the price — the opportunity cost — of a dramatically lower standard of living.

Trade-Offs between Pollution and Living Standards   Once we admit a willingness to live with some pollution, the question becomes: How low a standard of living are we willing to "pay" in order to reduce pollution? Small reductions in pollution like eliminating lead from gasoline and paint, or conserving energy to reduce output from coal-fired electrical plants, don't cost much. But to get to zero pollution, the opportunity cost is huge — eliminating all cars and airplanes, outlawing all power except solar, wind, and hydroelectric power, and shutting down most factories. As we eliminate more and more pollution, there comes a point when the additional (opportunity) costs become greater than the additional benefits of lower pollution.

Economists conclude that some level of pollution is "efficient" — there is a smart choice that balances the costs of a lower standard of living against the benefits of lower pollution. Let's see how to smartly draw the line for acceptable levels of pollution — the equivalent of the line between the offers of $1 and $1 million — and hopefully convince environmentalists not to turn away in disgust from the economists. (Incidentally, David Suzuki agrees with the economist's position — see Economics Out There on page 293.).

John Heller / Getty Images

▲ Money becomes an incentive for people to do things they would never normally do. How much money would it take to get you to eat mealworms and crickets?

NOTE
"Efficient pollution" balances the additional environmental benefits of lower pollution with the additional opportunity costs of reduced living standards.

Economics *Out There*

A Useful Poison?

DDT is an effective, potent pesticide that persists in the environment — it accumulates in animals that eat insects and is now banned in many countries, including Canada. So should DDT be banned everywhere, or is it just like the goal of zero pollution? Without more information, we tend to think, yes, it should be banned everywhere. But all choices have opportunity costs.

DDT is by far the most effective tool in fighting malaria because it kills the mosquitoes that spread the disease. In the 1950s and 1960s, widespread use of DDT all but eliminated malaria in most countries, and by 1970 had saved an estimated 500 million lives.

Since then, DDT has been banned in many countries, and malaria outbreaks have increased significantly. In Mozambique, malaria infection rates are 20 to 40 times higher than in neighbouring Swaziland, which never stopped using DDT. The World Health Organization estimates that roughly 500 million people currently suffer from malaria, most in sub-Saharan Africa. About 2 million die per year.

So, should DDT be banned everywhere?

Never make a choice, including environmentally friendly choices, without considering the opportunity costs.

Source: Based on "A Useful Poison," *The Economist*, December 14, 2000.

Efficient Combinations of Output and Pollution

The rule for an efficient combination of output and pollution is a simple refinement of Key 1 that accounts for *all* costs, including negative externalities. For any product or service (output) whose production also creates a negative externality, the rule for smart choices is:

Choose the Quantity of Output Where

Marginal Social Cost = Marginal Social Benefit

$$(MSC) = (MSB)$$

There are two new concepts in the rule — **marginal social cost** and **marginal social benefit** — which are related to the definitions of *social cost* and *social benefit* in section 11.1.

Marginal Social Cost When there are negative externalities, social costs are greater than private costs. When we focus on *additional* costs and benefits (Key 2), that relationship is

Marginal Social Cost (*MSC*)	=	Marginal Private Cost Directly Paid by Producers (*MC*)	+	Marginal External Cost Imposed on Others

Let's look at the example of a pulp mill. The mill's decisions about quantities to produce and prices to charge depends on the opportunity costs the mill pays directly — labour, wood, power, and so on. But the mill's smokestacks also emit sulphur dioxide — causing acid rain and air pollution, and contributing to global warming. The marginal external cost per tonne of pulp produced is the price of preventing or cleaning up the damage from the pollution. *Marginal social cost* (*MSC*) is the sum of the *marginal private cost* (*MC*) and the *marginal external cost*.

Marginal Social Benefit When there are positive externalities, social benefits are greater than private benefits.

Marginal Social Benefit (*MSB*)	=	Marginal Private Benefit Directly Received by Consumers (*MB*)	+	Marginal External Benefit Enjoyed by Others

Your post-secondary education provides you with private benefits like an increased lifetime income. But there are also external benefits to employers and government. The marginal external benefit is the value of the reduced average training costs and reduced government expenditures (more in section 11.4).

The pulp mill in our example does *not* produce positive externalities, so the *marginal social benefit* is the same as the *marginal private benefit* (*MB*). It is the value of the pulp bought and sold in markets.

Pulp Industry Challenge Figure 11.1 provides some simple, made-up numbers for the daily output of all the mills producing for the pulp market. The left three columns show market demand, and the right three columns show market supply. The first column on both the demand and supply sides is *Output*, the different quantities of pulp the businesses might produce. The rule for making a smart choice focuses first on the *quantity to produce and the associated levels of pollution.* That's why the first column on both the demand and supply sides is quantity, instead of (as in Figure 4.1) price.

Figure 11.1   Demand, Supply, and Negative Externalities in the Pulp Market

Demand			Supply		
Output (tonnes/day)	Marginal Private Benefit (MB)	Marginal Social Benefit (MSB)	Output (tonnes/day)	Marginal Private Cost (MC)	Marginal Social Cost (MSC)
1	$140	$140	1	$50	$ 80
2	$120	$120	2	$60	$ 90
3	$100	$100	3	$70	$100
4	$ 80	$ 80	4	$80	$110
5	$ 60	$ 60	5	$90	$120

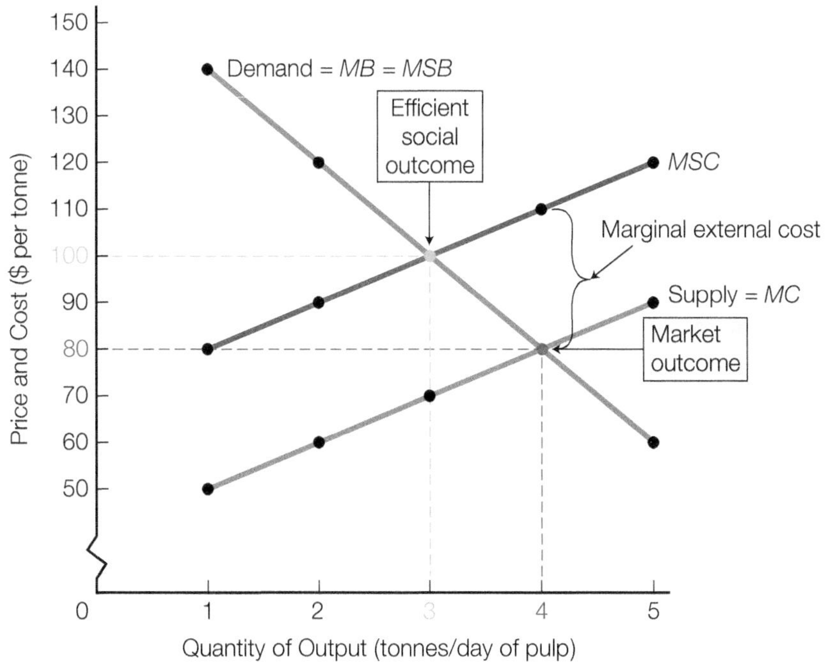

Demand The second column, *Marginal Private Benefit* (*MB*), shows, for each quantity, the maximum price consumers or buyers are willing and able to pay. The private benefit of the first tonne of pulp is $140, but that marginal benefit diminishes for each successive tonne. The downward-sloping *marginal private benefit* curve graphs these numbers. Remember, you read a marginal benefit curve up and over — from quantity up to the marginal benefit curve and over to the maximum price people are willing and able to pay.

You can also read the first two columns of numbers as a demand curve. Think of column 2 as *the price buyers are willing and able to pay* for the different quantities of pulp in column 1. When the price is $140 per tonne, quantity demanded is only 1 tonne. As the price falls, quantity demanded increases. So the *marginal private benefit* curve is also a demand curve.

The third column, *Marginal Social Benefit,* is the same as *Marginal Private Benefit* because there are no positive externalities. So the downward-sloping curve in Figure 11.1 has three identities — it is a *marginal private benefit* curve, a demand curve, and a *marginal social benefit* curve. Hence the label Demand = *MB* = *MSB*.

Supply Supply curves can also be read two ways — as marginal cost curves and as supply curves. Column 5, *Marginal Private Cost* (*MC*), shows the costs the pulp mills actually pay for additional labour, wood, power, and other inputs for each additional tonne of pulp. Notice the pattern of increasing marginal cost as output increases. The upward sloping *marginal private cost* curve graphs these numbers. You read a marginal cost curve just like a marginal benefit curve — up and over.

You can also read columns 4 and 5 as a supply curve. *Marginal private cost* is the minimum price the business will accept to supply that additional quantity — price must cover all marginal opportunity costs of production. As the price rises, the quantity supplied increases. So the *marginal private cost* curve is also a supply curve, hence the label Supply = *MC*.

Marginal Social Cost Again So far, the pattern of numbers for demand and supply is similar to Chapter 4, where the invisible hand works well. The big difference is in the last column, *Marginal Social Cost* (*MSC*). Let's say each tonne of pulp generates $30 of external costs — the costs of either preventing or cleaning up the damage from the pollution associated with that tonne of pulp. The pulp mills do not pay for these external costs. But these are costs to society that must be added to the *marginal private costs* to calculate marginal social cost. The upward-sloping *marginal social cost* curve combines quantities supplied with *marginal social costs*. *Marginal social cost* is $30 higher per tonne than the *marginal private cost*, due to the additional external costs of pollution.

Putting It All Together Figure 11.1 on the previous page tells the story, both in numbers and graphs, of what the market outcome will be, and what the smart social choice should be. Let's focus on the story in the graph.

For the private decisions of consumers and businesses, the market outcome is at the intersection of the *marginal private benefit* curve and the *marginal private cost* curve. Pulp sells for $80 per tonne and 4 tonnes are sold and bought. These numbers are highlighted in red on the table.

The smart social choice is at the intersection of the *marginal social benefit* curve and the *marginal social cost* curve. The smart social outcome has pulp selling for $100 per tonne and only 3 tonnes are sold and bought. These numbers are highlighted in green on the table.

NOTE
Market outcome — intersection of the *marginal private benefit* and *marginal private cost* curves

NOTE
Smart social choice — intersection of the *marginal social benefit* and *marginal social cost* curves

Understanding the Smart Social Choice The rule for a smart social choice is to choose the quantity of output where *marginal social cost = marginal social benefit*. The graph tells the story of why this rule works. For any quantity of pulp, starting with tonne 1, go up to the *marginal social cost* curve and *marginal social benefit* curve. *Marginal social benefit* is greater than *marginal social cost* for every quantity up to 3 tonnes. For any quantity greater than that, *marginal social benefit* is less than *marginal social cost*. Society should draw the line at 3 tonnes of pulp, accepting the associated "efficient" amount of pollution.

Compared to the market outcome, the smart choice for society means producing less of a product with a negative externality (3 tonnes of pulp instead of the market's 4 tonnes) and charging a higher price ($100 per tonne instead of $80 per tonne). These numbers illustrate the general result that *markets tend to overproduce products and services with negative externalities, and the price charged is too low* (because it does not incorporate the external costs).

NOTE
Markets overproduce products and services with negative externalities; the price is too low because it does not incorporate external costs.

Refresh 11.2

1. Explain the rule for coordinating private choices with smart social choices when there are negative externalities.

2. If the marginal external cost of pollution in Figure 11.1 were $60 per tonne instead of $30 per tonne, what would be the smart choice for society of pulp output? What would be the smart price of a tonne of pulp?

3. What position on DDT would you support (see story from Economics Out There, page 285)? What additional information might you need before deciding?

MyEconLab

For answers to these Refresh Questions, visit MyEconLab.

11.3

Liberating the Invisible Hand:
Policies to Internalize the Externality

Identify how government policies for polluters can internalize externalities to create smart social choices.

Because there are no clear property rights to the environment, individuals and businesses do not have to pay for the external costs their choices create. In fact, businesses usually save money and improve profits by ignoring external costs like pollution, soil contamination, and global warming. Businesses actually have *incentives to take actions that make society worse off.* Businesses that produce at lower cost because they ignore external costs are rewarded with more sales to price-conscious consumers. And without having to pay for your personal contribution to global warming, individuals like you and I are more likely to buy Honda Civics instead of taking public transit.

When markets work well, our self-interest leads us to make smart choices that turn out also to be good for everyone else, and markets produce the products and services we most desire at the lowest possible cost. With negative externalities, markets fail and self-interest leads to social problems like environmental damage.

What can be done to restore the power of the invisible hand?

Government Support for the Invisible Hand

Just as private property and contract laws are necessary rules of the game for markets to function at all, government has a crucial role to play in correcting the market failures caused by negative externalities.

Roads are a commonly shared space, just like the environment. If there were no traffic laws — no rules of the (road) game — self-interested drivers would not have to stop at intersections, signal turns, or obey speed limits. There would be traffic chaos as each driver tried to get where she was going without any concern for other drivers. Government traffic laws improve the functioning of roadways to the benefit of all drivers.

Create Property Rights   Government can also improve the functioning of the environment. It can effectively create social property rights by making it illegal to pollute the atmosphere or waterways. With pollution laws, government can protect the environment by "punishing" those who pollute. The punishment might be criminal penalties (jail time) or, more commonly, financial penalties (fines or taxes).

The key principle for any government policy is to set the environmental rules of the game in a way that aligns smart private choices with smart social choices. Smart government policies lead self-interested individuals and businesses to choose outcomes that are also best for society. For any product or service with negative externalities, that means policies that get everyone to voluntarily choose the quantity of output where *marginal social benefit* equals *marginal social cost.*

Carbon Taxes and Cap-and-Trade System for Emissions

Two important environmental polices that lead individuals and businesses to choose the quantities of outputs (and associated levels of pollution) that are best for society are

- carbon taxes.
- a cap-and-trade system for emissions.

Both policies force polluters to pay the cost of preventing or cleaning up the external damage they cause to others.

Carbon Taxes   Noxious emissions cause negative externalities, whether in the form of carbon dioxide increasing global warming, sulphur dioxide causing acid rain, or harmful chemicals causing cancers and other health problems. **Emissions taxes** are designed to pay for the external cost of preventing or cleaning up the damage from emissions. A **carbon tax**, paid by anyone using carbon-based fossil fuels (like oil, gas, or coal) is the best-known example of an emissions tax.

emissions tax   tax to pay for external costs of emissions

carbon tax   emissions tax on carbon-based fossil fuels

Let's look at how a government carbon tax would affect the choices of the pulp mills in our previous example. A smart carbon tax is set at an amount equal to the marginal external cost of the damage associated with a tonne of pulp. If that marginal external cost is $30 per tonne, the tax should be $30 per tonne.

Figure 11.2 (on the next page) reproduces the numbers in Figure 11.1, with one change. The last column is now labelled *Marginal Private Cost + Tax*. This column lists the costs the mill must now pay for each additional tonne of pulp it produces. For the first tonne (output = 1), the mill pays $50 in *marginal private costs* for inputs like labour, wood, and power, and the $30 emissions tax to the government, for a total of $80. This last column is the sum of the marginal costs (including the carbon tax) that pulp mills must now pay for producing the first tonne of pulp.

Given the new tax, which changes the rules of the game, what is the market-clearing output and price for the pulp industry? Look at the graph in Figure 11.2, which is similar to Figure 11.1. The only difference is that the red *marginal social cost* curve is now also the supply curve, including private marginal costs and the emissions tax. Businesses now choose to produce at the intersection of the demand and supply curves, where *marginal social benefit* equals *marginal social cost*. The efficient price and quantity for the pulp market is $100 per tonne and 3 tonnes per day. These numbers, highlighted in green, are also the market-clearing price and quantity. The pollution associated with 3 tonnes of pulp per day is the "efficient" amount of pollution.

By forcing producers to pay the external marginal cost of the negative externalities, emissions taxes get producers to voluntarily choose the socially best combination of output and price and associated level of pollution. There is a wonderfully descriptive and catchy (for an economist) phrase that describes how emissions taxes induce the best social outcome — we say that the emissions tax **internalizes the externality**. Remember that phrase. The tax transforms the external cost into a cost the producer must pay to the government.

internalize the externality   transform external costs into costs the producer must pay to the government

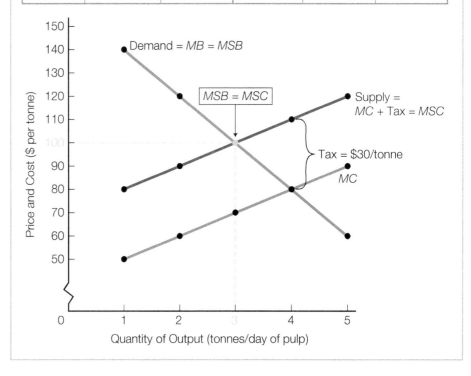

Figure 11.2 Pulp Market with $30/Tonne Emissions Tax

Demand			Supply		
Output (tonnes/day)	Marginal Private Benefit (MB)	Marginal Social Benefit (MSB)	Output (tonnes/day)	Marginal Private Cost (MC)	Marginal Private Cost + Tax
1	$140	$140	1	$50	$ 80
2	$120	$120	2	$60	$ 90
3	$100	$100	3	$70	$100
4	$ 80	$ 80	4	$80	$110
5	$ 60	$ 60	5	$90	$120

Cap-and-Trade System for Emissions A smart social choice of an efficient amount of pollution involves a combination of output, price, and associated levels of pollution. While emissions taxes increase the price (and cost) of products and services to reflect internal and external costs, cap-and-trade policies focus on the level or *quantity of emissions*.

In a **cap-and-trade system** for emissions, the government (or an international agreement among governments) establishes property rights to the environment and restricts the emission of pollutants. The system sets a limit, or *cap,* on the quantity of emissions that businesses can release into the environment. Businesses must have permits to pollute, which the government auctions off to the highest bidders. The total quantity of emissions allowed by the permits is set equal to the government target for emissions.

cap-and-trade system limits the quantity of emissions businesses can release into environment

A market for emissions permits is established, where businesses can buy and sell (that is, *trade*) permits. Businesses that reduce their emissions can sell permits they don't need to other businesses. Those other businesses are willing to pay the costs of additional pollution permits because the products or services they produce are sufficiently valuable that consumers will pay higher prices. The cap-and-trade system gives businesses a choice of reducing pollution themselves or buying pollution permits.

In theory, the price of an emissions permit reflects the marginal external cost of the pollution produced. Since this becomes a private cost to the business that buys the permits, a smart cap-and-trade system internalizes the externality, just like an emissions tax, and leads to the choice of output, prices, and pollution that is best for society. Although the initial focus of the cap-and-trade system is on the quantity of emissions, the additional costs businesses pay for emissions permits eventually turns into higher prices for consumers.

Licence to Pollute?   A common objection to the cap-and-trade system is that it allows businesses to "buy a licence to pollute" — and we are told pollution is always bad. But think back to the TV reality show of paying people to do weird things and the principle of zero pollution. Once we give up on the idea of a world with zero pollution because the associated standard of living is unacceptably low, there will be some pollution. To achieve the efficient amount of pollution, pollution must have a price that reflects the marginal external cost of the damage done. Pollution that is "priced" or "licensed" enables individuals and businesses to make smart choices that are also smart for society.

What's the Dif?   Does it make any difference which policy a government uses — a carbon tax or a cap-and-trade system?

There is a difference in who pays *initially*. With a carbon tax, anyone using energy, whether consumers filling up gas tanks or businesses buying energy for their factories, pays the tax up front. With a cap-and-trade system, businesses pay initially for emissions permits. But consumers pay eventually as the additional cost is passed on in higher prices for products and services.

A carbon tax makes the cost of a negative externality directly obvious to consumers and businesses. The costs of emissions permits in a cap-and-trade system are far less obvious to the final consumer. This hidden quality makes cap-and-trade systems more popular with politicians, who want to be seen to be supporting the environment, but don't want to be blamed for higher prices!

All of these cars congested on highways around Toronto pollute the air for free. As Suzuki says, they are treating the atmosphere as a dumping ground. Should drivers pay for the carbon they dump into the air?

Economics *Out There*

Make Polluters (Including You) Pay

The David Suzuki Foundation offers very clear background information about the motivation for a carbon tax or cap-and-trade system. The Foundation's website states that a fundamental problem is that "the atmosphere is treated as a free dumping ground for harmful, heat-trapping emissions," and that Canada is doing poorly at reducing these emissions because it has relied on voluntary measures to do so. According to the Foundation, most of the country's emissions come from burning fossil fuels. It supports pricing emissions using a carbon tax or a cap-and-trade system: "seeing that cost, and making it real, will give us new incentives to change the technologies and habits that created global warming in the first place."

Source: www.davidsuzuki.org

A cap-and-trade system sets a quantity limit for emissions, allowing targets to be set and progress toward those targets to be clearly measured. A carbon tax sets an estimated price on the costs of negative externalities, but the quantity of total emissions depends on the interaction of all the choices made by individuals and businesses. Quantities of emissions are more uncertain with a carbon tax.

Both government policies to internalize the externalities of pollution — a carbon tax or a cap-and-trade system — have three shared benefits:

- As carbon-based energy becomes more expensive, less carbon-based energy will be consumed. The law of demand applies — when something gets more expensive, people economize on its use and look for substitutes.
- Carbon taxes and emissions-permit auctions raise revenues that can be used by government to repair the environmental damage, or for other environmentally friendly initiatives.
- Higher carbon-based energy prices make solar, wind, and hydro power more competitive, and encourage businesses to search for alternative (cheaper) energy sources.

NOTE
Carbon taxes and emissions permits give pollution a price reflecting the marginal external cost of damage done, so smart individual and business choices become smart social choices.

Green Trade-Offs of Efficiency versus Equity

Smart government policies like a carbon tax or a cap-and-trade system raise the prices of products and services to include indirect external costs to the environment on top of direct costs of production. That helps restore the power of the invisible hand to coordinate smart private and social choices.

But the law of demand still applies. As prices rise, the quantity demanded decreases because fewer people are willing *and able* to buy at the higher prices. As government policies raise gasoline and other energy prices, fewer people can afford to buy. This is part of the trade-off between achieving less pollution at the cost of a lower standard of living.

Those hurt most by higher energy prices are often those least able to afford them. Once again (Chapter 6), it is a question of balance between efficiency and equity. Policies that are smart in yielding an "efficient" amount of pollution may also be inequitable by hurting lower-income consumers more than higher-income consumers. There is no "magic-bullet policy" that can significantly reduce pollution without also reducing living standards, especially of those who are poorest, or those in energy-sensitive industries like trucking, taxis, air travel, or automobile production.

Economics *Out There*

Carbon Taxes Make Ireland Even Greener

Ireland imposed a carbon tax in 2008, immediately raising prices for oil and natural gas. Yearly car registration fees also rose steeply in proportion to the vehicles' emissions. The good news is that the Irish quickly shifted to greener fuels and cars — emissions dropped more than 15 percent in just 4 years. Automakers like Mercedes found ways to make powerful cars more fuel efficient, and higher prices for fossil fuels made renewable energy sources like wind power competitive.

The bad news is that gas and oil prices rose 10 percent, which is hardest on the poor. And industries complain the higher prices hurt their competitiveness when selling outside Ireland. But the government provided subsidies for low-income families; the wealthy, who consume the most, pay the most in carbon taxes; and exporters have survived.

Why were Irish politicians able to do this when North American politicians run away from carbon taxes as fast as they can? One reason is timing. The global financial crisis caused the Irish economy to collapse, and tax revenue fell by 25 percent in 2009. Facing a huge government budget deficit, the carbon tax raised nearly 1 billion euros, giving the government 25 percent of the tax revenue it needed to close the budget gap and avoid income tax increases. The carbon tax was not only good for the environment, but also for the budget and the government.

One Irish economist said, "You don't want to waste a good crisis to do what we should be doing anyway."

Source: Elisabeth Rosenthal, "Carbon Taxes Make Ireland Even Greener," *The New York Times,* December 27, 2012.

1. Explain what the the phrase "internalize the externality" means for a polluting business. Give an example of how government policies like emissions taxes "internalize externalities" for polluters to create smart social choices.

2. Some environmental groups try to expose businesses that pollute while supporting environmentally friendly businesses by posting information and photos on public websites. Explain how this strategy may "internalize the externality" for the polluters even without government action.

3. While carbon taxes and cap-and-trade systems have the same objective, governments and political parties differ over which policy they support. Which policy would a political party have to adopt to gain your vote? Explain your reasons.

MyEconLab

For answers to these Refresh Questions, visit MyEconLab.

Why Lighthouses Won't Make You Rich: Free Riders and Public Goods

11.4

Explain how positive externalities create the free-rider problem of public goods and cause markets to fail.

Internet scams offering to make you rich are everywhere — emails alert you to forgotten prize winnings, foreign lottery payoffs, oppressed billionaires who direly need your assistance, and cheap stocks about to take off. I hope you ignore them, even though some are temptingly believable. But if you ever get an email promising you riches from a fabulous lighthouse investment opportunity, I can promise you it's a scam. Here's why I'm so sure.

The Free-Rider Problem

Think about the business case for lighthouses. They provide an extremely valuable service. They prevent ships from running aground or sinking, thereby saving millions of dollars every year in lost or damaged cargo (and ships and sailors!). Sounds like a service that ship owners would gladly pay for.

But think about the *decision to buy* lighthouse services from the viewpoint of a cost-conscious ship owner. Sure, the service is valuable — but once the lighthouse is operating, the ship owner can get the "service" for free! No one can be excluded from seeing an operating lighthouse signal beacon. Why be a fool and pay — let other foolish or naive ship owners pay to start up the lighthouse, and then free ride on the light. All ship owners will figure out this free-riding strategy eventually, so any private lighthouse business will end in bankruptcy.

Public Goods Lighthouses are a classic example of what economists call a public good. **Public goods** can be consumed simultaneously by everyone; no one can be excluded. National defence is another example. Once a country has a standing army in place, everyone benefits and no one can be excluded. If the United States attacks Canada — say, to take control of oil reserves in Alberta — the Canadian Armed Forces won't protect just the citizens who have paid taxes while ignoring those who haven't paid. Even though public goods provide valuable services, markets will not produce them because no business can make a profit from them. Public goods like lighthouses and national armed forces are extreme cases of positive externalities.

public goods provide external benefits consumed simultaneously by everyone; no one can be excluded

Positive Externalities   Positive externalities create a similar, less extreme free-rider problem for education and public transit. While the private benefits of your post-secondary education include higher lifetime earnings for you, there are also external benefits to employers (who do not have to spend as much money and time training you), and to governments and citizens (because you will require less assistance and will better participate in democratic activities). When you take public transit instead of driving, others benefit from reduced traffic jams and cleaner air without having to pay. All these "others" receive positive benefits from your choices, but "free ride" by not having to pay.

Positive externalities are not as "in-your-face" a problem as negative externalities. The problem with negative externalities is clear — markets produce too many "bads," like acid rain, global warming, and traffic jams. For products and services with positive externalities, the more subtle problem is why markets don't produce *more* such "goods" like education, public transit, and vaccinations. This is the **free-rider problem** — markets tend to underproduce products and services with positive externalities, and the price charged to buyers is too high and to sellers is too low. Let me explain.

free-rider problem   markets underproduce products and services with positive externalities

Efficient Combinations of Output and External Benefits

The rule for finding an efficient combination of output and external benefits is the same as for an efficient combination of output and pollution. For any product or service (output) whose production also generates a positive externality, the rule for smart choices is

Choose the Quantity of Output Where

Marginal Social Cost = Marginal Social Benefit

$$(MSC) = (MSB)$$

Let's look at an example of *privately* provided post-secondary education (the reason why I use this example of private education will become clear in section 11.5). The schools produce "educational services" that are sold to students.

Recall the definition:

Marginal Social Cost   =   Marginal Private Cost   +   Marginal External Cost
    (*MSC*)   Directly Paid by   Imposed on Others
                               Producers (*MC*)

The schools pay for instructors, buildings, computer systems, energy, and other inputs. These are *marginal private costs*. We will assume the schools are "green" and, unlike the pulp mills, do *not* produce any pollution or other external costs (marginal external costs = 0). For these schools, *marginal social cost* (*MSC*) equals *marginal private cost* (*MC*).

When there are positive externalities, social benefits are greater than private benefits:

Marginal Social Benefit   =   Marginal Private Benefit   +   Marginal External Benefit
    (*MSB*)   Directly Received by   Enjoyed by Others
                                  Consumers (*MB*)

The main private benefit to students of post-secondary education is increased lifetime income. But there are also external benefits, like reduced training costs for employers and reduced government expenditures on crime fighting and social assistance. The marginal external benefit is the value, per student educated per year, of the reduced training costs and reduced government expenditures. (See Economics Out There on page 298 for calculations of the marginal external benefit of roads.)

Figure 11.3 provides some simple, made-up numbers for the yearly output of all the schools producing in the private post-secondary education market. Like Figure 11.1, the left three columns show market demand, and the right three columns show market supply. The first column on both the demand and supply sides is *Output,* showing the different quantities of educational services (measured in students educated per year) the schools might choose to produce.

Figure 11.3 Demand, Supply, and Positive Externalities in a Private Post-Secondary Education Market

Demand			Supply		
Output (students/ year)	Marginal Private Benefit (MB)	Marginal Social Benefit (MSB)	Output (students/ year)	Marginal Private Cost (MC)	Marginal Social Cost (MSC)
100	$7 000	$10 000	100	$4 000	$4 000
200	$6 000	$ 9 000	200	$4 500	$4 500
300	$5 000	$ 8 000	300	$5 000	$5 000
400	$4 000	$ 7 000	400	$5 500	$5 500
500	$3 000	$ 6 000	500	$6 000	$6 000
600	$2 000	$ 5 000	600	$6 500	$6 500
700	$1 000	$ 4 000	700	$7 000	$7 000

Economics *Out There*

Infrastructure as Public Good

Ever wonder how much certain industries benefit from the infrastructure — like roads, bridges, sewers, water systems — that governments provide as a public good? No? Well, the information illustrates the idea of marginal external benefit. Statistics Canada estimated the "private production cost savings associated with the use of public infrastructure" and found that the biggest "winner" industries were transportation (42-cent payoff for every government dollar spent), retailers (34-cent payoff), and wholesalers (33-cent payoff). And this was on top of "money . . . earned from government purchases to build the infrastructure"! All 37 industries in the study received at least some marginal external benefit.

Source: Bruce Little, "Infrastructure as Public Good," *The Globe and Mail*, Nov. 24, 2003.

▲ Massive government infrastructure investments like this highway system provide external benefits for many private companies. Is this type of public good paid for by all of us a good use of tax dollars?

Demand   The second column, *Marginal Private Benefit (MB)*, shows the maximum price students (the buyers) are willing and able to pay for each quantity. The private marginal benefit of the first 100 student-years of education (output = 100) is $7000, but that marginal benefit diminishes for successive years. The downward-sloping blue *marginal private benefit* curve graphs these numbers.

Think of column 2 as *the price buyers are willing and able to pay* for the different quantities of education in column 1. When the price is $7000 per student-year, quantity demanded is only from 100 students. As the price falls, quantity demanded increases. So the *marginal private benefit* curve is also a demand curve.

Marginal Social Benefit   Compared to a market where the invisible hand works well, the third column, *Marginal Social Benefit (MSB)*, contains the important difference in the numbers. Let's say each 100 student-years of education generates $3000 in external benefits — the cost savings to employers and governments in training and assistance payments. Employers and government do not have to pay (they get a free ride) for the benefits, but these benefits must be added to *marginal private benefits* to calculate *marginal social benefits*. The downward-sloping green *MSB* curve shows *marginal social benefit* for any quantity demanded. For any quantity of educational services, *marginal social benefit* is $3000 higher per 100 student years than the *marginal private benefit*.

Supply   Supply curves can be read two ways — as a marginal cost curve and as a supply curve. Column 5, *Marginal Private Cost (MC)*, shows the costs the schools actually pay for instructors, buildings, computer systems, energy, and other inputs for each additional 100 students per year. Notice the pattern of increasing marginal cost as output increases. The upward-sloping *marginal private cost* curve graphs these numbers. *Marginal private cost* is the minimum price the schools will accept to supply that additional quantity — price must cover all marginal opportunity costs of production.

You can also read columns 4 and 5 as a supply curve. As the price rises, the quantity supplied increases. So the *marginal private cost* curve is also a supply curve, hence the label Supply = *MC*.

The last column, *Marginal Social Cost (MSC)*, is the same as *marginal private cost* because there are no negative externalities. So the upward-sloping blue curve in Figure 11.3 has three identities — it is a *marginal private cost* curve, a supply curve, and a *marginal social cost* curve. Hence the label, Supply = *MC* = *MSC*.

Putting It All Together   Figure 11.3 tells the story, both in numbers and graphs, of what the market outcome will be, and what the smart social choice should be. Let's focus on the story in the graph.

For the private decisions of students and schools, the market outcome is at the intersection of the *marginal private benefit* curve and the *marginal private cost* curve — educational services sell for $5000 per year and 300 student-years are sold and bought. These numbers are highlighted in red.

The smart social choice is at the intersection of the *marginal social benefit* curve and the *marginal social cost* curve. The smart social outcome has educational services selling for $6000 per year, and 500 student-years are sold and bought. These numbers are highlighted in green.

NOTE
Market outcome — intersection of the *marginal private benefit* and *marginal private cost* curves.

NOTE
Smart social choice — intersection of the *marginal social benefit* and *marginal social cost* curves.

Understanding the Smart Social Choice   The rule for a smart social choice is to choose the quantity of output where *marginal social cost = marginal social benefit*. The graph tells the story of why this rule works. For any quantity of education services, starting with 100 student-years, go up to the *marginal social cost* curve and *marginal social benefit* curve. *Marginal social benefit* is greater than *marginal social cost* for every quantity up to 500 student-years. For any quantity greater than that, *marginal social benefit* is less than *marginal social cost*.

Compared to the market outcome, the smart social choice is to produce more of products with positive externalities (500 student-years of education instead of the market's 300 student-years).

Is There a Smart Social Price?   There is no market-clearing price that can provide incentives to coordinate demand and supply for 500 student-years of output. To be willing to buy (demand) the smart social quantity of 500 student-years of education, students will pay only $3000 per year — the value of their *marginal private benefits* only, because students are not compensated for their external benefits to others. But to be willing to supply the smart social quantity of 500 student-years, schools need to receive $6000 per student-year. Market failure occurs because externalities drive a wedge between individuals' smart choices and the smart choice for society as a whole.

These numbers and the graph illustrate the general result that *markets tend to underproduce products and services with positive externalities*. Furthermore, the market-clearing price is too high for buyers to be willing to buy the quantity of output best for society, and too low for sellers to be willing to supply that socially best quantity (because neither buyers nor sellers are being paid for the external benefits their exchange creates). Is there a government policy that can solve this problem?

NOTE
Markets underproduce products and services with positive externalities: For the socially best quantity output, the market-clearing price is too high for buyers to be willing to buy and too low for sellers to be willing to supply.

Refresh 11.4

1. Explain how the free-rider problem of public goods causes markets to fail.

2. Smart students often don't like group projects. Explain why, using the concept of free riding.

3. Two physically identical houses can have very different values depending on their neighbourhoods. How do positive (or negative) externalities help explain this difference in property values?

MyEconLab

For answers to these Refresh Questions, visit MyEconLab.

11.5

Identify how government subsidies can internalize positive externalities to create smart social choices.

Why Your Tuition Is Cheap (Really!): Subsidies for the Public Good

When there are positive externalities, markets fail. Market-clearing prices do not reflect the external benefits associated with producing products and services we desire. Smart choices for individual consumers and businesses are not the same as smart choices for society.

Because of the free-rider problem, other individuals and businesses do not pay for the external benefits created by your private market exchanges. Smart individual choices leave society with too few products and services with positive externalities. If only there were a way to "internalize the (positive) externalities," everyone could end up better off.

Adam Smith's Vote for Government

Government has as much, if not more, of a role to play correcting market failures from positive externalities as from negative externalities. Adam Smith, the father of the invisible hand, recognized this back in 1776 when he explicitly gave government ("the commonwealth") the responsibility for providing valuable public goods that markets would not supply (see the quote in the margin). There is a reason why lighthouses are operated by governments.

The key principle for government policy is to set the rules of the game to combine smart private choices with smart social choices. Government needs to remove the wedge that positive externalities drive between prices for buyers and sellers, so that self-interested individuals and businesses choose the outcomes that are also best for society as a whole. That again means policies that get everyone to voluntarily choose the quantity of output where *marginal social benefit* equals *marginal social cost*.

The two main policy tools to accomplish this are

- subsidies.
- public provision.

Subsidies

How can private individuals and businesses whose choices create positive externalities be compensated for the benefits that go to others outside the original exchange? Governments can do that, and internalize externalities, by granting **subsidies**, or payments, equal to the value of the positive externality. Subsidies are the opposite of taxes. Instead of government adding a cost on individuals or businesses equal to the damage done by their negative externalities, subsidies reward those whose choices create positive externalities for others.

External benefits are widely spread over many, many others, so government can act on behalf of all ("the commonwealth"), taxing the general public to raise revenues to pay the subsidies to those whose actual choices generate positive externalities.

Let's look at how a government subsidy affects the choices of students and schools in the market for post-secondary educational services. A smart subsidy equals the marginal external benefit — the savings to others associated with a student-year of education. In our example, that marginal external benefit is $3000 per student-year, so that is the subsidy. To get a smart social outcome, the government can pay the subsidy to *either* the demanders or suppliers.

The third … duty of the … commonwealth is … erecting and maintaining those public institutions and those public works, which, though they may be in the highest degree advantageous to a great society, are, however, of such a nature that the profit could never repay the expense to any individual …

— *Adam Smith*

Wealth of Nations

subsidy payment to those who create positive externalities

NOTE
Smart subsidy = marginal external benefit of savings to others associated with activity.

Subsidy to Suppliers   Let's look at what happens when the government pays the subsidy to the schools for each student-year of education supplied. Figure 11.4 reproduces the numbers in Figure 11.3, with one change. The last column is now labelled *Marginal Private Cost – Subsidy*. This column lists the costs schools pay for each additional student-year of education *after subtracting the subsidy* received from the government. For each of the first 100 student-years, the schools pay $4000 in *marginal private costs* for inputs like instructors, buildings, computer systems, and energy, but they now receive a payment of $3000. So the net *marginal private cost*, with the subsidy, is $1000. For all other quantities of output, the numbers in the last column equal the *marginal private cost* minus the subsidy of $3000 per student-year.

Figure 11.4   Post-Secondary Education Market with $3000 Subsidy to Schools

Demand			Supply		
Output (students/ year)	Marginal Private Benefit (*MB*)	Marginal Social Benefit (*MSB*)	Output (students/ year)	Marginal Private Cost (*MC*)	Marginal Private Cost – Subsidy
100	$7 000	$10 000	100	$4 000	$1 000
200	$6 000	$ 9 000	200	$4 500	$1 500
300	$5 000	$ 8 000	300	$5 000	$2 000
400	$4 000	$ 7 000	400	$5 500	$2 500
500	$3 000	$ 6 000	500	$6 000	$3 000
600	$2 000	$ 5 000	600	$6 500	$3 500
700	$1 000	$ 4 000	700	$7 000	$4 000

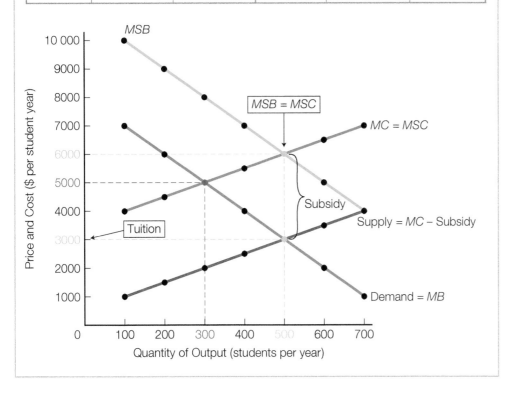

The new subsidy changes the rules of the game by affecting the private costs of the schools. What does the subsidy do to the market-clearing output and price for the post-secondary education? Look at the graph in Figure 11.4. The main difference from Figure 11.3 is the new red supply curve labelled *MC – Subsidy*. Because subsidies to suppliers lower total input costs, there is an increase in supply (section 3.4). The vertical distance between the original supply curve (*MC*) and the new supply curve (*MC – Subsidy*) is the amount of the subsidy — $3000 per student-year of education. (You can review the effects of a tax on supply and demand curves in section 5.3.)

This new supply curve, which takes *marginal private costs* and subtracts the subsidy, intersects the unchanged private demand curve (Demand = *MB*) at the efficient outcome of 500 student-years and a price of $3000 per student-year (in green numbers and on the graph). At the quantity of 500 student-years, going up to the *marginal social benefit* curve shows the *marginal social benefit* of $6000 per student year.

With the subsidy, both student-demanders and school-suppliers choose to produce the socially efficient quantity of educational services. Students pay the $3000 price equal to their private benefits, and schools receive that $3000 plus the $3000 subsidy from government. That total of $6000 going to the schools covers their marginal opportunity costs.

▲ With fewer cars on the road, public transit vehicles move more people faster, reduce commute times, and do it with less pollution. Do you think drivers would accept a tax to pay for more public transit?

NOTE
Subsidies remove the wedge positive externalities drive between prices for buyers and sellers, getting individuals and businesses to voluntarily choose the quantity of output best for society.

Subsidies Remove the Wedge   By paying the schools for the marginal external benefits the educational services provide to others beyond the students, government subsidies get students and schools to voluntarily choose the socially best combination of output and price and the associated level of external benefits. The subsidies remove the wedge that positive externalities drive between prices for buyers and sellers, so that self-interested individuals and businesses choose the outcomes that are also best for society.

Paying subsidies to the students instead of the schools also achieves an efficient social outcome. See the Refresh question at the end of this section.

Economics *Out There*

Should Drivers Be Taxed to Pay for Public Transit?

When the chairman of the Toronto Transit Commission proposed a tax on drivers to finance more public transit, drivers were outraged. After all, they argued, we don't take the transit, why should we pay for it?

Do you agree?

Before answering, think about externalities, both positive and negative.

Transit riders provide positive externalities to drivers by reducing traffic congestion, commute times, and pollution.

So drivers benefit from more public transit, and the tax is a way of forcing drivers to pay for the positive externality they receive from transit riders.

Drivers, though they don't intend it, create traffic jams and increased commute times, imposing a negative externality on other drivers. A tax forces drivers to pay for those negative externalities and also encourage some to switch to transit, reducing traffic problems.

Public Provision

Instead of paying subsidies to private suppliers or demanders, governments may choose to directly provide a product or service with positive externalities. Education from kindergarten to grade 12 falls into this category, as well as most public infrastructure like roads, bridges, streetlights, public transit, and lighthouses. Economists call this **public provision**. Governments provide these services when positive externalities are widespread and important for citizens, and/or when it is difficult to collect revenues from users. Basic education is the foundation for a literate and socialized workforce and citizenry, so government pays the entire cost. Economics Out There on page 298 about public infrastructure shows the broad benefits to most industries from having roads and bridges, and industries provide widespread jobs and tax revenues. While tolls or user fees can work for highways and bridges when there are few entry and exit points, toll booths and separate charges for marginal external benefits don't make any sense for city streets (or for streetlights, or lighthouses).

public provision government provision of products or services with positive externalities, financed by tax revenue

Public provision means governments *pay* for these products or services. But government can also run the business itself (most primary and secondary schools) or contract out the actual operations (hiring private contractors to build roads and bridges). Public provision is based on the same principle as subsidies — set policies that get everyone to voluntarily choose the quantity of output where *marginal social benefit* equals *marginal social cost*.

This is where the earlier example of private post-secondary schools is important. As an alternative to paying subsidies to private suppliers, governments instead can directly run the post-secondary schools. That is roughly what happens in Canada, where post-secondary education is the responsibility of provincial governments, and there are almost no private institutions. The smart policy choice is the same as with subsidies. Choose the quantity of output (of educational services) where *marginal social benefit* equals *marginal social cost*. Public colleges and universities still have input costs and choices to make about prices (tuition). A publicly operated college or university should make the same choices as a private post-secondary industry with government subsidies.

What Does Your Education Cost?   Speaking of tuition, how many of you think your tuition is expensive? OK, you can all put down your hands. Well, it depends on what you mean by expensive. If you mean more than you can easily afford, you may be right. But if you evaluate what you pay in tuition relative to the total cost of providing your education, then you are dead wrong. Tuition covers less than 25 percent of the cost of delivering post-secondary education. In that sense, you are getting a bargain, which the government is subsidizing and providing to you below cost because of the massive positive externalities associated with your education.

Paying for Externalities Government pays for public provision using tax revenues. If the external benefits are widespread, as they are for education, governments may use general tax revenues or property tax revenues to finance public provision. In the case of roads, governments often use a tax on gasoline to finance construction and upkeep of city streets, on the principle that motorists benefit most from having good roads. (See Economics Out There on page 302 about whether it is fair to tax motorists to pay for public transit they don't use.)

IMPLICIT
COSTS &
EXTERNALITIES

When there are externalities — negative or positive — markets fail. Smart private choices (using Keys 1 and 2) are different from smart social choices (Keys 1, 2, and 3). Because private individuals or businesses don't pay for external costs and don't get paid for external benefits, they do not have incentives to make choices that are good for society, and the invisible hand fails to coordinate individual choices to balance social benefits with social costs.

Smart government policies that internalize the externality through taxes, emission controls, subsidies, and public provision are essential for liberating the invisible hand to allow markets to produce more of the "goods" we desire and fewer of the "bads."

Refresh 11.5

MyEconLab

For answers to these Refresh Questions, visit MyEconLab.

1. Explain how government subsidies can internalize positive externalities to create smart social choices using education as your example.

2. What if the government gave the $3000 subsidy from Figure 11.4 directly to students instead of to schools? Construct a table like Figure 11.3, and discover whether the students' private choices would still be the same as the smart choice for society. [*Hint*: The *Marginal Private Benefit* column shows willingness to pay. Create a new column showing willingness to pay *with the subsidy* (*Marginal Private Benefit + Subsidy*).]

3. Some European countries have free tuition for post-secondary education. If you were a member of parliament defending this policy (knowing that any money needed to provide "free" education had to be raised by new taxes), what arguments would you make? If you defended the Canadian system, where students must pay some tuition, what arguments would you make?

Study Guide

11.1 Handcuffing the Invisible Hand: Market Failure with Externalities

When externalities exist, prices don't reflect all social costs and benefits; markets fail to coordinate private smart choices with social smart choices.

- **Negative externalities (external costs)** — costs to society from your private choice that affect others, but that you do not pay.

- **Positive externalities (external benefits)** — benefits to society from your private choice that affect others, but that others do not pay you for.

- Externalities occur when clear property rights are missing.
  - *Tragedy of the commons* — the overuse and depletion of a resource that no one can be excluded from because of missing property rights.
  - *Free riders* — those who consume products or services without paying.

- When externalities exist, prices don't reflect all social costs and benefits, and markets fail to produce efficient outcomes. Instead markets produce:
  - too many products and services with negative externalities (second-hand smoke, pollution, traffic jams).
  - too few products and services with positive externalities (vaccinations, education).

11.2 Why Radical Environmentalists Dislike Economists: Efficient Pollution

For an efficient market outcome when there are negative externalities, choose the quantity of output where *marginal social cost* equals *marginal social benefit*.

- "Efficient pollution" balances the additional environmental benefits of lower pollution with the additional opportunity costs of reduced living standards.
  - The socially desirable amount of pollution is not zero; at some point the additional opportunity costs of reducing pollution are greater than the additional benefits of lower pollution.

- The market quantity and price are determined at the intersection of the *marginal private benefit* and *marginal private cost* curves.

- For any product or service that generates an externality, the rule for a smart choice is: Choose the quantity of output where *marginal social cost* equals *marginal social benefit*.
  - **Marginal social cost** *(MSC)* = marginal private cost *(MC)* plus marginal external cost
  - Marginal external cost = price of preventing or cleaning up damage to others external to the original activity
  - **Marginal social benefit** *(MSB)* = marginal private benefit *(MB)* plus marginal external benefit
  - Marginal external benefit = price of the value or savings to others external to the original activity

- Markets overproduce products and services with negative externalities; the price is too low because it does not incorporate external costs.

11.3 Liberating the Invisible Hand: Policies to Internalize the Externality

If polluters are forced by government to pay the marginal external costs of their pollution, this internalizes the externalities/costs into private choices, creating smart social choices.

- Without property rights to the environment, businesses have incentives to save money and improve profits by ignoring external costs like pollution and global warming.

- Governments can remedy market failures from externalities by creating social property rights to the environment, making polluting illegal, and penalizing polluters.

- **Emissions tax** — tax to pay for external costs of emissions
  - **Carbon tax** — emissions tax on carbon-based fossil fuels
  - Smart carbon tax = marginal external cost of damage from emissions

- **Cap-and-trade system** — limits the quantities of emissions businesses can release into environment.
  - Government auctions off pollution permits to the highest bidders.
  - Total quantity of emissions allowed by permits = emissions target.
  - Businesses buy and sell emissions permits. Permit price becomes a private cost to business reflecting the marginal external cost of pollution.
- **Internalize the externality** — transform external costs into costs the producer must pay to the government.
- Carbon taxes and emissions permits give pollution a price reflecting marginal external cost of damage done, so smart individual and business choices become smart social choices.
- Carbon taxes and cap-and-trade systems are smart policies for efficient pollution, but may be inequitable in hurting lower-income consumers most.

11.4 Why Lighthouses Won't Make You Rich: Freeriders and Public Goods

With positive externalities, buyers and sellers are not paid for the external benefits their exchange creates. The market-clearing price is too high for buyers to be willing to buy the socially best quantity of output, and too low for sellers to be willing to supply.

- **Public goods** — provide external benefits consumed simultaneously by everyone; no one can be excluded.
  - Public goods like lighthouses and national defence are extreme examples of positive externalities.
- **Free-rider problem** — markets underproduce products and services with positive externalities.
  - Price charged to buyers is too high.
  - Price received by sellers is too low.

- The smart social quantity of output with positive externalities is at the intersection of the *marginal social benefit* and *marginal social cost* curves.
  - With positive externalities, no single price can coordinate smart individual choices and smart social choices.
  - The market-clearing price is too high for buyers to be willing to buy and too low for sellers to be willing to supply.

11.5 Why Your Tuition Is Cheap (Really!): Subsidies for the Public Good

When there are positive externalities, government subsidies can get everyone to voluntarily choose the socially best quantity of output where *marginal social benefit* equals *marginal social cost*.

- **Subsidy** — payment to those who create positive externalities.
  - Smart subsidy = marginal external benefit of savings to others associated with an activity.
  - Subsidies remove the disconnect between prices for buyers and sellers caused by positive externalities, leading individuals and businesses to voluntarily choose the quantity of output best for society.
  - Subsidies to either suppliers or demanders can achieve an efficient social outcome.
- **Public provision** — government provision of products or services with positive externalities, financed by tax revenue.

TRUE/FALSE

Circle the correct answer. Solutions to these questions are available at the end of the book and on MyEconLab. You can also visit the MyEconLab Study Plan to access additional questions that will help you master the concepts covered in this chapter.

11.1 Market Failure with Externalities

1. Social costs are sometimes ignored because decision makers do not have to pay for external costs or benefits.　　T　F

2. Drivers impose a negative externality on non-drivers.　　T　F

3. Smokers impose a positive externality on non-smokers.　　T　F

4. Markets underproduce products and services with negative externalities.　　T　F

11.2 Negative Externalities and Efficient Pollution

5. Economists believe the efficient amount of pollution is zero.　　T　F

6. Small reductions in pollution come at a higher opportunity cost than large reductions in pollution.　　T　F

7. The marginal external cost in the pulp market is the cost of preventing or cleaning up the damage from the pollution.　　T　F

8. Marginal social cost is the same as marginal private cost if there are no positive externalities.　　T　F

11.3 Policies to Internalize Negative Externalities

9. With carbon taxes the government sets the quantity of emissions; with cap-and-trade systems the government sets the price. T **F**

10. Smart carbon taxes lead individuals and businesses to voluntarily choose the quantity of output where marginal private benefit equals marginal private cost. T **F**

11. A carbon tax on fossil fuels raises their relative price and encourages alternatives. **T** F

11.4 Free Riders and Public Goods

12. Lighthouses are a public good. **T** F

13. It is not profitable for businesses to provide public goods. T **F**

11.5 Subsidies for the Public Good

14. A post-secondary education is an example of public provision. **T** F

15. A college education is an example of a subsidy. **T** F

MULTIPLE CHOICE

Circle the best answer. Solutions to these questions are available at the end of the book and on MyEconLab. You can also visit the MyEconLab Study Plan to access similar questions that will help you master the concepts covered in this chapter.

11.1 Market Failure with Externalities

1. **Which of the following is *not* a negative externality?**
   a) Jimbo blasts hip-hop music from his souped-up Honda as he cruises through his neighbourhood late at night.
   b) Jericho sings along to hip-hop music on the bus (and everyone on the bus thinks he is horrible).
   c) Jeremiah listens to hip-hop music in his room with his headphones on and his door closed.
   d) Jerry blasts hip-hop music in the common area while his roommate is studying for a test.

2. **All the following statements are true, *except*:**
   a) there is too much pollution in the world.
   b) there are too many cars on the road during rush hour.
   c) there are too many people smoking.
   d) there are too many people getting vaccinations.

11.2 Negative Externalities and Efficient Pollution

3. **The opportunity cost of reducing pollution includes the costs of**
   a) taking shorter showers.
   b) taking public transit rather than your car.
   c) shutting down factories.
   d) all of the above.

4. **If there is a negative externality and no positive externality, marginal private cost**
   a) *equals* marginal social cost, *and* marginal private benefit *equals* marginal social benefit.
   b) *is less than* marginal social cost, *and* marginal private benefit *is less than* marginal social benefit.
   c) *is less than* marginal social cost, *and* marginal private benefit *equals* marginal social benefit.
   d) *equals* marginal social cost, *and* marginal private benefit *is less than* marginal social benefit.

5. **If there is a positive externality and no negative externality, marginal private cost**
   a) *equals* marginal social cost, *and* marginal private benefit *equals* marginal social benefit.
   b) *is less than* marginal social cost, *and* marginal private benefit *is less than* marginal social benefit.
   c) *is less than* marginal social cost, *and* marginal private benefit *equals* marginal social benefit.
   d) *equals* marginal social cost, *and* marginal private benefit *is less than* marginal social benefit.

6. **If there is a positive externality and a negative externality, marginal private cost**
   a) *equals* marginal social cost, *and* marginal private benefit *equals* marginal social benefit.
   b) *is less than* marginal social cost, *and* marginal private benefit *is less than* marginal social benefit.
   c) *is less than* marginal social cost, *and* marginal private benefit *equals* marginal social benefit.
   d) *equals* marginal social cost, *and* marginal private benefit *is less than* marginal social benefit.

7. Smart cap-and-trade systems
   a) internalize the fraternity.
   b) internalize the externality.
   c) externalize the majority.
   d) externalize the externality.

8. Smart carbon taxes
   a) equal the marginal external cost.
   b) equal the damage of the negative externality.
   c) lead to prices and pollution levels that are best for society.
   d) all of the above.

9. Carbon taxes are inequitable if
   a) lower-income consumers are affected more than higher-income consumers.
   b) higher-income consumers are affected more than lower-income consumers.
   c) lower-income consumers receive a tax break.
   d) energy-sensitive businesses like trucking, taxis, air travel, or automobile production receive a tax break.

11.4 Free Riders and Public Goods

10. Free riding occurs when there are
    a) negative externalities.
    b) positive externalities.
    c) horses.
    d) unicorns.

11. Public goods are
    a) for the public.
    b) free.
    c) underproduced.
    d) all of the above.

12. Which of the following is *not* a public good?
    a) parks
    b) national defence
    c) clothes
    d) vaccinations

11.5 Subsidies for the Public Good

13. Smart subsidies for public goods equal the amount of the
    a) marginal social cost.
    b) marginal social benefit.
    c) marginal external cost.
    d) marginal external benefit.

14. Subsidies are
    a) the opposite of taxes.
    b) paid by the government.
    c) rewards for those creating positive externalities for others.
    d) all of the above.

15. All of the following are examples of public provision by the government, *except*
    a) Canadian education up to grade 12.
    b) Canadian post-secondary education.
    c) streetlights.
    d) public transit.

12

What Are You Worth?

Inputs, Incomes, and Inequality

LEARNING OBJECTIVES

After reading this chapter, you should be able to:

12.1 Explain four types of income and how they are determined in input markets.

12.2 Explain the importance of marginal revenue product for labour income and for smart business hiring decisions.

12.3 Explain how to calculate present value and how it informs smart capital investment choices.

12.4 Describe economic rent, and explain its importance for determining land and superstar income.

12.5 Explain the sources of poverty and describe trade-offs in policies to help the poor.

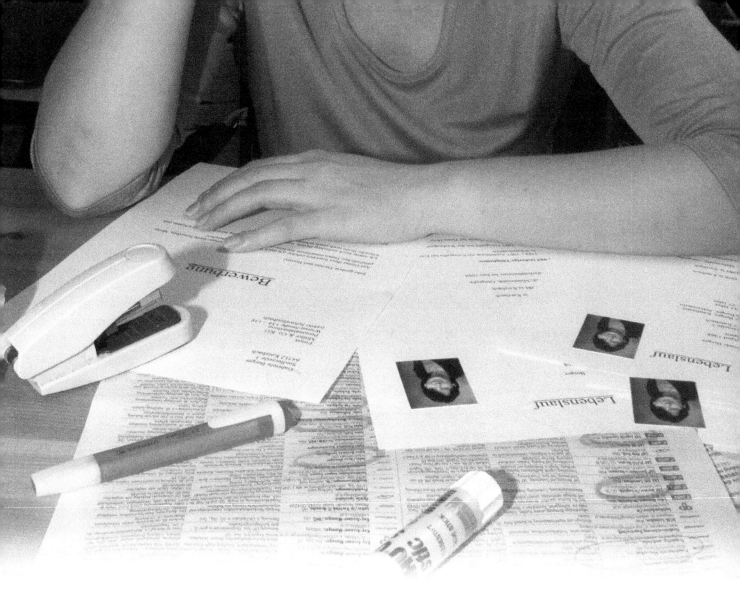

WHATEVER YOU WANT OUT OF LIFE —

riches, fame, love, adventure, a successful career, to make the world a better place — economics, and the Three Keys to Smart Choices, will help you get it. But no matter how smart your choices, *how much you earn* largely determines whether you reach your material goals for life.

Markets provide the products and services we want to buy, as well as jobs and investment opportunities for us to earn money. In *output markets,* consumers are the demanders and businesses are the suppliers. This chapter shifts focus to *input markets,* markets for labour, capital, and other inputs used to produce outputs. In input markets, businesses are the demanders, and consumers (or households) are the suppliers. What you are worth, in a market economy, is what the market is willing to pay for your inputs. Your income depends on your inputs and productivity, and in this chapter you will learn what you can do to improve both.

Output markets can fail due to economies of scale, monopoly, or externalities. Input markets can also fail in different ways, resulting in poverty and inequality. Input markets for labour and capital can work well to coordinate smart choices of consumers and businesses, ensuring businesses have the inputs they need to produce the products and services consumers want. Adam Smith's invisible hand of competition applies to input markets too. But even when businesses get the inputs they need, the resulting distributions of income and wealth may not be equitable. Government policies can help remedy inequality and poverty, but even smart policies to help the poor have opportunity costs that should be evaluated.

12.1 Switching Sides: Incomes Are Prices and Quantities in Input Markets

Explain four types of income and how they are determined in input markets.

We began our economics road trip in Chapter 1 with the map of the circular flow of economic life (reproduced in Figure 12.1), the simplest "big picture" of how an economist thinks about economic choices.

Finding Your Way Around the Circle

All the complexity of the Canadian economy is reduced to three sets of players — households, businesses, and governments. Households and businesses interact in two sets of markets — *input markets* (where businesses buy from households the inputs they need to produce products and services) and *output markets* (where businesses sell their products and services to households). Governments set the rules of the game and can choose to interact, or not, in almost any aspect of the economy. When markets work well, self-interest and the invisible hand of competition coordinate the smart choices of households and businesses in both sets of markets.

We have now come full circle (pun intended) back to this road map, but we are switching sides to focus on input markets, where households are the sellers and businesses are the buyers.

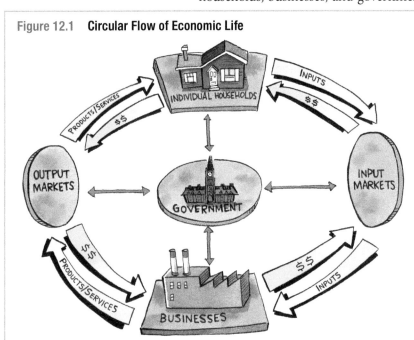

Figure 12.1   Circular Flow of Economic Life

Input Markets   Good maps or models like Figure 12.1 help you find your way by focusing on the most important information. Let's follow the circle, beginning at the top. Individuals in households sell or rent out their labour (ability to work), capital, land, and entrepreneurial abilities to businesses. In exchange, businesses pay households wages, interest, rent, and other money rewards. These exchanges, or trades, happen in input markets, where households are the sellers and businesses are the buyers.

Output Markets   Businesses (at the bottom) use those inputs to produce products and services to sell to households. In exchange, households use the money they have earned in input markets to pay businesses for these purchases. These exchanges, or trades, happen in output markets, where households are the buyers and businesses are the sellers.

At the end of the trip around the circle, households have the products and services they need to live, and businesses end up with the money. That sets the stage for the next trip around the circle, where businesses again buy inputs from individuals in households, produce outputs that households buy — and the flow goes on.

Inputs and Income

What does this circular flow have to do with the income you earn? Everything! Incomes are determined by prices and quantities in input markets. Figure 12.2 summarizes the four types of inputs that households supply in input markets, and the forms of income that households receive from businesses for using those inputs.

Figure 12.2   Inputs and Incomes

Input	Income
Labour	Wages
Capital ($)	Interest
Land (and other resources)	Rent
Entrepreneurship	Profits (normal and economic profits)

Labour   If you earn $12 per hour at Mr. Sub and work 25 hours per week, your income for the week is $300. To calculate income, you normally multiply the price you receive for your input times the quantity of the input that you sell. In the labour market, that price is the wage rate you receive, and the quantity is the number of hours you worked.

Capital   If you loan $5000 for a year to a business (your own or someone else's), at an interest rate of 8 percent (0.08) per year, your income is $400 per year from the input market for capital. The interest rate is the price of capital (capital here means money for investment purposes) and the quantity is the number of dollars you loan. If instead you put that money in a savings account and earn interest, the total amount of interest earned would likewise be income to you.

Land   If you own 10 hectares of land that you rent out to a farmer for $500 per hectare per month, your income is $5000 per month from the input market for land.

Income Is a Flow, Wealth Is a Stock

When we calculate income as price × quantity for whatever the input — labour, capital, land, or other resources — the resulting number is meaningful *only when there is a time dimension attached*. If someone tells you that her income is $50 000, what does that mean? It makes a big difference if it is $50 000 a year, or $50 000 a month, or $50 000 an hour! When a measurement — like income — makes sense only when there is a time dimension attached, economists call it a **flow**. A flow is measured as an *amount per unit of time*.

flow   amount per unit of time

On the other hand, your wealth — the total value of all the assets you own — is a **stock**. It is an *amount at a moment in time* — like a photo. When you read reports about Bill Gates being the richest person in the world (estimated wealth in 2014 of $76 billion), the rankings are based on wealth, which is measured as an amount at a moment in time. Your wealth is the total value of all the things you own.

stock   fixed amount at a moment in time

Here's how to think about the difference: *Income is what you earn; wealth is what you own.*

One Concept for Each Income   We will talk more about income and wealth — and who earns and owns what — in the final section of this chapter. Before that, we will explore the most important concept determining each type of input's income — marginal revenue product for labour, present value for capital, and economic rent for land and other resources.

Entrepreneurs' Income Is Different

Entrepreneur's income is the one type that does not fit the *price × quantity* formula. Individuals in households supply entrepreneurial talent or services to businesses (often their own). Those services, which involve the entrepreneur's time, are often accompanied by an investment of his or her own money too. The reward, or "payment," for this entrepreneurial input into production usually takes the form of *profits*.

Entrepreneurs are smart to offer their services only when they expect to make at least *normal profits*. Normal profits are what an entrepreneur could have earned in the best alternative use of his time and money.

But entrepreneurs are really after *economic profits,* profits over and above normal profits. What sets economic profits apart from all other types of income is that economic profits — the reward for innovation and risk-taking — are a *residual*. They are what is left over from revenues after all opportunity costs of production (including normal profits) have been paid for.

Refresh 12.1

MyEconLab

For answers to these Refresh
Questions, visit MyEconLab.

1. What are the two types of markets in the circular-flow road map? Identify the buyers and sellers in each market.

2. If you have $10 000 in a savings account, and no other assets, what is your income from capital if the interest rate is 8 percent per year? What is your wealth *at the end of the first year*?

3. When Wahid (Chapter 7) started his own web business using his savings and a small inheritance from his grandfather, he played multiple roles on the circular-flow road map. Identify those roles as he set up his business, and the roles he continues to play as the business begins producing web services. What are his types of income?

12.2 What Have You Done for Me Lately? Labour and Marginal Revenue Product

Explain the importance of
marginal revenue product for
labour income and for smart
business hiring decisions.

Income depends on prices and quantities. But what do prices and quantities depend on? The answer here is the same as it was in Chapter 4 . . . drum roll . . . prices (and quantities) come from the interaction of demand and supply. The only difference is that now we are looking at demand and supply in input markets instead of output markets. Businesses are now the demanders, and households are the suppliers. The resulting prices and quantities determine the income of that input.

Back to the Future of Wahid's Web Wonders Business

Labour markets are the most important input markets. The prices are wage rates, and the quantities tell us how many people are employed. There is a different labour market with its own wage rate and quantity of labour employed for each type of labour — markets for retail sales, construction, accountants, auto mechanics, chefs, and so on.

Let's look at the labour market for web designers, and go back to the Chapter 7 example of Wahid's Web Wonders. Wahid's business is booming, and he needs to hire additional web designers to increase his output of webpages. As long as he keeps his webpage prices competitive, there seems to be no limit to how much he can expand his output and sales. How many new designers should he hire? To answer that question, for Wahid or any business, we need to known more about supply and demand in labour markets.

Show Me the Money (Again): Supply of Labour

Recall the story in Chapter 3 about your boss calling you in a panic on Sunday night and wanting you to work as many hours as possible in the week ahead? As she increased the wage she was willing to pay you from $10 per hour to double time to triple time, the number of hours you were willing to work increased. In general, a rise in price (the wage rate) increases quantity supplied — the *law of supply*.

Paying Increasing Marginal Opportunity Costs
As you shift your time from alternative uses to work, *the marginal cost of your time increases*. You first give up the least valuable time, and continue giving up increasingly valuable time as the price you are offered rises. The market wage is determined when supply decisions of all households are combined with demand decisions of all businesses in a labour market.

To hire any input, including labour, a business must pay a price that matches the best opportunity cost of the input owner. Wahid is competing with other design businesses to hire workers. So he must pay at least what other businesses are paying web designers. Suppose the usual market wage for web designers is $50 per hour.

Wahid knows what additional workers will cost, but what will they *do* for him?

IT'S SIMPLE TO FIGURE OUT THE ADDITIONAL COSTS OF WEB DESIGNERS, BUT HOW DO I CALCULATE THE ADDITIONAL BENEFITS AND PROFITS THEY BRING TO MY BUSINESS?

Why Your Boss Wants You: Derived Demand for Labour

Businesses' demand for workers is not quite the same as consumers' demand for doughnuts. When you buy a tasty doughnut, you own it, you eat (consume) it, it's gone, and you are no longer hungry. When businesses buy labour, they don't own the labourer — that would be slavery. Businesses don't generally hire you because you taste good or look good (well, except for the modelling business). Businesses demand labour for the services the labourers provide. Workers help produce outputs that can be sold to earn revenues and (hopefully) profits for the business. The demand for labour is a **derived demand**, because businesses are not interested in the labour for its own sake (like a doughnut), but for the output and profits the business owner can derive from hiring labour.

derived demand demand for output and profits businesses can derive from hiring labour

Wahid is a demander, or buyer, in the labour market because he wants to employ web designers to produce webpages to sell to customers to earn revenues and profits. How does Wahid make a smart choice about the quantity of web designers to hire?

Smart Business Choices in Hiring Labour

The first two keys to smart choices are also key to Wahid's decision about hiring web designers. Although I am sure you know the two keys by heart by now, here they are again:

Key 1: Choose only when additional benefits are greater than additional *opportunity costs.*

Key 2: Count only *additional* benefits and *additional* costs.

Additional Costs and Additional Benefits   The cost, or supply-of-labour, side of the cost-benefit comparison is easy. What is the additional opportunity cost of a web designer to Wahid? It is the $50 per hour he must pay to attract a designer away from the designer's best alternative employment. The marginal cost of each additional designer is $50 per hour.

The *additional benefits* are derived from the additional output of webpages the designer can produce, and the revenues and profits from selling those additional webpages.

Figure 12.3 contains the information Wahid needs to decide how many web designers to hire. Column 1 lists the quantity of designers Wahid is considering hiring, from zero to five. In column 2, **marginal product** measures the additional *productivity* of this designer (labourer) — how much additional product (measured in webpages per hour) his or her work adds to output.

marginal product   additional output from hiring one more unit of labour

Diminishing Marginal Productivity   While the first designer has a marginal product of six webpages per hour, subsequent designers each have lower marginal products. Economists call this **diminishing marginal productivity**, and it occurs in most businesses that have some fixed inputs. As you add more of a variable input to fixed inputs, the marginal product of the variable input eventually diminishes.

diminishing marginal productivity   as you add more of a variable input to fixed inputs, the marginal product of the variable input eventually diminishes

Wahid has limited office space, only one printer, and a part-time technical support person. Plus, there is only one Wahid to supervise all the designers. As the office starts to get more crowded, there are problems sharing the printer, designers have to wait longer for technical support for computer problems, and each receives less supervision. Each additional designer stresses the sharing of these fixed inputs a bit more, causing the decreasing marginal productivity.

Figure 12.3   Labour Hiring Decision for Wahid's Web Wonders Business

Column			
1	2	3	4
Quantity of Labour (designers)	Marginal Product (MP) (additional webpages per hour)	Price (P_{output}) (per webpage)	Marginal Revenue Product ($MRP = MP \times P_{output}$) (additional revenue per designer hour)
0			
	6	$15	$90 120
1			
	5	$15	$75 100
2			
	4	$15	$60 80
3			
	3	$15	$45 60
4			
	2	$15	$30 40
5			

Column 3 lists the market price (always $15) that Wahid can sell each additional webpage for in the output market for web design services. Wahid's output market is close to perfect competition (Chapter 8), so he has little pricing power. That's the bad news. The good news about being a small competitor is that Wahid can increase his output and sales without having to lower his $15 price per webpage. For Wahid, price equals marginal revenue.

Marginal Revenue Product   Column 4 contains the most important concept for Wahid's smart hiring choice. **Marginal revenue product** is calculated by multiplying marginal product (column 2) times price of output (column 3). The first designer produces six additional webpages per hour, each of which can be sold for $15. Hiring that first designer adds $90 of revenue per hour. Just like marginal products, *marginal revenue products* diminish as Wahid's business adds more designers.

marginal revenue product
additional revenue from selling output produced by an additional labourer

Recipe for Profits for Hiring Inputs   With the information about additional costs of hiring a web designer ($50 per hour), and additional benefits in the form of marginal revenue products, what is Wahid's smart choice? The simple recipe for maximum profits is:

Hire additional inputs when
marginal revenue product is greater than marginal cost.

Figure 12.4 shows the numbers from Figure 12.3 in a graph. In Figure 12.4a, the marginal revenue product per hour for each designer is represented by a green (for revenue) bar, and the wage rate for each additional hour of designer labour is the red (for cost) line at $50 per hour.

NOTE
The simple recipe for hiring inputs is "Hire additional inputs when marginal revenue product is greater than marginal cost."

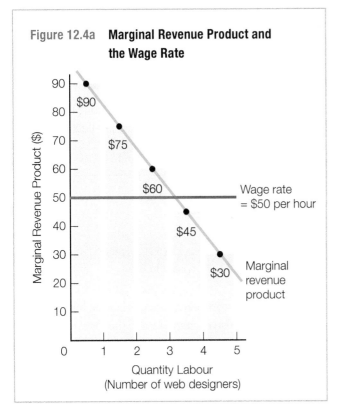

Figure 12.4a   Marginal Revenue Product and the Wage Rate

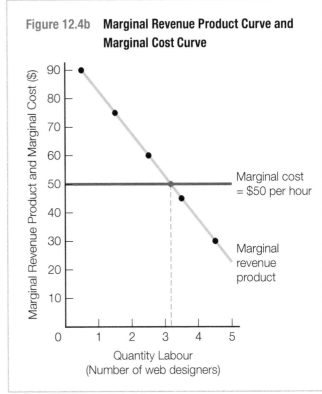

Figure 12.4b   Marginal Revenue Product Curve and Marginal Cost Curve

Use Figure 12.4a to evaluate Wahid's choices, designer by designer. If he hires the first web designer, Wahid's revenues go up by $90 per hour, while his costs go up by only $50 per hour. This is clearly a smart choice that adds to profits, since additional revenues are greater than additional costs. Hiring the second and third web designers each adds more to revenues than to costs. But if Wahid hires a fourth or fifth designer, costs go up by more than revenues.

Figure 12.4b presents the same information about marginal revenue product and the wage, but graphed as a marginal revenue product curve and a marginal cost curve. Like all marginal values, marginal revenue product is plotted halfway between quantities of labour, because it measures the additional revenue per hour moving between designers. The downward slope of the green marginal revenue product curve is due to diminishing marginal productivity. Because each additional designer costs the same $50 per hour, the marginal cost curve is the horizontal red line at $50 per hour.

Up to three designers, marginal revenue product is greater than marginal cost, adding to total profits. Beyond three designers, marginal cost is greater than marginal revenue product, reducing total profits. Not smart. Wahid should hire three designers.

Marginal Productivity and Income

Your boss wants you (your labour) for your productivity, and there is a close connection between how much you are paid in wages and what you contribute to the productivity, revenues, and profits of your employer — your marginal revenue productivity.

Refresh 12.2

MyEconLab

For answers to these Refresh Questions, visit MyEconLab.

1. In your own words, define marginal revenue product.

2. In the example from Chapter 3, your boss is willing to pay you triple-time wages for working extra time. Explain the calculation she must have made in offering you that much money, assuming she was making a smart decision.

3. In the example in Figure 12.3, what would happen to Wahid's hiring decision if the price for which he could sell webpages rose from $15 per page to $20 per page? Declined from $15 to $10? Explain your answers.

12.3 All Present and Accounted For: Interest on Capital and Present Value

Explain how to calculate present value and how it informs smart capital investment choices.

Most income depends on the wage or salary you earn for your labour, but I hope you will accumulate some savings to invest to also earn income in the form of interest. If you invest your "capital" of $5000 in a savings account that pays 4 percent interest per year, the calculation of your interest income uses the simple *price* × *quantity* formula, where the price of capital is the interest rate and the quantity is the number of dollars. At the end of the year, you earn $0.04 \times \$5000 = \$200$ in interest income.

Comparing the Present and Future

Most investment calculations are not so simple because the payoffs from today's investments extend far into the future. When businesses build new factories that last decades, or invest in expensive machine tools that improve productivity and output for years to come, how do they decide whether those are smart investment choices? If someone offers to sell you a small apartment building with six tenants who pay a total of $9000 in rent per month, how much should you pay today for that building? These long-lived investments produce a stream of revenues over many years, yet the business or investor is faced with a single purchase price in the present. How do we apply Key 1 for smart choices, "Choose only when additional benefits are greater than additional opportunity costs," when the benefits are spread out over the future and the cost is in the present? How do you simplify that future stream of revenues to a single number today you can compare with the cost today to make a smart choice?

ADDITIONAL BENEFITS VS. OPPORTUNITY COSTS

The key concept for that simplification is called **present value**. Let's work through some examples to help you to make sense of it.

The **present value** of a future amount of money is the amount that, if invested today, will grow as large as the future amount, taking account of earned interest.

present value   amount that, if invested today, will grow as large as the future amount, taking account of earned interest

From Present to Future

Even if you don't yet understand the definition of present value, you can see that interest rates play an important role. One of the reasons present value is confusing is that it reverses the way we usually think about time, money, and interest rates. Present value uses interest rates to convert a future value of money to a value in the present — today. Usually, we think about an amount of money we have in the present — today — and how much it will worth in the future after earning interest. Let's start there, with the more usual move from present to future.

Suppose you have $1000 today, and your bank is offering a special interest rate of 12% on savings accounts. How much will your $1000 be worth in the future, after one year? You calculate the interest you will earn, which is $0.12 \times \$1000 = \$120$. Add that interest to your original $1000 and you will have $1120 at the end of the year. That number, $1120, is the answer to the question, "What is the future value of $1000 in the present?" To calculate the future value of money today, we take account of earned interest.

From Future to Present: Key 3 and Implicit Costs to the Rescue

Now, let's answer the reverse question — "What is the present value of that future $1120?" You already know the answer from the example above! If the interest rate is 12%, the present value is $1000. The definition says:

The present value of a future amount of money ($1120) is the amount ($1000) that, if invested today, will grow as large as the future amount, taking account of earned interest ($120).

But what if you want to do a future-to-present calculation, and don't know the present-to-future numbers? There is a formula to calculate the present value of any future amount of money.

Suppose Wahid is thinking about buying a colour laser printer for producing sharper-looking printed reports for customers. The printer costs $1000 and wears out entirely after one year. During that time, Wahid estimates that, because of the beautiful-looking reports, customers will pay him an additional $1100 in revenues. This sounds like a good investment according to Key 1, since $1100 in additional revenues is greater than $1000 in additional costs.

But that comparison of revenues and costs does not take into account the role of time and interest. If Wahid's bank is offering the same special 12 percent interest rate on savings accounts, then the printer investment decision does not look so good. If Wahid invested the $1000 today in the savings account instead of the printer, at the end of the year he would have $1120 guaranteed ($0.12 \times \$1000 = \$120$ in interest, added to the $1000) instead of his expected $1100 in additional revenues the printer would bring in.

IMPLICIT
COSTS &
EXTERNALITIES

Implicit Costs   Key 3 comes back here, "Be sure to count *all* additional benefits and additional costs, including implicit costs and externalities," especially Chapter 7's *implicit costs of forgone interest*. The $1100 value for future income does not take into account implicit costs — the interest Wahid could have earned if he had saved the $1000 cost of the printer in the present and then collected the interest after a year.

Present value takes that interest into account, and allows us to reduce, or discount, Wahid's stream of future income into a number he can compare with the $1000 cost to see if buying the new printer is a smart choice.

Even though I haven't finished explaining present value, I am going to give you the formula for making the calculation that Wahid — and any investor — will use:

$$\text{Present Value} = \frac{\text{Amount of Money Available in } n \text{ Years}}{(1 + \text{Interest Rate})^n}$$

In the formula, n stands for the number of years the investment pays revenues. If a machine is expected to last 10 years, $n = 10$. This formula is scary looking but, for our simple example where $n = 1$, it is not so scary.

For Wahid's example, where $n = 1$ year and an interest rate of 12 percent (0.12), the formula becomes

$$\text{Present Value} = \frac{\$1100}{(1 + 0.12)} = \frac{\$1100}{1.12}$$

$$\text{Present Value} = \$982.14$$

This is the answer to the question, "What is the present value of $1100 in the future?" Going back to the definition of present value, $982.14 is the amount of money that, if invested today, will grow to be as large as $1100, taking account of earned interest.

So how does this tell us whether Wahid is making a smart investment choice? The modification of Keys 1, 2, and 3 for investment decisions comes down to this:

3 KEYS
TO SMART
CHOICES

1 CHOOSE ONLY WHEN ADDITIONAL BENEFITS ARE GREATER THAN ADDITIONAL OPPORTUNITY COSTS.

2 COUNT ONLY ADDITIONAL BENEFITS AND ADDITIONAL OPPORTUNITY COSTS.

3 BE SURE TO COUNT ALL ADDITIONAL BENEFITS AND COSTS, INCLUDING IMPLICIT COSTS AND EXTERNALITIES.

Invest when the present value of the stream of future earnings
is greater than the price of the investment.

For Wahid, the present value of $982.14 is *less than* the price of the investment ($1000), so it is not a smart choice. Wahid would make more money if he put his $1000 in the bank ($120 instead of $100).

What happens to the choice when the interest rate changes? If the interest rate falls to 5 percent (0.05), while everything else about the investment stays the same, the present value calculation becomes

$$\text{Present Value} = \frac{\$1100}{(1 + 0.05)} = \frac{\$1100}{1.05}$$

$$\text{Present Value} = \$1047.62$$

Now the present value of $1047.62 is *greater than* the price of the investment ($1000), so it becomes a smart choice. You can check the wisdom of this choice by calculating what Wahid would earn in the bank if he invested his $1000 for one year at 5 percent interest. This is the simpler present-to-future question: What is the future value of $1000 in the present? At the end of the year he would have $1050 from the bank, which is *less than* the $1100 he would have from investing in the laser colour printer. (To keep things simple, I am assuming Wahid believes there is a 100 percent probability he will get the $1100, so there is no need to add the complication of risk compensation.)

Intuition Behind Present Value Don't be concerned about other complications of the formula for investments with longer payoffs (when n is greater than 1), or uneven amounts of money available in different years. That's what accountants (and calculators and accounting software) are for — you don't need to master those calculation details. But it is important to understand the *idea* of present value, which underlies all those calculations. Understanding present value calculations is essential for any business owner or investor. The intuition behind present value is that $1 in the future is not worth as much as $1 today because if you had the dollar invested today you could be earning interest on it. That's why, to calculate the *value today* of a stream of future revenues, you can't simply add up those future revenues. They are not worth as much as the same sum today because they don't take into account the interest that you could have earned if you had invested that sum today.

NOTE
Revenues available in the future are not worth as much as revenues today, because today's revenues earn interest.

Discounting Accountants (and economists) would say you have to **discount** the future revenues to adjust for forgone interest. In the simple savings example, your revenues of $1120 at the end of the year in the bank are discounted to be worth only $1000 in the present, taking into account forgone interest. Wahid's revenues of $1100 next year from the printer are discounted to be worth only $982.14 in the present, taking into account forgone interest.

discount reduction of future revenues for forgone interest

The concept of present value gives you, and any investor, a method to simplify the future stream of revenues from an investment to a single number today. Present value converts a *flow* of future revenues into a *stock* concept, into a value at a moment in time — today — that you can compare with cost today to make a smart choice. And, to repeat, the recipe for a smart investment choice is:

Invest when the present value of the stream of future earnings
is greater than the price of the investment.

Refresh 12.3

1. In your own words, explain present value. Using the formula, compute the present value of $2000 earned one year from now if the interest rate is 5 percent per year.

2. What is the comparison problem that the concept of present value helps solve?

3. Suppose someone offers you a bond that will pay you $2000 at the end of a year. If the interest rate is 7 percent (0.07), what is the most you would be willing to pay for the bond today? Why?

MyEconLab

For answers to these Refresh Questions, visit MyEconLab.

12.4 Why Sidney Crosby Plays by Different Rules: Land, Economic Rent, and Superstars

Describe economic rent, and explain its importance for determining land and superstar income.

economic rent income paid to any input in relatively inelastic supply

What does the rent you pay your landlord have in common with Sidney Crosby's (the hockey super star) income? More than you think.

Economic Rent

Economists have a concept called **economic rent**, which is a form of income that is paid to any input in relatively inelastic supply. Elasticity is about responsiveness, and inelastic supply means, as I'm sure you remember, that the quantity supplied is *un*responsive to a rise in price. As the price rises, the quantity supplied hardly increases at all.

Land is a classic example of an input in inelastic supply. Consider a block of land at the corner of Burrard and Alberni streets in downtown Vancouver. No matter how high rents go for that piece of land, it won't cause more land to grow at the corner of Burrard and Alberni. The retail shops on this block pay very high rents to the landowners, and the shops also charge very high prices for the products and services they sell to the consumers who shop in this neighbourhood.

How do we explain these high prices — both the high rents paid to landlords and the high prices of products and services sold in the shops? The usual answer for an economist is that . . . drum roll . . . prices (and quantities) come from the interaction of demand and supply. But it turns out that for inputs like land in inelastic supply, the answer is different — prices are effectively determined by demand only.

For most outputs and inputs, the law of supply applies. A rise in price increases quantity supplied. And if the price rises high enough to generate economic profits, more businesses enter the industry (an increase in supply), and the price falls until businesses just earn normal profits. The invisible hand of the market adjusts quantities so that once again demand and supply balance, and the market provides the products and services we value most along with the inputs necessary to produce those outputs.

With land and other inputs in inelastic supply, there is no supply response. If demand increases, the price of the input rises but there is no increase in quantity supplied. Even with economic profits, there can be no increase in supply. If demand for the input decreases, the price of the input falls but there is no decrease in quantity supplied. This lack of responsiveness does strange things to the relationship between high rents and high prices for products and services sold in the high-rent shops.

Mike Stobe/Contributor/NHLI via Getty Images

▲ Superstars and expensive condominiums located on prime real estate are good examples of inelastic supply. What other examples of inelastic supply do you see every day?

High Input Prices Cause High Output Prices   For most products and services, high input prices cause high output prices. If businesses have to pay higher prices for inputs like energy or labour or raw materials, they usually pass on those higher costs to consumers in the form of higher output prices. If I asked you to explain the high prices of products and services in the shops in downtown Vancouver, you, and most people, would probably say, "The high prices for products and services are caused by the high rents the shopkeepers have to pay to landlords." But you would be dead wrong.

High Output Prices Cause High Input Prices   When an input like land is in inelastic supply, it goes to the highest bidder (demander). Why would shopkeepers be willing to pay such high rents, when they know cheaper rents are available elsewhere in the city? They know that in real estate, the three most important factors are location, location, and location. A good location generates high customer traffic, and this location brings in many high-income, free-spending customers. Smart shopkeepers know they can charge these customers high prices for products and services, so the shopkeepers bid up the rents.

NOTE
For most products and services, high input prices cause high output prices. For inputs in inelastic supply, high output prices cause high input prices — high economic rents.

For inputs like land in inelastic supply, high output prices cause high input prices (economic rents). The shopkeepers have to earn normal profits, or they wouldn't continue at that location. But it is the landlords, the owners of the input in inelastic supply, who really do well. The price, or rent, paid for the land is not proportional to the productivity of land as an input, as is the case for labour. Rents are demand driven, determined by "what the market will bear." Owners of inelastically supplied inputs are like mini-monopolists with barriers to entry. Their economic rents, like economic profits, stay high because no new competitors can enter. You can't build two buildings on one piece of land.

Is Sidney Crosby a Landlord?

What does this have to do with Sidney Crosby, and the income he and other superstars earn? Sidney Crosby, Ronaldo, Angelina Jolie, Madonna, and landlords actually have much in common — they all own inputs that are in relatively inelastic supply.

When salaries go up for professional athletes and entertainers, there is a large, elastic response in the quantity supplied of people with average talent. But superstars have rare talent that is not easily reproduced. Fans will pay plenty to see superstars, but very little for average talent. That means much of superstars' income takes the form of economic rent, rather than wages paid for their marginal productivity. Superstars, like landlords, are like mini-monopolists with barriers to entry. Their talents go to the highest bidders, and their incomes are largely demand-determined, just like the rent on land.

Are Superstar Salaries to Blame for High Ticket Prices?

In 2012, Sidney Crosby signed a 12-year, US$104.4-million contract with the Pittsburgh Penguins, earning an average of $8.7 million per year. He also has tens of millions of dollars in product endorsement income from Gatorade, Nike, and other companies. Fans love to complain about astronomical superstar incomes. Economics Out There describes fan anger during a National Hockey League lockout of players that cancelled a complete season. Fans blamed the players for being too greedy, and continue to believe that high player salaries are to blame for the high ticket prices that make NHL games unaffordable for your average fan.

Economics *Out There*

Fans Stick It to NHL Players

The 2004–2005 hockey season lives in infamy for its lockout of players. During the dispute, fans were vocal with their opinions. When player rep Bob Goodenow went on live television to field fans' questions, he heard variations on one theme: The players are paid too much, causing ticket prices to be too high, and should accept a salary cap. Polls showed that fans blamed the lockout on the players. Goodenow explained that ticket prices are dictated not by the players' salaries, but by the team owners' assessment of what fans are willing to pay — what the market will bear. Goodenow was correct to point out that in the World Cup of Hockey, owners priced top tickets in Toronto at $650 even though the players were paid only expenses and a contribution to their pension fund. According to *The Globe and Mail* writer David Shoalts, Goodenow is right, and fans have to realize that "owners charge $200 a ticket and $12 a beer in some cities because you will pay it," not because of player salaries.

Source: David Shoalts, "Fans Stick It to NHL Players," *The Globe and Mail*, September 23, 2004.

But fans are making the same mistake you made if you explained high retail prices in trendy Vancouver shops as being caused by the high rents the shopkeepers have to pay landlords.

Why are NHL owners willing to bid against each other to sign Sidney Crosby and other superstars to high-priced contracts? The owners know that fans will pay a lot of money to see real talent on the ice, and those fans who can't afford to go to the games in person will flock to screens to watch. That means owners can sell the broadcast rights to the games for even more money. Fan willingness to pay so much to watch superstar hockey players causes high ticket prices; tickets are priced to "what the market will bear." In turn, high ticket prices (and broadcast revenues) are the reason why owners bid against each other and drive up superstar salaries. *The Globe and Mail* sportswriter in Economics Out There knows his economics!

The salary cap implemented after the 2005 lockout was designed not to prevent players from being too greedy but to limit the bids owners could make for players, to ensure some of the economic rents earned by scarce superstars would end up with the owners instead of the players. Since incomes of inputs in inelastic supply are entirely demand determined, the salary cap limited the demand by owners and thereby limited (believe it or not) superstar salaries, leaving more of the ticket and broadcast revenues for the owners.

Economic rent is an important concept for understanding not only incomes from land and real estate, but also incomes of superstars and the economics of industries like professional sports, music, and entertainment.

Refresh 12.4

MyEconLab

For answers to these Refresh Questions, visit MyEconLab.

1. Define economic rent.

2. For most products and services, what is the relationship between input prices and output prices? For inputs in inelastic supply, what is the relationship between input prices and output prices?

3. Music groups usually go on tour to promote a new album. Given the availability of digital album downloads, what is the difference in the elasticity of supply of albums versus the elasticity of supply of concert performances? Where are (talented) musicians more likely to earn economic rents?

What *Should* You Be Worth?
Inequality and Poverty

In all your hopes and dreams about what you want out of life, do you ever dream of being poor? So why do 3.2 million Canadians (almost 1 in 10 individuals) live in poverty in the midst of a market economy that supposedly does such a good job of efficiently providing the products and services we desire?

Connected through the circular flow, we all depend on markets to provide outputs supporting our standard of living, and to provide jobs and investment opportunities to earn money to buy those outputs. The income you earn depends on the quantities of inputs you own — labour, capital, land, and entrepreneurship — and the prices you can sell them for in input markets. Poverty results from those same quantities and prices — but from *not* owning enough of a labour skill or asset that the market values, or from *not* getting a high enough price for what you do own.

In this last section, we will look at data on who is rich, who is poor, and how equally or unequally incomes and wealth are distributed among the population. We will briefly explain why incomes vary, what might be done to help the poor, and the trade-offs in so doing.

The interconnectedness of the circular flow is important in thinking about these questions. What you *are* worth depends on the prices the market places on what you own, which are derived from the prices the market places on the outputs that can be produced using your inputs. What you, or any human being, *should be* worth, and whether governments *should* help those who are poor, are normative questions that economics does not answer but that you must answer as a citizen evaluating policy choices or charitable commitments.

What Do We Earn and Own?
Measuring (In)Equality of Income and Wealth

Statistics Canada (www.statcan.gc.ca) collects data on all aspects of the Canadian economy, including income and wealth. The most recent comprehensive data were collected for 2010. These numbers, which are organized by family, not individuals, give an idea of how your family's income and wealth compare to that of other Canadian families.

Income   Figure 12.5 displays data for average market income in 2010. Market income consists of income (*before* taxes and government transfer payments) from selling on markets the inputs we described — wages from labour, investment income from capital and other resources, and entrepreneurial income from self-employment. For families as a whole, the majority of income comes from labour earnings. Of every $100 earned, $78 comes from employment and $10.10 comes from investment income. The remainder comes from self-employment and other income sources.

Statistics Canada arranges all families in order, from lowest to highest earning, and then divides the population into five equal groups called quintiles. The lowest quintile is the 20 percent of all families earning the lowest incomes. The highest quintile is the 20 percent of all families earning the highest incomes.

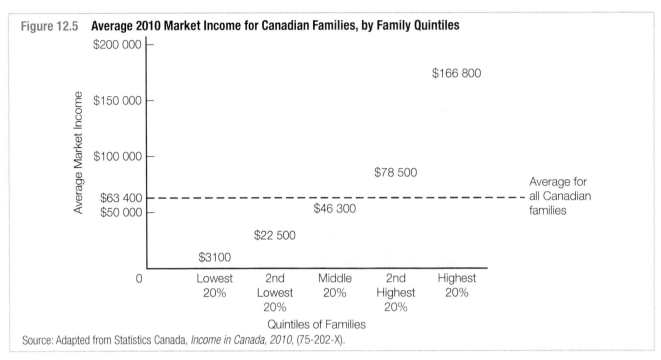

Figure 12.5   Average 2010 Market Income for Canadian Families, by Family Quintiles

Source: Adapted from Statistics Canada, *Income in Canada, 2010*, (75-202-X).

The average market income for all Canadian families in 2010 was $63 400. But that average comes from combining very different incomes. As you can see, the average market income was only $3100 for the poorest 20 percent of families, $46 300 for the middle 20 percent, and $166 800 for the richest 20 percent of families.

One way statisticians measure inequality is by calculating what *percentage of total income earned in Canada* is earned by each quintile. When you add the percentages for all five quintiles, it sums to 100 percent. If income were distributed perfectly equally, each 20 percent of families would earn 20 percent of total income. Figure 12.6 shows what those calculations look like for 2010.

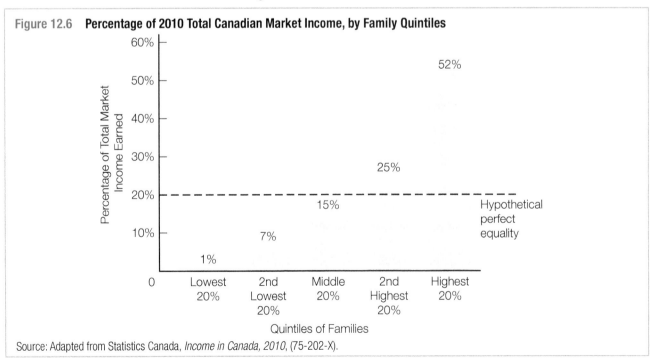

Figure 12.6   Percentage of 2010 Total Canadian Market Income, by Family Quintiles

Source: Adapted from Statistics Canada, *Income in Canada, 2010*, (75-202-X).

The poorest 20 percent of families earned 1 percent of total income in Canada, the middle 20 percent earned 15 percent of total income, and the richest 20 percent earned 52 percent of total income.

Wealth   Income is what you *earn,* while wealth is what you *own.* Wealth is the net value of all your assets, minus any liabilities of what you owe (student loans, that outstanding credit card balance, other debts).

After ranking families in order from lowest to highest wealth, Statistics Canada divides Canadian families into deciles — 10 groups with equal numbers of families in each. The statisticians use deciles instead of quintiles because the distribution of wealth is even more unequal than the distribution of income, and quintiles would hide large differences between families *within* each quintile, especially among wealthier Canadians. Figure 12.7 measures the percentage of total wealth in Canada owned by each decile of Canadian families in 2006. Because the bottom 40 percent of Canadian families owned almost none of the total wealth, they are lumped together to keep the graph simpler.

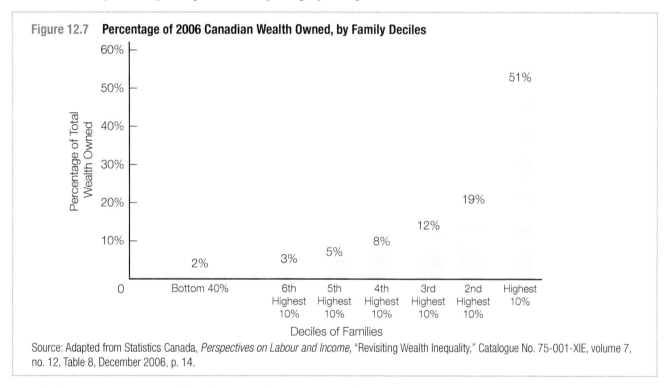

Figure 12.7   Percentage of 2006 Canadian Wealth Owned, by Family Deciles

Source: Adapted from Statistics Canada, *Perspectives on Labour and Income,* "Revisiting Wealth Inequality," Catalogue No. 75-001-XIE, volume 7, no. 12, Table 8, December 2006, p. 14.

The bottom 40 percent of families owned 2 percent of the total wealth. The top 10 percent of families owned 51 percent of all wealth in Canada. The top decile masks even more inequality, as within that group, the top 1 percent of families owned about 24 percent of all wealth in Canada.

Other Wealth Issues   Besides these dramatic differences in quantities of wealth, there are also differences in the kinds of assets owned. Wealth owned by the bottom half of families consists largely of the value of their automobiles, and some savings. For the wealthy, assets consist largely of equities, bonds, real estate, life insurance, and pension plans.

There is also a connection between wealth and income. The capital and land assets you own as wealth also produce a flow of income in the form of interest, dividend, and rent payments. For families in the higher range of the income distribution of Figures 12.5 and 12.6, more of their income consists of investment income — making money from their money, thus increasing their wealth. For families in the lower ranges, most of their income consists of labour income.

Why Are You (Not) Rich?

Besides wealth, what accounts for inequalities in income — what factors are connected with being poor and being rich? Let's start by defining what it means to be poor in terms of income.

Poverty   The income and wealth data show dramatic differences between families but do not clearly identify who is poor. There are many different definitions of poverty, and poverty is a relative concept. Families considered poor in Canada would be considered extremely wealthy in many African or Asian countries, where millions survive on less than $1000 per year. Statistics Canada defines low-income families as those who spend at least one-fifth *more* of their income than the average family on the basic necessities of food, shelter, and clothing. For a family of three in Toronto, that makes the "poverty line" $29 699.

In 2011, 3 million people in Canada lived below the poverty line, about 9 percent of the population. 8.2 percent of all children lived below the poverty line. Of those low-income individuals, 56 percent lived in a family whose major income earner was female.

There are many possible explanations for poverty that go beyond the scope of this book — discrimination, cultural factors, immigration adjustments, health and disability difficulties, to list just a few. We will focus only on the key *economic* factor that helps explain both lower and higher incomes — human capital.

Human Capital   Most Canadians' incomes come from employment, and the price you receive in the labour market depends on your productivity. Your productivity, your value to your boss, and your income all increase with your experience, your training, and your education. Economists use the term **human capital** to capture the increased earning potential individuals acquire through work experience, on-the-job training, and education.

Figure 12.8 shows the impact on lifetime income — compared to a high school graduate — of the education component of human capital.

human capital   increased earning potential from work experience, on-the-job training, education

Figure 12.8   Lifetime Earnings Premiums Relative to High School Education

Education	Lifetime Earnings Difference Relative to High School Graduate
Less Than High School	– $214 900
High School	———
Trades or Apprentices	$103 720
College	$221 360
University below Bachelor Degree	$394 000
University Bachelor Degree	$745 800
Post-Bachelor Study	$1 165 280

Data from Premium Relative to a High School Graduate over 40 Years, by Province, Joseph Berger and Andrew Parkin in *The Price of Knowledge* 4th edition 2009 http://qspace.library.queensu.ca/bitstream/1974/5780/1/POKVol4_EN.pdf

NOTE
Improving human capital through education and training treats the underlying cause of poverty, lack of inputs the market values.

For 2005, the average wealth (versus income) of a Canadian without a university education was $214 700. The average wealth of university graduates was $364 800.

Of the choices under your control, your choice to pursue an education is a smart one when it comes to increasing your income, wealth, and ability to reach your material goals in life.

What Can Be Done to Help the Poor?

What can be done to address inequality and poverty? Let's look at this *positive* question before confronting the *normative* question of whether governments *should* use tax revenues to help the poor and change the market distribution of income. If, as a society, we want to reduce inequality and poverty, two of the most powerful policy options are 1) education and training, and 2) a progressive system of taxes and transfers. Let's look at each.

Education and Training   Poverty means not having enough income. But lack of income is only a symptom of the underlying problem — a lack of inputs that the market values. Enhancing a person's human capital addresses this underlying problem. Government support for programs that increase human capital, whether through apprenticeships, training, or education, increase a person's ability to earn income and rise above poverty lines.

In addition, as shown in Chapter 10, education and training have positive externalities, with benefits to employers, governments, and citizens who are not directly involved in the programs that improve human capital. Education and training are win–win policies for the poor and for society as a whole. Economics Out There on page 157 of Chapter 6 suggests that early childhood education is so valuable that it actually eliminates the trade-off between efficiency and equity.

Progressive Taxes and Transfers   Governments can also directly reduce poverty and inequality by using the tax system to implement Robin Hood's motto — take from the rich and give to the poor.

In principle, a tax system may be progressive, regressive, or proportional. Both the federal and provincial tax systems use **progressive taxes**, meaning that as your income increases, you pay a higher percentage in tax. With **regressive taxes**, as your income increases you pay a lower percentage in tax. **Proportional taxes** — often called flat-rate taxes — charge the same percentage regardless of your level of income.

> **progressive taxes**   tax rate increases as income increases
>
> **regressive taxes**   tax rate decreases as income increases
>
> **proportional (flat-rate) taxes**   tax rate the same regardless of income

Both the federal and provincial governments have progressive tax systems that take more from the rich than from the poor. While tax rates vary from province to province, the combined federal and provincial income tax rates look something like this. The poorest Canadians pay no income tax at all. The tax rate on *additional* dollars earned (the **marginal tax rate**; see the word *additional*?) is roughly 25 percent up to $40 000, 35 percent up to $80 000, and 45 percent over $130 000. That means, for example, for every dollar you earn between $40 000 and $80 000, the government takes 35 cents and you keep 65 cents.

> **marginal tax rate**   rate on additional dollar of income

The progressive income tax is combined with a system of **transfer payments** that redistribute the tax revenues to those toward the bottom of the income distribution. Transfers are like negative income taxes. The main types of transfers occur through welfare programs (Canada Child Tax Benefit, Canada Assistance Plan), social security programs for seniors (Old Age Security), and Employment Insurance (for the unemployed).

> **transfer payments**   payments by government to households

As a direct result of the progressive tax and transfer systems, the distribution of income *after transfers and taxes* is more equal than the market distribution of Figures 12.5 and 12.6. Figures 12.9 and 12.10 show the income distribution data for 2010 *after transfers and taxes*.

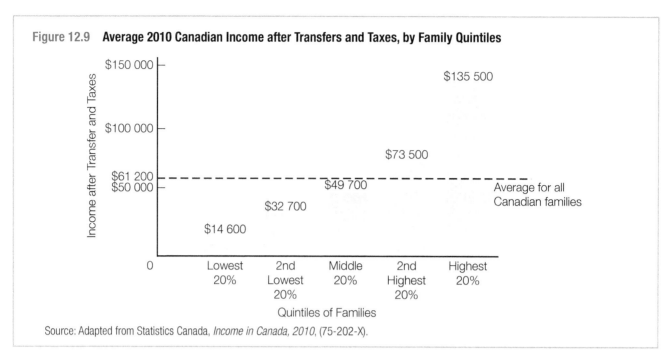

Figure 12.9   Average 2010 Canadian Income after Transfers and Taxes, by Family Quintiles

Source: Adapted from Statistics Canada, *Income in Canada, 2010*, (75-202-X).

In Figure 12.9, the average income of the lowest 20 percent of families rises from $3100 (in Figure 12.5) to $14 600 after taxes and transfers are applied. The second-lowest 20 percent of families' average incomes rise from $22 500 to $32 700. And the average income of the highest 20 percent of families *falls* from $166 800 to $135 500 after taxes and transfers. The result is that income shares, compared to Figure 12.6, move slightly closer toward the hypothetical equality where each quintile of families earns 20 percent of the total income in Canada. In Figure 12.10, after taxes and transfers, the share of total income for the lowest quintile of families rises from 1 to 5 percent, the share for the second-lowest quintile of families rises from 7 to 11 percent, and the share for the highest quintile of families *falls* from 52 to 44 percent.

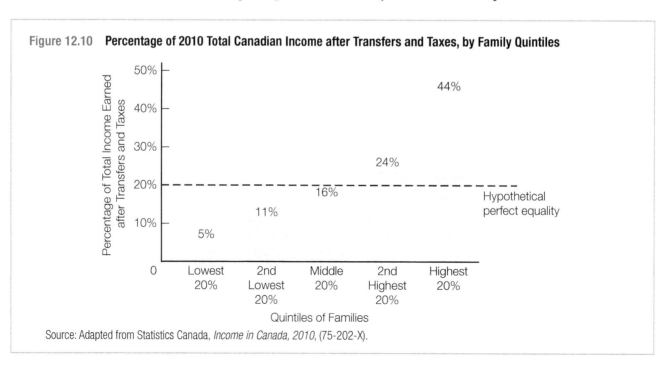

Figure 12.10   Percentage of 2010 Total Canadian Income after Transfers and Taxes, by Family Quintiles

Source: Adapted from Statistics Canada, *Income in Canada, 2010*, (75-202-X).

Incentive Effects of Redistribution   This redistribution of income from the rich to the poor is not as straightforward as it appears because of incentive effects and the interconnectedness of input and output markets through the circular flow. When governments take some of your income in taxes, leaving you less, it reduces the incentives you have to provide inputs and produce outputs. A market economy is based on the coordination of self-interest — and from a self-interest point of view, taking home 65 cents on the dollar is not as good as taking home all 100 cents. Because of incentive effects, taxes do not simply redistribute an unchanged quantity of products, services and income. If taxes cause some individuals to supply less to the market, because the rewards aren't as high (that's the law of supply), then input owners earn less and output markets will produce fewer products and services. To sum up the incentive effect in a phrase, "A more equally shared pie may result in a smaller pie."

Economists disagree about just how significant the incentive effect is, but unlike the largely win–win nature of education and training policies, this is a trade-off that must be considered when government is thinking about implementing tax and transfer policies.

What Should Be Done to Help the Poor? Equity and Efficiency One More Time

Clearly, there are policies for reducing poverty and inequality. But *should* governments use tax revenues for that purpose? This normative question is not as coldhearted as it might sound. True, most religions throughout history have treated helping the poor as a moral obligation. Basic human compassion inclines us to help others in need, and the Golden Rule — do unto others as you would have them do unto you — even suggests an element of self-interest in charity. But if I have taught you anything, it's that every choice involves trade-offs. To know whether government policies to reduce poverty and inequality are smart choices, we must once again apply Key 1. Are additional benefits greater than additional costs?

ADDITIONAL BENEFITS VS. OPPORTUNITY COSTS

Comparing costs and benefits is relatively easy for personal choices, where you alone pay the costs and reap the benefits. But policies to help the poor are different, as the costs and benefits apply to different people. How you feel about Robin Hood's motto depends considerably on whether you are being taken from or given to. And a personal choice to be charitable is different from a social choice by a government (even a democratically elected government) to implement a progressive tax and transfer system that takes from some to give to others.

One of the policy trade-offs that arises from the analogy "a more equally shared pie may result in a smaller pie" is the classic efficiency versus equity trade-off from Chapter 6. Let me remind you that when we say markets are efficient in producing the products and services we value the most, with the least waste, we mean outputs go to those most *willing and able to pay*. An efficient market outcome may include people who are unable to pay for basic necessities like shelter or food or medical care. An efficient market outcome is not necessarily fair or equitable.

Suppose the incentive effect of a progressive tax and transfer policy is large, and a more equal income distribution and reduced poverty come at the expense of slightly lower standards of living for everyone else in Canada. What is the smart policy choice? Economics alone does not provide the answer. The answer, which will be different for different people, depends on the *value* you place personally on efficiency versus equity. If you value efficiency far more than equity, you may not be willing to sacrifice lower standards of living for all to benefit those who are most in need. If you value equity more than efficiency, the policies will seem desirable and the trade-offs acceptable.

What Is Equity?   These differing valuations of efficiency and equity are also combined with differing views about equity. You are not likely to hear abstract philosophical debates about the meaning of equity, but you will hear politicians opposing or supporting tax and transfer policies — and you have to decide for whom to vote.

The two most common definitions of equity (section 6.5) emphasize *equal opportunities* or *equal outcomes*.

A conservative politician on the right of the political spectrum might oppose progressive taxes and transfers because she believes the efficiency of markets is more important for generating the economic prosperity that will ultimately help the poor. She might also believe that markets are already equitable because they provide everyone with *equal opportunities* (and fully expects that each person's accomplishments in life and income will differ with differences in talents, initiative, and luck). From her perspective, inequality and poverty are the result of either personal choices, failures, or misfortunes. They are not systemic "market failures" that require government intervention to correct. Personal charity is a more appropriate response for personal misfortune.

A left-leaning politician might favour progressive taxes and transfers because he believes *equal outcomes* are more important than efficiency. He is concerned with improving the equality of incomes, and does not believe poor children have the same opportunities as rich children. Inherited wealth stacks the rules of the game in favour of children who are born into wealth, and he believes the misfortune (only from an income perspective) of being born into a family with a single, female parent should not condemn such children to a lifetime of poverty. He thinks all individuals are worthy of having the basic necessities, and takes issue with the market principle that what you are worth is simply what the market is willing to pay for the inputs you provide. From his perspective, poverty and inequality are market failures, failures of a market system that responsible, democratic governments should correct.

You cannot decide that one politician is right and the other is wrong just on the basis of facts, or by using the Three Keys to Smart Choices. What you can — and, as a citizen, *must* decide — is which politician's *values* best match your own.

Refresh 12.5

MyEconLab

For answers to these Refresh Questions, visit MyEconLab.

1. Explain the differences between income and wealth.

2. What are the two main policy options for reducing poverty and inequality? What other policies can you think of to address other causes of poverty?

3. Where does your family fit into the Canadian distribution of income? Of wealth? Are you surprised?

Study Guide

12.1 Switching Sides: Incomes Are Prices and Quantities in Input Markets

Incomes are determined by prices and quantities in input markets, where households supply to businesses labour, capital, land, and entrepreneurship in exchange for wages, interest, rent, and profits.

- In input markets, households are sellers and businesses are buyers.

- Income — what you earn — is a flow.
  - **Flow** — amount per unit of time.
  - Income for labour, capital, and land
    = price of input × quantity of input

- Wealth — total value of assets you own — is a stock.
  - **Stock** — fixed amount at a moment in time.

- Key concepts for explaining input incomes are
  - *marginal revenue product* for labour
  - *present value* for capital
  - *economic rent* for land

- Entrepreneurs earn profits. Economic profits are a residual — what is left over from revenues after all opportunity costs of production (including normal profits) have been paid.

12.2 What Have You Done for Me Lately? Labour and Marginal Revenue Product

For maximum profits, businesses should hire additional labour when marginal revenue product is greater than marginal cost.

- To hire labour, business must pay the market wage reflecting the best opportunity cost of the input owner.

- Business demand for labour is a **derived demand** — demand for output and profits businesses can derive from hiring labour.

- **Marginal product** — *additional* output from hiring one more unit of labour.
  - When businesses hire additional labourers there is **diminishing marginal productivity** — as you add more of a variable input to fixed inputs, the marginal product of the variable input eventually diminishes.

- **Marginal revenue product** — additional revenue from selling output produced by an additional labourer.
  - marginal revenue product
    = marginal product × price of output.
  - Marginal revenue product diminishes for additional labourers.

- Recipe for maximum profits for business — hire additional inputs when marginal revenue product is greater than marginal cost.

12.3 All Present and Accounted For: Interest on Capital and Present Value

Present value tells you what money earned in the future is worth today. Present value compares the price you pay for today's investment against the investment's future earnings. For a smart choice, the present value of the investment's future earnings is greater than the investment's price today.

- The **present value** of a future amount of money is the amount that, if invested today, will grow as large as the future amount, taking account of earned interest.

$$\text{Present Value} = \frac{\text{Amount of Money Available in } n \text{ Years}}{(1 + \text{Interest Rate})^n}$$

- Revenues available in the future are not worth as much as revenues today because today's revenues earn interest.
  - **Discount** — reduction of future revenues for forgone interest.

- Present value simplifies the future stream of revenues from an investment to a single number today. It converts the flow of future revenues into stock concept, a value today that you compare with cost today to make a smart choice.

- Recipe for a smart investment choice — invest when the present value of the stream of future earnings is greater than the price of the investment.

12.4 Why Sidney Crosby Plays by Different Rules: Land, Economic Rent, and Superstars

Income for any input in inelastic supply, for example land or superstar talent, is economic rent, which is determined by demand alone.

- **Economic rent** — income paid to any input in relatively inelastic supply.

  - Land is a classic example of an input in inelastic supply.

- For inputs like land in inelastic supply, prices are effectively determined by demand alone.

- For most products and services, high input prices cause high output prices.

- For inputs in inelastic supply, high output prices cause high input prices — high economic rents.

12.5 What *Should* You Be Worth? Inequality and Poverty

Government policies to address the market's unequal distributions of income and wealth involve trade-offs between efficiency and equality.

- "What are you worth?" is a positive question; depends on quantities of inputs you own and prices markets place on those inputs.

- "What *should* you, or any person, be worth?" is a normative question you must answer as a citizen.

- Poverty results from not owning labour skills or assets that the market values, or from not getting a high enough price for what you do own.

- Policy options to reduce inequality and poverty: education, training, progressive tax and transfer system.

- Improving human capital through education and training addresses underlying cause of poverty: lack of inputs the market values.

  - **Human capital** — increased earning potential from work experience, on-the-job training, education.

- Federal and provincial tax systems use **progressive taxes** — tax rate increases as income increases.

  - **Regressive taxes** — tax rate decreases as income increases.

  - **Proportional (flat-rate) taxes** — tax rate the same regardless of income.

  - **Marginal tax rate** — rate on additional dollar of income.

  - **Transfer payments** — payments by government to households.

- Due to incentive effects, "A more equally shared pie may be a smaller pie."

- An efficient market outcome is not necessarily fair or equitable. May include poor people unable to pay for basic necessities like shelter, food, medical care.

- Governments can reduce poverty and inequality using tax–and-transfer systems to take from rich and give to poor (like Robin Hood).

  - Costs and benefits of policies to help the poor apply to different people. How you feel about Robin Hood's motto depends on whether you are being taken from or given to.

TRUE/FALSE

Circle the correct answer. Solutions to these questions are available at the end of the book and on MyEconLab. You can also visit the MyEconLab Study Plan to access additional questions that will help you master the concepts covered in this chapter.

12.1 Prices and Quantities in Input Markets

1. What you are worth, in a market economy, is what the market is willing to pay you for the inputs you provide.   T   F

2. If you earn $10 per hour and work 50 hours per week, your weekly income is $500.   T   F

3. Income is a stock of earnings received by an individual.   T   F

12.2 Marginal Revenue Product

4. Businesses' demand for labour is derived from the input market.   T   F

5. For maximum profits, a business should hire labour only when the marginal revenue product is greater than the wage.   T   F

6. An employer will hire more workers if the price of output rises.   T   F

12.3 Interest on Capital and Present Value

7. If someone offers you $1 today or $1 tomorrow, it is smart to prefer $1 tomorrow.   T   F

8. When interest rates rise, present value increases.   T   F

9. If interest rates fall, an investment that was smart before the decrease may no longer be smart.   T   F

12.4 Land, Economic Rent, and Superstars

10. For most products and services, high input prices cause high output prices.   T   F

11. Superstar salaries are to blame for high ticket prices.   T   F

12.5 Inequality and Poverty

12. In Canada, income is more unequally distributed than wealth.   T   F

13. A regressive income tax redistributes income from the rich to the poor.   T   F

14. Compared with the market distribution of income, government transfers and taxes reduce the inequality of income distribution.   T   F

15. Earnings from work account for the majority of income in Canada.   T   F

MULTIPLE CHOICE

Circle the best answer. Solutions to these questions are available at the end of the book and on MyEconLab. You can also visit the MyEconLab Study Plan to access similar questions that will help you master the concepts covered in this chapter.

12.1 Prices and Quantities in Input Markets

1. Wealth differs from income because
   a) income is a stock; wealth is a flow.
   b) wealth is derived from income.
   c) income is what you earn; wealth is what you own.
   d) income is what you own; wealth is what you earn.

2. Which of the following statements is *false*?
   a) Wealth is income received from supplying labour.
   b) Rent is income received from supplying land.
   c) Normal profits are income received from supplying entrepreneurial abilities.
   d) Interest is income received from supplying capital.

12.2 Marginal Revenue Product

3. The additional benefits from hiring an additional web designer are derived from the additional
   a) output of webpages she can produce.
   b) revenues from selling those additional webpages.
   c) profits from selling those additional webpages.
   d) all of the above.

4. Consider Figure 12.3 on page 316. How many designers (which cost $50 per hour) should Wahid hire if he can charge $20 per webpage sold, rather than $15 per webpage sold?
   a) 2
   b) 3
   c) 4
   d) 5

5. Economic rent is
   a) paid only for the use of land.
   b) paid only for the use of capital.
   c) determined only by supply.
   d) income paid to any input in relatively inelastic supply.

12.3 Interest on Capital and Present Value

6. An investment choice is smart when the
   a) future stream of revenues is greater than the price of the investment.
   b) future stream of revenues is less than the price of the investment.
   c) present value of the future stream of revenues is greater than the price of the investment.
   d) present value of the future stream of revenues is less than the price of the investment.

7. The present value of a future amount of money is
   a) a stock concept.
   b) less than the future amount because future revenues are discounted to adjust for forgone interest.
   c) the amount that, if invested today, will grow as large as the future amount, taking account of earned interest.
   d) all of the above.

12.4 Land, Economic Rent, and Superstars

8. Rents are determined by
   a) demand.
   b) input prices.
   c) the price of capital.
   d) all of the above.

9. For inputs in inelastic supply, such as land or superstar talent,
   a) there is no supply response to higher prices.
   b) the price paid for the input is not proportional to its productivity.
   c) input prices are explained by output prices.
   d) all of the above.

10. During the lockout that cancelled the 2004–2005 hockey season, fans blamed
    a) the players.
    b) the owners.
    c) the CBC.
    d) themselves.

11. During the lockout that cancelled the 2004–2005 hockey season, fans *should* have blamed
    a) the players.
    b) the owners.
    c) the CBC.
    d) themselves.

12.5 Inequality and Poverty

12. Which of the following statements about the distribution of market income in Canada is *true*?
    a) The poorest 20 percent of families earn 1 percent of total market income.
    b) The middle 20 percent of families earn 10 percent of total market income.
    c) The poorest 40 percent of families earn 15 percent of total market income.
    d) The richest 20 percent of families earn less than half of total market income.

13. Which of the following statements about the distribution of wealth in Canada is *false*?
    a) The bottom 50 percent of families own 5 percent of total wealth.
    b) The bottom 40 percent of families own 20 percent of total wealth.
    c) The wealthiest 10 percent of Canadian families own 51 percent of total wealth.
    d) The wealthiest 1 percent of Canadian families own 24 percent of total wealth.

14. If the marginal tax rate increases as income increases, the income tax is defined as
    a) progressive.
    b) proportional.
    c) negative.
    d) regressive.

15. Which of the following statements is *false*?
    a) A family of three in Toronto that makes less than $29 699 per year is considered to be in poverty.
    b) More than 50 percent of individuals in poverty live in a family whose major income earner is female.
    c) More than 9 million people in Canada lived below the poverty line in 2011.
    d) One out of 12 children lived below the poverty line in 2011.

SUMMING UP

In a very real way, you and I took an economics road trip in this book, providing you direction to better understand how to make smart choices in life. Together, we toured around the circular flow of economic life:

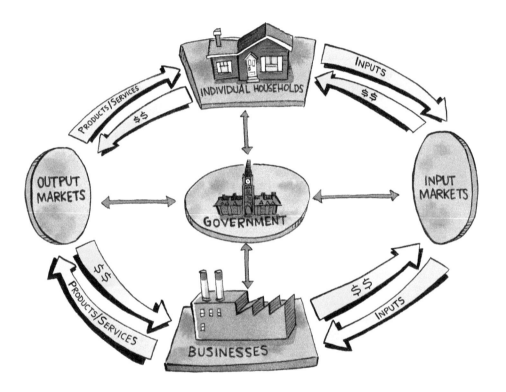

We visited individuals, businesses, and governments as they made choices to get what they wanted, and we looked at how those choices interact in output and input markets.

Most importantly, you saw how to use the Three Keys to Smart Choices as guides in your decision making. Good road maps make travel easier, and good economic models make smart choices easier. The Three Keys are a model for your personal smart choices and for society as a whole.

The Three Keys are like a map, helping you choose a direction at key decision points — forks in the road. The Three Keys focus you on the information that is most useful to make a smart choice.

3 KEYS TO SMART CHOICES

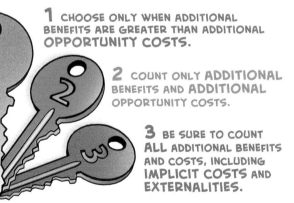

1 CHOOSE ONLY WHEN ADDITIONAL BENEFITS ARE GREATER THAN ADDITIONAL OPPORTUNITY COSTS.

2 COUNT ONLY ADDITIONAL BENEFITS AND ADDITIONAL OPPORTUNITY COSTS.

3 BE SURE TO COUNT ALL ADDITIONAL BENEFITS AND COSTS, INCLUDING IMPLICIT COSTS AND EXTERNALITIES.

GeorgSV/Fotolia

We constantly make choices in life — as individuals, businesspeople, and citizens. Use the Three Keys model to achieve more personal success in life. You will also be a better citizen through understanding the social consequences of your decisions, and by intelligently and systematically evaluating the benefits and costs of policies that governments offer. You may yourself become a politician or policymaker, and use the Three Keys model to make smart decisions.

Simply understanding the Three Keys to Smart Choices does not guarantee you will get the most out of life. Setting goals based on your personal values is just as important. Do you value efficiency more than equity? Which system of health care is best for Canada? Are you willing to change your standard of living for a greener planet? Should governments redistribute income to help those who are poor? These decisions grow from your personal values. But, once you decide on a political position or social goal, the Three Keys model (economic thinking) identifies smart policy or personal actions to efficiently reach it.

While our microeconomics road trip together is done, your life trip is ongoing. By learning to think like an economist (using the Three Keys to Smart Choices), the key "roads" to making smart choices become clearer, and difficult decisions become simpler and more manageable. The economic way of thinking presented in this book will help you choose paths in life that lead to more satisfying and successful destinations — economics for making the most of life.

The only way for me to know how close I've come to my goal of helping you make smart choices is to hear from you. Let me know what works for you in this book — and, more importantly, what doesn't. You can write to me at **avicohen@yorku.ca.** In future editions I will acknowledge by name all students who help improve *Economics for Life*.

Professor Avi J. Cohen
Department of Economics
York University
University of Toronto

Glossary

A

absolute advantage: the ability to produce a product or service at a lower absolute cost than another producer (p. 9)

accounting profits: revenues minus obvious costs (including depreciation) (p. 169)

average total cost: total cost per unit of output (p. 191)

B

barriers to entry: legal or economic barriers preventing new competitors from entering a market (p. 189)

breakeven point: business just earning normal profits (no economic profits, no economic losses) (p. 175)

C

cap-and-trade system: limits the quantity of emissions businesses can release into environment (p. 292)

capture view: government regulation benefits regulated businesses, not public interest (p. 269)

carbon tax: emissions tax on carbon-based fossil fuels (p. 291)

cartel: association of suppliers formed to maintain high prices and restrict competition (p. 263)

caveat emptor (**"let the buyer beware"**): the buyer alone is responsible for checking quality of products before purchasing (p. 266)

collusion: conspiracy to cheat or deceive others (p. 263)

comparative advantage: the ability to produce a product or service at lower opportunity cost than another producer (p. 10)

comparative statics: comparing two equilibrium outcomes to isolate the effect of changing one factor at a time (p. 95)

competition: active attempt to increase profits and gain the market power of monopoly (p. 195)

complements: products or services used together to satisfy the same want (p. 42)

consumer surplus: the difference between the amount a consumer is willing and able to pay, and the price actually paid (p. 97)

copyrights and **patents:** exclusive property rights to sell or license creations, protecting against competition (p. 189)

creative destruction: competitive business innovations generate economic profits for winners, improve living standards for all, but destroy less productive or less desirable products and production methods (p. 199)

cross elasticity of demand: measures the responsiveness of the demand for a product or service to a change in the price of a substitute or complement (p. 124)

Crown corporations: publicly owned businesses in Canada (p. 258)

D

deadweight loss: the decrease in total surplus compared to an economically efficient outcome (p. 101)

decrease in demand: decrease in consumers' willingness and ability to pay (p. 40)

decrease in supply: decrease in business's willingness to produce; leftward shift of supply curve (p. 68)

demand: consumers' willingness and ability to pay for a particular product or service (p. 29)

demand curve: shows the relationship between price and quantity demanded, other things remaining the same (p. 35)

depreciation: tax rule for spreading cost over lifetime of long-lasting equipment; decrease in value of equipment over time because of wear and tear and because it becomes obsolete (p. 168)

derived demand: demand for output and profits businesses can derive from hiring labour (p. 315)

diminishing marginal productivity: as you add more of a variable input to fixed inputs, the marginal product of the variable input eventually diminishes (p. 316)

diminishing returns: as output increases, decreasing productivity increases marginal costs (p. 213)

discount: reduction of future revenues for forgone interest (p. 321)

E

economic losses: negative economic profits (p. 173)

economic profits: revenues minus all opportunity costs (obvious costs plus hidden opportunity costs) (p. 172)

economic rent: income paid to any input in relatively inelastic supply (p. 322)

economics: how individuals, businesses, and governments make the best possible choices to get what they want, and how those choices interact in markets (p. 4)

economies of scale: average total costs of producing fall as quantity (scale) of production increases (pp. 191, 201)

efficient market outcome: consumers buy only products and services where marginal benefit is greater than marginal cost; products and services produced at lowest cost, with price just covering all opportunity costs of production (p. 101)

elastic demand: large response in quantity demanded when price rises (p. 109)

elastic supply: large response in quantity supplied when price rises (p. 120)

elasticity (or price elasticity of demand): measures by how much quantity demanded responds to a change in price (p. 108)

elasticity of supply: measures by how much quantity supplied responds to a change in price (p. 120)

emissions tax: tax to pay for external costs of emissions (p. 291)

equilibrium price: the price that equalizes quantity demanded and quantity supplied, balancing the forces of competition and cooperation, so that there is no tendency for change (p. 85)

excess demand (or shortage): quantity demanded exceeds quantity supplied (p. 82)

excess supply (or surplus): quantity supplied exceeds quantity demanded (p. 83)

explicit costs (or obvious costs): costs a business pays directly (p. 168)

external benefits (or positive externalities): benefits to society from your private choice that affect others, but that others do not pay you for (p. 282)

external costs (or negative externalities): costs to society from your private choice that affect others, but that you do not pay (p. 281)

externalities: costs or benefits that affect others external to a choice or a trade (p. 21)

F

fixed costs: do not change with the quantity of output produced (p. 217)

flat-rate (proportional) taxes: tax rate the same regardless of income (p. 329)

flow: amount per unit of time (p. 313)

free-rider problem: markets underproduce products and services with positive externalities (p. 296)

G

game theory: a mathematical tool for understanding how players make decisions, taking into account what they expect rivals to do (p. 260)

government failure: when regulations fail to serve the public interest (p. 272)

H

human capital: increased earning potential from work experience, on-the-job training, education (p. 328)

I

implicit costs: hidden opportunity costs of what business owner could earn elsewhere with time and money invested (pp. 20, 169)

incentives: rewards and penalties for choices (p. 6)

income elastic demand: for normal goods that are luxuries, the percentage change in quantity is greater than the percentage change in income (p. 126)

income elasticity of demand: measures the responsiveness of the demand for a product or service to a change in income (p. 125)

income inelastic demand: for normal goods that are necessities, the percentage change in quantity is less than the percentage change in income (p. 126)

increase in demand: increase in consumers' willingness and ability to pay (p. 40)

increase in supply: increase in businesses' willingness to produce; rightward shift of supply curve (p. 66)

inelastic demand: small response in quantity demanded when price rises (p. 108)

inelastic supply: small response in quantity supplied when price rises (p. 120)

inferior goods: products or services you buy less of when your income increases (p. 42)

inputs: the productive resources — labour, natural resources, capital equipment, and entrepreneurial ability — used to produce products and services (p. 14)

internalize the externality: transform external costs into costs the producer must pay privately to the government (p. 291)

L

law of demand: if the price of a product or service rises, quantity demanded decreases, other things remaining the same (p. 34)

law of supply: if the price of a product or service rises, quantity supplied increases (p. 62)

living wage: $20 per hour, enough to allow an individual in a Canadian city to live above the poverty line (p. 148)

long-run market equilibrium: quantity demanded equals quantity supplied, economic profits are zero, no tendency for change (p. 177)

M

macroeconomics: analyzes performance of the whole Canadian economy and global economy, the combined outcomes of all individual microeconomic choices (p. 18)

marginal benefits: the additional benefit from a choice, changing with circumstances (pp. 20, 30)

marginal cost: additional opportunity cost of increasing quantity supplied, changing with circumstances (p. 52)

marginal opportunity costs: additional opportunity costs from the next choice (pp. 20, 58)

marginal product: additional output from hiring one more unit of labour (p. 235)

marginal revenue: additional revenue from more sales or from selling one more unit (p. 206)

marginal revenue product: additional revenue from selling output produced by additional labourer (p. 317)

marginal social benefit (*MSB*): marginal private benefit plus marginal external benefit (p. 286)

marginal social cost (*MSC*): marginal private cost plus marginal external cost (p. 286)

marginal tax rate: rate on additional dollar of income (p. 329)

market: the interactions between buyers and sellers (p. 78)

market demand: sum of demands of all individuals willing and able to buy a particular product or service (p. 34)

market equilibrium: quantity demanded equals quantity supplied, economic profits zero, no tendency for change (p. 177)

market failure: when markets produce outcomes that are inefficient or inequitable (p. 257)

market power: business's ability to set prices (p. 184)

market structure: characteristics that affect competition and pricing power — availability of substitutes, number of competitors, barriers to entry of new competitors (p. 187)

market supply: sum of supplies of all businesses willing to produce a particular product or service (p. 61)

market-clearing price: the price that equalizes quantity demanded and quantity supplied (p. 85)

microeconomics: analyzes choices that individuals in households, individual businesses, and governments make, and how those choices interact in markets (p. 18)

minimum wage laws: example of price floor — minimum price set by government, making it illegal to pay a lower price (p. 148)

model: a simplified representation of the real world, focusing attention on what's important for understanding (p. 14)

monopolistic competition: many small businesses make similar but slightly differentiated products or services (p. 194)

monopoly: only seller of product or service; no close substitutes available (p. 184)

N

Nash equilibrium: outcome of a game in which each player makes her or his own best choice given the choice of the other player (p. 261)

natural monopoly: economies of scale allow only single seller to achieve lowest average total cost (p. 257)

negative externalities (external costs): costs to society from your private choice that affect others, but that you do not pay (p. 281)

normal goods: products or services you buy more of when your income increases (p. 42)

normal profits: compensation for business owner's time and money; sum of hidden opportunity costs (implicit costs); what business owner must earn to do as well as best alternative use of time and money; average profits in other industries (p. 172)

normative statements: about what you believe should be; involve value judgments (p. 17)

O

obvious costs (explicit costs): costs a business pays directly (p. 168)

oligopoly: few big sellers control most of the market (p. 193)

opportunity cost: cost of best alternative given up (p. 5)

P

patents and **copyrights:** exclusive property rights to sell or license creations, protecting against competition (p. 189)

perfect competition: many sellers producing identical products or services (p. 185)

perfectly elastic demand: price elasticity of demand equals infinity; quantity demanded has an infinite response to any change in price (p. 110)

perfectly elastic supply: price elasticity of supply equals infinity; quantity supplied has infinite response to a change in price (p. 121)

perfectly inelastic demand: price elasticity of demand equals zero; quantity demanded does not respond to a change in price (p. 110)

perfectly inelastic supply: price elasticity of supply equals zero; quantity supplied does not respond to a change in price (p. 121)

positive externalities (external benefits): benefits to society from your private choice that affect others, but that others do not pay you for (p. 282)

positive statements: about what is; can be evaluated as true or false by checking the facts (p. 17)

preferences: your wants and their intensities (p. 28)

present value: amount that, if invested today, will grow as large as the future amount, taking account of earned interest (p. 319)

price ceiling (or rent controls): maximum price set by government, making it illegal to charge higher price (p. 144)

price discrimination: charging different customers different prices for same product or service (p. 220)

price elasticity of demand (or elasticity): measures by how much quantity demanded responds to a change in price (p. 108)

price floor: minimum price set by government, making it illegal to pay a lower price (p. 148)

price maker: pure monopoly with maximum power to set prices (p. 184)

price taker: business with zero power to set price (p. 185)

prisoner's dilemma: a game with two players who must each make a strategic choice, where results depend on other player's choice (p. 260)

producer surplus: the difference between the amount a producer is willing to accept, and the price actually received (p. 97)

product differentiation: attempt to distinguish product or service from those of competitors (p. 188)

production possibilities frontier: maximum combinations of products or services that can be produced with existing inputs (p. 9)

progressive taxes: tax rate increases as income increases (p. 329)

property rights: legally enforceable guarantees of ownership of physical, financial, and intellectual property (p. 79)

proportional (flat-rate) taxes: tax rate the same regardless of income (p. 329)

public goods: provide external benefits consumed simultaneously by everyone; no one can be excluded (p. 295)

public provision: government provision of products or services with positive externalities, financed by tax revenue (p. 303)

public-interest view: government regulation eliminates waste, achieves efficiency, promotes public interest (p. 269)

Q

quantity demanded: amount you actually plan to buy at a given price (p. 33)

quantity supplied: the quantity you actually plan to supply at a given price (p. 56)

R

rate of return regulation: sets a price allowing the regulated monopoly to just cover average total costs, including normal profits (p. 258)

regressive taxes: tax rate decreases as income increases (p. 329)

rent controls: example of price ceiling — maximum price set by government, making it illegal to charge higher price (p. 144)

S

scarcity: the problem that arises because we all have limited money, time, and energy (p. 4)

short-run market equilibrium: quantity demanded equals quantity supplied, but economic losses or profits can lead to changes in supply (p. 176)

shortage (or excess demand): quantity demanded exceeds quantity supplied (p. 82)

stock: fixed amount at a moment in time (p. 313)

subsidy: payment to those who create positive externalities (p. 300)

substitutes: products or services used in place of each other to satisfy the same want (p. 41)

sunk costs: past expenses that cannot be recovered (p. 54)

supply: businesses' willingness to produce a particular product or service because price covers all opportunity costs (p. 55)

supply curve: shows relationship between price and quantity supplied, other things remaining the same (p. 62)

surplus (or excess supply): quantity supplied exceeds quantity demanded (p. 83)

T

tax incidence: the division of a tax between buyers and sellers (p. 128)

total cost: fixed costs plus variable costs (p. 235)

total product: total output labour produces when working with all fixed inputs (p. 235)

total revenue: all money a business receives from sales, equal to price per unit (P) multiplied by quantity sold (Q) (p. 113)

total surplus: consumer surplus plus producer surplus (p. 99)

transfer payments: payments by government to households (p. 329)

V

variable costs: change with changes in the quantity of output produced (p. 235)

Answers to the Study Guide Questions

CHAPTER 1

TRUE/FALSE

1. True. Definition of economics.
2. False. Even people who win the lottery can never satisfy all of their wants; they also face trade-offs and have to make smart choices.
3. False. The opportunity cost is the value of what you give up to take that path, action, or activity.
4. False. The grant covers the money cost of getting an apprenticeship but not the opportunity cost — the total value of what the individual gives up by taking an apprenticeship, which includes the money that the individual could have earned in a job.
5. False. Women have a larger incentive because the return on post-secondary education — the gap between incomes of post-secondary graduates and high-school graduates — is higher for women than for men.
6. False. If men held a comparative advantage in housework then traditional gender roles would be reversed (men would be doing the housework) because individuals should specialize in the activity where they have a comparative advantage.
7. False. Possible to produce but not maximum combinations.
8. False. Lower opportunity cost.
9. False. There are benefits for both people from trade.
10. True.
11. False. Economists must instead build models that assume all other things are unchanged.
12. True. The word *should* is a sign of a normative statement.
13. False. They are microeconomic choices.
14. True. Microeconomics focuses mostly on individual decisions.
15. False. They are the costs that affect others.

MULTIPLE CHOICE

1. **d)** We all have limited time, energy, and money.
2. **d)** Even Bill Gates faces the problem of scarcity.
3. **b)** Economics is about people (also in businesses and government) making choices.
4. **d)** All are scarce.
5. **a)** Paid tuition is the same for either choice.
6. **d)** See *Economics Out There* on p. 6.
7. **b)** Going to college means giving up *fewer* good jobs. With fewer good jobs in a weaker economy, the opportunity cost of going to school decreases.
8. **b)** Differences in opportunity costs key to gains from trade.
9. **a)** Formula on p. 10.
10. **c)** Chloe's opportunity cost of muffins (2 cookies per muffin) lower than Zabeen's (3 cookies per muffin).
11. **a)** Notice the word *should*.
12. **d)** See pp. 14–15.
13. **a)** Macroeconomic choice by government.
14. **c)** International exchange rates are a macroeconomic topic.
15. **b)** The past is the same no matter what choice you make now.

CHAPTER 2

TRUE/FALSE

1. False. Demand is a stronger word, meaning willing and able to pay.
2. True.
3. False. Also depends on your time and effort.
4. True. Marginal means additional.
5. True. Flat fee is not an additional cost.
6. False. Marginal benefit equals average benefit only in special circumstances. For example, if a basketball player with a shooting percentage of 50 percent successfully makes one out of her next two shots, then the additional points she adds are equal to the amount of points she usually (on average) adds.
7. True. Willingness to pay changes with circumstances.
8. False. Quantity demanded is a much more limited term than demand. Only a change in price changes quantity demanded. A change in any other influence on consumer choice changes demand.
9. True. Only a change in price changes quantity demanded.
10. True. Add up all individual demands at any price to get market demand.
11. False. Slope downward to the right.
12. True. For any quantity, maximum willing to pay is now less.

13. False, for normal goods. A decrease in income decreases demand. But True, for inferior goods.
14. False. As the holidays get nearer, people's willingness and ability to pay for certain products or services increases for any given price. Therefore, an increase in demand drives the rising prices.
15. False. Statement is true for normal goods, false for inferior goods.

1. **d)** Definition of preferences.
2. **b)** *Give up* includes money, time, effort.
3. **d)** Intensities of your wants.
4. **c)** Each additional plate brings less satisfaction.
5. **d)** Marginal costs greater than marginal benefits.
6. **a)** Quantity demanded is not wants. Must be willing and able to pay.
7. **d)** Price depends on marginal benefits, not total benefits.
8. **c)** With switch to cheaper substitutes, quantity demanded decreases.
9. **d)** Rising price is movement along demand curve for garbage collection.
10. **b)** Definition of substitutes.
11. **a)** Buy less as income increases, switching to better food that was previously unaffordable.
12. **c)** Price changes quantity demanded, not demand.
13. **b)** Cars and tires are complements.
14. **d)** (a) for inferior goods, (b) for normal goods.
15. **d)** Price only affects quantity demanded. Change in income changes demand.

CHAPTER 3

TRUE/FALSE

1. False. Workers with fewer alternatives may accept lower wages.
2. True. Choose to produce when additional benefits are greater than additional opportunity costs.
3. True.
4. True. Forgone opportunity is now more valuable.
5. False. Rent payments are sunk costs not relevant to the decision of how much to produce.
6. False. Sunk costs are the same no matter what choice you make.
7. True. Not willing to supply if prices don't cover marginal opportunity costs.
8. False. Opportunity cost equals what you give up divided by what you get.
9. False. As you spend more time in any activity (working instead of relaxing), the marginal opportunity cost of that activity increases.
10. True. Opportunity cost is a short form of marginal opportunity cost.
11. False. Start with quantity and go up and over to price (marginal cost).

12. True. Shifts supply curve leftward.
13. False. Rise in price decreases market supply of the other product.
14. True. Higher expected future prices decreases supply today.
15. False. Increase in quantity supplied.

1. **c)** The 30 minutes of studying you must give up become more valuable with an exam tomorrow.
2. **b)** $15 is the best forgone opportunity to make money.
3. **c)** Sunk costs are in the past, cannot be changed, and are not additional costs.
4. **b)** Previous money lost makes no difference to smart choice on next turn.
5. **c)** Tattoo remains whether he breaks up or not. (Are tattoos a sunk cost if they can be removed?)
6. **c)** Marginal cost is constant.
7. **d)** All describe a relationship between rising price and increasing quantity of hours supplied.
8. **a)** Law of supply.
9. **c)** If inputs *not* equally productive, opportunity cost increases.
10. **c)** Price changes quantity supplied.
11. **a)** Only **(a)** shifts supply curve rightward. **(b)**, **(c)**, **(d)** shift supply leftward.
12. **a)** Rightward shift in supply for **(b)**, **(c)**, **(d)**.
13. **a)** Rightward shift of supply curve.
14. **b)** Other answers change demand.
15. **d)** Piercing and tattoos are related products produced.

CHAPTER 4

TRUE/FALSE

1. False. Transactions would not be voluntary and there would be no incentive to supply the product to consumers.
2. False. Price should cover all opportunity costs.
3. False. Price and quantity adjustments do not require the consumer or business to know anything about anyone's personal wants or production capabilities.
4. True. Surplus, with quantity supplied greater than quantity demanded.
5. True.
6. True. Definition of market-clearing price.
7. False. May not be willing or able to pay the equilibrium price.
8. True. Quantity demanded equals quantity supplied.
9. False. Increased supply causes equilibrium price to fall and quantity to increase.
10. False. Increase in demand and increase in supply increase market-clearing quantity, but effect on price uncertain.
11. False. Increased supply lowers the price of grey seals, reducing the cost of producing seal coat fur, resulting in a lower price.

12. True. Reduced qualifications increases supply.
13. False. Price minus marginal cost.
14. False. Decrease in total surplus compared to economically efficient outcome.
15. True. Maximum total surplus and zero deadweight loss.

MULTIPLE CHOICE

1. **d)** Definition.
2. **d)** Price must cover marginal opportunity cost of seller and be less than marginal benefit of buyer.
3. **c)** Government guarantees of property rights allow markets to function.
4. **d)** When prices change, so do smart choices and quantities.
5. **c)** Price adjustment.
6. **c)** Excess demand and frustrated buyers.
7. **d)** Market-clearing price.
8. **a)** No one is kicking himself about wanting to buy or sell more.
9. **a)** Draw rightward shift demand and leftward shift supply.
10. **d)** Draw leftward shift demand and rightward shift supply.
11. **c)** Falling price increases quantity demanded and decreases quantity supplied.
12. **b)** Exercise and reading books are substitute activities for a child's time.
13. **b)** Area under the marginal benefit curve and above the (market) price actually paid.
14. **b)** Consumer surplus plus producer surplus.
15. **c)** For any quantity greater than the equilibrium quantity, read up to marginal cost and marginal benefit curves.

CHAPTER 5

TRUE/FALSE

1. True. More substitutes means more elastic demand.
2. True. Greater than 1 is elastic.
3. False. Fewer substitutes mean more inelastic demand.
4. True. You will respond strongly (shopping elsewhere) to a small change in price.
5. True. Raising the price of an inelastic good increases total revenue.
6. False. Slope is constant — elasticity changes.
7. True. Leftward shift supply increases price. If total revenue increases, demand is inelastic.
8. False. Prices rises will increase total revenue.
9. True. Quantity supplied has infinite response to change in price.
10. True. Increase in quantity supplied of work is greater for women than men. More work equals more income.
11. True. Percentage change in quantity supplied (40) greater than percentage change in price (10).
12. True. Cross elasticity of demand is negative for complements used together.

13. False. Has negative income elasticity of demand.
14. False. Necessities have income inelastic demand.
15. False. Sellers pay more because consumers will substitute rather than pay higher price with tax.

MULTIPLE CHOICE

1. **a)** Better substitutes mean more elastic demand.
2. **b)** Use midpoint formula. Percentage change in quantity = 20%. Percentage change in price = 10%.
3. **c)** Use simple formula. Price and quantity demanded inversely related.
4. **b)** Also longer time to adjust and easier to find substitutes.
5. **b)** Fall in price decreases total revenue for inelastic demand.
6. **c)** Bathroom demand likely inelastic — small decrease in use from price rise.
7. **c)** Unit elastic demand.
8. **d)** Supply shifts rightward. Equilibrium quantity increases, price falls, and, with inelastic demand, total revenue decreases.
9. **c)** Large rise in price produces no change in quantity supplied.
10. **b)** More available inputs.
11. **d)** More production times means more inelastic supply.
12. **c)** Almost perfect substitutes.
13. **a)** Use simple formula. Positive for normal goods.
14. **a)** Income elastic.
15. **b)** Seller pays entire tax because buyers will not pay more.

CHAPTER 6

TRUE/FALSE

1. True. Change in quantity of tenants with no change in prices (rents).
2. True. Can check if true by looking at what actually happens to available quantity and quality of rentals when rent ceilings introduced.
3. True. Empirical statement that can be checked against facts.
4. True. Statement about facts that can be checked.
5. False. Unsatisfied demand from the controlled market spills over to the uncontrolled market, pushing rent levels there even higher.
6. False. Statement cannot be evaluated as true/false because a value judgment is necessary to define what is a problem.
7. False. The word *should* indicates a value judgment.
8. True. Effect on young and unskilled can be measured.
9. False. Elasticity of demand for teen labour is highest; zero elasticity of demand for labour over 25 years old.
10. True. Wage inequality can be measured.
11. True. Higher wage increases quantity of labour supplied and decreases quantity demanded by business.

12. False. Longer waiting times are a trade-off Canadians make for a more *equitable* health care system that does not discriminate on the basis of ability to pay.
13. True. Crime, health care, and productivity can be measured.
14. False. Statement cannot be evaluated as true/false because it is a value judgment.
15. True. Equity of outcomes.

MULTIPLE CHOICE

1. **b)** Price ceiling below equilibrium price creates shortage with quantity demanded greater than quantity supplied.
2. **a)** Government-set price prevents price from falling to equilibrium price and creates surplus.
3. **d)** Businesses may immediately decrease supply from this rise in the price of an input. With time, find cheaper substitutes for labour.
4. **a)** Rent controls are only effective if price is set below the equilibrium price.
5. **d)** Create incentives to reduce quantity and quality of rental units.
6. **d)** Rent controls reduced the quantity and quality of private housing.
7. **c)** As rents rise, quantity supplied increases first and as new housing is built, supply also increases.
8. **d)** Unintended consequences of law.
9. **d)** Rent ceilings reduce the quantity and quality of private-sector housing.
10. **c)** Price floor prevents prices from falling, but allows prices to rise. With quantity demanded greater than quantity supplied, price will rise to equilibrium price.
11. **d)** Minimum wage is already below the poverty line.
12. **c)** For demand, must be willing and able.
13. **c)** Can measure improvement in income and effect on unemployment.
14. **b)** Positive statement with prediction that can be tested against data.
15. **b)** Greatest inequality between top and bottom of income distribution.

CHAPTER 7

TRUE/FALSE

1. False. Depreciation.
2. False. Cost is value of best alternative use of her time in that year.
3. False. You could have invested the borrowed money in a bank and earned interest instead.
4. False. The reverse is true.
5. True. Need a higher risk premium.
6. True. Could be interest foregone or return on investing money elsewhere.
7. False. Best alterative use of the owner's time.
8. True. Definition of normal profits.

9. False. Economic Profits = Accounting Profits − Hidden Opportunity Costs = $20 000 − ($50 000 × 10%) = $15 000
10. False. Remain in business if accounting profits are greater than normal profits (or hidden opportunity costs). Suppose accounting profits are $15 000. If you could be earning $20 000 in a different job then owning the business is not the smart choice.
11. True. More revenues increase likelihood of normal or economic profits.
12. False. Time to adjust economic profits to zero. Only normal profits in long run.
13. True. Economic profits are a green light for businesses to enter an industry.
14. False. Businesses are at the breakeven point when revenues equal the total of all opportunity costs (including obvious costs and hidden opportunity costs).
15. False. Businesses making economic profits of zero will remain in the industry since they are earning normal profits — covering all opportunity costs of production.

MULTIPLE CHOICE

1. **c)** Accountants do not subtract implicit costs.
2. **d)** Revenues more than all opportunity costs.
3. **c)** Best he could earn working somewhere else.
4. **d)** Interest paid is an obvious cost accountants subtract from revenues when calculating accounting profits.
5. **b)** Gambler has a low risk premium.
6. **d)** By definition.
7. **a)** Explicit costs are obvious, not hidden.
8. **c)** Economic profits subtract hidden opportunity costs from accounting profits.
9. **d)** See definitions on p. 172.
10. **b)** Economic Profits = Accounting Profits − Hidden Opportunity Costs.
11. **d)** If hidden opportunity costs are greater than accounting profits, economics profits are negative (economic losses).
12. **d)** All definitions of positive economic profits.
13. **c)** Economic profit signals can be green (enter), yellow (no change), or red (exit).
14. **d)** Profits are the same as average profits in other industries.
15. **b)** Businesses exit the industry, so the supply curve shifts leftward.

CHAPTER 8

TRUE/FALSE

1. False. Monopolist's market power is limited by what buyers are willing and able to pay.
2. True. The only seller can be in an output or input market.
3. True. But even monopoly price-makers must live by the law of demand.
4. False. A seller may earn more revenues by cutting prices instead of raising them if demand is elastic.

5. True. Businesses prefer to be price makers rather than price takers.
6. True. Barriers create the monopoly.
7. False. This would increase economies of scale.
8. True. Higher pricing power comes from more inelastic demand.
9. False. There are differentiated substitutes.
10. True. Because of product differentiation.
11. False. Consumers are more sensitive to price changes in monopolistic competition because there are more businesses selling similar substitutes.
12. False. The gaming industry is an oligopoly. A few companies — Nintendo, Microsoft, and Sony — control the market.
13. True. Businesses must at least match the competitive actions of rivals.
14. False. Businesses look for new ways to *beat* rivals, not just match them.
15. True.

MULTIPLE CHOICE

1. **d)** Definitions.
2. **b)** Even price-makers must live by the law of demand.
3. **c)** Narrow the definition of the market.
4. **d)** All are barriers to entry.
5. **c)** Barriers to entry.
6. **c)** Songs and poems get copyrights, products get patents.
7. **c)** A made-up, not real, word.
8. **d)** No barriers to entry.
9. **d)** More elastic demand = lower pricing power.
10. **d)** Great many sellers producing identical products.
11. **d)** All businesses are price takers. Zero pricing power.
12. **a)** Definition.
13. **d)** Active attempts of creative destruction.
14. **b)** Creates product differentiation, reducing consumer willingness to substitute other products or services.
15. **c)** Improve living standards for all, but destroy less productive production methods.

CHAPTER 9

TRUE/FALSE

1. False. Profits increase only if marginal revenue is greater than marginal cost.
2. True. Resale creates competition.
3. False. For products that can be easily resold, even monopolists must live by the one-price rule.
4. True. Businesses near capacity have increasing marginal costs.
5. False. Although there are marginal costs of adding passengers since additional snacks are served and fuel consumption increases — when each additional ticket is sold, marginal cost is constant as long as the airplane is below 100-percent capacity.

6. False. Total costs increase by the same amount when quantity increases.
7. True. Smart to increase quantity only when marginal revenue greater than marginal cost.
8. False. A change in fixed costs does not change smart decisions about price or quantity.
9. False. Quantity decision comes first. Then set highest price that allows you to sell that quantity.
10. True. Definition.
11. False. Products are more likely than services to be resold. Things that can easily be resold tend to have a single price.
12. False. Discounts should be given to the elastic-demand group, which is sensitive to prices.
13. False. Efficient market structures have normal profits only.
14. False. There are benefits (product variety, innovations raising living standards) to inefficient market structures that must be compared with costs of inefficiency.
15. True. Transfers some consumer surplus to producer surplus, but also creates deadweight loss.

MULTIPLE CHOICE

1. **a)** Marginal revenue is additional revenue from more sales or from selling one more unit.
2. **b)** Easily resold and less differentiated than services listed in other choices.
3. **b)** Because they are small, businesses in perfect competition can increase sales without lowering the (market-set) price.
4. **d)** Notice the word *additional* for all. Fixed costs are not part of marginal costs.
5. **d)** Due to diminishing returns or switch to more expensive inputs.
6. **a)** Indicates business is not operating near capacity.
7. **d)** To sell more, must lower price not just on last unit sold, but on all units sold.
8. **a)** For the first four hours of studying, marginal revenue is greater than the marginal opportunity cost of $10 per hour for working. For the fifth hour, you make more by working than by studying ($6).
9. **b)** Marginal revenue of hours of studying still $30 for 1st hour, $24 for 2nd, $18 for 3rd, $12 for 4th. Marginal opportunity cost now = $15, so only 3 hours of studying is smart, leaving 2 hours for work.
10. **d)** Recipe for successful price discrimination.
11. **c)** And higher prices for customers with inelastic demand.
12. **c)** Demand for business travel is more inelastic.
13. **b)** Maximum total surplus for perfect competition and deadweight loss for other market structures.
14. **a)** No deadweight loss, product differentiation, or innovation.
15. **d)** Same recipe for profits; inefficient but with benefits of creative destruction.

CHAPTER 9 APPENDIX

TRUE/FALSE

1. False.
2. False. Individual business demand curve is horizontal line at market price.
3. True. No need to lower price to sell more.
4. True. Normal market supply curve, with upward slope due to the law of supply.
5. False. Total costs equal fixed costs plus variable costs.
6. False. Marginal product of variable input eventually diminishes.
7. True. Cause of upward-sloping MC curve.
8. True. Marginal cost is pulling up average total cost.
9. False. Average total cost is at its minimum.
10. True. A business only has a quantity decision, no price decision.
11. False. In general, the marginal cost curve is the supply curve.
12. True. Rule for quantity choice in recipe for profits applies to all market structures.
13. True. $P = MR$ curve intersects both the MC curve and ATC curve at minimum point on ATC curve.
14. True. Businesses exit the industry. Industry supply curve shifts leftward.
15. False. Economic profits are zero and businesses earn just normal profits.

MULTIPLE CHOICE

1. **d)** All businesses produce identical products in perfect competition.
2. **d)** MR = price because business does not have to lower price to sell more.
3. **a)** Horizontal line at the market price.
4. **b)** Marginal product (number of additional meals) of the variable input (workers) diminishes.
5. **c)** Fixed costs do not change. (a) would be correct if total cost *per unit of output*.
6. **b)** Additional costs are ($310 – $200).
7. **b)** MC is below ATC and is therefore pulling down ATC.
8. **c)** Diminishing marginal productivity increases marginal costs.
9. **b)** Businesses are price-takers in perfect competition.
10. **a)** Choose quantity where price = marginal cost.
11. **c)** Recipe for profits.
12. **a)** MR equals price. ATC include normal profits. Since $P > ATC$, price covers all opportunity costs of production, leaving extra for economic profits.
13. **c)** A quantity to the right of the breakeven quantity.
14. **d)** Product is produced, revenues cover all opportunity costs of production, including implicit costs and no tendency for change.
15. **b)** With economic losses, businesses will exit industry, so industry supply decreases.

CHAPTER 10

TRUE/FALSE

1. True. Definition of market failure.
2. True. Economies of scale allow only a single seller to achieve lowest average total cost.
3. False. Crown corporations also exist in industries that are publicly important for political or social reasons (for example, alcohol control, lotteries).
4. False. The payoffs do depend on the other prisoner's choice.
5. True. Due to non-trust.
6. False. If players could trust, would be better off denying.
7. True.
8. False. They will prevent a merger if the costs of decreased competition exceed the benefits of increased efficiencies.
9. False. Penalties for *criminal* offences include prison sentences. Penalties for civil offences are limited to fines and legal prohibitions.
10. False. It means consumers, not government, are responsible for monitoring quality ("let the buyer beware").
11. True. But consumers can be harmed before that happens.
12. False. While for many products or services the costs exceed the benefits of regulation, for products like nuclear power and medicine the benefits exceed the costs.
13. True. With public interest view, regulation keeps prices low.
14. False. This supports the capture view, because the regulated industries were operating like a cartel, restricting output and raising prices.
15. False. Higher profits in regulated industries would support the capture view of government regulation.

MULTIPLE CHOICE

1. **d)** Definition of market failure.
2. **c)** So only a single seller can reach lowest average total cost.
3. **b)** Only example without high fixed costs.
4. **b)** Must allow a single seller to get efficiency, but prevent profit-maximizing high prices of monopoly.
5. **d)** Only a single seller can achieve lowest average total cost.
6. **c)** 2001 Oscar for Best Picture.
7. **b)** If prisoners can trust each other.
8. **c)** Switch back and forth between two smart choices of trust and lack of trust.
9. **d)** Tension between cheating and cooperating.
10. **c)** Prevent collusion and price-fixing.
11. **d)** Punished by prison time and fines.
12. **c)** CRTC appointed by government.
13. **b)** Regulation produced inefficiencies.
14. **d)** See descriptions of capture and public interest views.
15. **d)** All are positive questions.

CHAPTER 11

TRUE/FALSE

1. True. Individuals only consider private costs and benefits.
2. True. Pollution, noise and traffic congestion.
3. False. Smokers impose a negative externality on non-smokers.
4. False. Markets overproduce products and services that have negative externalities and underproduce those that have positive externalities.
5. False. Zero pollution means eliminating all cars and airplanes, outlawing all power except solar and hydroelectric power, and shutting down most factories. Therefore, some level of pollution is desirable.
6. False. It becomes increasingly difficult and costly to reduce pollution levels.
7. True. Definition.
8. False. Marginal social cost equals marginal private cost if there are no negative externalities; if there are no positive externalities, marginal social benefit equal marginal private benefit.
9. False. With carbon taxes the governments sets price, and with cap-and-trade systems the government sets quantity.
10. False. Smart taxes lead individuals and businesses to choose the outcomes that are best for society as a whole, where marginal *social* benefit equals marginal *social* cost.
11. True. The higher price is why carbon taxes are unpopular.
12. True. Provide external benefits consumed by everyone; no one can be excluded.
13. True. Because of free-rider problem.
14. False. Post-secondary education is not directly provided by the government (but is subsidized by the government).
15. True. Government subsidizes costs of colleges and universities.

MULTIPLE CHOICE

1. c) No cost to others.
2. d) Markets underproduce services like vaccinations with positive externalities.
3. d) Opportunity costs of reduced living standards.
4. c) Use rule for smart social choices.
5. d) Use rule for smart social choices.
6. b) Use rule for smart social choices.
7. b) General policy rule for achieving best social outcome.
8. d) Internalize the negative externality.
9. a) Make fuel more expensive for those who cannot afford to pay more.
10. b) Cause markets to underproduce products and services with positive externalities.
11. d) Underproduced because of positive externalities.
12. c) No positive externalities to clothes.
13. d) Smart subsidy internalizes the positive externality.
14. d) Definition.
15. b) Governments in Canada mostly use subsidies to help supply post-secondary education.

CHAPTER 12

TRUE/FALSE

1. True. Incomes are earned in input markets.
2. True. Price × Quantity.
3. False. Income is a flow.
4. False. Businesses' demand for labour is derived from the output market — from profits from selling output.
5. True. Recipe for profits for hiring inputs.
6. True. Higher output price increases màrginal revenue product of each worker.
7. False. $1 today is more valuable because you could be earning interest on it.
8. False. If interest rates increase, you have to further discount future revenues to adjust for more forgone interest.
9. False. When interest rates decrease, present value increases. Therefore, an investment that was smart before the decrease would become even more profitable.
10. True. Price must cover all opportunity costs of production.
11. False. What price sports team owners can get for output (ticket prices) determines what owners are willing to pay for inputs (player salaries).
12. False. Wealth is more unequally distributed.
13. False. Regressive taxes take proportionately more from the poor.
14. True. See tables with data.
15. True. Over three-quarters of income comes from working.

MULTIPLE CHOICE

1. c) Income is a flow, wealth is a stock.
2. a) Wages are income from labour.
3. d) All are related to marginal revenue product.
4. c) Marginal revenue product of 1st worker is now $120, 2nd $100, 3rd $80, 4th $60, 5th $40. Compare with marginal cost of $50.
5. d) Definition.
6. c) Recipe for smart investment choice.
7. d) Definition.
8. a) Because supply is relatively inelastic and does not change.
9. d) Income earned is a monopoly rent; not proportional to marginal revenue product.
10. a) Fans mistakenly believed high input prices (salaries) caused high output prices (tickets).
11. d) Fan willingness to pay high ticket prices leads to high superstar salaries.
12. a) See Figure 12.5.
13. b) See Figure 12.7.
14. a) Definition.
15. c) See paragraph on Poverty on page 328.

Index

long-run equilibrium, 248
long-run market equilibrium, 177, 178
luxury, 112, 126

M

macroeconomics, 18–19
The Magic Christian, 119, 120
maps, 13
marginal benefit, 20, 30
 change with circumstances, 30–31
 and consumer surplus, 96
 decrease with quantity, 31
 and efficient market outcome, 101
 greater than marginal cost, 99
 less than marginal cost, 99
marginal benefit curve, 37, 96
marginal choices, 30–32
marginal cost, 52, 58–59, 206
 and average total costs, 241
 constant marginal cost, 213
 diminishing returns, 213
 and efficient market outcome, 101
 graphs, 216–217
 greater than marginal benefit, 99
 increasing marginal cost, 212–213, 237–238
 intersection with marginal revenue, 217
 less than marginal benefit, 99
 less than marginal revenue, 206, 214–219
 maximum economic profits where $MR=MC$, 243–244
 patterns, 212
 and producer surplus, 97
 and total costs, 240
marginal cost curve, 62, 63, 97, 242–244
marginal external cost, 286
marginal opportunity costs, 20, 57–61, **58,** 315
marginal private benefit, 286, 287, 288, 299
marginal private cost, 286, 288, 291, 296, 298, 299, 301
marginal product, 235–237, **316**
marginal productivity, 318
marginal revenue, 206–211
 graphs, 216–217
 greater than marginal costs, 206, 214–219
 intersection with marginal cost, 217
 and market structure, 207
 maximum economic profits where $MR=MC$, 243–244
 and price, 234
 price maker, 209–211
 revenue from selling more than one unit, 208
 time machine explanation, 210

total revenue, 207, 211
 when equals price, 208
 when less than price, 208–211
marginal revenue curve, 208, 210–211
marginal revenue product, 317
marginal social benefit, 286, 288, 289, 291, 296, 298, 299, 303
marginal social cost, 286, 288, 289, 291, 296, 298, 299, 303
marginal tax rate, 329
market, 78–79
 broad markets, 187
 competition, 78
 cooperation, 78
 efficient market outcome, 101, 154–156
 and fairness, 153–156
 free markets, 79
 input markets, 14–15, 149, 311, 312–314
 labour market, 15, 149, 150, 315
 narrow markets, 187–188
 outcome, 288
 output markets, 14–15, 311, 312
 rules of the game, 79, 80
 and substitutes, 187–188
 trade-offs between efficiency and equity, 153–156
market-clearing price, 85, 96, 97
market-clearing wage, 151
market demand, 34
market demand curve, 35, 96
market economy, 197
market equilibrium, 176–178
market failure, 257
 efficiency *vs.* equity, 257
 with externalities, 280–284
 vs. government failure, 272–273
 invisible hand, failure of, 281
market power, 83, 184, 191
market structure, 187
 available substitutes, 187–188
 barriers to entry, 189–191
 changes in, 193
 competitors, number of, 188–189
 efficiency, 225
 inefficiency, 226
 and marginal revenue, 207
 and maximum profits, 225–227
 monopolistic competition, 194
 monopoly, 184–185, 226
 oligopoly, 193
 perfect competition, 185–186, 225, 234
 and pricing power, 191–192
market supply, 61
market supply curve, 97, 244
Marshall, Alfred, 13
Marx, Karl, 198–199
mergers, 265
microeconomics, 18–19
midpoint formula, 111, 115–117, 122

minimum wage laws, 148
 alternatives, 152
 benefits and costs, 149–150, 152
 and inefficiency, 151
 past and present, 148
 and unemployment, 151
 unintended consequences, 151
model, 14–16, 17–19, 94–95
money, opportunity cost of, 169–170
monopolistic competition, 194
monopoly, 184–185, 226, 258
 see also natural monopolies
Morgenstern, Oskar, 260
movies, 221

N

Nash, John, 260
Nash equilibrium, 261–262
National Farm Products Council (NFPC), 270
National Hockey League, 41
natural monopolies, 257, 259
necessity, 112, 126
negative externalities, 21, 279, **281,** 282, 289
new products, 227
norm, 157
normal goods, 42, 126
normal profits, 172, 314
normative choices, 273
normative question, 329
normative statements, 17, 157

O

obvious costs, 168–169
oligopoly, 193
one-price rule, 207, 209, 220
opportunity cost, 5
 vs. additional benefits. *See* keys to smart choices
 best alternative use, 146
 calculation of, 10
 and comparative advantage, 10
 marginal costs as, 58–59
 marginal opportunity costs, 20, 57–61, 315
 vs. money cost, 5–6
 mutual benefits from trade, 7
 paying for, 60
 of pollution, 285
 willingness to work, 52–53
 of your money, 169–170
 of your time, 169
output markets, 14–15, 311, 312
output prices, 323
ownership. *See* property rights

P

patent, 189–190
payoffs, 261